D0262109

Crisis in International News: Policies and Prospects

245928

Crisis in International News:
Policies and Prospects

JIM RICHSTAD and
MICHAEL H. ANDERSON Editors

PN
4736
C7

COLUMBIA UNIVERSITY PRESS　　New York, 1981

Library of Congress Cataloging in Publication Data
Main entry under title:

Crisis in international news.

   Bibliography: p.
   Includes index.
   1. Journalism—Political aspects—Addresses, essays,
lectures.   2. Foreign news—Addresses, essays, lectures.
3. Communication, International—Addresses, essays,
lectures.   4. News agencies—Addresses, essays,
lectures.   I. Richstad, Jim, 1932–   . II. Anderson,
Michael H., 1945–
PN4736.C7   070.4′33   81-677
ISBN 0-231-05254-5
ISBN 0-231-05255-3 (pbk.)   AACR2

Columbia University Press
New York   Guildford, Surrey

Copyright © 1981 Center for Cultural and Technical Inter-
change Between East and West, Inc.
All rights reserved
Printed in the United States of America

Printed on permanent and durable acid-free paper.

Contents

Acknowledgments

THIS COLLECTION of articles has its origins in international communication seminars conducted with journalists from Asia, the Pacific, and the United States during the Jefferson Fellowship Program at the East-West Center in Honolulu during the years 1975 to 1978. The ideas examined during the seminars were used as an organizing concept for advanced seminars on international communication in the Communication Policy and Planning Project in 1978 and 1979 at the East-West Center. Project members contributed their support to the collection. In particular, Dr. Syed Rahim, project leader, reviewed the early manuscript and offered substantive comments.

Selected journalism and communication faculty and directors from Asia and the United States reviewed an early manuscript in April 1979, and offered important comments on what the final manuscript should contain.

The final manuscript was put together in early 1981, with the addition of some materials from the International Commission for the Study of Communication Problems (MacBride Commission).

Several persons reviewed materials written by the editors, and we would like to add special thanks to them for their insightful comments: Stanley Swinton, Vice President and Director, World Services Division, the Associated Press; Professor Roger Tatarian, Journalism Department, California State

University at Fresno, former Editor-in-Chief, United Press International; Dr. Albert Hester, School of Journalism, University of Georgia; and Jakob Oetama, Editor-in-Chief, *Kompas*, Jakarta, Indonesia.

Dr. Sang-Chul Lee at the Communication Institute helped to complete the bibliography.

The final typing of the manuscript and much of the earlier work was coordinated by Phyllis Watanabe, project secretary.

To all these wonderful and helpful people, we offer our deepest thanks.

Foreword
A First World View
STANLEY M. SWINTON

THIS IS THE AGE of Information. Like oil, information is unequally distributed in our imperfect world. The developing world has less than its share, and this situation should be remedied. But is equal access to information an impossible dream?

No, in my view. It could come true. However, the media professional has learned from pragmatic experience that a chasm stands between the technical ability to distribute information and the ability of a world of vastly differing societal and cultural levels and political perspectives to absorb it.

How to democratize the ability to *utilize* information seems to me the heart of this vastly important problem, which this useful collection, evolving out of the East-West Communication Institute, highlights. Such democratization is vital to the developing world's economic aspirations, for information is basic to development. As development progresses, information becomes increasingly important.

But how, for example, does a Papua New Guinea highlander living in a near Stone Age society utilize information

Stanley M. Swinton is Vice-President and Director, World Services Division, the Associated Press.

even if given access? In a world where man's total knowledge doubles in a few decades, the sheer bulk of information flow is overwhelming.

It is the purity and veracity of information which makes possible the human value judgments on which successful economic and social development depend. If government, business, religion, or international bodies restrict or pollute information, then utilization is imperiled—and with it national development.

The gut problem is to turn the flood of raw information into a manageable stream of news and usable information which will have maximum possible relevance to the world's disparate cultures and societies. How to do this? Throw out the baby with the baby water? Start anew?

Information today is distributed on the broadest basis in the history of man. Imperfect as is the existing system, a learning process of more than 2,000 years was required to reach present levels.

Just as the Chinese invented gunpowder, China conceived the forerunner of the news agency. A plausible case can be made that the news agency is the more important of the two. It was during the Han dynasty, between 200 and 300 B.C., that the emperor ordered provincial administrators to send messengers regularly to Peking with reports on regional developments.

That information was for government only. Government continued to have sole access to systematically collected information for nearly 1,800 years. Eventually the first newspaper appeared in Germany. Not until the mid-nineteenth century did the progenitors of the Associated Press, United Press International, Reuters, and Agence-France Presse evolve. Their rapid growth was due in great part to the coincidental invention of the telegraph. Telegraphic costs were high. Media users could meet the expense only by banding together in what later matured into the major international, or transnational, news agencies. Today those news agencies provide the world with the great bulk of its international news.

News is only a small part of information flow, of course.

Books, the entertainment component of television and radio, advertising, statistical data, scholarly and specialized publications, and a multitude of other components are vastly important. Ways must be evolved for the developing world to not only gain equitable access to such information but to maximize absorption and utilization of all of them.

This thoughtful volume provides an overview of the total debate surrounding the flow of information from the Western industrialized world to the Third World. The flow of news, however, is the storm center of the controversy and I will address myself to it.

Basically, the dispute is between the traditional Western commitment to a free flow of information independent of government constraints and the widely held desire of the developing world for an information flow balanced on the basis of population distribution, national aspirations, and cultural independence.

Let me utilize forty years' experience in the international news field, much of it in the developing world, to offer a possible path toward ultimate solutions.

First, the time has come to move on from the rhetoric—from the sound and fury of the past ten years—and write a scenario for progress.

An essential first step is to broaden literacy so that the citizens of the developing world universally will be able to absorb and utilize information.

Next would come the establishment of media on a far broader basis in the Third World. Each country should have broadcast stations which can reach all the citizenry—and all the citizenry should have receivers. The number of newspapers should be increased not only in the cities but, even more, in rural areas, many of which lack print media. These papers should be aimed at local needs. They should help solve problems in the fields of agriculture, public health, urban development, cultural matters, and other essential areas of contemporary life—and at the same time, inform the populace of area, national, regional, and international developments.

After establishment of a media base—even a small one—national news agencies should be established to meet the nation's specific needs.

Once effective national agencies exist widely (for many today are ineffective), regional agencies should follow—at first there might be simple exchanges between the agencies of neighboring countries with mutual interests. Regional agencies (such as that which now exists in the Caribbean) would come next.

By the time an effective and operative Pan African News Agency, a Latin American news agency, or an Association of Southeast Asian Nations (ASEAN) news agency was established, experienced staffs and a healthy media base would be available. Today such broader agencies exist in theory but are not major functioning parts of daily media life in their areas.

Young agencies tend to divert scarce resources to posting correspondents in the "prestigious" news centers of London, Washington, or the United Nations. The existing international news agencies have far larger staffs, and more efficient communications for such coverage. Let me cite an example. The major agencies are unlikely to have a correspondent in Mauritania—yet Tunisia and Morocco are deeply interested in that African nation. Would it not be wiser to use regional resources for a correspondent in Mauritania and let the world agencies cover nations further afield? Scores of similar cases exist.

The international agencies are eager to broaden their foreign coverage. That is one reason why AP, Reuters, AFP, and UPI all are outspoken in their support of the national news agency concept. In the past year, the Associated Press alone provided training programs for journalists from eighteen developing countries without charge. True, an element of self-interest is involved on the part of the big agencies. Access to the coverage of individual national agencies enables the transnational agencies to strengthen and broaden their world coverage. Cooperation between agencies of the developed and developing world thus has mutual benefits. Access to the news coverage of national agencies—even if it is far from perfect in many cases—provides the major world agencies and ultimately the public with coverage of countries and areas that even a large and nonprofit agency like AP simply cannot afford to staff on a day-by-day basis. The more news voices heard the better, and new national and regional agencies are welcomed.

Within the total information picture, news agencies—with all their problems and constraints—constitute a small but vital sector. National news agencies are uniquely qualified to provide news which the societies of their nations can *utilize*. The global news agencies, while far from perfect, are consciously striving to be accurate and balanced, and their international news just happens to be the best thing there is available.

Man's progress comes in small, practical steps. If the constructive intranational changes outlined herein are added together, the world's media will have taken a long stride toward resolving existing media imbalances, by establishing the infrastructure through which the developing world's media will play a far more equal role. I feel priority should be given to these and other down-to-earth actions rather than to the cliches and the verbal acrobatics of those who talk about a "New International Communication" or "Information Order" and yet still cannot define it in terms that the journalist and the average citizen can understand.

A Third World View
NARINDER K. AGGARWALA

A EUROPEAN EDITOR recently portrayed the New International Information Order (NIIO) as a figleaf used by "Third World despots" to cover "their greed, inefficiency and exploitation" so that they could be "left in peace to exploit their

Narinder K. Aggarwala is Regional Information Officer for Asia and the Pacific, the United Nations Development Program.

subjects while they attract Western aid to bolster their private accounts." Mervyn Jones, a British journalist and novelist, took a little kinder but no less hostile an attitude. Writing in the British daily, *The Guardian*, he saw the controversy as a conflict between the backers of two traditions. Arrayed on one side, according to him, are the champions of the free press who consider the media's primary function as "offering unfettered controversy and fearless scrutiny of the intentions of the powerful." The "black hats" are the governments, primarily of developing countries, who view the media solely as a means of "convincing people to use fertilizers, kill mosquitoes and have two children instead of six." While these views may contain a grain of truth, they present a very false and distorted picture of the NIIO.

Ever since the phrase "New International Information Order" and its semantic variations became entrenched in the world diplomatic parlance, it has horrified Western media leaders. While most of them frankly admit their inability to define or understand what NIIO is, this has rarely inhibited them from hurling poisonous darts at NIIO, its protagonists, or its alleged Mephistophelian progenitor and mentor, Unesco. But Unesco is no more an instigator of NIIO than the United Nations is of the New International Economic Order (NIEO). Both these movements, if they could be described as such, are mere reflections of the Third World's long-simmering desire to change existing systems which militate against the interests of the developing countries.

Western media leaders seem to perceive NIIO solely as a ruse on the part of Third World governments to take over their domestic media and hamstring journalists responsible for the flow of news across national borders. But this is a myopic and self-centered view. The new order deals with the totality of information—technical, political, social, and economic. It covers all means of information—media, books, films, data banks, documentaries, and all kind of instructional material. It encompasses all aspects of information technology—communication satellites, press cable rates, telecommunications, as well as national and international press regulations. Media, print and electronic, are but a small—though admittedly most controversial—part of NIIO which its protagonists envision as a process for "intellectual decolonization" of the Third World.

NIIO is also seen by its critics as an attempt to impose uniformity in terms of structure and press policies and practices by the Third World not only over their domestic media but also over nonnational or transnational media, particularly the four major wire services—AP, UPI, Reuters, and AFP. Inherent to this perception is what Gerald Long, managing director of Reuters, calls "two fundamentally different views of the role of information in society." The first, according to him, "sees information as a carrier of freedom. The best expression of that view is the United States Constitution and in particular the First Amendment. The second view is that information is a carrier of power, and must be used by governments as a way of carrying out their policies."

Long charges that Unesco, and by implication NIIO, want to "transfer media technology to the countries that do not have it, while encouraging them to use that technology to control information for the purpose of the government." Unfortunately, Long's two-tone picture ignores the presence of large areas of gray. He paints all Third World countries with the same brush; hooded figures conspiring to exercise thought-control over their populations. But the Third World does not constitute a monolithic ideological, cultural, or political bloc. While agreeing on the objectives of NIIO, developing countries do pursue widely differing media policies and practices.

Freedom of the press is not something absolute. Even in the United States, there has been a continuing debate over the nature of, and limits to, the freedom of the press under the First Amendment. Some of the recent decisions of the Supreme Court of the United States on cases involving the media seem to reaffirm the thoughts expressed by Justice Oliver Wendell Holmes:

All rights tend to declare themselves absolute to their logical extreme. Yet all in fact are limited by the neighborhood of principles of policy which are other than those on which the particular right is founded, and which become strong enough to hold their own when a certain point is reached.

This is so in the case of the right of freedom of speech, expression, and thought. It is fundamental but not absolute.

The process of establishing equations and corelationships between various fundamental rights is going on throughout the world all the time, much more so in the Third World where the concepts of fundamental rights are being defined and interpreted by the powers that be in terms of each country's own national, historical, and cultural needs. While the media leaders are justified in striving for maximum freedom of the press, the degree of freedom enjoyed by the press in a given country will depend entirely on its leaders' perception of the country's political and security needs. Examples can be found in the Western world as well. Media freedom is treated differently by various Western countries, according to their own historical development.

In stating the above, one does not in any way minimize the seriousness of the threat to press freedom that exists in many developing countries. A free press is essential for assuring all other rights and for economic and social development in the Third World. But those governments which believe in the subservience of the media to the State do not need NIIO to acquire control over the media, although they may use NIIO as a ready-made excuse to justify such action.

Third World leaders, at least some of them, have very genuine and valid reasons for questioning the existing international information order or the lack of such an order. Most of them are worried about the media's influence in shaping or changing social and cultural values, particularly of the youth in their countries. They view NIIO as a means of freeing themselves from their total domination by and dependence on the Western media, through the creation of national, regional, and interregional news exchange systems. The proposed news systems may not, for example, conform to the models of Britain's Fleet Street journalism but they do represent the first feeble step in the Third World's desire to produce and disseminate news with Third World perspectives, to look at world developments with their own, rather than Western, eyes.

The general public in the West gets to look at world events through the prism of their media. In the developing countries also, people come to see their own world through the eyes of the Western media. Quite often, the media transmit single-dimensional, fractured images perceived by viewers as reflections of the whole. Partly this is due to the nature of the craft and partly due to an overemphasis on spot or action news in international news dissemination systems. Even noncrisis news is often reported with undertones of crisis. Western media leaders insist that noncrisis news is of little interest to the general public. But news is what happens, and the most important thing happening in the Third World today is the struggle for economic and social change. It is imperative for the survival of a free press that journalists and media leaders find ways to cover development news interestingly and adequately. Richard Critchfield, an American journalist who has spent nearly twenty years covering the Third World, made a very telling observation recently after spending five months in rural Java:

What is happening in village Asia is indeed "a revolutionary enterprise of the most momentous consequence." Americans need to know a lot more about what is going on in the world's two million villages where 80 percent of the Third World lives.

What is true of Americans is true of everyone in the world. The media, if they are to remain relevant to the public, will have to redress the situation.

The coverage of social and economic development processes in the Third World is of utmost significance in correcting what is often referred to as the imbalance in international news flows. As a journalist, I yield to none in defending the right of an editor, and at his level, that of a correspondent, to determine what is news. However, journalists and editors do not make their decisions about what is news in isolation. Their training, upbringing, environment, and value systems all play a substantial role in the ultimate determination of what is news. It is necessary for the media professionals to look at how news is identified, defined, and graded and to make the necessary changes to better serve the information needs of the public. This is true in the industrialized as well as in the developing countries.

Perhaps Western correspondents would be able to report from and about the Third World with greater empathy and understanding if they were to remember the time it took for social, economic, and political systems to evolve in their own countries. Although they may not find exact parallels in what is happening in many parts of the Third World and what happened in the past in their own countries, they may be surprised to discover quite a few similarities. The slow, zigzag, and often frustrating evolution of political democracy in the Third World will probably look less catastrophic, incomprehensive, and demonic given the centuries it took for the similar process to reach the present stage in North America and Western European.

The question of perspective in international news reporting is fundamental to the understanding of the causes of the Third World demand for a new order. The real justification for the NIIO lies not in the political or security needs of the Third World but in the poor or deficient state of the art of journalism itself.

Media leaders should look at NIIO as a challenge to identify the weaknesses of their profession and take corrective measures. Imbalances in the international information flows are now recognized by all but the most rabid defenders of the existing media setup. This in itself is a major achievement of the NIIO controversy. What critics of NIIO perhaps most react to is the regimentation and imposed conformity implied by the use of the word order. Diplomats, not unlike journalists, are often enamoured of neat phrases which express their often nebulous and vague ideas or give form to not-clearly defined but seemingly exciting or visionary concepts. Over a period of time, such phrases are defined, fleshed out, often with due deliberation, sometimes willy-nilly. Some such thing is happening in the case of NIIO which, despite more than five years of international conferences, workshops, and seminars, has still not been clearly defined. A few persons, perhaps, can tell in general terms what NIIO's salient features are but there is no consensus as to its exact meaning. There is even less agreement on how NIIO is to be brought about and by whom. Perhaps, once the politicians and the diplomats have had their fill of the subject, the task of defining and implementing the various components of NIIO would be handed over—either by choice or by default—to information technocrats and professionals.

In some ways, the process of defining NIIO has already begun. This book represents one such effort in better understanding and defining one very important aspect of the new order—international news. In this collection, journalists, communicators, and academicians view from different perspectives the need for a fresh look at the role, the functions, and the practices of the media in an ever-shrinking world in which—to quote from a statement made by Erskine Childers, director of information of the United Nations Development Program, at a recent Unesco conference—live satellite television has become "a factor in international diplomacy" and in which a five-minute video transmission, spanning our earth in an instant, could overwhelm "the techniques of quite diplomacy" and jeopardize the "climate for development cooperation."

Preface

OUR PURPOSE in this volume is not to address news as an isolated, professional area or to review the basic value and ideological differences inherent in the debates over news and the evolving new communication order. Rather, it is to emphasize—amidst a plurality of contrasting views—that national and international policy opportunities exist and that exciting possibilities for innovative, multiway flows of news and communication are emerging. There is reason to believe that significant progress is being made toward a greater consciousness of the existing realities and diverse perspectives of the 1980s.

A significant crisis in international news emerged during the 1970s, and was seen by many to be a threat to world stability, and particularly to stable relations between the industrialized world and the developing world. The linking of a New International Economic Order and a New International Communication Order was both a cause and result of the crisis in international news. The working out of the new orders will be critical to defusing the news crisis.

The policy context for the new order in international news is complex and changing, and there is no consensus on how nations, media, governments, or individuals should act in concert to change how communication is structured. The new order is not something that will suddenly appear one day in the 1980s, without discomfort and adjustments. And there are real dangers in some of the directions of the new order. Its final shape is still far from clear, and additional discussion and study of changes and reforms will be necessary in the years ahead.

But already, responsible change in the role and control of news and information *is* in the air. Policies *are* being reassessed, old vertical communication patterns *are* being broken, and new questions *are* being raised. The overall result is increased sensitivity among policy-makers, journalists, and others. There is a wider willingness among the developed countries to share communication resources and to talk frankly about strengths and vulnerabilities and future human possibilities.

As the spirit of international communication cooperation expands, however unsure or slow, better ways can be found to harmonize policies at various levels and across different cultures. Progress along these lines can enhance objective and independent global news flows in promoting development, understanding among peoples, and peaceful relations among nations.

Jim Richstad and Michael H. Anderson

Crisis in International News:
Policies and Prospects

Introduction

INTERNATIONAL NEWS policies and practices have only recently become a highly controversial, priority global issue verging at times on dangerous confrontation between the industrialized countries of the West and the newly emerged Third World.

This collection of readings focuses on a serious, emerging crisis over news collection, dissemination, and policymaking within and between nations—North and South, East and West, rich and poor, socialist and capitalist.

By "crisis," we simply mean that the world—for better or worse, depending on one's ideological and cultural perspectives—reached during the 1970s a turning point in its perception of the people's right to be informed and to use and regulate the communication resource known as "news." Throughout the past decade, longstanding rules and assumptions of how this scarce resource is gathered and distributed throughout an increasingly interdependent world were under intense scrutiny. International communication affairs—like those of energy, economics, and politics—were at a crucial juncture as the 1980s began. Information—like petroleum, gold, the seabed, or outer space—had suddenly been recognized as having a close correlation to both national and international power. Especially in the Third World, this recent concern reflects the urgent need for policies and plans to help efficiently use limited resources for national development, and to gain what many see as a global equity in use and control of communication systems and resources.

Significant changes and inevitable strains over new and changing concepts, structures, and attitudes were evident in the way the existing communication and news systems or orders worked. By the early 1980s, it was clear that the "good, old days," when a few agencies in developed nations virtually controlled international news flows, would never return. Out of the "disorder" of the 1970s is emerging, in the view of many observers, a more just and effective "new order" with different structures to correct deep-rooted imbalances and change some of the news-gathering procedures and communication channels that have existed since the colonial era.

This volume looks at the policy context for the still imprecise, evolving, concept of the New International Communication (or, as some prefer, Information) Order—the events and the ideas that gave rise to it, the contradictions surrounding it, the values represented by it, the communication environment it grew from, the main actors or forces that are involved in the crisis and in the formidable job of developing international communication policy and taking practical actions. In particular, we are focusing on how the new order concepts are interacting with international news processes and structures.

As the following essays will illustrate, a wide range of perspectives has evolved as this crisis emerged, and many practical measures and sophisticated developments are underway to move toward a more just and equitable world news policy and structure.

By the 1980s, various confrontational approaches, ideological positions, and national and international policy issues and media problems (including finances, technology, and training) were crystallizing.

More significantly, some of the acrimonious debate and tension surrounding Unesco activities had subsided—at least temporarily. Earlier, considerable international controversy had surrounded the 1976 Unesco General Conference in Nairobi and the controversial Soviet-backed draft mass media declaration that the United States contended would reduce freedom of the press. In 1978, the Unesco General Conference in Paris agreed to a compromise declaration and virtually saved the international organization as a credible forum for debate and action on international news issues. The work of the Unesco-initiated International Commission for the Study of Communication Problems (the MacBride Commission) on various imbalances and inequalities in world communication also provided important perspectives. Made public in 1980, the commission's recommendations for communications development in the world of tomorrow helped set the agenda for various efforts to quantitatively *and* qualitatively improve the world's news and information supply and flow. The MacBride report was approved by consensus at the twenty-first general conference of Unesco in Belgrade in October 1980. The conference also approved establishment of a formal International Program for the Development of Communication (IPDC). Operating within the framework of Unesco, IPDC is to serve as a mechanism through which financial and technical assistance might be channeled to developing countries to help improve their communicaton capabilities.

After about a decade of conferences, debates, international organizational voting, research, and dialogue, the time is right for a concise one-volume book that summarizes issues and solution areas and reflects political and cultural pluralism. This volume on international news is part of the editors' work with journalists, policy-makers, and scholars in the Communication Policy and Planning Project of the East-West Center's Communication Institute in Honolulu, Hawaii. Again and again, participants in various Project activities and other colleagues told us of the great need for more light and less heat about the news crisis. Without their ideas and perspectives and Communication Institute resources, this collection would not have been possible. We gratefully acknowledge their collaboration and assistance.

This collection of readings traces the events of the 1970s and early 1980s and addresses future prospects. It consciously strives to present the many viewpoints and value systems at operation in the flow of news, and combines a mixture of scholarly and "real world" perspectives from both the developed and developing worlds. It emphasizes that new issues are likely to emerge as the dialogue and debate, particularly over the new order concept, become even more truly international in the 1980s.

As Sean MacBride of the MacBride Commission noted, there are entrenched interests, and changes will not be easy or fast in some areas. Yet, in just a few years, there has emerged a global awareness of the international news issues, and significant changes are under way in both understanding the problems and in improved practices of news flow, many of them initiated by the major transnational and national news agencies. Various hard-and-fast positions are softening, although some are considered irreconcilable, and the search for common ground has assumed a more pragmatic, less emotional tone.

Materials in this collection include both published and unpublished items written during the 1970s and early 1980s. Some of the materials are "classics" or official international documents, and others are hard-to-find perspective pieces or original analyses and abridged reports on research findings that narrow the gap between problems and solutions, the present and the future, the quantitative and the qualitative.

The volume is organized into four parts, plus appendices, and a selected bibliography.

Part I, "Global Perspectives," presents essays sketching the broad international context out of which Third World dissatisfaction over the uneven distribution of news and other communication resources has emerged. Several key concepts ("the New International Communication Order," "domination," "free flow," "interdependence," "pluralism," "right to communicate") that recently have gained widespread academic, professional, and political attention are closely examined.

Part II, "News and Information," focuses specifically on the debate surrounding the free and balanced flow of news within and between societies.

Part III, "Transnational News Agencies," examines the

major internationally active news agencies and addresses various news policy and practice questions that have developed around these influential organizations headquartered in a few Western, industrial societies.

Part IV, "Evolving Directions in International Communication," looks to the rest of the 1980s and beyond to emerging trends that should affect news and policy making at national, regional, and international levels.

Appendixes A–F present six basic international declarations or document extracts highlighting how news and information emerged as an international issue during the 1970s. Items include a 1970 Council of Europe statement linking communication with human rights and Unesco resolutions on the importance of communication to international peace and national development. The reader should note that the wording of these various international documents is often convoluted. That is, it is frequently vague and even contradictory. If the language were clear, one if not more of the national representatives would not agree, and international compromise or consensus in this world of sharply conflicting ideologies would be impossible.

Finally, a selected bibliography points to additional reading and reference materials.

Part I

Global Perspectives

NEWS PROBLEMS cannot be easily solved or even discussed in isolation from broader communication and other problems.

The purpose of Part I is to outline the multidimensional global nature of the complex issues behind the present-day international communication crisis and its effects on human progress. As a group, these essays present a broad range of perspectives on the fundamental issues that affect international news and communication. Also, they present a global framework for the news crisis that emerged in the 1970s and that continued to be highly visible and politically charged in the 1980s, as developing nations struggled to strengthen their communication capabilities.

By appreciating the different implicit and explicit value bases inherent in these sharply conflicting, culture-bound perspectives, one can understand why what are called "irreconcilable" North-South differences (not to mention the more obvious political disagreements between East and West) will persist as the debate over news and related information issues continues.

Some of the essays focus on the traditional American commitment to free flow of information and the right to hear and be heard. Others emphasize the Third World concern for balanced flow and the right to national sovereignty and cultural identity.

Since neither of these major perspectives is likely to prevail, and there have been so many changes in the global environment in recent years, much of the international communication debate and policy making in the years ahead will emphasize accommodation. Unesco and its controversial International Commission for the Study of Communication Problems (the MacBride Commission) have tried to provide a context for the emergence and acceptance of not only the new order concept but also the principle of a "free flow and wider and better balanced dissemination of information," as contained in the 1978 Unesco Mass Media Declaration.

1

Policy Context for News and a "New Order"

JIM RICHSTAD and
MICHAEL H. ANDERSON

Richstad and Anderson argue that the international news crisis can be seen in a broader policy context that is framed by many of the concerns expressed in the loosely organized New International Communication Order concept. The magnitude of the news crisis surprised many in the West, and more voices are being heard in world debates on international news and communication policy. Many of these new voices are challenging the value base and consequences to the developing world of the prevailing order. "The world is for the first time looking at its communication policy on a global scale," and this presents a challenge to policy development. The essay reviews the various organizations involved in news policy, and notes that the relationships among the groups "are highly complex and interactive."

THE FLOW OF NEWS has always been a sensitive topic of both theoretical and policy interests at national levels, but

Jim Richstad is a research associate at the East-West Communication Institute and Michael H. Anderson is an information consultant with UNICEF. This essay and volume grew from their collaboration in the Communication Policy and Planning Project at the Communication Institute. Both are former newspapermen and university teachers of journalism and have had a long interest in international news policy.

only during the 1970s did it become a central international agenda item.

Only very recently have fundamental questions about news collection and circulation become pressing concerns within highly visible international organizations like Unesco and transnational news agencies like the Associated Press and Reuters.

The flow of news between nations has become a politically sensitive subject over the past several years as an increasingly frustrated Third World has spoken out loudly and clearly about the urgent need to reorder rules and assumptions governing news. Al Hester of the University of Georgia described this transitional situation well when he wrote:

Basically many Third World leaders desire to have a bigger share of the news and information pie—and they want the pie to be more to their taste, too. They are tired of going to the same old international communications "bakery" and having always to eat the pastries which are what the monied, developed nation customers always seem to order.[1]

India's Indira Gandhi, at the height of her Third World influence, spoke for many developing nations' leaders when she stressed the importance of information self-reliance:

We want to hear Africans on events in Africa. You should similarly be able to get an Indian explanation of events in India. It is astonishing that we know so little about leading poets, novelists, historians and editors of various Asian, African, and Latin American countries while we are familiar with minor authors and columnists of Europe and America.[2]

By the start of the 1980s, there had evolved a strong, global movement for restructuring international news and commu-

---

1. Al Hester, "Inter Press Service: News For and About the Third World," Studies in Third World Societies, Publication #9, Third World Mass Media: Issues, Theory and Research. William and Mary College, Department of Anthropology, 1980, p. 2.
2. Indira Gandhi, "Self-reliance in Information," Communicator (April–July 1976), 11(2–3): 16.

nication. Pressures for basic changes have come from outspoken Third World leaders, journalists, and others in both developed and developing societies. A consensus is gradually emerging that recognizes that many countries and people have not fully or even partially participated in the development of policies about the news they need for their security and well-being.

The magnitude of the crisis in international news came as a surprise to most journalists, political leaders, and communication researchers. In just a few years, the rather obscure issue moved to the center stage in Unesco and other organizations. While this much is clear, there were many early signs that all was not well with the international news systems, and several organizations were making important but, looking back, wholly inadequate progress toward a better and more equitable flow of world news.

The first clear data base for the one-way flow concept, for example, came with the historic flow-of-news study by the International Press Institute.[3] IPI, founded in the 1952 cold war atmosphere, through the years has strived for a Western style free press system, has improved news flow, has helped found national press institutes and organizations in developing areas of Asia and Africa, and has worked on journalism training and news exchanges.[4]

Unesco, too, had programs to improve journalism in the developing world long before the crisis erupted. The pre-1970 focus was on the practical skills of journalism, and not much attention was paid to the more political concerns that dominated the seventies. A private organization, the Thomson Foundation in Britain, has since 1963 been providing various levels of practical training for Third World journalists, again without a political framework.[5] The U.S. government, through

3. International Press Institute, The Flow of News (Zurich: International Press Institute, 1953).

4. Kurt Koszyk, "The Development of the International Press Institute," in Heinz-Dietrich Fischer and John C. Merrill, eds., International and Intercultural Communication (New York: Hastings House, 1976), pp. 372–76.

5. Don Rowlands, "The Practical Approach." Paper for the Conference on International Exchange and Training of Journalists, Honolulu, October 17–22, 1976.

the then United States Information Agency and the State Department, had programs of journalism exchange and visits to the United States, although on a much different level than now.[6]

So, while the political crisis in international news exploded in the 1970s, there were early warning signs, mainly overlooked and ignored, and some early but clearly inadequate efforts to improve international news flow.

Issues for the 1980s

At the start of the 1980s, the trend around the world was clearly toward news cooperation. A widely shared feeling among journalists, policy-makers, and scholars was that the turbulent period of confrontation should end and that attention should be focused on realistic strategies fostering new patterns of communication and cooperation. The issues are volatile, however, and the move toward cooperation is filled with uncertainties. A proposal by a high U.S. government budget official in early 1981, for example, called for U.S. withdrawal from Unesco, partly over the free flow of information issue.

Developments in the 1980s are centered around three broad issue areas of international news flow:

1. Issues of *impact* of international communication on national and subnational cultures, social systems, political stability, economic progress, development goals, value systems, and other areas.

2. Issues of *control* over communication on sovereignty, rights, responsibilities, privacy, access, dominance-dependency, participation, free and balanced flow, and other areas.

6. Early USIA and State Department activities can be found in John Henderson, *The U.S. Information Agency* (New York: Praeger, 1969); Ronald Rubin, *The Objective of the U.S. Information Agency* (New York: Praeger, 1966); Constance Stuart, "U.S. Department of State Exchange of Journalists Programs 1937–77." Paper for the Conference on International Exchange and Training of Journalists, Honolulu, October 17–22, 1976.

3. Issues of communication *resources* in development of new structural patterns and infrastructures, program materials, exchange agreements, technology transfer, training, loans and aid, spectrum allocation, news pool, and exchanges.

Widespread and growing discussion of these interrelated concerns has demonstrated the importance of knowledge about how news flows—or does not flow—from the First to the Third World and how the national and international news systems are linked.

Much of the global discussion focuses on the structures and practices of news agencies (transnational, regional, and national) and how they operate vis à vis the Third World. Material on these issues is scarce and much of it is out of date and insensitive to Third World concerns. The debate needs to focus increasingly on international and national communication policies, both implicit and explicit. While the comprehensiveness of policies varies greatly from country to country, communication policies are being approached systematically in many countries. This concern over communication policy is very recent, and reflects the need in new and developing countries to efficiently utilize limited communication resources for national social and economic development. Even in a highly developed Western country like the United States— with an extensive open communication system largely run by private interests—there is an increasing need to develop a comprehensive policy to meet international and domestic pressures.[7]

A clear understanding of how and why news has been recognized as politicized is necessary to help resolve misunderstandings over the flow of news and the rapid rise of national communication policies that build outward to regional and international policies. Progress toward solving the host of exceedingly difficult and interrelated problems affecting how people, news organizations, and societies send, receive, and regulate news is only possible once existing realities, diverse perspectives, and practical alternatives are appreciated.

7. Glen O. Robinson, ed., *Communication for Tomorrow: Policy Perspectives for the 1980s* (New York: Praeger, 1978).

Various actors in the news crisis of the 1970s and the challenges of the 1980s include those who want government to control media versus those who favor laissez-faire; those who stress freedom versus those who stress responsibility; those who perceive communication as a form of power versus those who see it as a human right; those who view news as a means versus those who see it as an end; those who use news as a private commodity versus those who view it as a precious public resource; and those who want to maintain the status quo versus those who want a new communication order.

Conflict over the new order is particularly critical because many Third World nations have made structural change in communication systems a priority. Communications-rich, information-based societies like the United States, the Soviet Union, Europe, and Japan are under great pressure to share their resources under the new order.

The examination of international news policy and practice goes beyond the collection and dissemination of news between the have and have-not nations, to the evolving, policy-related concept of the New International Communication Order.[8] Because it is not clearly or universally defined, this relatively new concept warrants special attention.

New Order

As a communication policy concept, the new order has both strengths and weaknesses. The vagueness of the post-1970 concept allows a wider input of ideas about how news and communication systems should be organized and run.

Much of the discussion about international news—implicitly, if not explicitly—concerns the policy context for the new

8. Several formulations for the concept have been developed and present similar but different perceptions of what is meant by the new order. Some of these are: new international information order, new world information order, new world communication order, and new world communication and information order. Several of the essays in this volume deal with the new order.

order, and the first question that comes up is whether we have an information order now and if so, what is it.[9] Concerns have been strongly expressed by First and Third World journalists that the new order should not provide a new basis for more government control of news in the Third World.

The predominant concept or principle of the present or "old order" is the free flow of information, as embodied in the United Nations constitution, the Universal Declaration of Human Rights, and many other international and national documents. At the beginning of the 1970s, free flow reigned as the basis of international news policy. The predominant structural form of the order was built on mass media systems, which created basic contradictions with the free flow principle.[10] These contradictions and changes in ways of thinking about communication, a broader global political base, and development of new technology have all led to the move toward a new order.

The free flow concept is viewed largely as a European or American principle, and one that was well suited in the post-1945 period to the people and countries that controlled most of the international communication and news systems.[11] In practice, free flow became almost a one-way flow from the industrial countries to the rest of the world, and, by the early 1970s, the one-way flow and its corollaries were a major international political issue. The concept of unrestricted international communication systems under private control and responsibility was never accepted by many countries—socialist and others—and calls for a new order increased.

Many changes in the political and communication environments were also occurring during that period, and it be-

9. See, for example, Roland Homet, "Goals and Contradictions in a World Information Order," Intermedia (March 1979), 7:2.

10. L. S. Harms, "A Note on the Evolution of Communication Orders." Paper for Advanced Summer Seminar on International Communication Policy and Organizations, East-West Communication Institute, Honolulu, July 5–August 4, 1979.

11. Herbert I. Schiller, "Freedom from the 'Free Flow,'" Journal of Communication (Winter 1974), 24(1):110–17. See also his essay "Genesis of the Free Flow of Information Principles," in this volume.

came increasingly evident by the mid-1970s that the prevailing news and information order was in a state of crisis.

The major political development was the emergence of new nations from colonialism. With independence came sharpened concern over the rights of sovereignty and recognition that "communication imperialism" was a matter to deal with before full sovereignty was possible. More voices were heard in the world debates on international news and communication policy, and many of the new perspectives were challenging the value-base and consequences of the prevailing order. At the heart of the existing order was an undeniable fact of international communication life: the ubiquity of American media. William H. Read has explained:

That American news agencies, magazines, films and TV programs have spread themselves worldwide must be obvious even to the most casual observer. Some of the statistics on this phenomenon are mind boggling: data available in the mid-1970s revealed that *Time* was more popular in Canada than in the United States, UPI was being translated into 48 languages, the world's movie theaters were devoting more than 50 percent of their screen time to American films, the amount of TV programs exported from this country was estimated to exceed 100,000 hours a year, the *International Herald Tribune* was circulating in some 70 countries, and so on. It is virtually impossible to escape the reach of U.S. media in the world. Even Peking's official news agency, Hsinhua, has exchange agreements with U.S. news services and Moscow has done business with the American television networks.[12]

Changes in the communication environment also provided an important policy context for the emergence of the new order, and provided further reasons to question the prevailing system. Many of these changes apply broadly to international relations and in particular ways to communication rights and the movement toward a new international com-

12. William H. Read, "U.S. Private Media Abroad," *The Role and Control of International Communications and Information,* Report to the Subcommittee on International Operations of the Committee on Foreign Relations, United States Senate (Washington, D.C.: GPO, June 1977), p. 1.

munication order. They also apply to what Daniel Bell calls "a post-industrial society based on services" in which "what counts is not raw muscle power, or energy, but information."[13] This notion of information power and its economic, political, and security implications is particularly important to the United States. By 1977, a U.S. Senate report emphasized that information was "a resource often ignored in American foreign policy debates" and pointed out:

The question of international communications and information is of grave import to the United States, where Department of Commerce statistics show that the information sector of the U.S. economy has grown to include over 40 percent of the GNP (if education is included). It continues to spiral upward.[14]

Global and Communication Developments

During the 1970s, several general global developments emerged that were important in the way they influenced thinking about communication. These include:

- The concept of *interdependence* among peoples and nations
- The realization of *finite resources*
- The concept of a *common heritage* of humankind
- *Non-Aligned/Third World views*
- The broad concept of *participation*
- A global perspective of *human rights*
- An *information society*, or what Marc U. Porat refers to as an "information economy,"[15] in which problems relating to communication and information occupy a central place on the policy agenda

13. Daniel Bell, *The Coming of Post-Industrial Society: A Venture in Social Forecasting* (New York: Basic Books, 1973), pp. 126–27.

14. George McGovern, "Introduction," in *The Role and Control of International Communications and Information* (see footnote 12), p. iv.

15. Marc U. Porat, "The Information Society," Ph.D. dissertation, Stanford University, August 1976.

- A new sense of *sovereignty*
- The comparatively great influence of the United States on the world's media and the subsequent realization that, as British sociologist Jeremy Tunstall has argued, "the media are American"[16]

Along with the more general developments were many changes in communication and the ways in which communication was viewed.

Communication Developments

- The rapid emergence of communication *technology* with few limits, creating potential news and information abundance instead of scarcity
- Growth of *user-driven* and *transceiver* communication technology, compared to source-driven technology, this permits the user to select the news and information desired or needed
- The creation of "instantaneous and simultaneous" *global communication systems* and potentials, particularly point-to-point capabilities through satellite
- Wide potential for individual and group *access* to media and to information sources
- *Role of communication* seen as an indispensable element in all social organizations, and for social and economic development
- The concept of communication as a *multiway, interactive, participatory, horizontal process*, rather than as one-way sender-receiver, vertical transfer of information
- Increasing concern over *impact and control* of the international and global news systems, especially over "cultural imperialism," "neocolonialism," "information imperialism"
- Theoretical development of *dominance-dependency* in communication and culture, showing the consequences of news

16. Jeremy Tunstall, *The Media Are American* (New York: Columbia University Press, 1977).

imbalances and asymmetrical distribution of communication resources[17]
- Emergence of *communication policy science*, and recognition of the basic relationship of communication needs, rights, and resources
- View of communication as a *resource* for human and social development and enrichment, cultural pluralism, and other objectives
- View of the right to communicate as a *basic human right*, applying to individuals, communities, and nations and in relations between nations; people have a right to hear and be heard
- Growing recognition that telecommunications may be more a *precondition* than a consequence of industrial and social development

The movement toward a new order does not mean casting aside the free flow principle—the principle is deeply embedded in many national ideologies in the West and elsewhere. A new order would encompass the free flow principle, and seek to balance it with other values from around the world. In the Unesco terminology, for example, the drive has been toward a "free and balanced flow."[18]

Many of the attributes for a new order are clear—more equitable distribution of communication resources, better and fairer balance in the flow of news and communication, an emphasis on respect for cultures and national unity and stability, recognition of the role of the media in social and economic development, and promotion of peace and understanding among nations and peoples. A much fuller exposition of what the new order can mean is made by Mustapha Masmoudi,[19] the UNESCO-appointed MacBride Commission, and

17. Johan Galtung, "A Structural Theory of Imperialism," *Journal of Peace Research* (1971), 8:2.

18. Many observers make the point that the phrase contradicts itself—a flow cannot be free and balanced at the same time; but others have no trouble with it.

19. See Mustapha Masmoudi's essay, "The New World Information Order," in this volume.

many others. Many aspects put forth for the new order, however, have little broad support, and others are unclear and open to wide interpretations. While this may cause confusion in the policy context, it seems unavoidable at this early and evolving stage of the new order.

New International Communication Order (NICO)

- *New*—this signifies a clear break with the past, that a new paradigm for communication is recognized, and with it many and major changes in patterns, structures, and concepts of communication are occurring or will occur.
- *International*—this term can be seen in its traditional sense of communication between nations and also in the universal sense that the new order's principles apply within nations, as well as to everyone.
- *Communication*—this term is used in the broad sense to include the entire process and structure of communication, including but not limited to the information content and processes. Much of the impetus for the new order came from concern over news flow patterns, so in some ways it could be a news order as well as an information order. "Communication order" encompasses both, as well as other forms.
- *Order*—the term *order* can be simply understood as meaning how things within a given framework "fit together and work," and can refer to "public and civic orders, and local, national and world orders, and economic, social or communication orders." Orders, L. S. Harms notes, are concerned with "human values, and, in the world context of communication, on communication, on communication rights, including, for instance, a right to participate, a right to inform, and a right to privacy."[20]

The new order is deeply based in ethical and moral concerns of justice, freedom, equity, and human dignity, and the differing perceptions of how these values should be imple-

20. Harms, "A Note on the Evolution of Communication Orders."

mented give rise to much of the confusion and disagreement over the new order. Who would not subscribe to justice, freedom, equity, and human dignity? But, when human dignity is defined in a particular way, there may be disagreements. Read put the issue of human dignity this way:

At bottom there is an emotional issue of human dignity deriving from neocolonial feelings of always being talked to, always being on the receiving end, and always being imposed upon by foreign judgments as well as by foreign values.[21]

Equity can be seen in the light of a demand to share the communication resources of the planet more broadly, as well as the opportunity to acquire communication resources on the open market. A *right* to the communication resources is quite different than the *freedom* to acquire those resources.

Dealing with vastly different value bases and perceptions is a continuing task for all international organizations and in relations between states, and particularly so in the culturally sensitive area of human communication. One of the basic questions of human society is how it will organize its communication system, who can use it under what conditions, and where the rewards flow.

In the policy context, this is why many observers argue that news (or more broadly, communication) cannot be singled out as a separate problem—it is so closely interwoven with the rest of society that it must be considered in the overall societal context.[22]

The world is for the first time looking at its communication policy on a global scale, and this forces attention to the diverse and conflicting perceptions of news and communication and their role in various societies. From a policy standpoint, this means attention must be given to perception of the

21. William H. Read, "Information as a National Resource," *Journal of Communication* (Winter 1979), 29:1.
22. See, for example, Kaarle Nordenstreng, "Struggle Around 'New International Information Order'." Abridged version published in *Journal of Communication* (Spring 1979).

problem—what is the problem. For example, if some perceive the communication problem as being one of a lack of communication infrastructure in the developing world, it will make policy development and problem solution difficult if others view the problem as one of dominance-dependence, imperialism, neocolonialism, and so forth, growing from broad historical forces.[23]

From a theoretical standpoint, policy and problem statements develop from an implicit or explicit value base, and in communication this value base is closely locked in with the values of a society. The classic distinction that illustrates much of the difference in the East-West deadlock of communication policy is between the view of the human being as the center of policy development, and the view of the human-being-in-society as the center of policy development. The value systems behind primacy for the individual or for the community lead to quite different policies on all aspects of life, and certainly in the role of news and communication.

In the international debates and discussions on news policy and practice in recent years, an often expressed view is that the value bases in this area are so different—stemming from different premises into separate logical systems—that the differences are "irreconcilable."[24]

This is an often expressed position when the value systems of the West and of the Soviet group of nations are discussed. In the West, the news media and other communication systems generally are privately owned and operated, they are under a minimum of government control, and they perform as a critic or watchdog of government. Under the Soviet system, the media are considered parts of the government, in full

23. For examples of contrasting perspectives of the communication problem, see Kaarle Nordenstreng and Herbert I. Schiller, eds., *National Sovereignty and International Communication: A Reader* (Norwood, N.J.: Ablex, 1979); and John Reinhardt, "The Challenge for Communications Development." Policy statement to Unesco, Paris, November 3, 1978.

24. Leonard H. Marks, Remarks made at International Institute of Communications, Dubrovnik, September 11–14, 1978.

support of the government policies and practices, and they undertake a critic's role only in well-defined areas.[25]

Dealing with international communication issues and policy at that level, it is easy to see why certain issues seem irreconcilable.[26] The Soviet side would want government control and responsibility of all international communication; the West would want little or no government control, with the private media being the responsible parties. This point was illustrated in the final report of the MacBride Commission: the report called for abolishing censorship, and the Soviet commissioner objected, saying censorship is the concern of national interests.[27]

Yet, for a variety of reasons well understood in international relations, there is communication, however difficult, between these different groups of countries. At the international communication level, the "irreconcilable issues" are accommodated into an international as opposed to a national policy, and function with varying success.

So, operationally, ways are found around the sharply contrasting value systems. The controversy seems more critical when a proposal is put forth for a universal policy statement on communication, such as the Mass Media Declaration at the 1978 Unesco meeting.[28] In 1974 and 1976, the drafts of this declaration encompassed what were indeed irreconcilable po-

25. Fred S. Siebert, Theodore Peterson, and Wilbur Schramm, Four Theories of the Press (Urbana: University of Illinois Press, 1956); Yevgeny Prokhorov, "The Marxist Press Concept," pp. 51–58, and W. Phillips Davison, "The Role of Communication in Democracies," both in Heinz-Dietrich Fischer and John C. Merrill, eds., International and Intercultural Communication, (New York: Hastings House, 1976), pp. 29–36.

26. The use of the term irreconcilable can also be a rationale to shut off the discussion and result in polarization of issues. "These issues are irreconcilable, therefore we can't talk about them, or it does no good to talk about them."

27. "Unesco Study Asks Press Rights; Soviet Stand on Censorship Cited," New York Times, February 23, 1980.

28. For a sample of reactions, see Elena Androunas and Yassen Zassoursky, "Protecting the Sovereignty of Information"; Rosemary Righter, "Who Won?" and Kaarle Nordenstreng, "Behind the Semantics—A Strategic Design," under "Unesco's Mass Media Declaration: A Forum of Three Worlds," Journal of Communication (Spring 1979), 29(2):186–98. See Appendix F for text of Declaration.

sitions, to the point of serious consideration by the United States of withdrawing from Unesco if the 1976 version, viewed as sanctioning state control of international communication, were passed.

Crisis Reached

A crisis point was reached at the 1976 Nairobi meeting, with important ramifications for the policy context for international communication.

First, the United States media interest in particular and the West in general were fully and rudely awakened about the concerns over flow of information and news of the nonaligned and Third World countries. And the U.S. government and media interests engaged fully in the debate. The 1976 Nairobi meeting put international communication policy on the world agenda and opened participation to all.[29]

Second, out of the compromise to put off a vote on the 1976 declaration, the International Commission for the Study of Communication Problems was formed, and became known as the MacBride Commission, after its president, Irish diplomat/statesman Sean MacBride. The commission was charged with conducting a "comprehensive study of the problems of communication in the modern world." It published an interim report in 1978 and a final report in 1980.[30] An important aspect

29. This does not mean all peoples and nations have an equal voice on world communication policy. There are large numbers of people within countries excluded from any policymaking, and many countries have little to say on a global scale. The point here is that the debate on communication is recognized as a global one in which there should be opportunity for full participation by all. One of the major tasks of the new order is to make that participation closer to reality.

30. See International Commission for the Study of Communication Problems, *Interim Report on Communication Problems in Modern Society* (Paris: Unesco, 1978). The *Final Report* of the commission was completed in December 1979, although, except for the Recommendations section, the report was not publicly released until well into 1980. By the time of the twenty-first Unesco General Conference in Belgrade in September–October, the report had become available as a 312-page book, *Many Voices, One World: Communication and Society Today and Tomorrow* (London: Kogan Page, 1980).

of the commission was the scope of its task. It was charged with examining communication as a world problem. In the policy context, this truly put a global framework on the new international communication order and related issues.

In his first address to the commission, MacBride said "it is not only unavoidable, but resolutely necessary to approach communication problems globally." He also said communication cannot be separated between national and international levels—"to isolate one from the other . . . would not only be a mistake, but is really impossible." What goes on internationally in communication, he said, is related to what goes on nationally.[31]

During this time when everyone seems to be demanding different, often incompatible things from communication, the policy context of the new order must be seen as both international and national—between countries and within countries. By nature of its concern with global problems, the new order applies to all countries and peoples. Such a globally based communication policy was not even on the international agenda until the 1970s, and now represents one of the great policy problems in an interdependent world.

As the debate on the new order broadens to include more perspectives, it becomes increasingly important to open thinking to higher levels, and not to spend all the effort on trying to prove there is one correct perspective for international communication policy. In global communication problem assessment, "what seems to be required now is an inclusive process that recognizes that a complete picture is formed only in the integration of multiple perspectives, in effect, forming a new and large perspective."[32] It is important, too, to bear in mind that the policy-making process is incremental and time consuming. Laurence E. Lynn, Jr. has pointed out:

Policy making is not an event. It is a process that moves through

31. Excerpts from his inaugural address to the commission appeared as Sean MacBride, "A Formidable Task," *Intermedia* (February 1978), 6(1):7.
    32. Center for the Study of Social Policy, *Assessment of Future National and International Problem Areas* (February 1977), vol. 1.

time-consuming stages, beginning with public recognition that a problem exists, to the adoption of laws or a combination of measures aimed at dealing with aspects of the problem (which may take a long time and may never happen), to the establishment and operation of a program, to evaluation, review, and modification—but seldom death.[33]

Right to Communicate

The right to communicate and the new order activities within and outside of Unesco in the 1970s have moved the international communication policy debate and policy formation mechanism off dead center, where it was stuck—polarized between East and West—in the post-1945 era.[34] Both of these efforts stress multicultural perspectives in their policy development, and share many of the strengths and weaknesses of such an approach.

The right to communicate developed from widespread feelings of the inadequacy of a mass media communication order, particularly in the light of developments in technology.[35] The right to communicate is a complex and evolving concept but can simply be put as: "Everyone has the right to communicate." The right entails at least the right to inform and to be informed, the right of active participation in the communication process, the right of equitable access to com-

33. Laurence E. Lynn, Jr., "The Question of Relevance," in Laurence E. Lynn, Jr., ed., Knowledge and Policy: The Uncertain Connection. Study Project on Social Research and Development (Washington, D.C.: National Academy of Science, 1978), 5:17.

34. E. Lloyd Sommerlad, "Free Flow of Information, Balance, and the Right to Communicate," in Jim Richstad, ed., New Perspectives in International Communication (Honolulu: East-West Communication Institute, 1977), pp. 22–32.

35. For an introduction to the right to communicate, see L. S. Harms and Jim Richstad, eds., Evolving Perspectives on the Right to Communicate (Honolulu: East-West Communication Institute and distributed through University Press of Hawaii, 1977), and Harms, Richstad, and Kathleen A. Kies, eds., Right to Communicate: Collected Papers (Honolulu: Social Sciences and Linguistics Institute, 1977) distributed through University Press of Hawaii. See also Jean d'Arcy's "The Right to Communicate" essay in this volume.

munication resources and information, and the right of cultural and individual privacy from communication. It is premised on the shift in communication from a one-way, vertical system to a multiway, horizontal system with high levels of participation on individual and community terms—many of the same attributes behind the new order.

A key philosophical shift is that people have a right to communication resources necessary to their communication needs—that communication means beyond the interpersonal level should be equitably shared and not controlled by wealthy powerful groups, individuals, or nations. This position is also at the heart of the new order—communication is a basic human right. Everyone has a right to the news and information needed for survival, growth, and enrichment.

The right to communicate encompasses Article 19 of the Universal Declaration of Human Rights, and goes beyond it. The humanistic content of Article 19 is strongly moral and ethical. Article 19 imbues human beings—everyone—with freedom of opinion and expression, and the right to send and receive information and ideas in any way anywhere in the world. It does not provide for government, business, religious, or other forms of control, nor does it provide the essential means to enjoy the freedoms and rights.

Major Actors

From the policy context, it is important to look at the complex set of interrelationships and various organizations and individuals that played leading roles in shaping key concepts, particularly the new order and the right to communicate, which both have emerged out of the ongoing, international news and communication crisis.

The following list briefly outlines the key actors in the crisis affecting news and information:

1. *Nonaligned/developing countries.* This is where the impetus

for change is coming from, these are the aggrieved parties, this is the source of many of the new values that have to be built into the communication order. These countries have great impact through their international and regional organizations and groupings.

2. *Transnational (sometimes called multinational) communication enterprises.* These are the media organizations, carriers, and manufacturing units—Associated Press, Reuters, Visnews, IBM, Cable & Wireless, television and film distributors. They are being asked to change both their structures and processes to allow wider policy input and to reflect wider values and new elements in the communication environment. Throughout the 1960s and 1970s, a flood of literature and international debate—much of it critical of private transnationals— has analyzed the trend toward transnationalization of the media industry and relationships between corporations and decolonization of information. The transnational news agencies have come under particularly strong criticism.

3. *International organizations.* These have the official national representations for telecommunications, such as the United Nations and its organizations, particularly, in the case of news, Unesco, and the International Telecommunication Union (ITU). Policy can be made and sometimes enforced in these organizations and they present a forum for recognition, discussion, and weighting of the important international communication issues. They compile information and coordinate and conduct research.

4. *Nongovernmental organizations.* These include a wide variety of groups. In the communication issues area, there are the International Press Institute, International Organization of Journalists, International Institute of Communications, World Press Freedom Committee, the International Association for Mass Communication Research, and the International Communication Association, for example.

5. *National governments.* Although they may be part of regional or other blocs, many national governments have communication policies of their own that have varying impacts on international policy. The U.S. government policy (of little or no policy) on national media is a basic contextual factor in international communication policy. U.S. policy set by the State Department and the International Communication

Agency (ICA) is the center of much of the global debate.
6. *National media organizations.* While most of these have little direct international impact, indigenous organizations, especially national news agencies and media councils, are very important in shaping national positions.
7. *Specialized training, research, and policy institutes.* These provide special services and inputs into policy formation, and may be part of governments or other organizations. Included here would be the Press Foundation of Asia, the East-West Communication Institute, Asian Mass Communication Research and Information Center, the Edward R. Murrow Center of the Fletcher School of Law and Diplomacy at Tufts University, the Annenberg School of Communications at the University of Pennsylvania, Freedom House, the Thomson Foundation, and similar groups.

In the context of the international news crisis, Unesco and the transnational news agencies—as major subsets of two of these groups of actors—warrant special attention.

Unesco

Unesco is a key international organization that deserves careful analysis. It remains the major public organization where both concepts and specific policies are being developed in substantive programs at the same time, and where rich interaction between the two is likely to develop.[36]

Unesco has come under severe attack, particularly by Western media interests, over the past several years for its programs on communication policies, the Mass Media Declaration, national news agency development, the new order,

36. For an overview of Unesco, see Richard Hoggart, *An Idea and Its Servants: Unesco from Within* (London: Chatto and Windus, 1978). For a discussion of Unesco and the debate over news, see Rosemary Righter, *Whose News? Politics, the Press and the Third World* (London: Burnett Books, 1978). See also Robert P. Knight, "Unesco's Role in World Communication," in Heinz-Dietrich Fischer and John Merrill, eds. *International and Intercultural Communication* (New York: Hastings House, 1976), pp. 377–91.

the MacBride Commission, the International Program for the Development of Communication, and other matters. While some of these criticisms seemed to have subsided by the end of the 1970s, this was not the case for long. By the biennial Unesco General Conference in late 1980, heated ideological debate was once again the order of the day. Unesco came under intense Western criticism for its role as a so-called "propaganda forum" for the Soviets and for some Third World nations. As in earlier years, there was considerable talk that the United States should withdraw from Unesco to protest its communication activities.

All of these criticisms made broad understanding of the role of Unesco very difficult. Former Unesco official Gunnar Naesselund, for example, has challenged the argument that Unesco cannot do much in communication policy because world differences in information and news policies are as irreconcilable as the basic ideologies of the member states, and that it is simply impossible to conceive of a news philosophy or news distribution system acceptable to the Soviet bloc and the Western democracies. Naesselund says such thinking "reveals a basic misconception of Unesco's role and its means."

"The only 'news philosophy' within this program," Naesselund said, "is the concept of 'the right to communicate' as an extension within the potentials of modern technologies, of the freedom-of-information concept that was conceived in the age of newspapers and not electronics."

Unesco programs are the concerted action of its member states, he said, and Unesco must take account of the existing ideologies or social philosophies but is in "no way asked or obliged to present a common philosophy."[37]

While what Naesselund says is true of the Unesco formal structure, the influence of the Unesco communication staff on what the organization undertakes clearly is not simply a reflection of the members' wishes. This became particularly obvious during the MacBride Commission activities, when the

37. Gunnar Naesselund, "Unesco and the Press in the Third World," in Philip C. Horton, ed., The Third World and Press Freedom (New York: Praeger, 1978).

staff-prepared *Interim Report* was released in 1978 without full review by the commission members.[38]

The advantages Unesco has in a policy context are that it works closely with the national governments and professional organizations, and has accumulated information on communication equipment, training, manpower, and other aspects of communication needs. Also, Unesco provides an important forum for all members to participate in development of international communication policy.

One important role Unesco can fill is to go beyond reacting to crisis events, such as the Mass Media Declaration, and try to look ahead to serious problems in the future, and attempt to head them off through actions now. Such foresight, which the MacBride Commission was charged with, has done much to legitimize Unesco's role in international communication policy. Some media interests, however, continue to raise serious questions about Unesco's role and competence in news and information issues.

The News Agencies

Outside of Unesco, the other key actor affected by the whole crisis has been the transnational news agency (TNNA), a highly visible subset of the transnational communication enterprise.[39]

The prestigious, Western-based TNNAs warrant particularly careful consideration in the international debate over news. The four predominant transnational news agencies—the Associated Press (AP), the United Press International (UPI), Reuters, and Agence France-Presse (AFP)—and the two largest television news enterprises—Visnews and UPITN—are immensely powerful and influential organizations, far outpacing

38. Elie Abel, a member of the MacBride Commission, in remarks from the podium at the meeting of the U.S. National Commission for Unesco, Athens, Georgia, December 12–15, 1979, on the *Interim Report*.

39. Oliver Boyd-Barrett, "The Global News Wholesalers," in George Gerbner, ed., *Mass Media Policies in Changing Cultures* (New York: Wiley, 1977), pp. 13–20.

their operating budgets. These TNNAs are influential not only in effectively transmitting news around the globe but also, more subtly, in defining news values and styles. Journalism in much of the Third World is patterned after Western perceptions, values, and practices, especially the TNNA-style writing.

By TNNAs, we refer to those major, nonterritorial organizations that produce, process, and distribute news (and, increasingly, specialized information) in literally dozens of nations and that pursue a common, coordinated strategy of covering the news and tapping new markets wherever they operate. *Transnational* does not imply that either management or ownership is in the hands of more than one country. AP, UPI, and AFP, for example, are wholly owned within single Western, industrialized countries. Reuters, Visnews, and UPITN are owned by more than one organization—but always in a Western country. The term does imply influence and consequences—including an oligopolistic market situation—extending far beyond conventional, nation-state political boundaries. To their sharpest critics, for example, the TNNAs are devils incorporated and are as much "disturbers" as they are "distributors" of news. To their most ardent supporters, the TNNAs represent objective truth in an otherwise highly politicized and propaganda-heavy news flow, and do their best to maintain the highest ideals of Western press and individual freedom, private enterprise, and professional journalism.

For our purposes, the non-Western, state-owned news agencies like the Soviet TASS and Hsinhua, the New China News Agency, are excluded from our definition of TNNAs. Although these are relatively large and internationally active, they are part of an official government information and propaganda apparatus, and they do not sell their services in the same market-based way that AP or Reuters sell their news. By our definition, the TNNAs certainly are not value-free but they are widely perceived as being somehow more modern, objective, or neutral in their coverage than the overtly political news agencies in noncapitalist societies. Tunstall made this point when he emphasized the dilemmas facing the Soviets when they try to compete with the commercial Anglo-American media:

it is hardly surprising that the Soviet Union is a weak media exporter—with the partial exception of eastern Europe. No nation can more than marginally separate its domestic from its export media. The American trick is always to assume that if they go for it in Iowa and Illinois, they'll go for it worldwide. The Soviet media controllers have no such illusions; they're not at all sure that what's offered will go down at home, let alone abroad.[40]

In addition to such obviously important actors as the TNNAs and the others enumerated above, there are many organizations whose main activities are not in news or, even more generally, communication policy, but which may be highly influential or interested in particular areas.

Relationships among these groups are highly complex. It is not always easy to pick out the various policy strands as they interweave with each other and develop over the years through these organizations. No one theory or framework or even definition is adequate or without its problems.

In trying to assess the international and national policy context for communication, the International Institute of Communications stated:

Society as a whole is thus posed with a whole series of new challenges as complex and interdependent as those underlying other major issues now pressing on countries and on the international community. Seen in this perspective, questions of policy and of planning are obviously not only crucial, but urgent.[41]

In news, as in other areas of communication, priority should be given to policy (or, more accurately, series of pol-

40. Tunstall, The Media Are American, p. 200.

41. International Institute of Communications, "Comparative Account of National Structures for Policy and Decision-making in the Communications Field." A document prepared for the International Commission for the Study of Communication Problems (Paris: Unesco, 1978).

icies) if problems and prospects surrounding the contemporary crisis are to be understood. And if such an undertaking is to have relevance, knowledge-seeking and knowledgeable communicators, policy-makers, and researchers will need to join forces.

2

Communication Problems Today
INTERNATIONAL COMMISSION FOR THE STUDY OF COMMUNICATION PROBLEMS (THE MACBRIDE COMMISSION)

In late 1977, the Unesco-initiated International Commission for the Study of Communication Problems under chairman Sean MacBride, the Irish statesman, began its controversial work. The job of the study group—widely known as the MacBride Commission—was to review the "totality of the problems of communication in modern society" and suggest ways that a more just and effective new international communication order might be fostered. Many of the problems and trends of concern to the commission concerned the necessity for some change in the structure and practices that guide how news is defined, collected, and disseminated. The commission's formidable assignment was completed when its book-length final report was submitted to Unesco in December 1979. See "Communication Tomorrow" in this collection for the commission's recommendations, which were discussed at the Unesco General Conference in Belgrade in late 1980.

This essay, excerpted from the commission's 1978 Interim Re-

This is an excerpt from International Commission for the Study of Communication Problems, Interim Report in Communication Problems in Modern Society (Paris: Unesco, 1978), pp. 63–73. Copyright © 1979 Unesco. Reprinted by permission.

port, highlights major communication problems and challenges facing humankind as a whole. It emphasizes the gravity of various problems, including news imbalances and inequalities, and supports the growing realization that communication within and between societies has a major role to play in how individuals, communities, governments, and media work for greater independence, sharing, understanding, justice, and social change.

The MacBride Commission, by raising various deep-rooted problems, broadened the global dialogue on some intensely controversial matters and focused public attention on them as no other national or international group has done since the global news crisis began. Without the landmark efforts of the commission, the world in the 1980s would be a more politically uncertain place in terms of both North-South and East-West confrontations over international communication.

The Commission members at the time of the Interim Report were:

- —Sean MacBride, President of the Commission, (Ireland), barrister, politician and journalist, President of the International Peace Bureau, former Minister for Foreign Affairs, founding member of Amnesty International, United Nations Commissioner for Namibia, holder of the Nobel and Lenin Peace Prizes
- —Elie Abel (U.S.A.), journalist and broadcasting expert, former Dean of the Graduate School of Journalism, Columbia University, Harry and Norman Chandler, Professor of Communication at Stanford University
- —Hubert Beuve-Méry (France), journalist, founder of the newspaper Le Monde, President of the Centre de formation et de perfectionnement des journalistes, Paris
- —Elebe Ma Ekonzo (Zaire), journalist, Director-General of Agence Zaire-Presse
- —Gabriel Garcia Marquez (Colombia), author and journalist
- —Mochtar Lubis (Indonesia), journalist, President of the Press Foundation of Asia
- —Mustapha Masmoudi (Tunisia), Secretary of State for Information, President, Intergovernmental Coordinating Council for Information of the Nonaligned Countries
- —Michio Nagai (Japan), journalist and sociologist, former Minister of Education, editorialist of the newspaper Asahi Shimbun
- —Fred Isaac Akporuaro Omu (Nigeria), former head of the Department of Mass Communications, University of Lagos, Com-

missioner for Information, Social Development and Sport, Bendel State
- Bogdan Osolnik (Yugoslavia), journalist, politician, member of the National Assembly
- Gamal el Oteifi (Egypt), former Minister for Information and Culture, Honorary Professor, Cairo University, journalist, lawyer and legal adviser
- Johannes Pieter Pronk (Netherlands), economist and politician
- Juan Somavia (Chile), Executive Director, Instituto Latinoamericano de Estudios Transnacionales, Mexico City
- Boobli George Verghese (India), journalist and Gandhi Peace Foundation Fellow
- Leonid Mitrofanovich Zamiatin (USSR), member of the Supreme Soviet, ambassador, journalist
- Betty Zimmerman (Canada), broadcaster, Director of International Relations, Canadian Broadcasting Corporation

WITHIN THE PRESENT complex situation of communications . . . it will be useful to isolate . . . problems which are of particular importance today in the international debate, and which recur in different forms and to different degrees in many countries. In seeking to identify the problems which call for study and subsequent analysis in depth, the Commission considered that, since the media are all interconnected, the problems affecting individual media might be examined to greater purpose in terms of their interdependence, by taking an overall approach to communications.

Freedom of Information

The first, and undoubtedly the most significant, problem relates to freedom of information and to the associated concepts of free flow and balanced flow of information.

The very definition of the concept of freedom of information raises many problems, particularly of an ideological, political and legal order, and problems of a linguistic nature. . . . It is for this reason that the search for a universally acceptable definition has always met with failure. The fact that the word "freedom" has without doubt given rise to more interpretations than any other, and is used to describe, to stand as the objective of, or as the screen for, all types of political regimes amply reveals that the principles involved are themselves complex and ambiguous. In rough-and-ready terms, freedom of information would appear to embrace: the freedom to seek out information and ideas; the freedom to express opinions and to impart information by different means; the freedom to receive information. Inasmuch as having opinions only becomes tangible for other people when these opinions are expressed, freedom of expression goes hand in hand with freedom of opinion and is coterminous with freedom of information. Inasmuch as the act of expressing oneself means making known what one has to say, freedom of expression ties up with freedom of dissemination, i.e., the free flow of information, knowledge and ideas. In other words, the notion of freedom of information contains a number of overlapping, complementary and interacting elements, thereby rendering all attempts to isolate one from the others artificial. Whereas, the invention and development of printing added the right of expression and its corollary, freedom of the press, to the right to speech and opinion, the later development of the new media has given prime importance to the concept of freedom of information. Seen in this perspective, the order in which rights relating to information may be classified today bears the imprint of their historical development: opinion, expression, information. To this progression must be added—in order to take account of the technical evolution and extraordinary diversification of information sources—the right to free flow of information in all its forms and expressions, regardless of frontiers.[1]

1. In this connection, two United Nations texts may be quoted: Article 19 of the Universal Declaration of Human Rights (1948) stipulates: "Everyone has the right to freedom of opinion and expression; this right includes freedom to hold opinions without interference and to seek, receive and impart information and ideas through any media and regardless of frontiers." The International Covenant on Civil and Political Rights, adopted by the General Assembly of the United Nations on 18 De-

A MISAPPLICATION

The formulation of this fundamental aspect of freedom in United Nations documents occurred during a period when freedom of enterprise, heir to the doctrine of laissez-faire, appeared as the yardstick of all other freedoms, since it constituted the supreme value and touchstone of the business world—without it ever being wondered at whose cost this material success was obtained. A similar assimilation led to the misapplication of principles whose philosophical value remains undisputed. Hence, in the field of information, free flow between the strong and the weak, the haves and the have-nots cannot fail to have pernicious consequences for the latter, and hence at the international level for the developing countries. There may be cases where the freedom of the rich is in fact simply the reverse of the dependence of the poor.

INDIVIDUAL AND COLLECTIVE RIGHT

Freedom of information nevertheless appears to be the logical extension of freedom of thought. If freedom of thought is an individual freedom, freedom of information is both individual and collective, its composite character becoming increasingly pronounced as mass communication techniques become ever more diversified and sophisticated.

The paramount importance enjoyed by freedom of information in the family of human, and especially economic and social, rights is explained quite simply by the fact that the right to inform and be informed makes possible the exercise of all the other rights. . . .

Greater attention should be given to the persistence of the obstacles standing in the way of the full exercise of freedom of information. To underestimate the impediments and difficulties existing in this field could lead only to an aggravation

---

cember 1966, stipulates, in particular, that the right to freedom of expression: "comprises the freedom to seek out, to receive and to communicate information and ideas of all kinds, regardless of frontiers, whether in oral, written, printed or artistic form, or by any other means of the individual's choice."

of the present situation. According to recent reports, it would appear that, although of very different kinds, the obstacles recorded can be classified into two categories on criteria of objective evidence: (i) "evident" obstacles, curbs and pressures; physical pressure or obstruction; administrative measures; judicial procedures bound up with . . . news reporting; lawful monopolies; allegedly voluntary renunciation of freedom of information following acts of arbitrary interference; (ii) "nonevident" obstacles and impediments; economic and social pressures; interventions on the part of monopolies or pressure groups; political, financial and technological necessities; obstacles resulting from unequal relations between publishers and journalists, etc. Ultimately, any public or private, political or economic monopoly affecting the flow of information may constitute an at least potential threat to freedom of information.

The concept of free flow of information as it has been invoked for the past thirty or so years, and as it is applied today, can serve to justify a doctrine serving the interests of the powerful countries or groups which all too frequently enables them to ensure or to perpetuate cultural domination under the cloak of generous ideas; moreover, it is not accepted by all States, certain States subordinating it to respect of their national legislation. Once again, we are faced with the gulf between formal and actual rights—a gulf which is unfortunately tending to widen.

Responsibility in the use made of freedom of information, and in particular, the responsibility incumbent upon professional communicators, is of great importance. . . . This responsibility is not limited to the obligations imposed by law or by governments, but also includes those dictated by conscience, professional standards and ethics, or which stem from the social interests of a given community or even from the international community as a whole. This question should be discussed and explored in greater depth not only by those involved in the communication process but also by the decision-takers and by public opinion in general, since acceptance of responsibility must not lead to the unjustified curtailment of the freedom of information.

Moreover, it will be necessary to analyze situations where: (i) under the cloak of freedom of information some (countries, institutions, pressure groups, etc.) seek to violate the sovereignty of others; (ii) on pretext of "decolonizing" information, it is placed under the exclusive control of the State apparatus; (iii) national sovereignty is adduced as an absolute argument to justify infringements of the free exercise of human rights.

Accuracy and Distortion of Information

The accuracy—or inaccuracy—of news is governed by several factors: (i) access to information sources; (ii) the possible existence of a vested interest in misrepresenting events; (iii) the availability of multiple news channels; (iv) the gatekeeping and selection process that influences news content, emphasis and presentation; (v) the professional qualifications of news reporters; (vi) journalists' attitude toward professional codes of conduct and ethical norms; (vii) difficulties in understanding and interpreting the circumstances and situations obtained in foreign countries, which are bound up with ethnocentric tendencies; (viii) the general conditions governing accurate and comprehensive reporting.

On a more practical level, a typology of the phenomena of news distortion might be drawn up comprising for example the following categories:

(a) highlighting of events that have no real importance by interweaving the anecdotal, the irrelevant, and what is considered picturesque in the developed countries with facts of real national significance;

(b) making news by putting isolated facts together and presenting them as a whole, or presenting a sum of partial truths in such a way that it appears to amount to an overall truth;

(c) misrepresentation by implication characterized by the presentation of facts in such a way that the implicit conclusions are favorable to particular interests;

(d) distortion by "preconditioning" of events, specific facts being presented in such a way that unfounded or exaggerated fears and misgivings are created in order to condition later action by individuals, communities and governments;

(e) distortion by keeping silent on situations presumed to be no longer of interest to the public for whom the agencies' correspondents are writing; thus Vietnam has virtually ceased to be news in the international press after the defeat of the United States, despite the value and interest of its development work following so devastating a war;

(f) distortions arising from government control of news, from restrictions on the freedom of access to news sources, from censorship and from governmental authority infringing on press freedom.

Since absolute objectivity does not exist, the accuracy of information is probably less a measurable quantity and more a question of judgment or viewpoint. It is the perception of the person responsible for deciding what is news, how to present and transmit it, that forms for the reader or listener the picture—bright, dim or disfigured—of the cultural realities, events, and situations he cannot personally know. It is difficult to report facts without interpreting them.

However, this problem is also bound up with the question . . . of what constitutes news, and on what value judgment its definition is based. Some contend that there can be only one conception of "news value": it is a necessary and sufficient condition that it be comprehensive, accurate, and objective and relate to interesting and preferably exceptional or out-of-the-way events or phenomena. Conversely, there are many, particularly in the Third World, who consider that the criteria governing what is news vary in accordance with the needs of respective countries and publics, and that news value is ultimately a question of cultural perception.

In developing countries, it seems necessary to broaden the concept of news to include not only "events" but entire "processes"—hunger being a process, while a hunger strike is an event; a flood being an event, while a long struggle to control floods is a process—in the hope that reporters and journalists . . . will consent to give greater coverage to processes and to long-term trends. A new style of journalism, in which good news is considered just as worthy of interest as bad news, has become necessary. . . . If communication is essential in order for the development effort to receive the support and cooperation of the people at large, should not communicators not only objectively report events which constitute "valid" news but also serve as society's analysts and educators, thus playing a vital role in the national and international struggle to promote human progress.

INFLUENCE OF THE PUBLIC

Accuracy of news also depends on the value system of society or of certain groups within that society. While it is true that journalists seek to satisfy the market, taking account of their readers' desires and public demand in general, public opinion is not a phenomenon *sui generis*; it is molded partly by the government's policy and partly by the messages transmitted by the various media. . . . The volume and variety of news imported from foreign sources also affects the shaping of public opinion in each country. . . . Many distortions may appear deliberate, while others are inevitable. This is so firstly because they reflect the world as it really is, that is, a world divided, rent by the forces of domination and fraught with structural contradictions. Secondly, because they originate in the unconscious ethnocentrism of journalists or are rooted in the relativity of the concept of objectivity. This is not to say that distortions cannot or must not be reduced, or that efforts to devise and improve means of discovering or getting closer to the truth should be abandoned. . . . This question of defining the measures and mechanisms or seeking the means best suited to fostering such a process . . . calls for particular attention.

Balance and Imbalance in Communication

The problem of imbalance doubtless boils down to: (i) in all societies, much more information reaches the higher strata (urban areas, elites, and ruling groups) and is transmitted by them than in the case of the other strata; and (ii) a far greater amount of information flowing around the world is transmitted by the industrially advanced countries to the less industrially advanced than the other way around, and the effects of such one-way flow may be detrimental, if not disastrous for the cultural, intellectual and economic growth of the less developed countries. However, Japan's past experience and China's experience today suggest that certain benefits may be derived by developing countries from the information flow emanating from the technologically more advanced world. In other words, the imbalance is both an intranational and an international phenomenon. . . . But for the internal imbalances, the worldwide imbalance in news circulation would probably be less pronounced and less alarming.

Generally, when speaking of free flow of information and balanced flow of information, we place the discussion more at the international than at the national level. We also tend to consider that, at the international level, the quantitative aspects are more important than the qualitative aspects, volume predominating over content. This twofold tendency must surely be reversed. News imbalance is a historical phenomenon which is still reflected in present-day sociopolitical realities. Resulting from the present-day structure of societies, it has been affected at the same time by the emergence from colonialism and by the efforts of a large number of Third World countries, to achieve political, economic, social, and cultural independence. Most of them have recognized and come to feel increasingly intensely how deceptive and fragile the concept of "political freedom" can be within a global context of domination, which continues to exert an impact on every aspect of society. The pattern of appropriation and control of instantaneous, collective dissemination of messages and data to the benefit of a few is now seen as affecting not merely the way people form pictures in their minds, but also the way in which they work (or remain out of work), eat (or do not eat), and breathe, live, and die.

Should it not also be stressed that the communicators may themselves be responsible for certain aspects of news imbalance and distortion? The general rule being all too often to retain the public's attention or to attract a new potential audience, a tendency has emerged: (i) to trivialize programs; (ii) to give a superficial or stereotyped character to news; (iii) to isolate current events from their context; (iv) to make the message essentially ephemeral.

INTERPRETATIONS AND ISSUES

The various currents of thought and opinion would seem to concur today in acknowledging the existence of both a quantitative and qualitative imbalance in the flow of information between developed and developing countries although there was no agreement as to the reasons for this, nor to its consequences or to the most suitable way of overcoming it. The protagonists of this debate are many and various:

(a) representatives of the Western media and more particularly of the major news agencies;

(b) together with—but distinct from—them, representatives of certain media who are ready to consider controversial issues from a dialectical point of view;

(c) those representing more moderate viewpoints and searching for mutually acceptable improvements;

(d) those for whom news is inevitably distorted in a certain type of society and in the present-day world situation;

(e) representatives of the Third World, with the nonaligned countries as their chief champions, who, despite slight disparities in their approach and differences in their experiences, are close to one another in their choice of solutions.

However, this classification doubtless fails to reflect sufficiently accurately the diversity of opinions and the varying degree of vehemence with which they are expressed.

To reduce the debate to a "West-East" or a "North-South" confrontation seems in any case too simplistic and is bound to be harmful. The broadening of the dialogue on this controversial issue has already brought out: (i) the wide variety of views and feelings on this subject; (ii) the visible softening of rigid positions or hard-and-fast hostile standpoints; (iii) initial improvements in news circulation, as well as a certain decrease in the distortions noted, in particular as a result of pressure from developing countries.

May we not infer from the foregoing, still provisional considerations that, if they are to succeed, efforts to redress news imbalance and distortion presuppose: (i) social and political transformations involving a reduction of economic imbalances and the attenuation of social inequalities and disparities; (ii) the creation of a news-reporting potential in developing countries and a corresponding reduction in the gap separating them in this field from the more advanced countries; (iii) tangible evidence of a willingness on the part of industrialized countries to accept and to retransmit information emanating from or concerning the Third World on more liberal terms.

Professional Conduct and Professional Responsibility

In every country news reporting finds itself faced with certain ethical rules which may or may not be respected in everyday practice. This ethic is enshrined in the social and intellectual or spiritual traditions of each country. However, observance of it does not necessarily depend upon its being codified in specific regulations, or upon entrusting particular institutions with responsibility for keeping check on the practices deriving from it. It might, however, be worth exploring the potential utility and efficacy . . . of two specific measures:

> (a) formulating . . . codes as a means of self-imposition of ethical standards;

(b) establishing press councils concerned to take better account of the general interest by ensuring a certain measure of socialization of the media and of the information process as a whole.

INTERNAL NORMS

Adopted in many countries by journalists' and publishers' associations, by radio broadcasting and filmmakers' organizations, and by advertisers' associations, standards of conduct—whether or not they are enshrined in national deontological codes—are generally based on such key concepts as impartiality, objectivity, truthfulness, respect for private life, honesty, integrity, confidentiality, responsibility, and protection of the freedom of information. These norms may also be bound up with certain rights, such as right of access to information sources, or certain requirements, such as occupational training. The concept of . . . codes appears to have been prompted both by the concern to act rightly and by the feeling that control exercised by those concerned is to be preferred to rules imposed from outside. Thus, alongside rules laid down by the State, the media have established their own internal regulations. In certain countries, these constitute a major and sometimes predominant source of the right to communicate, particularly in those in which State intervention is limited to certain fields and where the media enjoy an autonomy recognized by law and play a major role. . . . Many national codes do not comprise principles governing journalists' duties and responsibilities toward the international community and foreign countries, or do not place sufficient stress on such principles [because] the codes are generally conceived in terms of an individualistic ethic, designed to regulate interpersonal relations (between those communicating and those receiving the information), and overlook the fact that news reporting and the responsibilities which it involves are social phenomena which concern the community as a whole, both at the national and international levels.

PROFESSIONAL RESPONSIBILITIES AND THE GENERAL INTEREST

These and other matters undoubtedly make it necessary to pursue in individual countries and to coordinate at the international level efforts to establish, clarify or improve the ethical norms governing communication. However inadequate they may seem to be, existing codes constitute a starting point for the generalization of such norms at the regional and international levels.

Concurrently, the trend has gradually become established to set up press councils, media councils or similar bodies, recalling the corporate bodies which regulated the exercise of the professions and crafts in the past. From this standpoint, such councils are part and parcel of a certain process of socialization and professionalization of communication, which may be accepted or rejected.

Although the first such body was established in Sweden in 1916, it was not until the start of the 1960s that the institution began to be generalized. The British Press Council has served as a model for many press councils. Over half the forty-odd national councils existing throughout the world were not established until the 1970s. Certain bodies composed of representatives of all the categories concerned play a role which transcends the framework of professional ethics and affects the regulation and arbitration of the activities of the media and of professional communicators. Such bodies pursue a two-fold objective: (i) to wrest from the political authorities (the legislature and executive) part of their powers and duties in matters of communication; (ii) to win acceptance of the necessity, in all democratic societies, of controlling the powers wielded by those who themselves control the media. . . .

The role of the State in formulating and applying a professional code of ethics would seem to be one of the cruxes of the problem. Can the State dissociate itself from questions which involve almost every aspect of man's existence? What place should be left to the other parties concerned? What limitations are to be set on the exercise of the rights? Who is to establish and enforce respect of such limitations? These and many other questions are bound up with the ultimate aims and ends of communication, which may vary from one country to another and according to real or supposed needs. Inquiry into this problem might be focused firstly on the advisability of taking at the regional or international level, measures similar to those described above: establishing codes, normative instruments, arbitration procedures, setting up international or regional councils, etc. Secondly, it might aim to identify certain common denominators of professional norms as applied in different countries so as to enable communication to contribute more effectively to a positive evolution in world affairs and to help solve the primary problems besetting mankind.

Specific Situations and Social Groups

It is self-evident that society is not equally and indifferently affected in all its components and in every situation by the emergence of the media and by the expansion of communication structures . . . or by the effects of the different forms of communication. . . . To be comprehensive, the study of communication problems must bear upon certain specific situations and social factors.

MINORITIES

Many minority linguistic and ethnic groups are not reached by communication networks and channels in a large number of countries. The same is true of a frequently large section of the rural population, living in geographically isolated areas or in extremely difficult material conditions, as well as of various marginal groups or groups poorly integrated into society as a whole. In several regions of the world, countries have to contend with difficulties stemming from multilingualism and the cultural fragmentation which results from it. This is undoubtedly a significant feature of the intranational imbalances in communication referred to above. In any case, these questions call for study: firstly in view of their intrinsic importance and secondly because they constitute a factor of discrimination, and sometimes of racial discrimination, for whose persistence the media are by no means wholly irresponsible. Indeed, they do not appear to be sufficiently committed to combating such prejudices, which, whether involuntarily or deliberately, overtly or covertly, they frequently help to perpetuate or to strengthen.

An equally far-reaching problem is that of women's place and role in communication, seen in terms of the diversity of cultures, the way they are represented and perceived and even exploited by the media. The aim here must be to determine the contribution which information could make to the adoption and generalization of norms and behavior patterns designed to modify stereotyped attitudes and reactions which affect women's dignity or which strengthen prejudices and negative attitudes rooted in male chauvinism.

Attention should also be given to the role and place of young people and particularly children in communication . . . .

LEISURE ACTIVITIES AND ENTERTAINMENT

The question of the tie-up between communication and leisure activities calls for careful scrutiny, despite or perhaps because of the enormous diversity . . . in the world. . . . Leisure activities may be seen as a passive form of communication. In many countries, particularly in the industrialized world, certain media play a dominant role in popularizing and organizing various forms of leisure activity, entertainment, and games. Indeed, in the case of the mass media and particularly television, entertainment, in the form of cultural and musical broadcasts, has become the main function.

VIOLENCE

What possible types of correlation exist between the content of media transmissions and certain phenomena occurring in modern societies beset by profound crises and transformations? This thorny question arises in particular in connection with the phenomenon of violence, and especially terrorist violence—even though such violence is by no means equally widespread throughout the world . . . .

Material Imbalances and Inequalities

Imbalances in the content and flow of information are obviously bound up with technological material, economic and financial imbalances and inequalities. For material conditions necessarily affect communication as a whole. Inequalities in this respect are flagrant, at all levels and in all dimensions: within each nation, between industrialized and developing countries, among developed countries and among Third World countries.

TECHNICAL SHORTCOMINGS

The media and networks used to disseminate messages . . . are most unevenly distributed between urban and rural areas. Communication channels are denser in a centrifugal than in a centripetal or circular direction. The links between former colonies and the metropolitan countries have been maintained and in certain cases strengthened, and in actual fact prevent—even if such is not the intention—further ties from being established among Third World countries and particularly between those not linked to the same metropolitan country.

Transmission costs are another major factor which help to cause or to amplify this inequality first because they are high, and also because they have a discriminatory effect. Originally, reduced tariffs had been introduced for certain means of transmission which are today largely replaced by new technologies. For instance, although point to multipoint transmission (broadcasting) is less expensive than point-to-point transmission, the advantages of the latter have led to its gaining predominance throughout the world. In principle, moreover, the rates are meant to be roughly the same in either direction between two given points. . . . However, they are mostly lower from developed to developing countries than in the other direction. . . . Actual communication costs represent a much heavier financial burden for the developing countries, given the fragility of their economies in general.

This problem . . . concerns the reduction of telecommunications tariffs and the measures to be taken to correct the many irregularities in tariff structures affecting news transmission and dissemination so as to take greater account of the interests of developing countries and of the need to broaden and diversify the international flow of information.

PRODUCTION AND CONSUMPTION OF GOODS

In respect to both the production and consumption of the materials and equipment used in communication, the imbalance between the different countries is tending to increase. Leaving aside tele-informatics, whose uneven development raises complex problems . . . , we shall confine ourselves here to the question of paper production and consumption, which governs the expansion of the press, the book industry, documentation, and many public and private communications and information systems. . . . Studies reveal a substantial increase in consumption in recent times (a 50 percent increase during the past decade) or in anticipated consumption in the coming years (the consumption of newsprint probably rising from 25.6 million tons in 1976 to 34.7 in 1985).[2] The elasticity of the paper supply on the international market should be studied in the light of the fact that only thirty-six countries are at present paper producers and only six export a significant fraction of the production. . . . The gulf between developed and developing countries is particularly striking in this area, those developed countries characterized by a market economy having consumed nine times more paper in 1974 than all the

2. Unesco Office of Statistics, *Consumption of Cultural Paper in the World Regions.* ST-78/WS/211.

Third World countries together[3]—which latter nevertheless produce 55 percent of the raw materials used by the paper industry. All possibilities of recycling and rational utilization of paper and all means of economizing it should therefore be carefully explored. . . .

Communications Technology

While the industrialized countries are undergoing a veritable revolution in communications technology which is disrupting institutions, transforming ways of life, providing enormous opportunities for individual enrichment and social advancement, but at the same time jeopardizing social values, the developing countries are benefiting only minimally and slowly from technological innovations. Moreover, these innovations are not designed to meet their development requirements, do not take account of their planning and management capacities, and are frequently introduced in haste, without regard either to problems of evaluation and transfer or to the interdependence of hardware and software. It is probably in communications that the gulf between developed and developing countries is widening most alarmingly—a gulf which is liable to have irreversible consequences if corrective measures are not promptly taken. This is in any case one of the most important features of the strategy of securing a more equitable distribution of resources and potentialities which underlies the new international economic order.

POSITIVE IMPLICATIONS

Man is a symbol-using being. Of all the environments that he creates (and pollutes) that of symbols and messages is one of the most crucial. The means that shape our symbol systems today are about to undergo a veritable revolution, in which a

3. *Ibid.*

series of interacting technological changes affecting communications may occur on such a scale and at such speed as virtually to dwarf all past changes.

Innovation in the field of communication revolves around the development of semiconductors. High-performance solid state material has now outdated the older, electron-tube-dominated technology, thus opening up the way for much more efficient bidirectional communication systems, and particularly for lightweight communication and control equipment in the field of strategies and advanced technology. Sophisticated integrated circuitry is now capable of condensing a multitude of electronic functions into tiny, microscopic chips of silicon or some other material; these mass-produced prefabricated elements can be incorporated into a wide range of apparatus, from computers to television cameras, for use in space. This circuitry has greatly enhanced the reliability of digital technology, which is now making its entry into sound and visual recording (numerical analysis). The ever-increasing demands made on the performance of data processing and space circuitry create pressure for the improvement and development of electronic components, thereby opening up a vast field of application in the field of communication. . . .

At the international level, it should be possible to produce a "freer" and more balanced flow of information. Unwisely applied, technology may create the worst of messes; correctly assessed in terms of its benefits, costs and consequences and adapted to suit the needs of those involved, it can make a major contribution to the solution of many problems. In general, communication technology can have positive effects. . . .

NEW CONCERNS

Although scientific discoveries and technological innovations are constantly opening up new vistas, three main questions remain which are tending to become increasingly serious:

(a) the first concerns the real value of technological change and

its relationship to other human, and particularly political and social, activities which should have priority over technology;
(b) the second concerns transfers of technology and the socio-cultural impact which they exert . . . ;
(c) the third concerns the wisdom of massive technology transfers from the industrialized countries to the developing nations . . . .

Communication is certainly one of the areas which have benefited from such transfers; however, there is another side to the picture, since technology transfers: (i) have consisted primarily in simple exportation of Western technology, which reflects the economic and social conditions and practices of one part of the world only; (ii) have generally tended to be capital rather than labor-intensive; (iii) have created dependence upon foreign capital, foreign supply sources, and foreign tastes and expectations; (iv) have been effected mostly by multinational corporations, which have maintained control over the technology; (v) have benefited elite sectors (newspapers, television, telephone) more than the masses; (vi) have contributed little to economic self-reliance and cooperation among developing countries; (vii) have fostered the rural exodus and increased urban migration.

3

World Communication Issues
ROSEMARY RIGHTER

In her essay, the British journalist builds upon some of the world's "big issues" to introduce more specific concerns having to do with the often hostile confrontations between Third World nations and the more economically developed nations of the West. She focuses on Unesco and Western press freedom as major factors in the ongoing worldwide debate over news and a "new order."

She says there is no easy response for the West—either by staunchly defending Western-style free press or being tolerant of diverse news values and tight national controls on the press. She suggests that the West concentrate on practical programs for improvement of "Third World access to information," which she calls a "fundamental right."

THE QUESTION of communications—and their control—is rapidly becoming one of the most intractable areas of disagreement between developing countries and the West. In 1976, the nonaligned governments issued a call for a New World Information Order, as "an integral part of the overall struggle for

Rosemary Righter, development correspondent of the *Sunday Times*, London, is the author of *Whose News? Politics, Press, and the Third World*.

This essay, updated in June 1980, originally appeared as "Newsflow International," *The Political Quarterly* (July–September 1979), 50(3):302–15.

political, economic and social independence."[1] At the time, the call went largely unheard; those in the West who did take note were united in viewing it as a serious threat to the free flow of information. Since then there has been little progress towards defining the possible implications of such a "new order"; but demands for its establishment have surfaced in almost every international forum, from Unesco to the United Nations General Assembly.

There are two basic claims underlying the Third World attack on the existing information structure. The first, which needs to be taken extremely seriously, is that developing countries' news and points of view should have greater access to the international news flow. The second is that the role of the media must be radically revised. At the international level, codes of conduct should be devised to regulate the activities of the "transnational" media, and the free flow of information should be tempered to the requirements of national sovereignty. At national level, policymakers in a number of countries are already seeking to ensure that the press is used for the general good (as governments perceive it)—as a tool for mobilizing the masses for development and the task of nation building.

The attack focuses therefore not just on the power of the Western press, its supposed influence on Western decision-making and on public opinion in the developed countries, or even on its impact on the cultures and economies of developing societies. The system of news values, and the structure of an independent press, which have evolved in the context of Western democracy, are being rejected as inappropriate and undesirable models by a growing number of Third World governments. The challenge to the Western press is a symbol of the growing distrust of Western values and lifestyles, of the very balance between individual rights and the constraints of power which an independent press exists to protect. The special difficulty for Western governments in meeting this challenge is that—unlike protectionism, aid, or the stabilization of

---

1. Official Communique, Fifth Non-Aligned Summit, Colombo, August 1976.

commodities prices—the press is not their province. It is one thing to offer help in building up the infrastructure of communications (and some governments are seeking to provide such assistance); it is quite another to concede that questions of news values and news content belong on the international agenda at all. In the confrontation which has inevitably resulted, the genuine grievances are obscured by the rhetoric of freedom versus sovereignty.

The Bitterness Felt

The roots of this confrontation lie in the bitterness felt by many people in the Third World at the end of the first U.N. Development Decade. Not only had the poverty gap widened, but Third World dependence on the industrialized West in terms of technology, finance, and trade had if anything increased. Their share of world trade was under 17 percent, of manufacturing a mere 8 percent. The outcome of developing countries' frustration was the call in 1974 for a New International Economic Order (NIEO)—a concept which has been generally interpreted as a demand for a fairer share of the world's resources. So it is: but it has been accompanied in some countries at least by a search for "alternative" development models, and by a deep distrust of Western financial power and economic prescriptions.

To the extent that the NIEO represents a struggle to break the chain of dominance forged by the industrialized West, it was bound eventually to focus on the press. It is worth noticing how recently these resentments have come into political focus. The nonaligned turned their attention to communication only at the 1973 nonaligned summit at Algiers, in the context of their Program for Economic Cooperation. The national media, they agreed, must be strengthened as part and parcel of their efforts to "eliminate the harmful consequences of the colonial era."From the outset, the attack on the information structure has been explicitly linked with the call for a new economic order.

Progress on the economic front has been extremely slow; the West has proved remarkably successful at breaking up global claims into small parcels for negotiation. During the long and inconclusive North-South conference in Paris which followed the 1975 U.N. Seventh Special Session, Western leaders stalled over what seemed to developing countries' negotiators as self-evidently just demands, saying that their public opinion was simply not prepared for major concessions. One consequence of this lack of progress is that—as the meeting of the Group of Seventy-Seven at Arusha in February 1979 demonstrated—Third World governments are beginning to reject the concept of an interdependent world, just as leaders in the West are belatedly beginning to support it. (It is instructive, in this context, that the Brandt Commission, which reported in 1980, skirted round phrases like interdependence and preferred to speak of "mutual interest.") Leaders of developing countries increasingly argue that since the system is pitched against them, their road to true independence will require the forging of new economic and cultural models.

The second consequence is that the role of the international press is coming under attack as a form of "cultural imperialism." Western reporting of Third World affairs is widely held to be responsible for the miserly attitude to trade, aid, and financial reforms taken by Western political and business leaders. If public opinion in the industrialized world is not prepared for structural change, the argument runs, it is because the international press is failing to report the crucial political evolution of this century. It may be a slightly naive assumption that, if only the publics of the West were fully and properly informed of the implications of a new international economic order, they would rush to lobby their governments in its favor. But there is some force in the accusation by Third World governments that the international press is failing to explain the reasons behind the pressures for change and to put across Third World arguments. This failure to put the case, they assert, also extends to the international reporting directed to developing countries themselves via the news agencies.

For all these reasons, our ideas about a free press are increasingly rejected both as alien to developing countries, and as a fraud. The doctrine of the "free flow of information," Third World leaders charge, is simply a comfortable moral screen for the protection of our vested interests. Since the overwhelming bulk of the world's international news is collected and distributed by a handful of Western news agencies, networks, and newspapers, the free flow concept has simply enabled the rich and the powerful to impose their views, and their market economies, on developing countries. And within the Third World, the imported model of a free press sows dissent instead of promoting the unity which they claim is vital to development and countering the instability inherent in societies undergoing rapid economic change.

Cultural Imperialists

The basic resentments begin with the fact that there is an imbalance in the flow of information which favors the North. The fact of Western dominance of the news flow is real enough. Between 80 percent and 90 percent of the international news is supplied by Reuters, the Associated Press, United Press International, and Agence France Presse. (TASS is rarely mentioned in the same context as the "Big Four," probably because TASS is not widely perceived as offering a *news* service.) This dominance of the market places a particular responsibility on the news agencies to free their reporting of national or Western bias. This they claim to do. But critics point out that an "international" language which describes a rise in coffee prices as a "coffee crisis" is patently biased. News agencies, and above all Western newspapers, do tend to talk about Orderly Marketing Arrangements where our own manufactured products are concerned, and about cartels where primary producers seek to organize their markets. When they do so, they accurately reflect the language used by government negotiators; but the corollary is that they are suspected of supporting their governments' *goals*. There is a language barrier between North and South; and one of the telling complaints about the Western press is that it helps to maintain that barrier.

The sheer volume of output by the major international agencies is enormous. It has been calculated that a newspaper office which sifted through the world services of the Big Four and TASS would have to sort 300,000 words a day—over fifty pages of broadsheet newspaper without the advertisements. Hilary Ng'Weno, a Kenyan editor whose support for the independence of the press is total, nevertheless reminds us that "Third World people have come to feel a great sense of impotence over the cultural influences which permeate their relations with the Western world throughout the mass media. It is an unrelenting one-way flow of ideas from the Western countries to the Third World, with little opportunity given to Third World nations to examine the content of the materials which daily flood their own presses."

This point can be overdone. In practice, a good deal of vetting goes on—and not by newspaper offices. As Professor Elie Abel, a former NBC correspondent and dean of the Columbia University School of Journalism, now at Stanford, points out: "Most developing countries do not allow their newspapers or broadcasting stations to subscribe directly to foreign agency services. The subscriber in most cases is the government, or government-controlled agency. In short, the picture of passive millions in the developing countries awash in a tidal wave of alien information is somewhat fanciful. . . . Governments, presumably, have a need to know what is happening in the world, even when they take special steps to 'protect' the inpopulation by filtering this information."[2] In about three-quarters of the nonaligned countries, the agencies' material goes through this filtering process.

2. Elie Abel, "Communication for an Interdependent, Pluralistic World." Paper for International Commission for the Study of Communication Problems, 1978.

The existence of national censorship, however, is not a complete answer to the basic charge: which is that news is selected in terms of Western attitudes and interests, if for no other reason than the need to cater to the main news markets. The agencies point out that their only editorial policy is to discover what news their clients want, and to supply it. This principle is imperfectly carried out in developing countries. . . . If governments continue freely to subscribe to the international agencies, it is because they are the best thing around, not because they provide an adequate diet of regional news.

Part of the problem is that although the agencies are under attack both for their success in penetrating international markets and their failure to provide an international service, they are in a sense being criticized for what they cannot possibly do. All four Western agencies between them operate on less than $300 million a year: They cannot pretend to cover the globe, nor do they do so—whatever Mark Twain said about God and the AP. The interests of developing countries are bound to be imperfectly treated in international reporting geared to the parochial demands of national media; the flow of international news is, if anything, more a trickle than a torrent despite the enormous number of words flowing over the wires. Worldwide, newspapers devote about 25 percent of their total space to international news: The agencies offer the basic ingredients for a thin diet. And the costs of international reporting operate as a further deterrent to more comprehensive coverage. It remains true that the bulk of the agencies' correspondents are located in the northern hemisphere.

The nub of the "cultural imperialism" thesis concerns quality even more than quantity. Not only do the international news media neglect whole countries or regions for months on end, the argument goes; they will rush to cover any calamity. This focus on droughts, earthquakes, and coups negates the claims of the Western press to provide accurate and objective reporting. The daily struggles of developing countries, with hunger, poverty, illiteracy, and the imperatives of development are either ignored, or treated superficially and in terms of Western criteria of what might constitute success or failure in tackling them. Most of the reporting from the Third World is ill-informed, biased, and sensationalized.

There is a lot of truth in this, although the major agencies have in recent years responded to the criticisms, and are making serious efforts to shed their reputation for "negative" reporting. But the difficulty is that, although everybody is agreed on the nature of bad news, there are as many versions of "good" news as there are editors and government censors. It is only too easy for an Asian diplomat, explaining why a visa is slow in emerging for a correspondent, to say that a previous article in *The Sunday Times* had referred to the involvement of the ruling family in corruption, and that "in the Orient, to name names is an offence to cultural values." Anything can be alien to cultural sovereignty which is perceived to be embarrassing.

The Real Problems

The real problems are more mundane, and more pervasive. Even where there is no intended bias in a report, journalists use a shorthand which can infuriate. Third World readers find their governments too easily labelled Marxist or right-wing, West-leaning or Soviet-supporting; their one-party political systems too easily dismissed as dictatorships, and organized liberation movements too automatically branded as terrorists. Two-dimensional reporting—typically emphasizing the impact on East-West relations, or on oil supplies, of a national or regional crisis—may be inevitable, but it stings. And beyond that, our concept of neutral reporting—and this is particularly true of the agencies—has its drawbacks. Between the pressures of the market and the emphasis on what journalists call hard news, there is a strong tendency to stick to stories which can be cleanly pegged to the particular event (coups are easier to make vivid, and to report, than agricultural programs). All correspondents seek to report what they expect will interest the news editor (and there is a possibly too unquestioned

assumption that what interests him will interest the public).
The spike is a great censor. Much Third World news simply
does not fall into this category of finite happenings, and is
largely ignored. Western-style reporting continues to be based
on the exceptional: "journalism of exception" can give a false
picture when the context is missing.

The more the Western press claims, realistically enough,
that there are limits to the coverage it can give developing
countries' affairs, the more likely Third World governments
are to close their frontiers to foreign journalists. This is already
beginning to affect the flow of news; and it is beside the point
to insist that Western news organizations should hire more
nationals of the countries in question. Most do this when they
can (apart from other advantages, it is cheaper to do so); but
in many countries, a national will be under strong pressure
not to file in certain circumstances, or to file a version of
events which fits with the government's line. The second demand—access to the Western press for news from Third World
media—has every theoretical justification. It may well be true
that only when such reporting reaches the publics of the industrialized world directly will any improvement in their understanding of Third World affairs occur.

This is where the key question arises: *what* news? Whatever the shortcomings of the Western press, editors fear that
they are being asked to accept propaganda in place of news.
They are not being merely fanciful or obstructive. The problem with a new world information order is not with the demand for access, but with the nature of national news organizations and the concept of the "new" news. The paradox
inherent in the Third World challenge is that in the name of
a number of so-called Western values—such as national sovereignty, self-determination and equality—Third World governments are demanding the right to exercise sovereignty over
news, internationally as well as nationally. They see the duties
of the press not as supporting the rights of the public to fuller
knowledge of national affairs, but as didactic, even ideological,
explaining to the people their part in forging a new social
order.

What this means, in a growing number of countries, has been described by an African journalist writing anonymously in a 1978 issue of *Afrique:* "The role given to the press in Africa is that of spreading among the population government propaganda calling for national unity and productive labor. The policies which underlie this propaganda are not put forward for discussion. National unity demands unanimity." As another journalist from Liberia puts it, "the press cannot criticize the government because it is part of the government." Many journalists in the Third World do not share this view. There is a lively debate between those in developing countries who believe that the journalist's responsibilities to national development come first, and those who argue that he can only exercise those responsibilities in a climate of independence from government control. But policies are not made in newsrooms. They are made in government offices, and governments have a strong tendency to believe, against all the evidence of history, that a controlled press promotes political stability. The "new order," as it is promoted within developing countries, may not increase the diversity of news sources, but create a kind of cultural nationalism in which government-regulated "national perspectives" exercise a monopoly over the citizens' view of the world.

This is already happening, and, where governments are used to controlling their own media, they find it inconceivable that the press is not similarly used, by Western governments, for the malign ends of Super-Power politics. The natural corollary of this approach to the press at home is that a number of states—notably among the nonaligned group—is attempting to win international support for the concept of a "guided" press, and to devise international agreements for that purpose. News, crudely, has ceased to be treated as neutral, and has become a commodity (like washing machines, but more important because more insidious in its effects on a society's attitudes) which must be subject to regulations governing its import, export, and even its basic design and safety features.

The dilemma is that the underlying resentments have a solid basis which we cannot ignore, but the remedies proposed threaten the flow of news and the freedom and independence of the press. There is no "solution," as Gerald Long, Reuters' chief executive, said in a speech in April 1979: "No agreement, even if one were possible, would reorder the great formless sprawl that is international communications. You might as well undertake to reform an oak tree or a camel." Yet the complaints are not just the invention of tinpot dictatorships, even though some of those who attack the system in the name of cultural emancipation may well have more effective control in mind. Nor are they merely a piece of international rhetoric: they are becoming institutionalized in ways which embed them in international politics.

Reforming the Camel

The first organization to question the international news flow was Unesco, a body of the U.N. committed by its constitution to promoting the "free flow of ideas by word and image." In 1970, Unesco turned its attention from the technical problems of the media—from training journalists and advising governments on communication infrastructures—to the content of news and the role of the media in society. Unesco also announced a major communications program to encourage governments to formulate national policies, with the express purpose of using the media more effectively for development. This switch in policy was initially ignored by Western governments—largely for the familiar reason that Western societies treat information as an area for the private sector; but also because of a generalized indifference to Unesco (which has been well described by Richard Hoggart).[3]

Belatedly, the West woke up when a Unesco "Declaration on the Media" was introduced which implied the setting of international standards and also a degree of state control of the press which directly threatened the principle of the free

3. Richard Hoggart, *An Idea and Its Servants: Unesco from Within* (London: Chatto & Windus, 1978).

flow of information. This declaration was something of a red herring: it did not arise out of Unesco's communications program. It was originally proposed by Byelorussia in 1972, with the narrow aim of bringing U.N. pressure to bear on foreign broadcasts to the Soviet Union and Eastern Europe. It challenged Western assumptions in two ways.

First, Western governments at Unesco took the view that even to negotiate on the functions of the press would be to accept the premise of state intervention in the content of news and the conduct of the media. Secondly, the successive drafts of the declaration which surfaced between 1974 and 1978 directly advocated state control. The declaration thus came to symbolize the growing pressures against the free-flow principle. In 1976, amid international outcry, the declaration came up to the Unesco General Conference in Nairobi and was referred back to Unesco for redrafting. The core of the uproar was a paragraph which said that: "States are responsible, in the international sphere, for all mass media under their jurisdiction."[4]

Unesco declarations are not legally enforceable, but they have a way of setting the terms of international discussion. This particular declaration was important because, in the name of a number of worthy goals such as the promotion of peace and the fight against racism and apartheid, it imposed duties on the media which not only abrogated the editorial function (and subjected the reporting of international news, for example, to the principle of respect for the "dignity of all nations") but required states to use their powers to see that media conformed. In broader terms, the declaration imperiled reasonable discussion of Third World grievances by introducing the fundamental East-West controversy about the press, between those who see the press as a tool of the state, and those who see the press as a guardian of civil liberties, acting as a check to political power by informing the citizen and thus enabling him to make his own choices. The timing of the

---

4. The text of this draft, presented to the 1976 General Conference as Item 69 of the agenda, is published in the conference document 19C/91 (Paris: Unesco, 1976).

debates on the declaration, coinciding as they did with the formulation of Unesco's new communications policies and with the demand for a new world information order, also meant that what began as an East-West quarrel became a symbol of the North-South disagreements on the role of the media.

At the 1978 General Conference, to the surprise of most delegates, agreement on a declaration was reached. The final text turned the whole focus of the declaration around, emphasizing human rights, diversity of news sources, the free flow of information, and the journalist's right of access to news sources.

The final declaration,[5] arrived at after weeks of corridor negotiations, was therefore widely interpreted as a victory for the West. So, in a sense, it was, although the final document was little more than a masterly achievement in squaring the circle. The declaration left the basic issues unresolved; and this was a great improvement on any pretense that a U.N. resolution could reconcile fundamentally opposed positions.

The important lessons to emerge were first, for Western governments, that the debate about international communications is on the agenda, and that absentees have no influence. This implies much more careful monitoring of the political pressures on the information structure; and also action to meet legitimate Third World grievances. Agreement on a radically revised text of the declaration was possible only because the West implicitly recognized these grievances, even if they avoided direct reference to a New World Information Order; and because most governments made offers of assistance to build up Third World media. Even then, three consequences stem from the unanimous agreement to support the revised declaration:

(i) It sets a precedent for governments to pronounce on the functions of the media and the content of information (and Malta, immediately afterwards, indicated that it would call next for a declaration on an international right of reply, for states as well as individuals).

5. 20C/20 Rev. Documents of the 20th General Conference (Paris: Unesco, 1978).

(ii) Unesco's role in investigating communications structures and advising on communications policies was implicitly endorsed.

(iii) Nonaligned spokesmen are already claiming that the declaration endorses the New World Information Order.

What the declaration did was to give the developing countries assurances that their grievances will be taken more seriously by the rich; and it gave the West a short breathing space in which to attempt to build up mechanisms for cooperation. What can be done with the breathing space?

What Can Be Done?

The three imperatives for the West after 1978 have been, not necessarily in this order: to implement some of the promises to assist in improving Third World communications which were made in the course of the negotiations on the Declaration; to impress on Unesco that the price of Western cooperation is a switch toward more practical policies by Unesco itself; and, with that in mind, to prevent the call for a new world information order from developing into a further direct ideological challenge.

Even on the first issue, practical cooperation, it has been rough sailing. A series of meetings ended in agreement by governments in April 1980 to set up a new "mechanism" within Unesco to implement an international program. Largely through the lack of coordination between the Americans and the European Economic Community (EEC) countries at the final meeting, the new mechanism finished up vague as to mandate, unworkable as to structure, and without funds. The one thing that was clear at the end of ten days of meetings was that it was to be serviced by a Unesco secretariat, "governed" by a council of thirty-five states to be elected at the 1980 General Conference of Unesco in Belgrade, and directed by an appointee of the Director-General of Unesco, Amadou Mahtar M'Bow. The Western countries still hoped, as the conference ended, that the new body would be a clearinghouse, matching what the U.S. delegation called "this vast area of unmet needs" with the resources available. But the United States had fought in vain to make the new mechanism an interagency body, free of Unesco's control, on the grounds that Unesco had shown little competence in the past at assisting the developing countries' press—and had no experience in the technical area of telecommunications—and also that its record on the whole issue had been ideologically loaded.

They failed for two reasons. One was that the Europeans, rightly up to a point, dismissed the U.S. scheme as unworkable—and were in any case fairly indifferent: Unesco could have its "mechanism" if it wanted, so long as they did not have to put their hands in their pockets. The second was that for once the developing countries had put together an extremely well-coordinated document, for which they fought tenaciously and expertly; and they were unimpressed that even Unesco's own statistics showed that in terms of developing Third World communications, the big spending agencies were elsewhere (the World Bank contribution dwarfs those of all other U.N. organizations combined.)

If Western negotiators believed at the end of that April conference that, at least, they had succeeded in isolating practical tasks from the political morass, they were disillusioned even before they had dispersed, when M'Bow reminded them that it was "impossible to separate the media from the messages which they transmit" and made it clear that, for him, the issue of communications was linked with "the aspirations of Third World countries to dignity and sovereignty."

M'Bow also made it clear that a special fund would be needed; Unesco is not about to redirect funds from its regular budget from theoretical studies of dubious intellectual quality to technical assistance programs. More worrisome for the West, however, as the Unesco General Conference in Belgrade that autumn approached, was the way in which the MacBride Report would be fed into Unesco's communications strategy.

This report was born in controversy, at the height of the confrontation over the Declaration on the Media, when M'Bow was asked in 1976 at Nairobi to provide a comprehensive review of communication problems. He responded by setting up an "independent" international commission with sixteen members, under the chairmanship of Sean MacBride—Irish statesman, lawyer, holder of both Nobel and Lenin Peace Prizes, a man whose many qualifications did not include much knowledge of how the media actually function.

MacBride and his commissioners met eight times over two years. Much of their conversation ranged over general principles, and the drafting of their report was left to a secretariat provided by Unesco. Their remit was completely open-sided: they were to look at the totality of communications, considered, M'Bow suggested, as a "sociocultural problem" with "political, ideological and philosophical" dimensions. It was not, for all that, open-ended: they were to seek ways of establishing a new world information and communication order, and consider while they were at it how the media could better be used for objectives ranging from education to "safeguarding peace."

The Commission's first job—which had to be completed after a total of only eight days of meetings—was to produce an interim report for the 1978 Unesco General Conference. It was, not surprisingly, a tortuous, ill-written, and intellectually garbled document, and it betrayed, beneath the intellectual muddle and the appallingly obscure language, a distinct bias toward control of the media. It rightly, however, characterized the new information order as something essentially negative.

It could hardly have avoided reaching such a conclusion, given the paper presented to the commission by Mustapha Masmoudi, Tunisia's permanent representative to Unesco, a former president of the Nonaligned Committee on Information and a member of the MacBride Commission (although officially it was composed of "individuals") very much as the spokesman of the nonaligned. Masmoudi's new order, as he presented it, would (i) regulate the rights of those receiving information, (ii) endorse the principle that a nation should "choose its information in accordance with its own realities and requirements," (iii) prevent the "abuse" of the right of access to information, (iv) regulate the flow of news and data across national frontiers, and (v) give states the right to publish in foreign media corrections of reports a state felt were not "a faithful reflection of its concerns and aspirations."

The *Interim Report* was heavily criticized, and not only by Westerners. When the *Final Report* finally surfaced in May 1980, some of the criticisms had been met. Not only were many restrictive passages dropped, but the *Final Report* strongly condemned censorship, affirmed that the principle of freedom must be respected, and insisted that journalists must have access to "the entire spectrum of opinion within any country" (an assertion which lost some of its force since the Soviet commissioner, Sergei Losev of TASS, put in a strong note of dissent).[6]

But on the *practice* of freedom—what journalists could do with their information once they had obtained it—the report was more ambiguous. Certainly, journalists have responsibilities: but the commission laid on them heavy burdens: they must take care that their reporting promoted friendly relations between states, fostered cultural identity, enhanced the dignity of nations and peoples, respected national sovereignty, and promoted just causes like disarmament and liberation movements.

The report was addressed to the director-general, who could draw on any part of it to make recommendations to Unesco's member states at the 1980 General Conference. Even so, the commission's recommendations mattered more than its utterances of irreproachable pieties, or even than the generally didactic and even paternalistic tone which it adopted.

Many of these recommendations, contained in a final section, were greatly toned down by a minority of the commission's members, who fought determinedly to enlarge rather than restrict the flow of information. They argued, successfully, that their chairman's pet project, a draft charter for the protection of journalists, would subject journalists to the dan-

6. Excerpts from the MacBride Commission *Interim Report* and *Final Report* are published elsewhere in this collection of readings.

gers involved in a licensing system; they argued against international codes of ethics; they rejected the idea of a World Press Council. But much escaped them.

The commission could not have been expected to resolve the dichotomy between two approaches to information. But, for all its references to pluralism, its very first recommendation was that nations should formulate "comprehensive communications policies" and that these should be "linked to overall social, cultural, economic, and political goals." The implication was clear: the content of communications, including news, must be subjected to national planning, subordinated to national policy, used to fulfill "political goals." One of the commission's members, Gamal el-Oteify from Egypt, warned his colleagues that state coordination would mean state control. Perhaps in its desire to encourage the growth of communications facilities, the commission paid no heed.

And, for all its hopes that journalists would not be controlled, the commission recommended that "effective legal measures should be designed to . . . circumscribe the action of transnationals by requiring them to comply with specific criteria and conditions defined by national legislation and development policies." This is an open invitation to governments to circumscribe international news flows; it is as incompatible with free reporting as it is with the admirable phrases about censorship and access.

If these and other recommendations were not enough to concern supporters of a free press, the final section also included a strange endpiece: a subsection entitled "Issues for Further Study," compiled after the commission's last meeting on November 30, 1979, when it was formally dissolved.

This collection of "issues" was not, the report said, approved by the commission, was not in some cases even discussed. But in fact some of them *were* discussed, and were rejected. International codes of ethics, for example: it now seemed that the commission after all thought that journalists' organizations might fruitfully look into the possibility. And, in apparent contradiction to the main recommendations, there was the suggestion that "some mechanism" might be created, "ideally with adequate judicial authority" to which a journalist could appeal if "refused or deprived of his identity card." The proposals so carefully considered, and rejected, by the commission now crept back through a side entrance.

These niceties matter, because the report was intended from the start to be interpreted, and used. It was vital that it give no hostages to governments. The urge to regulate was still apparent in the *Final Report*, and this urge is dear to all governments. More than that, the commission had ideas about setting up the appropriate machinery for regulation. In a proposal that Professor Elie Abel called in a footnote "premature, unnecessary and unwise," the commission suggested that Unesco should set up a center for the study and planning of communications. (This proposal, coming forward just as the Unesco "mechanism" was being set up, increased the risk that the mechanism would be used for more than mere technical assistance programs.) And it said that Unesco should include "the elaboration of international norms" as a priority in its communications activities.

The effect of the report (although its almost 150,000 very long words would be digested by only the most dedicated few) was therefore to sharpen rather than smooth over the controversy behind the Declaration on the Media. It provided ample excuses to those who wished to strengthen the bureaucratic and political controls over news flows. And, precisely because it is both long and ambiguous, Western governments were again likely to be slow to respond to the challenge. They had little time in any case; for the *Final Report* was formally to be presented to the Belgrade Conference as an appendix to recommendations made by the director-general, and they were slow in coming.

Western governments were disinclined, in the summer of 1980, to believe that much could be amiss. They had, after all, insisted—at least in Western Europe—that they would be able to keep politics out of the 1979 World Administrative Radio Conference, and they had largely succeeded, even though critical issues about the use of the spectrum and particularly the geostationary orbit were referred to a future session. And they had, after all, paid lip service to the concept of some form of new information order and thereby, many bureaucrats believed, eased the pressures against the existing, disorderly web of communications misnamed the "old order."

Government reluctance to take either Unesco's activities or the MacBride Report's recommendations seriously is mistaken but—given Western traditions—natural. It is not their business, they say, and they are right. And in any case, there is no easy response for the West to these pressures, because there is no consistent strategy which makes sense. If governments were to base their policy on recognizing the diversity of news values, they would come close to conceding that news should be shaped to the dictates of national policy. This would not only weaken their defense of the concept of a free press in their own countries, but would undermine the position of journalists and others in the Third World who argue that independent reporting and open debate are not just Western luxuries but basic human rights.

On the other hand, policies which make the defense of press freedom their goal run into two separate difficulties. First, freedom is defended essentially negatively, by resistance to encroachments upon it—it cannot be protected by international agreement and it is a stranger to planning. Secondly, insistence on the importance of free expression sounds natural to Western ears but can sound threatening to developing countries. It also runs up against the growing distrust of Western motives: until the reporting by the Western press of Third World affairs shows markedly more sympathy and understanding, such preaching will meet with a hostile response.

Western governments can only concentrate on implementing practical programs which will improve Third World access to information, and to the means of disseminating it, and hope that these means will be used to disseminate news rather than propaganda. That issue—the content of information—will in the end be decided within the developing countries themselves. The best prospect for a free press lies in the fact that people everywhere have a way of knowing when they are being sold a load of old rope. Governments which curb open debate do not necessarily promote national unity and development: they are more likely to meet with apathy and disaffection. Given the means to communicate, pressures for more accurate information build up from below. But it is a patchy, long-term process.

The technological revolution in communications means that changes in news flows and news structures are inevitable; we are moving toward a "new order" of some kind. It is in this context that any international moves to regulate the press are vitally important. For Western governments to steer clear of ideological debate is wholly natural but the penalty is likely to be the endorsement of a new world information order which constricts rather than improves the flow of information. If governments shape their national media to an official ideology, creating tight monopolies in the name of the struggle against the domination of the news flow by the international press, the "new order" will imply a positive manipulation of the media which goes far beyond mere censorship. At stake is far more than the fortunes of the Western press: it is the ability of the citizen, in developing countries as in the West, to make his opinions heard and to make his own choices on the basis of knowledge. It is this fundamental right of access which the debate has so far largely obscured.

4

The New World Information Order
MUSTAPHA MASMOUDI

Ambassador Masmoudi undertakes the difficult task of defining what the still-emerging concept of the "new order" means to political sovereignty and national development. The essay offers a comprehensive list of grievances centered on various political, legal, technical, and financial imbalances in the present system.

Masmoudi's arguments deserve attention because of the great influence normative aspects in particular have had within international organizations, especially Unesco. Among Third World spokesmen, he undoubtedly has been the single most influential person challenging the consequences of the existing order. His views are frequently used to explain why Third World nations, especially in the 1970s, pushed so hard against lingering colonialism and for a major overhaul of prevailing economic and information orders.

To many in the West, Masmoudi's views are not merely controversial but also radical. His descriptions of what he sees as obvious

Mustapha Masmoudi, Tunisia's permanent delegate to Unesco, is a leading Third World advocate for a "new world information order." He was an influential member of the MacBride Commission and has been secretary of state for information of Tunisia and President of the Intergovernmental Coordinating Council for Information of the Nonaligned Countries.

This essay is taken from a longer article from the *Interim Report* of the International Commission for the Study of Communication Problems. Copyright © 1979 Unesco. Reprinted by permission.

abuses in the existing international system have been interpreted by Western media organizations and others as a serious threat to press freedom and an invitation to governments to take over media in the Third World. His sweeping indictments of the First World communication systems are often challenged. The paper itself addresses broad communication and political problems, well beyond news itself, but which are important to an understanding of the news crisis.

SINCE THE END of World War II, the world has undergone profound upheavals, due to a rapid transformation of political concepts as well as to a change of outlook in men, whether they belong to the developed or to the developing world . . . . At the economic level, present-day international society still suffers from a deep and serious inequality between developed and developing countries. In all other domains, the same imbalance is to be observed between the two groups of States.

The developing countries have rapidly become aware of the seriousness of this imbalance, and have launched new battles to establish a better international society. . . . These objectives could not be fully achieved if the reform movement failed to affect the international information system.

Information plays a paramount role in international relations, both as a means of communication between peoples and as an instrument of understanding and knowledge between nations. . . . However, what must be noted right away is that the present international information system shows a profound imbalance between developed and developing countries. . . .

This situation of imbalance has naturally prompted the wish for a radical overhaul of the present international information system and highlighted the need to establish a new world order for information. . . .

POLITICAL ASPECTS OF INFORMATION

In the political sphere, that is, in respect of the conception of information, these imbalances take many forms:

A flagrant quantitative imbalance between North and South. This imbalance is created by the disparity between the volume of news and information emanating from the developed world and intended for the developing countries and the volume of the flow in the opposite direction. Almost 80 percent of the world news flow emanates from the major transnational agencies; however, these devote only 20 to 30 percent of news coverage to the developing countries, despite the fact that the latter account for almost three-quarters of mankind. This results in a veritable de facto monopoly on the part of the developed countries.

An inequality in information resources. The five major transnational agencies monopolize between them the essential share of material and human potential, while almost a third of the developing countries do not yet possess a single national agency.

Inequality also exists in the distribution of the radio frequency spectrum between developed and developing countries. The former control nearly 90 percent of the source of the spectrum, while the developing countries have no means of protecting themselves against foreign broadcasts. . . . In respect of television, not only do 45 percent of the developing countries have no television of their own, but this disparity is aggravated still further by the broadcasting in these countries of a larger number of programs produced in the developing countries.

A de facto hegemony and a will to dominate. Such hegemony and domination are evident in the marked indifference of the media in the developed countries, particularly in the West, to the problems, concerns, and aspirations of the developing countries. They are founded on financial, industrial, cultural, and technological power and result in most of the developing countries being relegated to the status of mere consumers of information sold as a commodity like any other. They are exercised above all through the control of the information flow, wrested and wielded by the transnational agencies operating without let or hindrance in most developing countries and based in turn on the control of technology. . . .

A lack of information on developing countries. Current events in the developing countries are reported to the world via the transnational media; at the same time, these countries are kept "informed" of what is happening abroad through the same channels. By transmitting to the developing countries only news processed by them, that is, news which they have filtered, cut, and distorted, the transnational media impose their own way of seeing the world upon the developing countries. As a result, communities geographically close to each other sometimes learn about each other only via these transnational systems. Moreover, the latter often seek to present these communities—when indeed they do show interest in them—in the most unfavorable light, stressing crises, strikes, street demonstrations, putsches, etc., or even holding them up to ridicule. . . .

Survival of the colonial era. The present-day information system enshrines a form of political, economic and cultural colonialism which is reflected in the often tendentious interpretation of news concerning the developing countries. This consists in highlighting events whose significance, in certain cases, is limited or even nonexistent; in collecting isolated facts and presenting them as a "whole"; in setting out facts in such a way that the conclusion to be drawn from them is necessarily favorable to the interests of the transnational system; in amplifying small-scale events so as to arouse unjustified fears; in keeping silent on situations unfavorable to the interests of the countries of origin of these media. . . .

Likewise, information is distorted by reference to moral, cultural, or political values peculiar to certain States, in defiance of the values and concerns of other nations. . . .

An alienating influence in the economic, social, and cultural spheres. In addition to dominating and manipulating the international news flow, the developed countries practice other forms of hegemony over the communications institutions of the Third World. First of all, they have possession of the media through direct investment. Then, there is another form of control, . . . near-monopoly on advertising throughout the world exercised by the major advertising agencies, which operate like the media transnationals and which earn their income by serving the interests of the transnational industrial and commercial corporations, which themselves dominate the business world. A further form of domination is represented by the influence used to oppose social evolution; this is practiced quite openly by the institutions engaging in propaganda. Moreover, advertising, magazines, and television programs are today so many instruments of cultural domination and acculturation, transmitting to the developing countries messages which are harmful to their cultures, contrary to their values, and detrimental to their development aims and efforts.

Messages ill-suited to the areas in which they are disseminated. Even important news may be deliberately neglected by the major media in favor of other information of interest only to public opinion in the country to which the media in question belong. Such news is transmitted to the client countries and is indeed practically imposed on them, despite the fact that readers and listeners in these countries have no interest therein. The major mass media and those who work for them take no account of the real relevance of their messages. Their news coverage is designed to meet the national needs of their countries of origin. They also disregard the impact of their news beyond their own frontiers. They even ignore the important minorities and foreign communities living on their national territory, whose needs in matters of information are different from their own.

The fact cannot therefore be blinked that the present information order, based as it is on a quasi-monopolistic concentration of the power to communicate in the hands of a new developed nations, is incapable of meeting the aspirations of the international community. . . . All such political and conceptual shortcomings are worsened—when they are not actually justified—by inadequate international legal structures.

LEGAL ASPECTS OF INFORMATION

The traditional conception of rights in matters of communication is founded on individual considerations, to the detriment of collective needs. The present international legal framework is defective, and even nonexistent in certain fields. Moreover, the application of present-day legislation is arbitrary. It favors a small number of countries at the expense of the majority, thanks to a conception of liberty peculiar to those who own or control the communication media—and who are frequently the very same people who own or control the means of production. In this context, many questions need to be raised.

Individual rights and community rights. The philosophy which has prevailed to date has given prominence to the rights of a small number of persons or bodies specializing in this field. As a result, the rights and concerns of groups have been more or less disregarded. Yet, if it is true that the right to information is intrinsic to the human condition, it is nonetheless a natural right of every human community, in the sense that each people feels an overpowering urge to communicate with "the other," not only in order to come to terms with and to preserve its own personality but also in order to know and understand other peoples better. . . .

Freedom of information or freedom to inform. Freedom of information is presented as the corollary of freedom of opinion and freedom of expression but was in fact conceived as the "freedom of the informing agent." As a result, it has become an instrument of domination in the hands of those who control the media. In legal terms, it has resulted in the enshrining of the rights of the communicator, while disregarding his duties and responsibilities toward those to whom he is communicating.

Right of access to information sources. This right is understood in a one-sided manner, and essentially benefits those who have the resources to obtain and impart information. This de facto situation has allowed certain major transnational corporations to turn this right into a prerogative, and enabled the wealthy powers to establish their domination over the information channels.

The ineffectiveness of the right of correction. In contrast to the domestic law of certain countries, the right of correction is regulated very ineffectively by international law. . . . Regulations in this area are in fact restrictive and unfavorable to developing countries.

The absence of an international deontology and the defective character of the regulations governing the profession. In this context, the imbalance is also fostered by the absence of an international deontology. Attempts made to date by Unesco and the United Nations to institute an international code of ethics suited to the needs of the individual and the community have proved ineffectual.

Imbalance in the field of copyright. Matters of copyright have long been regulated by the Berne Convention of 1886, which is protectionist in its scope of application, in the duration of the validity of copyright and in the fewness of the waivers that may be applied to these provisions. The Universal Convention of 1952, revised in 1971 and administered by Unesco, provides for a less rigorous degree of protection. . . . Altogether, the international publishing and distribution system operating today has led, on pretext of protecting copyright, to the predominance of certain commercial interests in the developed countries and has indirectly contributed to the cultural and political domination of these countries over the international community as a whole.

Imbalance in the distribution of the source of the spectrum. The objective must be to denounce the provisions of Article 9 of the Radio Regulations, which enshrine vested interests in respect of the distribution of the spectrum, and so deprive in particular recently independent countries of satisfactory means of making their voices heard.

Disorder and lack of coordination in telecommunications and in the use of satellites, compounded with flagrant inequalities between States. In the absence of any effective regulation, the present inequalities in this field are likely to increase, while the rights of the more powerful will become consolidated in a manner beyond remedy. It hardly needs stressing that such great progress has been made in this field that, without adequate regulation, a veritable invasion of radio broadcasts and television programs must be expected, amounting to a violation of national territories and private homes and a veritable form of mental rape. . . .

TECHNICO-FINANCIAL ASPECTS OF INFORMATION

Because of the structures inherited from colonialism, the low volume of trade, and the laxity in economic relations, the telecommunications are far from having met the hopes of establishing closer links and a more intensive flow of information among developing countries. The developed countries benefit from the most efficient and least costly communications channels and resources. The developing countries suffer all the drawbacks of an organization which is both defective and costly to the communications system now operating. The developed countries' technological lead and the tariff system for international communications which they have instituted have enabled them to benefit from monopoly situations and prerogatives both in fixing the rates for transport of publications and telecommunications and in the use of communications and information technology. . . .

The advent of satellites is likely to intensify this imbalance if decisive international action is not taken and if technological aid is not furnished to the developing countries. This imbalance is particularly apparent in the following fields:

Telecommunications. The present structures and patterns of telecommunications networks between developing countries are based solely on criteria of profitability and volume of traffic, and so constitute a serious handicap to the development of information and communication. This handicap affects both the infrastructure and the tariff system.

With regard to the infrastructure, in addition to the absence of direct links between developing countries, a concentration of communication networks is to be observed in the developed countries. The planning of the infrastructure devised by the former colonial powers precludes, for certain developing countries, all possibility of transmitting information beyond their frontiers (earth stations allowing only reception of television programs produced in the industrialized countries, with no possibility of broadcasting toward these countries). . . .

Designed so as to disadvantage small outputs, the present tariff system perpetuates the stranglehold of the rich countries on the information flow. It is strange, to say the least, that, over the same distance, communications should cost more between two points within developing countries than between two others situated in developed countries.

Similarly, nothing can justify the fact that the same communication should cost less when transmitted from a developed to a developing country than in the opposite direction. . . . How can we accept the privilege enjoyed by the major news agencies, which secure, thanks to the density of their traffic, fulltime use of circuits at a cost that in certain cases does not exceed that of a daily average use of one hour? . . .

Satellites . . . the developing countries are still threatened by the anarchic use of extra-atmospheric space, which is liable to worsen the imbalance affecting the present telecommunications system.

Distribution of radio frequencies. The problem of allocating the frequency spectrum . . . arises today with particular urgency. The developing countries are . . . more determined than ever to challenge vigorously the rights that the developed countries have arrogated to themselves in the use of the frequency spectrum. They are also determined to secure an equitable sharing out of this spectrum.

It is common knowledge that almost 90 percent of the source of the spectrum is controlled by a few developed countries, and that the developing countries, although covering far more extensive areas, possess fewer channels than the developed countries. The power density per square kilometer is four times less in developing countries than in the developed.

Transport of publications. The imbalance observed in the telecommunications field also occurs in the flow of newspapers and publications:

  –Tariffs and distribution rates for newspapers are governed, as are those for all other mail, by the Universal Postal Convention, and all member countries of the Universal Postal Union are obliged to respect them.

—With regard to newspapers . . . the Universal Postal Convention allows member countries the option of granting a maximum 50 percent reduction in the tariff applicable to printed materials in respect both of newspapers and periodicals, books and pamphlets.

—In addition to the optional nature of this reduction, air mail is subject to a bottom rate which does not favor the transport of small-circulation publications, i.e., precisely those produced in the developing countries. . . .

The New World Information Order

. . . . This new order entails a thorough-going readjustment. It is no ready-made recipe, which could enable an unjust situation to be transformed overnight into one less unjust. . . . The aim must be rather to initiate a process at the national, regional, and international levels. Effective, concrete measures are called for rather than academic discussion. . . .

The new world information order founded on democratic principles seeks to establish relations of equality in the communications field between developed and developing nations and aims at greater justice and greater balance. Far from calling in question the freedom of information, it proposes to ensure that this principle is applied fairly and equitably for all nations and not only in the case of the more developed among them. . . .

FROM THE POLITICAL VIEWPOINT

In this respect, the aim must be to define a communications policy and the role of information, and to identify the measures to be taken in respect of news collection, editing, selection, and dissemination with a view to eliminating the aftereffects of the colonial era. It should be constantly borne in mind that information is a social need and not a mere commodity. . . .

In respect of developing countries. The aim must be:

—To define national communications policy, as being necessary to each country's economic and social development and of a nature to motivate its citizens on behalf of such development;
—To make provision, in the formulation of such national communications policies, for measures favoring optimum exchanges of news programs at the regional or subregional level, and fostering active and determined participation on the part of all developing countries in the operation of international communications and information centers and networks;
—To multiply exchange agreements between information bodies, training and research institutes and national, regional and international organizations directly or indirectly involved in the communications sector. . . ;
—To consolidate and develop the established structures, particularly among the nonaligned countries, while at the same time, helping, in cooperation with the developed countries and the international organizations concerned, to establish communications media, to train qualified personnel and to acquire suitable materials and equipment in a spirit of collective self-reliance;
—To institute and strengthen assistance to the least developed countries;
—To pay particular attention to the information supplied by the national news collection centers or news pools of the developing countries, on the problems which concern their respective regions or countries;
—To alert the media of the developed countries to the imbalances, deficiencies and imperfections of the present communications system, by arranging for meetings (conferences, seminars or symposia) between those responsible for the different media in the developed and developing countries;
—To launch a wide-ranging campaign in the field of communications in the universities of both developing and developed countries, aimed at training or retraining professionals and inculcating the values of the new international economic order and the new world information order;
—To democratize information resources and structures. At the horizontal level, this implies setting up national news agencies and machinery for cooperation and mutual assistance between

developing countries . . . and, on the vertical plane, curtailing the monopolies of the major press agencies by promoting . . . international agreements aimed at equal and fair utilization of all communications media, including satellites;

– To establish a system fostering free and equitable flow between developed and developing countries, from the point of view both of content, volume, and intensity;

– To implement a national policy to promote literary and artistic creation by instituting a tax system that is as favorable as possible;

– To encourage the setting up or development of national societies of authors aimed at ensuring optimum management for the countries concerned of the resources deriving from the exploitation of intellectual works in all their diversity.

In respect of the developed countries. The aim here must be:

– To call public attention to the action taken by the developing countries, emphasizing the ever-increasing interdependence of the different nations of the world. It is indeed unthinkable that public opinion in the developed countries should continue to be unaware of the widening gap between these and the deprived countries, or to adopt an attitude of indifference to the matter. . . ;

– To help "decolonize" information by taking a more objective approach to the aspirations and concerns of the developing nations. . . ;

– To help establish a balance in the information flow by devoting more space in newspapers and in radio and television programs to news concerning developing countries. . . ;

– To promote better mutual understanding by encouraging the media in the industrialized countries to devote greater attention to the content of their transmissions . . . to make the cultures and civilizations of other peoples . . . more widely known;

– To ensure that journalists and writers show the utmost prudence and themselves verify the reliability and authenticity of all material, data, or arguments used by them which might tend to intensify the arms race;

– To ensure that journalists respect the laws of the country and the cultural values of the different peoples, and acknowledge that the right of peoples to make known their own concerns and to learn about those of other peoples is as important as respect for individuals;

–To put an end to the pernicious activities of foreign stations established outside national frontiers;

–To give particular attention to information supplied by national newsgathering centers or news pools in the developing countries on events concerning their respective regions or countries . . . with a view to balancing and diversifying the news concerning these countries and in general increasing the space alloted thereto;

–To ensure that, prior to each mission, special correspondents acquire as comprehensive a knowledge as possible of the countries to which they are sent. . . .

In respect of the international organizations. Efforts should be aimed at:

–Enlarging and diversifying the scope of the aid given by Unesco and the other international organizations to developing countries and supplying means for linking up multilateral and bilateral assistance to these countries. . . ;

–Helping to promote the development of the media in developing countries both at the national and regional level, in a spirit of collective self-sufficiency;

–Enabling the developing countries to take advantage of the forums open to them in the international organizations . . . to make known their demands and to bring about the establishment of a new world information order;

–Supporting the efforts of developing countries to formulate and adopt national communications policies, to promote research, particularly on the implications of transfers of technology, and to set up documentation centers on communications;

–Instituting a tax in the developed countries which are exporters of literary and artistic works of all kinds, the proceeds from which would help to finance the international copyright fund which is to be administered by Unesco.

–Enlarging and diversifying the range of the aid granted to developing countries, and helping them to use the communication sciences to promote social evolution by undertaking studies

based on assumptions and methods which reflect the realities
and correspond to the needs of the developing countries;
—Granting maximum technical and financial assistance to institutions carrying out research on communications, in accordance
with the needs emerging in each country and each region;
—Implementing . . . in collaboration with the mass communications training centers which exist in all developing countries,
a program to draw up and coordinate the curricula of mass
communications institutes and departments and special voca-
tional training courses in this field. The essential purpose of
this program would be to adapt studies to the specific, practical
needs of each country and each region in respect of
communications. . . ;
—Promoting through the grant of fellowships and similar measures
an advanced university training course in the communication
sciences. Such training should be given in accordance with the
needs, objectives, and potentialities of developing countries. It
should help to imbue future generations of specialists with a
new vision of communication, and introduce a different theory
and practice capable of establishing national and international
relations that are nonauthoritarian and conducted between
equals;
—Helping to formulate research programs and to establish training
centers so as to enable developing countries to produce radio
and television programs designed to serve the aims of the New
International Economic Order;
—Granting the mass communications sector a status that corresponds to its undoubted importance and to its evident influence
on all other sectors of activity, so as to develop an easy and
harmonious relationship not only with the cultural sector but
also with the education sector and with others that are today
less closely linked thereto;
—Divising a clear-cut policy on the use of satellites transmission
systems, respecting in all cases the sovereign rights of individual
States;
—Encouraging the testing, evaluation, and dissemination of new,
low-priced and easy-to-use communications technology so as
to enable the message of development to reach the masses at
present cut off from all such information;
—Helping to establish historical documentation and archives centers in the developing countries.

FROM THE LEGAL VIEWPOINT

A new definition of the right to communicate. There can be no justice in international communications unless and until rights in this field are redefined and applied on an extensive scale.

Information must be understood as a social good and a cultural product, and not as a material commodity or merchandise. Seen in this perspective, all countries should enjoy the same opportunities of access to sources of information as well as to participate in the communication process. . . . Communication is like air or daylight: everyone should have the same right thereto. It is the common property of all mankind. The right to communicate must be obstructed neither by individuals nor by entities.

Information is not the prerogative of a few individuals or entities that command the technical and financial means enabling them to control communication; rather, it must be conceived as a social function intrinsic to the various communities, cultures, and different conceptions of civilization. Accordingly, the right of those receiving information should be so regulated as to sanction the functions of interaction and participation and to ensure free and balanced flow of information. . . .

Equity and equality. In this context, a number of measures should be promoted with a view to ensuring:

–Democratization of the media and information structures, which entails on the horizontal plane setting up national news agencies and machinery for cooperation and mutual assistance between developing countries, such as Press Agency Pool of the Nonaligned Countries and the regional unions (African, Arab, Asian, Latin-American), and on the vertical plane curtailing the monopolies of the major news agencies by promoting the conclusion of international agreements aimed at ensuring equal and equitable use of all communication media, including satellites;
–Respect for the rights of those receiving information, in particular the right to objectivity of information and balance in its presentation, so as to take account of their concerns and of the

cultural and moral values of the society to which they belong;
—Institution of a system fostering free and equitable circulation
between developed and developing countries, from the point of
view of the content, volume, and intensity of the flow;
—Establishment at the international level of the new world information order based on the principles of the equality and
sovereignty of States, these principles entailing the need to ensure equal access of all to communication media, a fair share
in the international communications environment and the right
of every State to see its internal order, its options, and objectives
respected.

Right of access to sources. The new world information
order must put an end to the imbalance between nations in
this field and promote a new conception of access to information based on the following principles:
  In respect of current news:

  —Regulation of the right to information by preventing abusive
  uses of the right of access to information;
  —Definition of appropriate criteria to govern truly objective news
  selection;
  —Regulation of the collection, processing, and transmission of
  news and data across national frontiers, and in particular of
  transnational processing, memorization, and storage systems so
  as to protect the individual's right to private life and to ensure
  respect for the dignity of communities and nations.
  —The new world information order must provide for the right of
  developing countries to restitution to their countries of origin
  of archives and historical documents concerning the history of
  these newly emancipated countries, in particular those in the
  possession of the former colonial powers. . . .

Professional deontology. The need to establish an international deontology governing information and communications is becoming ever more strongly felt. The self-regulation
of professional media organizations must, to be sure, be given
recognition in such a deontology. However, it cannot replace
a more wide-ranging formula, since no social group should have

the prerogative of not being held accountable to the community to which it belongs. . . .

Protection of journalists. The protection of journalists is a key element in the world communications and information system. Such protection should extend to the relations between the journalist and his employers and should enable him to safeguard his freedom of thought and analysis against all potential pressures. It must cover the journalist in the performance of his professional duties, whether he is working abroad or in his own country, undertaking a dangerous mission or operating in normal conditions.

The right of correction. The social function of information truly attains its objective only if the information transmitted is true and objective and squares with reality. The journalist betrays his mission if he gives information which is false, tendentious, or mutilated, or is dictated by concerns, criteria, and choices which are peculiar to himself. In such cases, the State concerned should have the right to publish or have published a communiqué rectifying and supplementing the false or incomplete information already disseminated so as to give an accurate picture of the facts and to situate these in their true context. . . .

The distribution of the electromagnetic spectrum and the use of satellites. . . . the natural resources of both the electromagnetic spectrum and the geostationary orbits are limited. This limitation makes it essential to revise the present allocation of the resources of the spectrum and to regulate the use of extra-atmospheric space for telecommunications purposes. . . .

For this purpose, it is essential to provide for:

–The safeguarding of the rights of countries still under domination to equitable access to the frequency spectrum;
–The revision of Article 9 of the Radio Regulations and the reappraisal of the rule of "first come, first served" where the frequency spectrum is concerned;
–A "moratorium" on the free-for-all use of extra-atmospheric space pending the conclusion of an international agreement

which satisfactorily guarantees the supply and use of modern telecommunications technical resources in general. . . .

Copyright. In this field, the conventions and regulations currently in force should be revised with a view to ensuring the necessary balance in the circulation of intellectual works between developed and developing countries. In particular the object must be to incorporate into the Florence Convention provisions on behalf of developing countries, as was the case in 1971 in the revision of the Berne Convention and the Universal Copyright Convention.

FROM THE TECHNICAL AND FINANCIAL VIEWPOINTS

The measures advocated above can be given concrete form only through an overall reappraisal of technical structures at the international level. In this perspective, the steps to be taken . . . may be defined as follows:

-Rethinking the present pattern of the international telecommunications network;
-Fostering the establishment of centers or nodes of communication in developing countries and setting up direct links whenever possible between developing countries;
-Working for the lowering of communication tariffs between developing countries;
-Revising the structure of international tariffs at present in force so as to cease to penalize low outputs, and providing for a tariff system favoring communication from developing to developed countries; . . .
-Ensuring that satellites are seen primarily as a means of alleviating certain telecommunications functions hitherto discharged by point-to-point, short-wave transmission;
-Using satellites for transmitting radio and television programs of developing countries which have hitherto been unable to ensure their adequate diffusion solely by conventional means; . . .
-Taking appropriate steps . . . [for] assistance from the developed countries in projects to launch satellites and in the transfer of technology. . . .

—Ensuring equitable redistribution of the spectrum, without taking any *faits accomplis* into consideration, on the basis of a balanced allocation between all regions of the globe; . . .
—Encouraging the exchange of newspapers between developing countries . . . and between these and developed countries. . . ;
—Taking joint action . . . to obtain new favorable terms for newspapers at the next congress of the Universal Postal Union; . . .
—Formulating an international code of conduct governing the transfer of technology. . . ;
—Improving the conditions of access to modern technologies and adapting them as appropriate . . . to the developing countries. . . ;
—Extending the assistance given by the developed to the developing countries in the form of research-and-development programs and by developing appropriate local technologies;
—Setting up a genuinely independent body responsible for advising developing countries on the choice, establishment and use of communications technology. . . .

The New International Orders

The technical advances achieved during the recent decades in all sectors of economic activity have not been equitably distributed between members of the international community. The income of the developed countries, in which 75 percent of the world's population is concentrated, at present represents only 30 percent of world income. Average per capita income in the industrialized countries today stands at $2,400 per annum, whereas that of the developing countries in which three-quarters of the world's population live, is a mere $180. More serious still, the twenty-four poorest countries have an annual per capital income not exceeding $100. . . .

The developing countries' share in world trade, already limited to 32 percent in 1950, has continued to diminish, dropping to a mere 17 percent within the framework of the United Nations Development Decade, [and] has been attended by a considerable increase in the Third World's debt. . . .

These phenomena were perceived by the developing countries as a continuation of political hegemony and an expression of the will to pursue neocolonialist exploitation. Conscious of the grave implications of this ever-widening gulf between Third World countries and industrialized countries, the United Nations proclaimed on May 1, 1974 their common determination to undertake the urgent task of establishing a new international economic order founded on equity and capable of redressing the flagrant inequalities of the present system. . . . the failure of these appeals for equity to produce a response or to gain a hearing has soon proved their essential inefficacy. Certain media . . . have frequently sought to make a mockery of the principles advocated by the Third World, when they have not simply ignored them. . . .

Accordingly, the establishment of a new world information order must be considered as the essential corollary of the new international economic order. In order to give concrete reality to this new approach and to enable the media to fulfill their task of educating and informing, measures must be taken both by the industrialized and the developing countries, as well as by the international organizations concerned. . . .

Is a new world information order a feasible proposition? The concept has continued to gain ground. However, its actual establishment and successful operation are contingent upon the full agreement, sense of responsibility, and realism of all those involved in the vast world of communication.

As far as the mass media are concerned, their aim must be to adapt to the new realities. Their contribution is not only desired; it is considered to be decisive. . . .

The process initiated is a complex one, and transformations will take time. What is essential is to familiarize public opinion with change and to promote a responsive awareness of it. . . . For the developing countries, self-reliance must be the watchword; this they can achieve by developing cooperation at the horizontal level so as to enable them to establish a balanced flow with the developed countries.

5

Communication for an Interdependent, Pluralistic World

ELIE ABEL

In this essay, the broadcasting expert and former journalist Elie Abel offers a vigorous exposition of the Western or American model of how international communication and media-government relations ought to work. Responding to some of fellow MacBride Commissioner Masmoudi's much-aired complaints, Abel argues for greater diversification in message flows and broader citizen and private sector participation. He cites a number of specific areas of possible concrete decision and joint cooperative action by both developed and developing nations. To Abel (and most Western media practitioners, policy-makers, and scholars), the remedy to various qualitative and quantitative communication imbalances does not lie with "measures to restrict and control the voices now being heard" or with "the adoption of a single standard for the control of communication systems throughout the world."

Elie Abel is a professor of communication at Stanford University and former dean of the Columbia School of Journalism. He was the American member of the MacBride Commission.

This is a shorter version of an article from the *Interim Report* of the International Commission for the Study of Communication Problems. Copyright © 1979 Unesco. Reprinted by permission.

CHANGES IN THE WAY this world communicates are necessary and indeed inescapable. They are dictated, in fact, by the forward march of technology and by the transformation of interstate relations since the end of World War II. There are today three times as many independent nations as there were when the United Nations was founded. The newly sovereign member states are properly making their voices heard, and their weight felt, in world politics and economics, as well as communications.

The role of the developing countries in world affairs is bound to grow and find expression in a variety of contexts—through bilateral and regional cooperation, through international organizations, and the nonaligned movement. Certain resource-rich developing countries have already assumed roles of major importance on the world stage. The series of challenges confronting the modern world—how to maintain peace, promote economic growth with equity, and preserve the common environment—will be more daunting than ever. Any serious attempt to master these challenges to all mankind will require abundant multilateral flows of information reflecting in their rich diversity all cultural and political perspectives.

To say that the technological revolution now underway in the field of international communication carried with it the seeds of change, regardless of ideology, is a truism. The marvelous new machines that man has invented disseminate truth and lies with equal facility. It is human intelligence, not the machine, that determines the message to be transmitted. In the space of three decades, we have seen the advent of television, computers, and satellites. To a degree these inventions have transformed the ways in which mankind works, perceives the world, is entertained and instructed. The new technologies also have transformed the global flows of news, and cultural and technical information, in quantity and quality.

While these technologies were first developed and applied in the advanced industrial countries, the benefits that flow from them are now beginning to be shared more widely. Far from constituting an element of increased imbalance between North and South, the new technologies can help in dramatic ways to redress the acknowledged present-day imbalance that is our central concern.

Even more rapid progress can be foreseen over the next two decades. By the end of the century, the existing boundaries between telecommunications, computing, broadcast, and print media can be expected to blur as integrated information systems of unprecedented capacity are developed and installed. All nations can benefit from these remarkable new opportunities, and employ them for social ends of their own choosing, by turning their attention to the promise of a more abundant future and putting behind them certain sterile arguments of the past.

Technology by itself, however, cannot be allowed to set the agenda for mankind in the twenty-first century. Once the possibilities and choices promised by technology have been understood, the [MacBride] Commission must come to grips with its mandate: to analyze and propose "concrete and practical measures" leading to action, measures that would inaugurate changes in the existing system of world communication toward the goal of a more just and efficient arrangement, with special benefits flowing to those countries whose infrastructures are as yet in an early stage of development.

The Myth of Passivity

The most ardent champions of a new information order have so far failed to provide us with a clear definition. One proponent concedes that it is not yet "a perfectly definable concept." Another has written:

This new order . . . is not ready-made recipe, which would enable an unjust situation to be transformed overnight into one less unjust. Because it is the product of a long history, the present situation cannot be put right quickly. The aim must be, rather, to initiate a process at the national, regional and international levels. Effective, concrete measures are called for, rather than academic discussion.[1]

There persists, nonetheless, in certain quarters a belief that the free circulation of information and ideas is, to say the least, a mixed blessing for mankind, one that must be brought under control through the proclamation of a new world order. Much is made of the notion that the output of the major international news agencies is of no interest or value to developing countries, because it is said to be superficial, irrelevant, ethnocentric, and somehow biased in favor of the countries in which these agencies are based. Consider this statement, for example:

Even important news may be deliberately neglected by the major media in favor of other information of interest only to public opinion in the country to which the media in question belong. Such news is transmitted to the client countries and is indeed practically imposed on them, despite the fact that readers and listeners in these countries have no interest in them.[2]

One might conclude from the statement just cited that:

a) Foreign news agencies have direct access to the eyes and ears of readers and listeners in developing countries;
b) Their output is so lacking in interest or relevance that no developing country would voluntarily subscribe to them.

Neither statement happens to be accurate.

In fact, most developing countries do not allow their newspapers or broadcasting stations to subscribe directly to foreign agency services. The subscriber in most cases is the government, or a government-controlled agency. In short, the picture of passive millions in the developing countries awash

---

1. Mustapha Masmoudi, "The New World Information Order," document presented to the International Commission for the Study of Communication Problems (Paris: Unesco, 1978), p. 10.
    2. *Ibid.*, p. 5.

in a tidal wave of alien information is somewhat fanciful. Table 5.1 is an attempt to show the real pattern.

Of eighty-five nonaligned countries in the sample, AP makes direct sales to 22 percent, UPI to 18 percent, and Reuters to 26 percent. The other side of the coin is that Reuters (the largest direct supplier of the three) enters 74 percent of these countries only through government, or government-controlled channels. The respective figures for the other agencies are—AP, 78 percent and UPI, 82 percent. Thus the majority of nonaligned countries and their populations are by no means "passive recipients" of unwanted foreign information. Their governments are, and have long been, in firm control.

These facts are difficult to reconcile with the wholly negative view of the Western news agencies cited above. Surely some information of value, at least to governments, moves on these circuits, else they would not subscribe. Much of this information appears, however, to be reserved for official use only. Governments, presumably, have a need to know what is happening in the world, even when they take special steps to "protect" the in-populations by filtering this information through national agencies of one sort or another.

Ascertainable facts of this kind must not be ignored if the commission wishes to be taken seriously. Where additional research is called for, we must not shrink from the effort of

Table 5.1 Sales to Nonaligned Countries by AP, UPI, and Reuters

	Number of countries	AP Direct	AP Govt.	UPI Direct	UPI Govt.	Reuters Direct	Reuters Govt.
Arab region	18	5	4	5	8	7	10
Africa	41	2	3	1	—	5	27
Asia	14	2	4	1	3	3	6
Americas	9	8	—	7	—	5	2
Europe	3	2	1	1	1	2	1
TOTALS	85	19	12	15	12	22	46

SOURCE: Edward T. Pinch, "The Third World and the Fourth Estate," a study done while Pinch was a member of the U.S. State Department Senior Seminar in Foreign Policy, 1977.

providing it. Recommendations based on nothing more solid than slogans can only invite derision among professional students and practitioners of the communication arts. It is not for the commission to decide whether in the fullness of time there will be a new, more widely distributed, world system of communications. Technology alone will see to that. Our task is to consider how those inevitable changes will be shaped: By whom? According to what principles? To what ends? If practical results are the goal, then the international community will have to focus on specific measures that are susceptible of cooperation and to tread warily in areas that tend to generate hostility or confrontation.

The Nature of News

News values differ from country to country, even within particular countries. There is no single, internationally accepted standard of news judgment. The interests and preoccupations of one nation may seem trivial, even foolish, by the standards of another. Articles describing the same event will be placed in very different positions, and treated at greater or lesser length, in different publications within the same city. . . .

While news is information, information is not necessarily news—unless it meets the tests of timeliness, wide interest, usefulness, freshness, and so forth. Any number of talented journalists have demonstrated that it is possible to meet these tests, thus ensuring publication, and still do justice to development news from the Third World. This calls on the part of the reporter for an effort to rise above the demands of "dailiness," as James Reston has called it. There is a need in the Western countries, no less than in the East or the South, for reports that fall into the "soft news" category, news of attempts to defeat hunger and disease in the form of long-term projects that may take years before fulfillment.

But "hard news" will continue to demand the attention of foreign correspondents and their audiences. A coup, a strike, a border war, the overthrow of any regime, must be reported, even at the risk of being labeled negative news by some. News of this kind will necessarily remain part of the international flow, but only a part. Whether the news is hard or soft, however, it requires access to countries and to sources of information within them. The accuracy and balance that members of the commission have demanded of foreign correspondents can be attained only when those correspondents are free to travel, to see and hear, to investigate conditions for themselves.

The Political Dimension

It is well to remember that although technological advances hold real promise for the future, we are not here dealing with technical issues. These are, instead, political issues of extraordinary sensitivity. Few decisions taken in the name of any people more accurately reflect their underlying political philosophy than those having to do with ownership and control of their information networks. Particular countries have chosen one model or another, because that model is in harmony with the economic and social system distinctive to that country. So long as the present diversity of system and belief persists, there can be no single, approved Unesco standard in these matters. A decent respect for the convictions of other societies is called for.

Indeed, the effective functioning of the international system under construction demands a degree of understanding round the world that can only be the product of more, and more accurate, information flowing freely between nations and regions. Mutual respect and understanding among peoples cannot be based upon ignorance. The truly free multidirectional flow of information we seek is a condition long desired, increasingly approximated, but still far from realization.

There is no real disagreement within the commission on certain shortcomings of the present incomplete system of worldwide communications. The necessary resources, whether

of infrastructure or trained manpower, are unevenly distributed. The reasons behind this uneven development are rooted
in the uneven history of industrialization. Some countries—in
the words of [fellow commissioner] Dr. Michio Nagai—were
starters on the road of development; others started late. Talk
of conspiracies to "dominate" information and culture flows
can yield no practical outcome, save increased polarization.
The current situation in the communications field is inescap-
ably linked with the uneven pace of economic development
generally. The remedy must, therefore be found in deliberate
national and international measures to advance the welfare of
those countries still locked in the grip of traditional poverty.

The present concentration in particular nations and institutions of the resources needed to communicate effectively
across national boundaries—and within them—is clearly undesirable. It results in the disproportionate voicing of certain
perspectives and the substantial ignoring of others. It is clear
that this situation does not suit the needs of an increasingly
interdependent, pluralistic world system of states. The remedy
does not lie, however, in measures to restrict and control the
voices now being heard. The developing nations will not
strengthen their own capacity to communicate by attempts to
block, or tear down, the capacities of others. Nor can the answer be found in the adoption of a single standard for the
control of communication systems throughout the world. The
worldwide need is for more voices, not fewer, in order that
citizens of all nations can make themselves heard even as they
listen to voices and messages from afar. The only constructive
response can be a massive international effort to increase the
capacity for communication at every level—the individual, the
community, the nation, and among nations.

Few would disagree with the proposition that a major
share of available resources should be invested in the developing countries. Agreement within the commission upon concrete measures for attacking this problem will necessarily demand open, honest discussion. Those spokesmen who condemn
the alleged monopoly of information flowing from the industrial countries all too often represent governments which im-

pose internal monopolies on all incoming and outgoing information. Stubborn adherence to this double standard of virtue can only sharpen existing differences.

Rights and Responsibilities

Traditional ideas with regard to human rights, including the right to inform and to be informed, together with the rights of free expression and of privacy, are undergoing significant reformulation in our time. The move toward expansion of these rights also brings into play new concepts affecting the responsibilities of individuals, institutions, and nations. The inherent contradictions between certain of these conflicting rights are being reevaluated in several countries, including my own. In the United States, for example, the courts are grappling with the contradiction between the reporter's right to protect the confidentiality of news sources and the government's right to information that is relevant to criminal investigation or prosecution. The individual citizen's right of privacy . . . also has come into conflict with the government's responsibility to inform the citizen of its own operations. Concentration of media ownership in certain communities, the product of laissez-faire attitudes in years past, conflicts increasingly with the responsibility of public authorities to foster a diversity of viewpoint and expression within those communities. Similar debates are taking place in other societies, based upon reinterpretations of their separate legal and moral value systems. These are highly complex issues. In attempting to resolve them, each society is bound to follow its own traditions.

Any attempt to decree a single planetary standard for resolving these issues must necessarily fail. The world community can, at best, undertake to seek out, and build upon, whatever elements of consensus may exist in this area, recognizing at all times the need to respect the diverse traditions that govern communication systems in each country.

Areas of Possible Concrete Decision

Mustapha Masmoudi and Bogdan Osolnik [the MacBride commissioner from Yugoslavia] between them have raised a number of matters that seem to me susceptible of agreement, leading to action. These include measures relating to international postal rates, telecommunication tariffs, universal access to satellite services, technology transfer, and financial and training assistance. It may be useful to comment upon these suggestions, one by one.

AIR POSTAL RATES

Reductions in the rates affecting newspapers, periodicals, and books could do much to increase the flows of information and cultural materials between developing countries, and between developing and industrial countries. Reduced mailing costs, moreover, could have the effect of stimulating increased production of such materials in the developing countries. At present, the Universal Postal Union allows its members to apply a 50 percent optional reduction for all printed matter. Material relief for the developing countries will probably require more drastic reductions, including specific preferential rates for small-run publications. Progress in this direction will not, however, be easily accomplished.

The Universal Postal Union is, of course, heavily influenced by the ministries of Posts and Telegraphs of the member states, the largest number of these from developing countries. Most ministries of post, telephone and telegraph (PTTs) lose money on their postal operations and can, therefore, be expected to resist any drastic revision of international agreements that would have the effect of cutting their revenues. To reduce, or remove, this impediment to the free flow of information from the developing countries, a concerted effort will be needed on the part of all governments, above all the governments of the developing countries themselves.

They will have to persuade their PTTs that the maintenance of present rate structures, for reasons of revenue alone, conflicts directly with the promise of desirable outcomes for the developing countries in telling the world of their aims and accomplishments. The UPU is a respected technical organization, which has been largely free of excessive political or ideological influence. If proposals for reform of the rate structure can be framed and put forward by a sufficient number of governments acting together, progress should be possible.

TELECOMMUNICATION TARIFFS

This is another area for concrete action. The present tariff structure is the outcome of a web of complicated agreements at the national and international level. It will require the active involvement of many institutions to bring about the reforms we seek. Probably the most important forum for discussion is INTELSAT, the international consortium created especially to provide international telecommunication services by means of satellite transmission. With a membership of some 100 states and its doors still open to others, INTELSAT answers to many constituents. It is an appropriate forum for discussion of proposals to equalize communication rates worldwide, to offer discounts for transmission of news, and to create preferential rates for certain types of transmissions from developing countries.

As in the matter of postal rates, however, the crucial persuading role may have to be played by the developing countries with their own PTTs. These ministries, quite apart from exerting considerable influence upon the positions taken by their governments within INTELSAT, also levy charges on international communications, and these invariably surpass the charges billed by INTELSAT for the international segment. . . .

The history of INTELSAT, brief though it is, has been marked by considerable technical and economic accomplishment, rather than political debate. For this reason, fruitful discussion within the organization will have to be conducted in the most objective terms possible. One caveat warrants special emphasis: To describe the treatment of small-scale users of telecommunication services as an "injustice" overlooks economic fact. It costs less, in real terms, to provide any such service in bulk than to start and stop the service repeatedly for small transmissions. It is this wholly economic factor, rather than malevolent intent, that explains why bulk users tend to pay less, per transmission. It will be difficult enough, in my judgment, to persuade the technical/financial personnel in the PTTs and in INTELSAT to override their normal inclinations, even if a powerful case can be made in favor of revising their tariff structures for reasons of social benefit. Vague complaints of injustice will make the task of persuasion even more difficult. The argument must be more compelling—nothing less than the absolute necessity of building a worldwide communication system in which the developing countries can make their presence felt as full partners, capable of transmitting as well as receiving, in common with the industrial nations.

ACCESS TO SATELLITE SERVICES

This broader issue is entirely appropriate for consideration through INTELSAT. In recent years, satellite communication capacity has been expanding rapidly and costs have been declining. This trend is likely to continue. INTELSAT has already begun to offer its members domestic as well as international telecommunication services. Several developing countries have used this service to great advantage. A number of highly technical questions, with direct implications for the matter of access, remain to be dealt with. For example, decisions must be taken with regard to the minimum technical standards for earth stations using present and projected INTELSAT satellites. An agreement on standards will directly affect the costs of expanding satellite communications beyond the capital cities of the developing countries. For countries now engaged in building or planning national news agencies, telephone networks, and rural development programs, the determination will be of crucial importance. On this and other issues of no less importance for the free flow of information between nations, and within them, INTELSAT seems the right forum for serious discussion. . . .

TECHNOLOGY TRANSFER

This is one more area for concrete action. Certain errors of the past have arisen from a lack of clarity regarding the needs of receiving countries and the supply of technology that proved inappropriate to those needs. The United States government, cognizant of the disappointments caused by certain of these transactions in years past, is now engaged in a major effort to upgrade in qualitative terms the official support given to technical cooperation between American enterprises and the developing countries. There is reason to believe that advice and suggestions from foreign government and international organizations on ways of improving procedures for the transfer of communications technology would be carefully considered. . . .

FINANCIAL AND TRAINING ASSISTANCE

Support for a major initiative in this area has been building . . . in the United States and other Western countries. Certain of the major international funding agencies are now actively reconsidering their past disinclination to support communication projects in Third World countries on the ground that such projects tended to favor the urban elites in recipient countries rather than the poorest of the rural poor. As a result of the rethinking now in process, it seems likely that more substantial funds will be allocated by the Agency for International Development (AID) in the United States, together with the other institutions mentioned, in response to statements of interest and need on the part of developing countries. Within AID there is considerable interest, for example, in communication programs that explore the educational and development applications of satellite technology. The success of

India's SITE project has pointed the way to new forms of North-South cooperation—the United States, in this case, supplying the satellite facilities with Indian educators in full control of the software.

We have learned through long experience that professional education and training for journalists and others involved in the communication arts are most effective when carried out within the regions in which the students feel at home, with instructors native to the region in control of the curriculum. Under a recent proposal put forward by the United States, the developing countries would be invited to identify regional training centers, with financial and technical support from the developed countries or international agencies. The United States has offered to send a senior American faculty member to each such center for a year, if requested, to serve as an adviser. Private news organizations in the United States also are prepared to underwrite visits of senior correspondents and editors, on rotating assignments, to help in skills training. Equipment needs, once identified, would be met through donations to the regional centers. The visiting instructors will be there to learn, as well as teach. Their direct exposure to the development needs and perspective of developing regions will stay with them when they return to their permanent assignments as teachers and gatekeepers in American journalism.

Issues of Political Sensitivity

The debate within Unesco, the scholarly community, and the commission itself has already exposed a number of questions which do not, in my judgment, lend themselves to solution by consensus. These are philosophical-political issues of a kind that generate strong passions and dogmatic assertions. Among these are the rights of access to countries and to sources of information within those countries, censorship, licensing of journalists, codes of ethics, the right of rectification, and demands for "equitable access" to the radio spectrum.

RIGHT OF ACCESS

From the libertarian perspective, this right is fundamental. It calls for measures that would guarantee the freedom of journalists to move about the world without hindrance, to interview sources (both official and nonofficial), and to transmit their reports as a matter of right without interference by governments or other authorities. The Stockholm seminar (April 1978) specified a right of access not only to government sources but to the "entire spectrum of opinion" within any country.

The concept of access for duly accredited journalists clearly implies a worldwide opening of channels. Certain spokesmen for the developing countries, however, see the matter quite differently. In discussing the right of access, they appear to be concerned with constricting, rather than opening, these channels of communication. Mr. Masmoudi, for example, lists three measures he would like to see adopted that plainly suggest restriction of access:

–Regulation of the right to information by preventing abusive uses of the right of access to information
–Definition of appropriate criteria to govern truly objective news selection
–Regulation of the collection, processing, and transmission of news and data across national frontiers

As a citizen of a country that has enshrined in its constitution certain rugged safeguards for the press, designed to insure its independence from government, I am bound to ask: Who would define "abusive uses" of the right of access? Who would determine the "appropriate criteria" for "truly objective" news selection? Who would regulate the flow of news across national frontiers? Does not each of his proposed measures invite official interference with the flow of information? Is he not, in effect proposing an elaborate new system of censorship?

Let there be no mistake about the response to these suggestions in my country, and in many others (including Third

World countries with a strong attachment to free institutions). We regard governments, and the men who lead them, as poor judges of journalistic objectivity. We must reject the notion that the right of access, which is still in the process of definition, must from the outset be qualified, regulated, some would say nullified, by unidentified agencies. Any sovereign nation has the right and the power to shape its domestic laws and regulations as it sees fit. Such a nation would, however, be ill-advised to expect passive acceptance of international standards based upon government control by countries that value a free and independent press.

LICENSING OF JOURNALISTS

This practice is not as yet widespread but it has gained sufficient ground in Latin America to be troubling. In much of the world, even in countries where mass media enterprises are subject to licensing, they remain free to employ as journalists persons they consider qualified for the task. The media institution itself is commonly considered the most appropriate source of knowledge regarding the particular demands of the job to be filled and the capabilities of the employee in question. For any outside body, officially constituted or sanctioned, to intervene in this process would be to negate the independence of the press, subjecting it to influence or control by persons whose motives may have nothing to do with the pursuit of disinterested reporting, or of truth.

Proposals for the licensing of journalists, moreover, must inevitably collide with the individual citizen's right to communicate. If that right is to be elaborated and confirmed in international law, access to the media cannot logically be restricted solely to those persons holding professional licenses. The individual who has been denied access to the columns of a newspaper for lack of a professional license has been effectively stripped of a basic right under Article 19 of the Universal Declaration of Human Rights, adopted by the United Nations General Assembly in 1948. It reads: "Everyone has the right to freedom of opinion and expression; this right includes freedom to hold opinions . . . and *to seek, receive and impart information and ideas through any media* and regardless of frontiers." (italics added)

THE RIGHT OF RECTIFICATION

In many countries, including the United States, it is unthinkable that the media should be compelled by the government to publish a retraction or correction of an earlier report. The government of the United States has, to my knowledge, never requested such powers. Along with its private citizens, who may feel offended or injured by a particular report, the government relies on the professionalism of the media to publish corrections or retractions voluntarily when they are justified. A right under international law to compel corrections or retractions at the request of foreign governments, or their citizens, has in my judgment absolutely no prospect of acceptance in the United States, or many other countries. Foreign governments are not, of course, debarred from requesting correction of false or distorted reports, but the decision to publish rests with the responsible editors of the publication in question. It would be naïve to assume that the United States government would countenance the extension to foreign entities of a right it does not claim for itself.

The major means of redress for persons who feel they have been maligned in the press or broadcast media is, of course, the traditional laws governing libel. In the United States at least, libel actions do not as a rule lead to published retractions. In successful cases the court awards financial compensation for damages caused by the publication.

While libel laws offer the only legal remedy in such cases, new avenues of accountability to the public have been developed voluntarily by newspapers and broadcasting stations in the United States and other countries. These include the establishment of press councils, which thoroughly investigate public complaints of false, distorted, or misleading reports and publish their findings; the appointment of ombudsmen assigned by many newspapers to investigate reader complaints and expose the shortcomings of their own newspapers in the treatment of specific news developments. . . .

There has been a parallel development in the recent proliferation of op-ed pages, so called because they tend to be published opposite the editorial, or leader, page in hundreds of newspapers across the country. These pages provide space for articles submitted by outside contributors, that is, nonjournalists (some prominent, others obscure) who freely express their views and observations on matters of public interest. There are, finally, letters-to-the-editor sections in virtually all American newspapers which invite and publish contributions from readers.

The purpose of citing these examples is not to persuade other countries that the American system is a perfect model for the world. It is only to show that there are several ways of dealing with the problem of false information, the more compelling in that they rest upon voluntary compliance, rather than compulsion. Any attempt to draft a right of universal application that would compel retraction or correction of offending articles risks direct contravention of a decent and durable tradition that is honored not only in the United States but in other countries as well. Such a measure, if proposed as an international norm, would certainly be unacceptable in the United States and elsewhere.

CODES OF ETHICS

There can be no objection, only encouragement, on the part of the commission to the voluntary elaboration of professional codes by journalists and journalistic organizations, so long as these codes apply within particular countries. Such codes exist and are observed, more or less, in a great many countries. In my own, the National Association of Broadcasters has a code of conduct; the American Society of Newspaper Editors has its Canons of Journalism. In addition to these industry-wide codes, many media enterprises, concerned with the maintenance of high professional standards, have their own codes.

To attempt the drafting of a universal code for journalists of all nations seems to me a fruitless task.

Given the radically different conceptions of the journalist's role in society that have become apparent in our own deliberations, it seems abundantly clear that any formula we could devise would be essentially meaningless. In the United States, for example, the press and three of the four television networks are privately owned. They remain independent of government, frequently serving as a check on abuses of government power. In the Soviet Union, on the other hand, the press is seen as a direct instrument of the State. It is difficult for me to imagine how representatives of societies with such disparate political and social systems can be expected to agree upon a single code of conduct for all journalists, everywhere.

Spokesmen for certain nonaligned countries have argued for a code of planetary scope in order that journalists might be held accountable to the entire world community. There have also been calls for a code to protect journalists from improper demands placed upon them by their employers. It strikes me as remarkable and somehow revealing, that nowhere in these documents is there mention of a code to protect journalists—and journalistic enterprises—from the dead hand of government control. . . .

The list of sensitive issues discussed above is not intended to be comprehensive. My purpose in raising these issues is to suggest that the commission would be well advised to separate the more intractable political and philosophical issues from those relatively value-free, on which consensus is possible and even likely.

Long-Term Perspectives

The most thoughtful of journalists and students of communication processes are fully aware of the historic dependencies, disparities, and imbalances that handicap the developing nations. They acknowledge that the present patterns of information flow, running heavily in one direction, must be altered for the benefit of all nations, developed and developing alike.

The news flow argument, however noisy and prolonged, will have served its purpose if it leads to the establishment of new national and regional structures above all in the developing regions of the world, that can serve as building blocks of the genuinely multidirectional world system that technology has put within our grasp. Wisely applied in a spirit of North–South cooperation, the new technologies can create an abundance of communication channels without precedent in human history. Greater and more diversified message flows and broader citizen participation are technically possible today. With each passing year, the productivity of communication technology rises as costs continue to drop.

In economic terms, the information technology possesses certain unique virtues. It is a resource created by human ingenuity that, unlike oil or coal or other nonrenewable materials, can never be exhausted. As it becomes ever more productive, hence cheaper, it can be universally available.

Seen in this hopeful perspective, the new multidirectional world system can become a primary agent of reform and reconstruction also affecting political and economic relationships among nations. Indeed the problem confronting generations to come may well be how to share the world's increasing abundance of communication resources, a more agreeable task than the familiar squabbles and power struggles over control of energy and other raw materials, which diminish year by year. It is by focusing on the prospects the future holds, rather than the legacies of the colonial past, that this commission can accomplish its assigned task.

6

The Right to Communicate

JEAN D'ARCY

This essay develops the global notion of each individual's basic "right to communicate" as an extension of the right of information. Described as "a concept of the future, still in the making," this potential right goes beyond the humanistic content of the U.N. Universal Declaration of Human Rights to encompass all the great freedoms of expression and the press and to add to them, "both for individuals and societies, the concepts of access, participation, two-way information—all of which are vital, as we now sense, for the harmonious development of man and mankind."

In the context of this volume on news, d'Arcy's observations are useful in reminding readers that many people in both developed and developing countries have "a mass media mentality." D'Arcy also offers an important perspective by emphasizing interrelationships on a worldwide scale and arguing that problems in an area as specialized as news cannot be separated from broader problems of communication structures, operations, contents, rights, duties, and freedom at different levels.

Jean d'Arcy is a French thinker and consultant on communication. He is president of the International Institute of Communications, London, and VIDEO-CITES, Paris.

This is an excerpt from an article in the *Interim Report* of the International Commission for the Study of Communication Problems. Copyright © 1979 Unesco. Reprinted by permission.

MAN'S "RIGHT TO COMMUNICATE" is an as-yet inchoate concept, a concept of the future, still in the making. Enunciated for the first time in 1969, it was then formulated in essentially forward-looking terms, as a possible line of research: "The time will come when the Universal Declaration of Human Rights will have to encompass a more extensive right than man's right to information, first laid down twenty-one years ago in Article 19. This is the right of man to communicate."[1]

This potential or future "right" has still received neither its form nor its true content. Far from being, as some apparently maintain, an already established principle from which logical consequences might, here and now, be drawn, it is still at the stage of being thought through in all its implications and gradually enriched. Once the potential applications of the hypothesis have been explored, the international community will have to decide what intrinsic value such a concept possesses. It will be required to recognize—or not—the existence of a possible new human right, one to be added to, and not substituted for, those that have already been declared.

For the notion of an ascending evolution of rights and duties is at the heart of the proposal. Our concern must be not to abolish one right in order to replace it by another, but rather to take cognizance of the current by which we are borne along. . . .

Today, we are suddenly becoming aware of the essential role played by communication in man's emergence and development, as though it had needed an explosion, a sudden transformation of the possibilities of communication such as we are now witnessing, in order for us to perceive the magnitude of the phenomenon; a phenomenon which had been permanently present from the very first, but whose function both for the individual and society could be identified only through its variations.

1. Jean d'Arcy, "Direct Broadcast Satellites and the Right to Communicate," *EBU Review* (November 1969) 118.

Communication Between Individuals, Societies

Man depends upon being able to communicate with his fellows. His emergence and subsequent full development appear to have been contingent upon a constant process of communication, and it may today be supposed that man's development as a species was closely governed from the start by the relational activities which he was gradually led to establish through the medium of touch, gesture, hearing, and later speech. . . .

Man has a specific, a biological, need to communicate. It therefore seems normal that his right to communicate be recognized, since it is upon the exercise of this activity that his very existence depends. Were the question of recognizing such a right to be raised in a society in which there existed only oral, interpersonal communication, without the mediation of machines, it would immediately receive an affirmative response. The intervention of the media today should in no way modify this essential factor, the biological, root datum.

The same is true of society. All societies spring from the communication established among their members. . . . To cut communications within a human group is equivalent to annihilating that group. To cut communications between it and other groups, to prevent it practically from expressing itself is tantamount, as in the case of the individual, to destroying its personality. For society as for the individual, there is undoubtedly a specific right to communicate. What is important is to win the recognition of this right.

Thus there are two forces at work: that which impels the individual, for his very existence's sake, to assert his right to communicate, thereby forming, through the communication established with his fellows, a society; and that which drives the society thus formed to work out, in order to be able to function and express itself, ever more elaborate means of communication leading to ever more highly developed social structures. It is from this tension between the individual's need to communicate and society's need to establish its own channels of communication and expression, from the tension between the two rights—that of the individual and that of society—to communicate, that successive rights, duties, and freedoms have sprung.

The Successive Freedoms

In the age of the agora and the forum, when communication was direct and interpersonal, there first emerged—a concept at the root of all human advancement and all civilization—freedom of opinion: "That is your opinion: though it is not my own, I nevertheless respect it." Ranged against this nascent freedom of opinion were the various social, religious, and political forces, as is attested by history's tale of inquisitions, martyrdoms, and persecutions. It nevertheless continued to gain ground as an essential and basic component of social life, and was to constitute, in the age of the Renaissance and the Reformation, one of the demands underlying all struggles against those in power. It is the oldest form of the right to communicate.

The advent of printing, the first of the mass media, gave rise, through its very expansion and in defiance of royal or religious prerogatives to exercise control, to the corollary concept of freedom of expression. A much shorter period of time—the three centuries which separated Gutenberg from the philosophers of the Enlightenment—was needed for it to win recognition and to gain its place, as a more elaborate formulation of a right to communicate, in the first Declarations of the Rights of Man.

The nineteenth century, which saw the extraordinary development of the mass circulation press, was marked by constant struggles to win freedom of the press. From barricades to revolutions, these struggles culminated in its recognition, in particular in France, where the Law of 1881, formally establishing the freedom of the press, enshrined the victory of the people over those in power and all forms of censorship.

The successive advent of other mass media—film, radio, television—and the abusive recourse to all forms of propaganda on the eve of war were rapidly to demonstrate the need for and possibility of, a more specific but more extensive right, namely, the right "to seek, receive and impart information and ideas through any media and regardless of frontiers." Barely thirty years separated the emergence of these new media from the proclamation by the international community of a new human right, the right to inform and be informed, as it results from the Universal Declaration of Human Rights of 1948.

Today, a new step forward seems possible: recognition of man's right to communicate, deriving from our latest victories over time and space and from our increased awareness of the phenomenon of communication. From the very first, this fundamental right was implicit in, and underlay, all the freedoms that have successively been won: freedom of opinion, freedom of expression, freedom of the press, freedom of information. The advent of machines, coming between men, caused us to forget its existence. Today, it is clear to us that it encompasses all these freedoms but adds to them, both for individuals and societies, the concepts of access, participation, two-way information flow—all of which are vital, as we now sense, for the harmonious development of man and mankind.

The Obstacles to Be Overcome

In every age, the powers that be, be they political, economic, or religious, have had to control communications in order to govern more effectively. The entire history of mankind bears witness to the fact: whoever controls communications controls society, whoever is master of the information flow ensures for himself—for a time—order and stability.

In this field, each new breakthrough, before it is finally reflected, as we have seen above, in a further extension of man's freedoms, in the possibility of better communication, has always been attended by the establishment or strengthening of controls. . . .

Initially, the press was inconceivable without censorship. Telephone communications rapidly became liable to tapping. Censorship, which had been abolished in the case of the press, was reestablished in the cinema, before disappearing here also. Public and private monopolies were established on radio communications and then on radio broadcasting. The advent of the satellite, *the* instrument of interdependence, has been attended by a reaffirmation of national sovereignties. And the list is not closed. . . .

Each time, however, a further step forward could be taken once public opinion realized that a larger freedom was possible without endangering life in society, and that this larger freedom was desirable for the very equilibrium of society. We have now reached another such stage.

THE MASS MEDIA MENTALITY

Over fifty years' experience of the mass media . . . have conditioned us, both at the national and international levels, to a single kind of information flow, which we have come to accept as normal and indeed as the only possible kind: a vertical, one-way flow from the top downwards of nondiversified, anonymous messages, produced by a few and addressed to all. This is not communication.

It has thus become difficult for us to realize what true communication could be, what indeed it was a century ago in our countries and still is today in its traditional forms in the majority of Third World countries: a horizontal, interactive flow, a process of give-and-take, weaving at the level of the village, the parish, and the neighborhood, among tribes and communities, a human web of social relationships in which people and groups live and participate, in the full possession of their own individual identity.

What urban dwellers and particularly the young reject, and Third World countries do not wish to be subjected to, is this vertical flow of information so common today, in which there can be no participation, and which generates passivity and frustration both among individuals and peoples.

Confronted by this problem, however, our "mass media mentality" reacts only by stepping up the vertical flow, increasing everywhere the number of newspapers, radio, and television receivers, and cinemas, especially in the developing countries, without recognizing that it is this very vertical nature of the flow which is at issue. Thus the definition of a new concept making possible a horizontal flow based on the right to communicate is an urgent task.

THE ESTABLISHMENT OF MONOPOLIES

From the outset, and by a process that to many appeared quite natural, communication over long distances, whether of a material or spiritual nature, became the property of a few. . . . The privilege of long-distance communication belongs to those who govern; it is one of the royal prerogatives of power.

The initially exceptional nature of such long-distance communication was largely responsible for the establishment of these monopolies; it was only natural that something so uncommon, which could exercise so powerful a social influence, should pertain to those in power. Moreover, the means involved in order to establish over an entire country the close-meshed links of these networks (coaching stages, the telegraph, the telephone, radio broadcasting, etc.) were so considerable that only the established power could undertake the task. And undertake it it must, if it wished to avert the creation of oligopolies, whose potential power would have made them a threat to all concerned.

Lastly, the feeling that whoever wished to communicate outside the power structure wished to do so in order to combat that power periodically led legislators to claim a monopoly on communications as a means of countering conspiracy. . . . The pattern is clear: those who had just assumed power were determined to use the monopoly in order to hold onto power.

What are their reasons worth today? What was rare, exceptional, and quasi-magical has become, thanks to the electronic revolution, common and plentiful. What was once costly is now cheap. . . .

As regards the conspiracy argument, it no longer holds for present-day societies; moreover, conspirators have at their disposal whatever modern coding techniques they may wish for. . . . The time now seems ripe not to abolish monopolies on telecommunications but rather to redefine them on the basis of a new fundamental principle: that of the right of the individuals and communities to communicate on their own, replacing the old principle whereby the right of communication was reserved for governments. . . .

The Concept at the International Level

. . . The association of the doctrine of free flow of information with the vertical, one-way flow mechanism which has predominated since the advent of the mass media has led on the one hand to abuses which the authors of the Universal Declaration could not have envisaged and, on the other, to the impasse which studies and discussions have now reached, from which the international community can escape only by resorting to new principles.

The Universal Declaration, proclaimed in 1948 in the immediate post-war period, bears the stamp of that period. Its authors were mindful of the war . . . which, in their view, had been made possible by propaganda operating in countries closed upon themselves and given over to fanatical nationalism. To their minds, the free flow of information was a precondition of peace. Moreover, it is essentially to the press and to the printed word that they were referring. The new horizons that electronics have since opened up in communications were then beyond their grasp. This emphasis on the press was to become still more pronounced some years later when the draft declaration and draft convention on freedom of information were presented to the United Nations. At the time, many already felt that these drafts did not reflect the phenomenon in its entirety. The discussions bogged down. . . . The same is true in the case of the other international bodies, and the concept of "freedom of information" can practically no longer be used without giving rise to bitter controversies.

In face of this impasse . . . new formulas have begun to emerge. . . . "Free and balanced flow of information" is one such formula. Although seemingly no less inadequate to describe the communication phenomenon as a whole, this expression reflects, through its two-way focus, one of the trends underlying the "right to communicate."

This latter concept, by virtue of the give-and-take "horizontal" nature of the flow which it implies, the concepts of access and participation which are intrinsic to it, and the fact that the right to communicate includes the right *not* to communicate, appears to be far more promising and better suited to . . . discussions on information flow. . . . The welcome which for some years has been given to the new concept at international meetings, particularly by the developing countries, would seem to prove this.

VARYING CONCEPTIONS OF INFORMATION

Within the community of nations, fundamental differences exist concerning the State's role in matters of information and, at a deeper level, concerning the conception itself of the State. These disparities have resulted in contrary positions regarding the role of the established powers in the field of information.

Some countries, whose history has been marked by the successive struggles waged by their peoples to do away with the royal prerogatives exercised by the executive power, consider that freedom of information and freedom of opinion are essential for the functioning of democracy, since they enable this power to be controlled. Their citizens do not recognize the existence of a "State" as this term is understood elsewhere and, by force of tradition, or even by constitutional means, they deny to the executive power all right to intervene in matters of information. In their view, control of the executive power by public opinion is the best guarantee of their freedom.

For them, this is an essential value, a national legacy won through bloody struggles, which it is their duty to preserve as an integral part of their heritage.

In other countries and particularly in those that are heirs to the traditions of Roman law, the existence of a State at the head of the nation is the sole means of ensuring its unity, defense, and development. Reasons of State are usually accepted as a matter of course. For the citizens, the State incarnated in the executive power is the sole agent responsible for their destiny and the sole arbiter of their internal conflicts, rising above all ideological, ethical, or religious considerations. In the last resort, it alone is capable of deciding right from wrong. It is therefore duty bound to control public opinion and thereby to ensure, in defiance of all private interests, that the general interest—to which all the nation's activities, including information, must contribute—shall prevail.

From these disparities in the conception of the relationship between the authorities and information spring fundamental differences between States concerning many international instruments, as was recently to be observed in connection with the "Draft Declaration on Fundamental Principles Governing the Use of the Mass Media. . . ."

Such oppositions are natural and genuine, despite the mutual accusations put forward on each side concerning hidden views and unavowed objectives. It would be vain for one of the parties to seek to convert the other: on either side, traditions, cultures, and structures stand in the way of any such initiative. The study of the question must be resumed on different bases, by frankly acknowledging these differences, formulating in clear-cut terms the aims pursued, and taking as a starting point a new and different concept, namely, the "right to communicate". . . .

ALLOCATION OF COMMUNICATION RESOURCES

Distribution among the nations of the world of the natural and limited resource constituted by the radio frequency spectrum has to date followed no other principle than that of "first come, first served." Only the World Administrative Radio Conference for Space Telecommunications, held in Geneva by the International Telecommunications Union (ITU) in 1971, has introduced a new provision, namely, "the registration with the ITU of frequency assignments for space radio communication services and their use should not provide any permanent priority for any individual country or group of countries and should not create an obstacle to the establishment of space systems by other countries." The same is true of orbital positions.

The adoption of this new rule, which to date has been restricted solely to space radio communications, is a preliminary step towards the recognition by and for States of a right to communicate. This was made possible by the fact that it was a new area, space, and a new range of frequencies which till then had been but little used which were involved. In the case of terrestrial radio communications and in particular radio broadcasting, no such principle exists. Each State considers itself to be the owner of the entire frequency spectrum, insists on using it as it sees fit, and accepts intervention on the part of the ITU through its International Frequency Registration Board (IFRB)—whose name alone is indicative of the approach taken—only in order to obviate jamming. Where there should be joint management, coordination alone is accepted.

In reality, there is no principle governing these communication matters at the international level. This has given rise, as a result of the lead gained by the industrialized countries, to a situation of flagrant injustice. The rule tacitly observed of first come, first served had obviously operated to the detriment of the developing countries, while their dependence in matters of technology and equipment as well as training has placed them, despite the efforts of the ITU, virtually in the hands of those in possession of the relevant technology, knowledge, and influence. . . .

Between now and the next Plenipotentiary Conference of the ITU, scheduled for 1982–83, whose task it will be to renew the International Conventions by which it is governed, it should be possible to identify a number of principles which can provide a basis on which to establish a charter and enable the Union to operate harmoniously and equitably to the benefit of all and not just of a few.

The essential decision would be to declare the frequency spectrum and the geostationary orbit—two limited natural resources—to be the common property of all mankind. Joint management of this capital by the ITU, thereby endowed with the necessary authority, would normally ensue. The simultaneous recognition of the right of individuals and nations to communicate would then become the basic principle, already foreshadowed by the ITU in 1971, by virtue of which frequencies would be assigned and joint management decisions taken. An international body of law governing communications would begin to be established.

RESPECT FOR CULTURES

After millennia marked by cultural expansionism, by the successive attempts of empires and religions to impose their own civilizations . . . our present age is slowly learning to respect others and is gradually realizing that, for mankind as a whole, our wealth derives from our diversity and not from any artificially imposed unity. . . .

Having learned, through two world wars, the hard lesson that the price of peace is equilibrium and respect for others, our generations are progressively equipping themselves with the instruments, structures, and laws required to preserve it. Such is the aim and function not only of the United Nations but of all its agencies. . . .

It has been noted above in connection with the ITU—though the remark is equally valid for Unesco—that there is virtually no principle governing communication at the international level. This was a good reason for the international community to recognize the right to communicate as a potential basis for the gradual establishment of a new international order in the field of communication.

By virtue of its pluralistic inspiration and the respect for other cultures which it presupposes by recognizing their right to communicate and their right not to communicate, this new concept can also help effectively to solve one of the urgent problems of our time, namely, that of the cultural identity of peoples and nations.

During recent years, the baneful consequences have in fact begun to emerge of encouraging the development of the mass media without thinking it out thoroughly. Through their levelling action, through the alien ways of life which they present—and which frequently appear as models—radio, film, and television encroach deeply upon the different cultures, cause them to be seen as belonging to the past, and gravely jeopardize the preservation of the cultural heritage of the various human groups.

Inadequately equipped with their own original means of production but compelled constantly to renew their programs, some countries feel obliged to seek their supplies elsewhere, thereby becoming dependent upon foreign countries not only for their news but also for their entertainment, their education, and their recreation. Rethinking this problem is today an urgent task. The concept of the right to communicate, which places the emphasis on give-and-take rather than on transmission, can make a useful contribution thereto. Henceforth, the objective must no longer be geared so much to diffusion (cinemas, radio, and television transmitters and receivers) as to the material and intellectual possibilities of creation—and this at every cultural level—in order that all cultures, whether national, regional, or local may thrive. . . .

The Concept at the Individual, National Levels

The technological explosion in communications which we have been witnessing for the past twenty years—destined as it is to contribute . . . to the eventual recognition of a right to communicate—is still far from having exhausted its full impact.

Three major trends underlying this revolution can be identified: a wealth of possibilities of communication following upon their former scarcity; the extension of these possibilities on a planetary or global scale . . . ; a trend towards individualization. What the new media—cassettes and records, cable television, teleinformatics, teleprinting, etc.—are bringing with them is the ever greater possibility for individuals to communicate directly with one another.

Little wonder, then, if legislators in many countries are already pondering the new structures with which communication should be endowed. At present, these are no more than signs pointing to a future transformation. Nevertheless, they deserve to be mentioned.

In France, the law of August 7, 1974, reforming the then ORTF [French broadcasting service] added for the first time to the three traditional aims of broadcasting—information, education, entertainment—a fourth: "the French national public television and radio broadcasting service shall undertake, within the fields of its competence, to meet the needs and aspirations of the population in respect of information, *communication*, culture, education, entertainment and the values of civilization as a whole." In this field, the law still remains to be applied. However, no agreement has yet been reached concerning its implications.

In Italy, the Constitutional Court, in dealing with cases of closure by the government of cable television networks and local radio and television stations set up without authorization, reversed its previous judgments regarding the monopoly on radio broadcasting and excluded such installations from the scope of the monopoly. . . .

In the United Kingdom . . . the systematic development of local radio, designed to meet the needs for self-expression, access, and participation of individuals and communities, has for several years been encouraged both by the British Broadcasting Corporation (BBC) and the Independent Broadcasting Authority (IBA).

As early as 1970 in Canada, the "Telecommission" was

pondering in its remarkable report to the government, the question of whether a "right to communicate" should not be recognized, and had begun to study the resources required and the means to be used in order that all Canadian citizens might exercise this right. The satellites providing the inhabitants of the Far North with telephone and television services constitute the practical application of this concept.

In the United States, the Federal Communications Commission (FCC) taken by surprise—as was indeed industry—by the explosive development from 1973 on of citizens' band radio—for which 23 till then little-used frequency bands had been made available as far back as 1953—decided in 1975 to increase this number to 40, and began to explore the feasibility of raising it to 100, thereby recognizing the right of citizens to communicate among themselves. In Europe, with the exception of Sweden and Switzerland where citizens' band radio has received more encouragement, such a policy appears unreasonable to the administrations. . . .

All these signs are indicative of an underlying movement. The world of communications is stirring, searching for new principles on which to build new structures. What is to be derived from that of the "right to communicate?"

A NATIONAL COMMUNICATIONS POLICY

If we take as our starting point the notion of a fundamental right of citizens and communities to communicate, then there is no doubt that an entirely new national policy governing communications must be established.

Where bodies responsible for formulating such a policy do not yet exist, they should be set up. Countries which already possess such bodies (e.g., Canada, the United States, Sweden, Australia) could provide a useful example or reference point.

Responsibility for taking decisions in this field can no longer be entrusted to a single administration—till now in most cases the postal and telecommunications service—or even to several. The social and economic implications of a communications policy are so far-reaching that it would be advisable to set up a national communications authority, established on a multidisciplinary basis and comprising a small number of suitably qualified persons.

The function of this authority should be both regulatory (planning, allocation of frequencies and licenses, formulation of technical and deontological norms, etc.) and arbitrational (disputes arising in connection with communications). Its essential task would first be to work out a long-term plan.

A NATIONAL COMMUNICATIONS PLAN

In a little-known work published in 1932, "Radiotheorié," the dramatist Berthold Brecht expressed himself at the moment of leaving Hitler's Germany, in the following terms:

> The radio must be transformed from a means of distribution into a medium of communication. Radio might be the most wonderful medium of communication imaginable for the public, a vast, close-meshed network. This it could become if it was not only to receive but also to transmit, a means given to the listener not only to listen but also to speak, a means of putting him in touch rather than isolating him.

The point worth noting here is not so much that the technical means for which Brecht was calling are now available to us in various forms (citizens' band radio, cable networks, teleinformatics, etc.), as that forty-seven years ago he was already pleading on behalf of what we are so conscious of today, man's need to communicate, and pointing to the isolation resulting from the use of the mass media.

Those who, in the 1920s and 1930s, were responsible in each country for making optimum use of available frequencies in order to establish radio broadcasting, set about their task with the then prevailing idea in mind of creating throughout the national territory a vertical, one-way network for the distribution of messages. Had the concept of the right to communicate come into being at that time, a completely different system of networks would have been established.

This is the task which must be accomplished today. What is needed is a new communications plan, allowing due place for mass radio and television broadcasting (for example with one or two channels providing national coverage, probably by satellite), but using the combined resources of radio and telecommunications in addition to enable individuals and communities to express themselves, communicating freely with one another.

COMMUNICATIVENESS

As we have seen above, half a century's experience of the mass media has marked us deeply. We are no longer able to conceive of any other means of communication. For many of us, the terms "means of communication" and "mass media" are synonymous, and interchangeable. It is this error that must, first and foremost, be correct. Communication is rooted in interaction and involves participation in a two-way process, which is the very opposite of the process by which the mass media operate. At best, these are means of information; all too frequently, however, they are but the vehicles of political or commercial propaganda.

The concept of communication and of the right to communicate must lead to the demystification of the medium and its agents, and the stripping away of the magic aura which still surrounds communicators and the tools of communication. Ultimately, machines are but an extension of our own senses: they are our own ears and eyes, hearing and seeing over long distances. This awe of machines which we have inherited from the nineteenth century, and the stardom enjoyed by those who operate them, must both be done away with. This is precisely what the new means now available to us make possible, always provided we are determined to use them in the service of greater freedom and no longer to subjugate; to promote greater democratization, access, and participation rather than a reinforcement of controls.

AT THE GRASS-ROOTS LEVEL

Questions concerning opportunities for self-expression at the local community level should be decided not in terms of mass media but in terms of communication. The concept of group media, in contradistinction to mass media, has been proposed to cover those media operating on a human scale, i.e., local radio and television stations, cable television networks, rural newspapers, etc. The term appears appropriate in the case of those media whose purpose is not to provide a centralized supply of information but to facilitate exchange among all concerned through easy access to, and participation in, the joint enterprise of living together in local communities: at that level of direct human relationships where whoever seeks a hearing is aware that he is known personally to those whom he is addressing and that he will meet them the following day, either at work or during his leisure time. There will thus be feedback—which so seldom occurs in the case of the mass media—regulating the entire process.

There can be little doubt that it is this very type of media which should be fostered today, both in the industrialized countries, overwhelmed by the mass media, where the advent of direct broadcast satellites should make it possible to reorganize frequency utilization, and in the developing countries, where the mass media are fortunately still becoming established only by slow and gradual stages. The costs of setting up a local radio station or a rural newspaper are small, and within the economic capacity of most countries.

For a large number of Third World nations, the concept of the right to communicate should lead to a revision of their planning and a reappraisal of the positive (national unity) and negative effects of the mass media, while at the same time encouraging communication rather than mere information, by focusing efforts primarily on the establishment of group media:

rural newspapers, local radio stations, local program production centers. . . .

CITIZENS' BAND RADIO

If they accept the concept of the right to communicate, our industrialized countries will surely be impelled one day to consider very closely the causes of the explosive development of citizens' band radio in the United States over the past five years. This is no mere superficial phenomenon of the consumer society: industry had not envisaged CB radio, and was taken by surprise. It was the users themselves who in 1973, began to discover possibilities of communciation. . . . Today, some 18 million transmitting/receiving licenses have been issued to American citizens by the FCC—a striking demonstration of man's need to emerge from his isolation and to communicate with his fellows, even though he may not know them personally. . . .

Focus on Electronics

As electronics continues to make new advances, through a process of miniaturization which was inconceivable a few years ago (e.g., computers), an increasingly powerful transmission capacity . . . and a flexibility of use which is becoming ever closer to that of living organisms, the various tools of human expression are increasingly converging upon or becoming geared to it. Teleprinting and the use of facsimiles in the case of the press, video transmission in that of the cinema are but two immediate examples. Ultimately, we shall probably witness a complete reorganization of existing structures. Instead of our present vertically diversified structures—the press, radio, film, television, data-processing, etc.—organized into major complexes each possessing their own resources and their own semiautonomous regulations, there will emerge quite different structures of a horizontal kind—the collection, production, and distribution of messages and replies—applying to all existing media without distinction, and giving uniformity to their regulations. We are moving away from the present structural pattern based on techniques—printing, sound-and-image-recording, and data-processing—and towards a new pattern based on functions, but operating through a single medium: electronics.

The telecommunications and data-processing structures in most countries being such that the governments control this necessary transition via electronics, it is essential for freedom of opinion, freedom of expression, and freedom of information that a new principle should be applied which reaffirms . . . the fundamental rights of individuals and communities by asserting their right to communicate freely. Today, moreover, legislation governing the press, the cinema, radio, and television as also data-processing differs from one country to another. In the short term, it will inevitably be unified.

This can and must be done only on the basis of a new principle applied to all means of communication, namely, the right to communicate. It is this right, indeed, which might provide the basis for a new body of laws guaranteeing existing freedoms but designed to take account of our most recent technological achievements. . . . The concept of the right to communicate can, here and now, provide a new psychological impetus, throw a fresh light on existing structures, and enable different objectives to be put forward. However, the entire legal edifice still remains to be built. This is the task which must be accomplished in the coming years, in order that one day we shall be able to proclaim this new freedom, which we know will not replace existing freedoms but rather embrace them all.

Part II

News and Information

THE QUANTITY AND QUALITY of the flow of news and other information between nations is at the heart of the present-day world communication problems. Some nations, groups, and individuals are more troubled and are in less privileged positions than others because communication resources and benefits are not being distributed equitably. One-way flows and other alarming imbalances affect communication worldwide and contribute to the contemporary crisis and policy debate. The role of news agencies nationally and internationally must be examined.

This section moves from fundamental global issues surrounding the totality of communication to a more specific conceptualization of news—this volume's area of major theoretical and policy focus. The collection, distribution, and control of news and information has become a highly controversial, central international agenda item. Today, much of the developing world remains very dissatisfied with what they perceive as dominance-dependency relationships that have been maintained by the developed countries in dealing with the Third World. The industrial, information-rich nations of the West are also deeply troubled. Their journalists and certainly their policy-makers realize that the existing international news system has major flaws, but they are apprehensive about the near-global, unmistakable trend toward greater restrictions on journalists and increased official control of local and foreign media. The often conflicting interests over international news have generated the still unfolding crisis.

Together, these essays explore the international communication "system" forces that bear upon the consistently observed patterns of flows. Directly or indirectly, they point out some of these system-related factors, such as established colonial traditions in foreign relations, poor communication links among developing nations and between them and the First and Second Worlds respectively, and market forces operating the international communication system. Redressing imbalances in the flow and content of information will require qualitative and quantitative improvements in national capacities to inform and be informed.

7

Information Imbalance: A Closer Look

Y. V. LAKSHMANA RAO

Dr. Rao helps conceptualize "imbalance" by explaining that the world's basic communication problems at all levels can be traced to the root problem of information imbalance. He argues that it is imbalance that has led so many, particularly in recent years through Unesco, to question the 1948 United Nations concept of freedom of information and its corollary, the free flow of information. He provides a useful list of major assumptions about today's urgent imbalance issues and suggests some "fair" solutions that might help alleviate present-day concerns.

Dr. Rao is also author of "Propaganda Through the Printed Media in the Developing World," in "Propaganda in International Affairs," The Annals, November 1971. The article was one of the first to raise Third World concerns over alien influences and one-way flow in international news and information.

I CAN DO WORSE in this necessarily brief paper than to summarize first of all some of the things I have already had the

Y. V. Lakshmana Rao is an Asian communication expert now with Unesco in Paris. He is a former secretary-general of the Asian Mass Communication Research and Information Center (AMIC), Singapore.

This is a slightly expanded and updated version of a paper given at the Conference on Fair Communication Policy for the International Exchange of Information, East-West Communication Institute, Honolulu, March–April 1978.

opportunities to talk and to write about. After doing that, I wish to raise some of the fundamental questions to which we need to find answers. Obviously, it is this second part which is going to be difficult. I do not mean the finding of the answers; I mean the very exercise of raising the so-called fundamental questions.

These questions seem to be fundamental to me, because I have not been comfortable with them churning in my head ever since I first got involved in this whole question of information imbalance, fair communication policy, the right to communicate, communication policies and planning, the "new order," etc. Under slightly different names and somewhat different focuses, I do believe that, even if they do not exactly mean the same thing, they do deal with highly related facets of the same broad concept. And, also, they are integrally related to the ongoing work of the United Nations, particularly Unesco, in international development strategy.

Communication and the United Nations

From the outset, the United Nations, seeking ways of establishing a lasting peace, acknowledged the role of communication as a potentially decisive factor in international understanding. The idea that the mass media should be enlisted in the task of promoting "the mutual knowledge and understanding of peoples" is embodied in the organization's constitution. It was for this reason that, as soon as it was founded, Unesco tackled the problem of finding out the conditions under which the development of communication might be likely to strengthen "the defenses of peace" in the minds of men. While the recognition of the role of communication in human and economic development may be particularly intense and relevant to the less-developed countries, it is by no means exclusive to them. It is this recognition that has gradually led all member states of Unesco to demand and work toward the establishment of a new world information and communication order which could both be assisted by and contribute to a new economic order.

Since 1946, developments have been swift and we are entitled to expect a great deal more of the mass media than "the free flow of ideas." But it must be emphasized that, historically, the media were ill-prepared for the task which now devolves upon them. Being products of industrialization, they scarcely affected the peoples of the developing region of the world who, by reason of their low purchasing power, were deprived of access to the media.

Information Imbalance

I would contend that information imbalance is at the root of the controversy over international communication. I say this because, whether they are at the international level, or at the regional, or even at the subnational, such imbalances have brought up all the other related questions. It is these imbalances that have gradually led us to question all over again the concept of freedom of information (which was heralded in 1948 as "the touchstone of all the freedoms to which the United Nations is working") and its corollary, the free flow of information. And it is these questions that have caused Unesco, which had successfully established agreements to facilitate the free flow of information around the world, today to go through the whole exercise again by initiating studies of more or less the same issues under the concept of "The Right to Communicate" and "The New World Information Order."

The ebb and flow of the various questions and issues surrounding the notion of information imbalance have been noted at a number of international gatherings. One of the earliest and most important of such efforts was the Regional Conference on Information Imbalance in Asia, organized by the Asian Mass Communication Research and Information Center, Singapore, and held in Kandy, Sri Lanka, in April 1975. For

that occasion, I was able to discuss a number of major assumptions concerning information imbalance that seem worth
repeating at the start of the 1980s. This list is not meant to be
exhaustive or definitive but merely to indicate the importance
and complexity of the issues involved.[1] Many of these issues
seem even more urgent and fundamental today than they were
when they first were explicitly raised, and only one of them,
the need for hard data on information imbalance, has been
partially resolved. All have been, in the years since 1975,
under discussion in many forums throughout the world.

First, concern continues to be expressed in Asia, as well
as other developing regions, that the concept of free flow of
information has generally worked solely to the advantage of
the industrially more advanced nations. But is this in fact the
case? Isn't there a great deal of material (news and features
rather than entertainment) now emanating from the developing countries? And, even if the assumption can be regarded
as essentially true, does it not appear that the parties involved
may be jointly concerned about this situation and are already
considering what might be done to change it? For example,
there seem to be indications that Americans (as well as other
exporters) may be as concerned about the attendant international publicity as the leaders of the developing countries are
about the implications for their own national plans and programs, values and beliefs. With regard to entertainment material, many exporting countries don't seem particularly happy
with the types of programs that seem to attract the greatest
popularity and thus the greatest demand from the developing
countries.

And when one talks of "advantage," does that mean a
primary emphasis on the economic factor? If it does, then it
seems worthwhile to investigate the reasons why such an outflow of financial resources is permitted by the developing
countries (either by government or by media units). Public
demand may not be the only reason involved; there may also

1. For a fuller account, see "Information Imbalance in Asia," *Media Asia* (1976),
pp. 78–81.

be a perceived need to fill the available space and time, which the developing countries are incapable of filling themselves. It seems most important to learn the basis on which decisions of this sort are made and at what levels in the communication hierarchies.

Or are worries about advantage based more on social and cultural considerations? Many of us seem worried that our publics will emulate the behavioral patterns and absorb the values and beliefs of the "alien invaders" of our cultures. But is it possible to come up with a clear and well-defined scale by which to measure this sort of cultural invasion? Is an "invader" anyone who comes from across a national boundary, or does the word only apply to one who crosses a regional boundary? Or perhaps the boundary of concern is that great one around all developing countries?

Second, despite such concerns, there had been few serious attempts by 1975 to look at the issues practically and realistically, and no basic data had been collected that would provide an accurate picture either quantitatively or qualitatively. This, of course, raises the question of whether it is possible to develop ways in which such a picture might be drawn in a realistic manner, and in the past several years, several data-rich flow studies have been conducted. This gives the policy-makers of the 1980s a distinct advantage over those of 1975 and earlier.

Third, it therefore seems apparent that the issue requires discussion, not only in greater depth, but from several separate but related points of view. It seems especially important that the discussion include those who are now directly involved in the practice of mass communication.

Fourth, the mass communication practitioner is generally aware both of the material available to him and of that desired by his present and potential audiences. He may not always be in a position to make formal decisions of the sort with which we are concerned here, but his function of transforming directives from higher authority into everyday action permits him some impact on the decision process. But is it within his capabilities and authority to generate material that can compete with products from abroad for the attention of his public? Is he in fact making any effort to progressively improve the quality of his products and, thereby, to reduce the quantity of products imported?

Fifth, it may be true that the real ratio of imported to indigenous informational and entertainment material is not as awesome as generally assumed. What is needed here is not only the hard data now available to some extent but also data that show trends over time. There are some signs that, however bad one may deem the present situation, it may be an improvement over what has been before.

Sixth, even if the ratio is found to be quite significant, there may be reasons why governments and media permit such imbalance to continue. The tendency is always to assume that they cannot help it when, in fact, they may see some advantages in it. For instance, they may regard some measure of international intercourse as inevitable, or they may hope to encourage their citizens to compete and catch up with the "haves" by learning their ways. If this is the case, then one must confront the issue of how to define and separate the "bad" from the "good," and prevent the former from slipping in along with the latter.

Seventh, if decision-makers in government and the media could get together to discuss the various issues, they might be able to find ways to correct the imbalances without too much further delay.

Eighth, detailed discussions on these questions might lead to more coordinated and concerted efforts at research on the social and psychological impact of media exposure on various audiences.

"Haves" and "Have-Nots"

As a result of information imbalance and the issues it has generated, there has been a growing perception of the world as a dichotomy. On the one side are the "haves" in information—those who export their (primarily informational and entertainment) material—and on the other are the "have-nots"—those who are mainly on the receiving end. The perception of their relative disadvantages has tended to draw the have-nots closer together and to lead them more actively to seek joint solutions to the problems of their disadvantaged state.

For example, the Kandy Conference brought together participants from sixteen Asian nations, territories, and institutions.[2] While they naturally represented a wide divergence of views, it is perhaps noteworthy that the keynote speaker "urged the participants to take a fresh and critical look from a regional point of view and in a cooperative spirit" at the problem. It also seems noteworthy that these participants were able to reach a consensus on various assumptions and recommendations reflecting what must appear to be something resembling the "regional point of view" and the "cooperative spirit" that had been called for—especially in connection with their aspirations vis-à-vis the haves. For example, there was agreement that:

- "For an Asian country, free flow of information still generally means that it has to be at the receiving end, with very little opportunity to explain its own position in any given situation."
- "As a result, the concept of free flow of information is not feasible in the Asian situation."
- In consequence, it "is important to take deliberate steps to regulate the flow of information in such a manner that will assist the development of information systems in Asian countries."
- Communication policy and planning must be developed primarily at the national level, with national objectives and goals in mind. However, at the same time, at "the sub-regional and regional levels, cooperative and coordinated efforts should be made to create greater interest among the people in the affairs

2. A report on the conference, from which all references herein have been taken, is found in *Media Asia* (1975), pp. 69–77.

of the countries of Asia and Africa in general, and in neighboring countries in particular."

Thus, the have-nots were becoming more vocal and perhaps even growing in numbers and weight. Perhaps in consequence, both sides—the haves and the have-nots—began to
recognize and to feel intensely the need for dialogue and the
need for compromise and working solutions between them.
They have realized that perhaps they are in the same boat—
and that it might easily tip over.

This may sound quite cynical, and even heartless in some
ways. I cannot help it. At one time, I had approached this
question quite idealistically, believe it or not. I had this great
belief in the innate goodness of Man, in his feelings for his
fellow man, etc. I had even argued that the have-nots must
learn from the haves (thank goodness, they exist)—learn from
their successes and avoid their mistakes—and develop their
own skills to match the excellence of their mentors.

In the course of time, I had argued, the imbalance will
right itself. We would have achieved Utopia. Now, as I progress
increasingly rapidly toward that point where I had expected
Utopia to be, I find that either Utopia has receded or that I
was perhaps walking the wrong road all the time. The gap
between ideology and reality has, in fact, widened. My first
fundamental question, therefore, is: Why? What happened?

I know I wasn't walking alone. My friends are lost too.
And we are all asking the same question. We wonder if it is
too late for some of us to seek the "right" road. Or make some
"fundamental" compromises and look for shortcuts—if we still
insist on reaching that goal we set out toward. We would, I
think, be satisfied to merely see a hazy outline of that goal
somewhere on the horizon. Our children and theirs may eventually make it.

This whole idea of shortcuts then came to me. Only partially has it been due to creeping old age, I would like to
believe, and to the realization that if I want to see that outline
on the horizon, I had better do something—fast. The more im-

portant factor, I think, has been the opening of my eyes to
Reality. While I was singlemindedly following my chosen
path, others have already found the shortcuts! What is worse
(or is it better?), they are about to convince me that I should
do the same—and pass on more peacefully.

I would like to share with you some of the implications
which strike me as being crucial to any intellectual decisions
I might make for myself. By taking a closer look, I hope to
salve my own conscience. Or, perhaps I am destined to continue to grope. Spelling out the dilemmas and paradoxes is
perhaps unnecessary in this day and age. Therefore let me
here confine myself to the real questions.

The Shortcuts

I would call the great call for free flow of information the
straight road. So also the efforts at the national level to increase
literacy, to use communication (technology and all) for social
change, for modernization, for development, etc. Combine the
international with the national. What has happened? Not a
great deal.

Of course *some* progress has been made. More people
know a little more about more things now than they might
have without all the free flow and without all the communication inputs. Even that, we cannot actually prove. There *are*
skeptics at the highest levels of decision-making. It is them we
have to reach and convince.

The decision-makers *have* already taken some shortcuts,
free flow or no free flow. They seem to be far more capable
of living with conflicting ideas and norms than some of us are.
They can sign a covenant with one hand and a whole set of
controls with the other. Is such ambidextrous capacity what
we need to develop if we are to comfortably live with ourselves? That is my next fundamental question. Or should we

just drop the one and live with the other alone—to be "realistic," "pragmatic," and "functional?"

What is fair? (That's the most fundamental question of all—but it may be quite unfair in itself.) It is fair, one can argue, to have high goals and aspirations. It is also fair, *meanwhile*, to resort to shortcuts and to controls and whatever may become necessary to speed the process leading to that goal. Only, the "meanwhile" doesn't seem to have any end. If anything, the controls are becoming greater—partly because the "gaps" of which people speak seem to be widening all the time instead of narrowing, which was the initial hope.

If the free flow concept is now slowly, and with a great deal of respect and dignity, being led unbeknown to itself toward a grave which took a large number of people to dig (including its own progenitors), is it because we have all accepted that it is untenable? The regional conference in Kandy on this subject frankly called it that. Others have also done so. If that is so, what is forcing us to more or less resurrect it (before a final verdict of death has been passed, let alone death actually having taken place!) under a new phrase, The Right to Communicate? My own feeling is that we all have this insatiable thirst for ideology. I am all for it. I raise it only because my first "why?" has not been answered.

Can we agree that a "preamble" or a "statement of objectives" should not be taken literally no matter what the circumstances are or no matter what the state of development is in any given country? Can we also agree that some controls on freedom of speech, freedom of expression, etc., are perhaps necessary and *fair*? If we do that, are we diluting the kind of absolutes on which we have been brought up? If this has happened in so many other areas (I can think of economics and sex as two of the most clearly visible) why not in information? After all, it *has* taken unto itself many of the characteristics of the other two fields I just mentioned. Information is an *industry* and some journalists have practiced the oldest profession for a long time (their members are increasing). I am not saying anything about "intellectuals," except perhaps this:

some of my brightest friends have gone into the "private sector!"

I am sorry that this essay has been perhaps overly provocative and even cynical. Let me say simply that it is cynical only because it is based on an ideology I find it increasingly hard to adhere to. I am trying, but I need help.

"Fair Solutions"

It may be useful for me to summarize the main points raised at several conferences in Asia and elsewhere, together with some "solutions" people see as being "fair—under the circumstances":

1. Developing countries should impose controls on flow of informational and entertainment materials:
    - to protect their own language, culture, behavioral patterns, values, beliefs, etc. (The highest degree of nationalism is apparent, with some concession made for regionalism);
    - to increase their own capabilities in production of materials (continued importation tends to make them complacent and lethargic);
    - to protect them from being brainwashed into looking at world events the way the major news networks see them;
    - to be forced to train the needed personnel for their own networks.
2. "Exporting" countries should impose restrictions on the quantity and quality of their own producers (public and private), especially with regard to what they sell or distribute freely abroad.
3. Equitable agreements (bilateral) with exporting countries, should be reached, that is, send some, take some.
4. Developing countries should work toward regional agreements within Asia for exchange of informational and entertainment material, so as to exclude "foreign" material and "influence."

5. Research is needed, both quantitative and qualitative, to gauge the impact of imported materials (trend studies may show that the imbalance is, in fact, already on the way down).

People's voices have been raised against throwing the baby out with the bathwater by restricting "good" programs—but people seem to have more concern for the bathwater than for the baby. "That is a price we may have to pay."

8

A Growing Controversy: The "Free Flow" of News among Nations
JOHN C. MERRILL

Professor Merrill's essay represents the pragmatic, mainstream American response to Third World criticism of the "free flow" of news among nations. In general, he rejects the argument that major changes are needed in the practices guiding news collection and dissemination. He points out that the basic conceptual differences between Western and Third World journalism are not sufficiently stressed in international communication debates and that "as long as countries go their different ideological ways, these differences will be reflected in their journalistic philosophies and systems." He concludes that it is unrealistic to expect news to flow in a balanced way between or within individual countries because "unevenness of flow is a basic characteristic of news—and not only of news flow, but of water flow, oil flow, money flow, population flow, and food flow."

John C. Merrill is director, School of Journalism, Louisiana State University and the author/editor of *The Foreign Press, Ethics and the Press, The Imperative of Freedom, International and Intercultural Communication,* and *The World's Great Dailies.*

This is an expanded version of "The 'Free Flow' of News Among Nations," *Nieman Reports* (Winter/Spring 1978).

IN THIS DAY when news flow is said not to be what it should be, there is at least one kind of information flowing freely: denunciation of Western journalism for alleged inadequate and biased reporting and news dissemination as relates to the so-called Third World—the "developing" or "nonaligned" countries. Largely propelled by Unesco conferences on the subject, proliferating throughout the world in recent years, a barrage of Third World criticism of Western news practices pounds upon the ear and has become a major theme in communications literature.[1]

Among the main targets are the big international news agencies of the West—the U.S.'s Associated Press and United Press International, Britain's Reuters, and France's Agence France-Presse. Quite simply, it seems, the Third World is greatly disturbed over what it sees as the unenlightened, biased, and inadequate journalistic theory and practice of the capitalistic Western nations—especially the United States. Hardly a day goes by that some editor or political leader in the Third World does not take a public swing at Western journalism for its "injustices" in the area of news coverage; and, it might be added, this criticism flows rather freely into the media journals and general press of the West.

The Fundamental Issue

What is the main problem? Actually, the Third World has a whole list of complaints against the Western press but at present the main target seems to be what is referred to as the "free flow" of news across national boundaries. According to Third

---

1. The terms "West" and "Western journalism" are used in this article to refer to the capitalistic industrialized nations of Western Europe and North America (and Japan); the journalism of this group of nations is contrasted to that of the Third World (developing, nonaligned, new) nations, some of which are certainly in the West. The West in this article is also contrasted with Communist nations such as the U.S.S.R., China, and Cuba, although the last-named is geographically part of the West.

World spokesmen, the Western news agencies—especially the
AP and UPI—are disrupting this free flow of news, are distorting
the realities of the developing countries, and are basically
presenting negative images of the Third World. This is the
basic criticism, although there are many others.

The leaders of these developing countries,[2] both political
and journalistic, recognize the great importance of mass communication, the potency of international information dissemination, and the impact of national images on the conduct of
foreign relations. They are, justifiably, sensitive to the kind of
press treatment they receive. And, by and large, they feel they
do not fare well in the Western press—especially in stories from
the big news agencies.

Individually, and through the international forum of
Unesco, these Third World countries are mounting an esca-
lating campaign against Western journalism.[3] They seek to
eliminate the impediments they see blocking the free flow of
information throughout the world. In other words, they want
to see news flow as freely *from* the Third World to the Western
countries as it flows from the West *to* the Third World. The
big Western news agencies, they say, have a virtual monopoly
on news dissemination and fail to provide the world with a
realistic picture of what is really happening in the Third
World. Too biased, they say. Too heavy on negative news—poverty, illiteracy, riots, revolutions, volcano eruptions, antics of
national leaders, kidnappings, etc. They ask: What about the
good things that are going on—bridge building, highway construction, new schools, and the like? Why is it that the AP and
UPI, and to a lesser degree Reuters and Agence France-Presse,
so grossly neglect these aspects of the Third World?

2. This term is often used to describe Third World nations; it is, of course,
somewhat fuzzy and even unfair, for there are many kinds of development. *All* countries are developing—and *all* countries are underdeveloped in many areas. What is
usually meant by calling the Third World nations "developing," I think, is that these
nations are intent on developing technologically, industrially, and economically.

3. It is indeed strange that the Third World and Unesco have little or no criticism
for the journalism of the Communist world; evidently the news flow to and from
these countries is satisfactory—balanced and free.

Basic Conceptual Differences

Having talked with journalists in some twenty Third World countries in the past several years, I have concluded that what they really mean by free flow of news is a "balanced flow." Western journalists mean something else by free flow. In other words, Western newsmen put the emphasis on the *free* and the Third World journalists stress the *flow*—with the main part of this flow relating to a desired *balance* or *equality* in the news that moves among nations and parts of the world.

This difference in concept is important, but it is not often stressed in discussions and debates. Western journalists, for example, have found many (most?) of the Third World nations to be highly restrictive and secretive societies whose leaders go to great lengths to keep correspondents (and not only *for-eign* ones) at arm's length. Sources in these countries are hard to reach; meetings are closed; leaders are secretive and touchy, and the record shows that in recent years foreign journalists have been threatened often with expulsion—and many have been expelled for reporting what in the West would be the most obvious kinds of news events. The Western journalists say that if there is a problem with news flow it largely rests with the controlled systems in which they are trying to report. How can Western journalists permit the news flow to be *free* when the Third World nations themselves do not have free societies with press systems which are free? In other words, a *free* flow of news must include the flow within countries themselves and not simply the flow between and among na-tions. It is the situation *within* countries that most often affects news flow, say the Western journalists trying to report the Third World.

Third World critics, of course, reject this Western per-spective, and they shift the emphasis from the internal restric-tive problems of the nations to the Western news agencies and foreign correspondents. So we are constantly told that Western reporters in the Third World are either biased or uninformed (or both), that they are too few, that they are too bound by traditional Western news values, that they are blinded to Third World developmental concerns, and that they are too warped in their reporting by extreme anticommunism and by suspicions that the Third World generally is not really "nonaligned."

What the Third World Wants

So, briefly, what the Third World seems to want from Western journalism is this: (1) a kind of "balanced" flow of news in and out of the Third World; (2) more thorough, incisive, and unbiased news coverage of their countries on a continuing basis, and (3) more emphasis on "good" or positive news of the Third World, including what has come to be called "development" news.

Western journalists readily admit that there is some truth in the indictments of the Western press. Certainly there *is* an unevenness in news flow among nations—but, say Western journalists, this is also true of news flow *within* individual countries. And, certainly, much international coverage can be said to contain bias—but, *all* reporting can be so indicted. Also, what the Third World means by development news is really not considered particularly newsworthy by Western standards—or, it may be said, that the Western concept of news would include *all* news in the concept of development of the nation—not just that dealing with obvious construction, educational innovations, scientific achievements, and the like.

To Western journalists it is naïve to expect the world to have a balanced flow of news. News simply does not flow evenly—for example, there is not as much news flowing from South America to Europe as from Europe to South America, or as much flowing from the northern Mexican town of Saltillo to Mexico City as the other way around. Who can talk of a "balance of news flow" in the real world? We do not have any balance in news flow even within a single country, so certainly we cannot expect to have it in the whole world. Why does the

Third World keep asking for such a balance? It is a strange request, indeed. One might as well ask why so much more news flows from New Delhi to Poona than flows from Poona to New Delhi. Unevenness of flow is a basic characteristic of news—and not only of news flow, but of water flow, oil flow, money flow, population flow, and food flow.

Flow of news is related to supply, consumers, and producers. News, like oil, flows mainly from where the supply is greatest; also it flows from where there are more workers "drilling" for it; and finally, it flows mainly to places where consumers seem to demand it. If, for instance, the Third World begins to be a producer of a news product desired by the West, then and only then will the news flow tend to become more balanced. At present this is not the case: the West is simply not interested in the more routine news of the Third World.[4] (It might be noted here that several researchers have found that one Third World country is not interested in development news of another Third World country.)

Also, it should be said that the Third World nations can help the flow imbalance by not relying so heavily on the Western agencies; they can do more to develop their own news organizations; they can cooperate in Third World news pools to a greater extent; and, if they really feel so antagonistic toward Western news agencies, they can stop using the agency material altogether.

The Third World also wants Western journalism to be "unbiased" and to present news on a "continuing" basis, eliminating the "piecemeal," sporadic nature of news coverage. This, of course, is a worthy goal for any journalism, but it is unrealistic in practice. And, certainly the existence of such news does not indicate any Western prejudice against the Third World. News is *always* piecemeal and biased as to real-

---

4. It is always interesting to observe in Third World newspapers the large portions of the news space given over to news from the West dealing with explosions, crashes and wrecks, murders, rapes and kidnapping, Hollywood escapades, and the like. In fact, content analyses have shown that in many Third World countries "Western" sensational news gets as big a play as it does in Western countries—in many cases a larger play.

ity, and is so because of *somebody's* perspective. A journalist—in *any* society—selects what will be news and fashions it according to his value system; this works within the United States and it works with news agency correspondents who report news internationally. Since journalistic decisions are strained through the journalist's subjectivity, it is safe to say that all news is biased in some way—unfaithful to reality and manipulated by journalistic judgment. It is unreasonable for the Third World nations—or any nations—to expect otherwise. There is certainly no proof that Western journalism maliciously and with premeditation biases news stories against Third World countries. If there is such proof, the Western news agencies would like to see it presented at Third World and Unesco conferences instead of the wild accusations and generalizations which are usually presented.

Then, there is the indictment of Western news agencies for not presenting enough positive or "good" news of the Third World. First, what do the critics mean when they talk of not "enough" news of the Third World? How much is enough, and who is to decide this quantity? As long as the Western agencies are operating in a free-enterprise system and are doing the collecting and transmitting, they are the ones who will make these decisions. It is not reasonable for anyone to think otherwise.

It may well be true that much (or even *most*) of the news emanating from the Third World has a "negative" character, but this can also be said (and *is* said) of news flowing within Western countries themselves. Certainly, the news agencies do not seem to play favorites in this respect. It should be noted also that this atypical, unusual, and often sensational nature of news is a very basic part of the West's definition of news; therefore it is completely natural for Western journalists to call on such a definition when collecting and sending news from a Third World country. The Marxist countries, of course, have their own definitions of news, and the Third World nations can use much more news from TASS and other such agencies if they find this definition of news compatible. Also, it should be said that the piecemeal coverage of news, by which the media jump from one news item to another without too much concern with relatedness of news items or continuing coverage, is very much a part of the nature of journalism in the West. It may be a weakness, but if so, it is a universal weakness.

And What About Third World Editors?

Third World editors who are critical of the West for the above practices themselves have basically the same values and do the same things. In selecting and printing stories, they generally agree with the Western concept of news (if they exercise any real freedom of editorial determination), for it is easy to see in their papers reflections of the same negative and sensational news—generally about *other* (usually Western) countries, of course. I have been told by editors of the Third World that they have to do this because all the news they have is from the Western news agencies. This is simply not true. These editors know full well that they themselves, in assigning local and national news and deciding which of it to put on their pages, generally use the more dramatic, more sensational, more atypical examples of this material. And they get foreign news from embassies, some of their own correspondents, their own national news agencies, and from other sources. If they use the Western news agencies in preference to other sources, it must be that they prefer their news coverage—in spite of what they say.

In many Third World countries—for example, India, Bangladesh, Indonesia, Malaysia, and the Philippines, to name a few in Asia—editors who complain of the kinds of news stories sent them by Western agencies also are having their own reporters write and submit (and they are predominantly used) stories *of the same* genre. If anyone doubts this, he is invited to take a look at the local and national news in the newspapers of these countries.

Of course, the editors may complain that through the years they have been "brainwashed" by the Western concept of news (or have studied journalism in the West); this, perhaps is to some extent true, but it seems clear that at least part of the blame lies with those who allow themselves to be brainwashed. And, certainly, no foreign journalist is coerced into studying journalism in the West.

However reluctant the editors in the Third World are to face it, they bear some responsibility. For example, the Western agencies send many stories about Third World countries. Surely, many Third World editors get more such stories than are used. In fact, the editors admit that few of these are used. Why? There are two general answers: (1) the stories are not written to suit the editors, and (2) the readers are simply not interested in such stories from other Third World countries. So, it seems that Third World editors themselves do not really have a dedication to presenting other Third World news in their papers; they simply want to use this as a stick with which to beat the Western news agencies. Almost every editor I have ever talked with in the Third World has admitted that his readers would not be interested in the bulk of "development" news coming from the Third World—even that which was happening right in the editor's own country. The fact that not much Third World news appears on the pages of newspapers (in or out of the Third World) is no proof that the Western news agencies are at fault.

Certainly, Western journalism is far from perfect. Nor do I believe that Third World editors are not sincerely concerned about improving journalism; I have been impressed by the obvious zeal and dedication of Third World journalists. But we are *all* concerned about the state of world journalism. It is just that we see the problems from different perspectives.

There is no doubt that the following research is needed: (a) definitional studies to find the main distinctions between Western definitions of news in Third World countries and the definitions of news in those countries themselves; (b) news flow studies that point out the quantity and type of news that actually crosses national boundaries; (c) "usage" studies that show what news in the flow is actually used by editors; (d) readership studies in various countries that indicate the real news values of readers. Such studies have been few and far between since the 1950s.

This whole matter of news flow is a tough one. Undoubtedly it will be one of the world's basic journalistic issues for a long time. For as long as countries go their different ideological ways, these differences will be reflected in their journalistic philosophies and systems.

9

Genesis of the Free Flow of Information Principles
HERBERT I. SCHILLER

Dr. Schiller pays particular attention to connections between national and international communication and policy making and examines the free flow of information concept in terms of American capitalism's past and present imposition of what he argues is communication domination on the formerly colonial countries. He contends that the ideals of the free flow of communication exist only for the privileged (both inter- and intranational "haves") and that the flow of information between nations is "to a very great extent a one-way, unbalanced traffic."

Like Masmoudi politically, Schiller academically represents those who outspokenly favor comprehensive national and international policies which diminish Western influence in the Third World and challenge the prevailing system's media structures and controls. Schiller's pioneering efforts at developing a critical perspective within American academia have made their marks on international communication debate.

Herbert L. Schiller, professor of communications at the University of California, San Diego, is a critical scholar concerned about communication as a source of media imperialism and political power in today's American-influenced world system. He is the author of such books as *Mass Communications and American Empire, The Mind Managers*, and *Communication and Cultural Domination*.

This essay originally appeared in *Instant Research on Peace and Violence* (1975, Tampere, Finland), 5(1):75–86.

Regardless of how many Westerners strongly reject the thinking of such individuals, both Schiller and Masmoudi have played leading roles in legitimizing alternative, wider, and essentially non-Western concepts of development and communication in the post-1970 era.

FOR A QUARTER OF A CENTURY, one doctrine—the idea that no barriers should prevent the flow of information among nations—dominated international thinking about communications and cultural relations. The genesis and extension of the free flow of information concept are roughly coterminous with the brief and hectic interval of U.S. global hegemony, an epoch already on the wane. As we look back, it is now evident that the historical coincidence of these two phenomena—the policy of free flow of information and the imperial ascendancy of the United States—was not fortuitous. The first element was one of a very few indispensable prerequisites for the latter. Their interaction deserves examination.

As World War II drew to a close, attention in the United States at the highest decision-making levels was already focusing on the era ahead. In 1943, two years before the war's end, it was clear that the United States would emerge from the conflict physically unscathed and economically overpowering.

In the most general terms, the more articulate exponents of what seemed to be a looming American Century envisioned a world unshackled from former colonial ties and generally accessible to the initiatives and undertakings of American private enterprise. Accumulated advantages, not all of them war related, ineluctably would permit American business to flourish and expand into the farthest reaches of the world capitalist system. The limits that the very existence of a sphere under socialist organization put on this expansion were, it might be noted, neither agreeable nor acceptable, at that time, to a self-confident North American leadership.

The outward thrust of U.S. corporate enterprise was economic, but the utility of the cultural-informational component in the expansion process was appreciated at a very early stage in the drama. The rapid international advances of U.S. capitalism, already underway in the early 1940s, were legitimized as unexceptional and highly beneficial expressions of growing freedom in the international arena—freedom for capital, resources, and information flows.

It was an especially propitious time to extol the virtues of unrestricted movement of information and resources. The depredations of the Nazi occupation had traumatized Europe and a good part of the rest of the world. Freedom of information and movement were the highly desirable and legitimate aspirations of occupied nations and peoples. And it was relatively easy to confuse truly national needs with private business objectives.

John Knight, owner of a major chain of newspapers in the United States, and in 1946 the president of the American Society of Newspaper Editors, made a point, which left out more than it explained, that many were expressing at the time:

Had not the Nazi and Fascist forces in Germany and Italy seized and dominated the press and all communication facilities at the start, the growth of these poisonous dictatorships might well have been prevented and the indoctrination of national thought in the direction of hatred and mistrust might have been impossible.[1]

Free flow of information could not only be contrasted to the Fascist mode of operations but also was associated with the hope for peace shared by war-weary peoples everywhere. Palmer Hoyt, another influential American publisher, declared a few months after the war's end:

I believe entirely that the world cannot stand another war. But I believe as completely that the world is headed for such a war and destruction unless immediate steps are taken to insure the beginning at least of freedom of news—*American style*—between the peoples of the earth. A civilization that is not informed cannot be free and a world that is not free cannot endure. (italics added)[2]

1. John S. Knight, "World Freedom of Information," speech presented in Philadelphia, April 16, 1946. Published in *Vital Speeches* (1946), 12:472–77.
2. Palmer Hoyt, "Last Chance," speech delivered before the Jackson County Chamber of Commerce, Medford, Oregon, September 18, 1945. Published in *Vital Speeches* (1946), 12:60–62.

U.S. advocates of ease of movement of information then capitalized heavily on the experiences and emotions of people freshly liberated from Fascist-occupied and war-ravaged continents. But accompanying the rhetoric of freedom were powerful economic forces employing a skillful political and semantic strategy.

In the first decades of the twentieth century, important sectors of domestic industry chafed impatiently at being excluded from vast regions preempted by the still-forceful British and French empires, i.e., the British global imperial preferences that tied together that colonial system's network of dependencies and sealed them off from possible commercial penetration by other entrepreneurs.

The decisive role played by the British worldwide communications network—both its control of the physical hardware of oceanic cables and its administrative and business organization of news and information—which held the colonial system together, promoted its advantages, and insulated it from external assault, had not escaped attention in the United States. It was against these finely spun, structural ties that an American offensive was mounted. Conveniently, the attack could avail itself of the virtuous language and praiseworthy objectives of "free flow of information" and "world-wide access to news."

But there was no mistaking the underlying thrust. For years Kent Cooper, executive manager of the Associated Press (AP), had sought to break the international grip of the European news cartels—Reuters, foremost, and Havas and Wolff. Cooper's book *Barriers Down*[3] described the global territorial divisions the cartels had organized and the limitations they posed for the activities of the AP. As early as 1914, Cooper wrote, the AP "board was debating whether the Associated Press should not make an effort to break through the Havas (French) control of the vast South American territory."[4] He recalled, "The tenacious hold that a Nineteenth Century ter-

---

3. Kent Cooper, *Barriers Down* (New York: Farrar and Rinehart, 1942), p. 41.
4. *Ibid.*, p. 41.

ritorial allotment for news dissemination had upon the world was evidenced by each year's discussion of the subject by the Associated Press Board of Directors, continuing until 1934."[5]

Cooper's indictment of the old cartels has an ironic quality today when U.S. news agencies largely dominate the flow of world information:

In precluding the Associated Press from disseminating news abroad, Reuters and Havas served three purposes: (1) they kept out Associated Press competition; (2) they were free to present American news disparagingly to the United States if they presented it at all; (3) they could present news of their own countries most favorably and without it being contradicted. Their own countries were always glorified. This was done by reporting great advances at home in English and French civilizations, the benefits of which would, of course, be bestowed on the world.[6]

Cooper also recognized the significance of Britain's domination of the oceanic cables:

The cable brought Australia, South Africa, India, China, Canada and all the British world instantaneously to London on the Thames. . . . Britain, far ahead of any other nation, concentrated on the cable business. First it tied its Empire together. Then it stretched out and tied other nations to it. And in harmony with Victorian practices, the news that went through this vast network of cables gave luster to the British cause![7]

Cooper was not alone in seeing these advantages. James Lawrence Fly,[8] chairman of the Federal Communications Commission during World War II, also drew attention to this subject:

Among the artificial restraints to the free development of commerce throughout the world none is more irksome and less justifiable than

5. *Ibid.*, p. 43.
6. *Ibid.*
7. *Ibid.*, p. 11.
8. James Lawrence Fly, "A Free Flow of News Must Link the Nations," *Free World* (August 1944), 8(2):165–69.

the control of communication facilities by one country with preferential services and rates to its own nationals. . . .

Great Britain owns the major portion of the cables of the world, and it is a fair statement that, through such ownership and the interlocking contractual relations based on it, that country dominates the world cable situation.[9]

This understanding of the power afforded by domination of communications was not forgotten. It was manifest two decades later when U.S. companies, with huge government subsidies, were the first to develop and then monopolize satellite communications.

The impatient U.S. press associations and governmental communications regulators found others in the country who recognized the advantages that worldwide communications control bestowed on foreign trade and export markets. *Business Week* reported:

Washington recognizes the postwar importance of freer communications as a stimulant to the interchange of goods and ideas. . . . In peacetime, reduced costs of messages will energize our trade, support our propaganda, bolster business for all the lines.[10]

The magazine summed up the business view by quoting approvingly a comment that had appeared in the London *Standard*: Control of communications "gives power to survey the trade of the world and . . . to facilitate those activities which are to the interest of those in control."

Of course, British power was not unaware of American interest in these matters. The influential *Economist* reacted tartly to Kent Cooper's expanding campaign, in late 1944, for the free flow of information: The "huge financial resources of the American agencies might enable them to dominate the world. . . . [Cooper], like most big business executives, experiences a peculiar moral glow in finding that his idea of freedom coincides with his commercial advantage. . . . De-

9. *Ibid.*, p. 168.
10. *Business Week* (August 4, 1945) 87:32, 34, 41.

mocracy does not necessarily mean making the whole world safe for the AP."[11] Nor did it mean, the *Economist* failed to add, retaining control for Reuters and British Cables.

The public official most directly concerned with formulating and explaining U.S. policy in the communications sphere immediately after the war was William Benton, the assistant secretary of state. Benton,[12] who was to become a U.S. senator and president of the Encyclopedia Britannica, outlined, in a State Department broadcast in January 1946, the government's position on the meaning of freedom of communications:

The State Department plans to do everything within its power along political or diplomatic lines to help break down the artificial barriers to the expansion of private American news agencies, magazines, motion pictures, and other media of communications throughout the world. . . . Freedom of the press—and freedom of exchange of information generally—is an integral part of our foreign policy.

The economic aspects of the free-flow-of-information policy certainly were no secret, though the media neither dwelt on the self-serving nature of its widely proclaimed principle nor made the implications of the policy explicit to the public. Instead, a remarkable political campaign was organized by the big press associations and publishers, with the support of industry in general, to elevate the issue of free flow of information to the highest level of national and international principle. This served a handsome pair of objectives. It rallied public opinion to the support of a commercial goal expressed as an ethical imperative. Simultaneously, it provided a highly effective ideological club against the Soviet Union and its newly created neighboring zone of anticapitalist influence.

It was obvious that the fundamental premise of free enterprise—access to capital governs access to message dissemination—would be intolerable to societies that had eliminated private ownership of decisive forms of property, such as mass

11. Quoted in "Charter for a Free Press," *Newsweek* (December 11, 1944), p. 88.
12. *Department of State Bulletin* (February 3, 1946), 14(344):160.

communications facilities. Therefore, the issue of free flow of information provided American policy managers with a powerful cultural argument for creating suspicion about an alternate form of social organization. It thus helped to weaken the enormous popular interest in Europe and Asia at the war's end in one or another variety of socialism.

John Foster Dulles, one of the chief architects and executors of America's Cold War policy, was forthright on this matter: "If I were to be granted one point of foreign policy and no other, I would make it the free flow of information."[13] This is a recurring theme in postwar U.S. diplomacy. For example, a couple of years later, the U.S. delegation to a United Nations Conference on Freedom of Information[14] reported:

It is the hope of the six of us that this Conference helped to turn the tide that has been running against freedom throughout much of the world. It is our conviction that in the future conduct of our foreign policy the United States should continue to take vigorous action in this field of freedom of thought and expression.

Certainly the chronology of the launching and steadfast pursuance of the free-flow doctrine supports the belief that the issue had been thoughtfully prepared and carefully promoted in the critical period immediately preceding the end of World War II and the few years directly thereafter. Those who select the interval beginning in 1948 as the start of the Cold War era overlook the earlier period when the groundwork was prepared in the United States for the general offensive of American capitalism throughout the world. This was the time, too, as we shall see, when the free-flow question first came to prominence.

Well before the war was over, American business had incorporated the issue of free flow of information into a formal political ideology. In June 1944, the directors of the powerful American Society of Newspaper Editors adopted resolutions

13. Quoted by John S. Knight, "World Freedom of Information," p. 476.
14. *Report of the United States Delegates to the United Nations Conference on Freedom of Information*, U.S. Department of State Publication 3150, International Organization and Conference Series 111.5 (Washington, D.C.: GPO, 1948).

urging both major political parties to support "world freedom of information and unrestricted communications for news throughout the world."[15] Thereupon, both the Democrats and the Republicans, in the next two months, adopted planks in their party platforms that incorporated these aims. . . .

In September 1944, both houses of Congress adopted a concurrent resolution that followed closely the recommendations of the editors and publishers. Congress expressed "its belief in the worldwide right of interchange of news by newsgathering and distributing agencies, whether individual or associate, by any means, without discrimination as to sources, distribution, rates or charges; and that this right should be protected by international compact."[16]

Having sought and secured congressional endorsement of their aims, the directors of the American Society of Newspaper Editors, meeting in November 1944, then declared that "most Americans and their newspapers will support government policies . . . and action toward removal of all political, legal and economic barriers to the media of information, and . . . our government should make this abundantly clear to other nations."[17] The group noted with satisfaction that the newly appointed secretary of state, Edward Stettinius, Jr., had announced that "the United States plans exploratory talks with other nations looking to international understandings guaranteeing there shall be no barriers to interchange of information among all nations."[18]

At the same time, the American Society of Newspaper Editors, in conjunction with the AP and United Press news agencies, announced an international expedition of a delegation to "personally carry the message of an international free press into every friendly capital of the world."[19] In the spring of 1945, while the war was still being fought, the delegation traveled 40,000 miles around the world, to twenty-two major

15. John S. Knight, "World Freedom of Information," pp. 472–73.
16. *Congressional Record*, 90th Congress, 8044:58 Stat. (Pt. 2), p. 1119.
17. *New York Times*, November 29, 1944.
18. *Editor & Publisher*, December 2, 1944, p. 7.
19. *New York Times*, November 29, 1944.

cities and eleven allied and neutral countries, "on first priority of the War Department on Army Transport Command planes."[20]

While the private group of U.S. press representatives was making its international journey . . . the directors of the Associated Press "placed a fund of $1,000,000 a year at the disposal of Executive Director Kent Cooper to make the AP a global institution."[21]

In fact, as the war drew to a close, preparations for the promotion of the free-flow doctrine shifted from the national to the international level. With congressional and political support assured and domestic public opinion effectively organized, the free-flow advocates carried their campaign vigorously into the channels of international diplomacy and peacemaking that were becoming activated with the end of hostilities.

One of the first occasions that provided an opportunity for an international forum for espousing the free-flow doctrine was the InterAmerican Conference on Problems of War and Peace convened in Mexico City in February 1945. Latin America, regarded for more than a century as a prime U.S. interest— with European economic influence practically eliminated as a result of the war—was a natural site for testing the new doctrine in a congenial, if not controlled, international setting. Predictably, the conference adopted a strong resolution on "free access to information" that was "based substantially on a United States proposal."[22]

The Western Hemisphere having been successfully persuaded of the merits of "free flow," attention turned to the rest of the world. International peacekeeping structures were being established; and the United States made certain that the newly created United Nations, and the related United Nations Educational, Scientific, and Cultural Organization (Unesco), would put great emphasis on the free-flow issue.

---

20. *Editor & Publisher*, June 16, 1945, pp. 5, 64.

21. *Editor & Publisher*, April 21, 1945, p. 15.

22. *Report of the United States Delegation to the Inter-American Conference on Problems of War and Peace*, Mexico City, February 21–March 8, 1945. U.S. Department of State Publication 2497, Conference Series 85 (Washington, D.C.: GPO, 1946), p. 21.

The utilization of the United Nations and its affiliated organizations as instruments of U.S. policy and, additionally, as effective forums for the propagation of the free-flow doctrine can best be understood in the context of the international economy thirty years ago.

In the 1970s, the United States often [was] on the minority side of the voting in the United Nations. . . . In the 1940s, affairs were quite different.

Fifty states were represented in the first meetings of the United Nations in 1945, hardly more than a third of the present 143-nation membership. Of the original fifty, two-fifths were Latin American states, at that time almost totally subservient to North American pressure. The Western European member states were economically drained, politically unstable, and heavily dependent on the United States for economic assistance. The few Middle Eastern, Asian, and African countries then participating in the U.N. were, with a few exceptions, still, in real terms, subject to the Western empire system. In sum, the United Nations, in 1945–48, was far from being universal, much less independent. In fact, it was distinguished by an "automatic majority," invoked whenever its heaviest financial supporter and economically strongest member desired to use it. . . .

In this atmosphere the U.N.'s endorsement of the free-flow doctrine was hardly surprising. It was also poor evidence that the principle had genuinely international support or that its full import was appreciated. Rather, it offered a striking example of how the machinery of international organization could be put at the disposal of its most powerful participant. What follows is a very brief review of the utilization of Unesco and the United Nations itself for the propagation of the free-flow doctrine.

The earliest proposals for the constitution of Unesco, which were drafted by a U.S. panel of experts and reviewed by the State Department, prominently espoused the free flow of information as a Unesco objective.[23] In an account of the

23. *Proposed Educational and Cultural Organization of the United Nations.* U.S. Department of State Publication 2382 (Washington, D.C.: GPO, 1945), pp. 5–7.

meetings of the U.S. delegation to the constitutional conference of Unesco in Washington and London in October and November 1945, the head of the delegation, Archibald MacLeish, repeatedly emphasized his (and the delegation's) conviction that the free flow of information was a basic principle.[24] There is no reason to doubt this. Many people in the United States, especially in the literary and humanistic arts, fully supported the concept of free flow, unaware of, or perhaps indifferent to, the central purpose the doctrine served or to which it was meant to be applied.

In this respect, the first report of the United States National Commission for Unesco (an appointed group, heavily representative of the cultural arts) to the secretary of state, in early 1947, is an unusual document. It contained a mildly worded qualification with respect to the free-flow doctrine. The commission recommended:

The American Delegation [to Unesco] should advance and support proposals for the removal of obstacles to the free flow of information in accordance with the report of the Committee of Consultants to the Department of State on Mass Media and Unesco. *The Commission differs, however, with the Committee of Consultants in believing that the organization should concern itself with the quality of international communication through the mass media and should give serious study to the means by which the mass media may be of more positive and creative service to the cause of international understanding and therefore of peace.* (italics added)[25]

The commission hastened to add, "The Organization should, of course, avoid at all times any act or suggestion of censorship."

The concern for *quality* rarely, if ever, found its way into official U.S. pronouncements on the desirability of the free flow of information. When suggested, as it regularly was by

24. Luther H. Evans, *The United States and Unesco; A Summary of the United States Delegation Meetings to the Constitutional Conference of the United Nations Educational, Scientific and Cultural Organization, in Washington and London,* October–November 1945 (Dobbs Ferry, N.Y.: Oceana Publications, 1971), p. 11.

25. *Report of the United States Commission for the United Nations Educational, Scientific, and Cultural Organization to the Secretary of State,* 1947.

the state ownership societies, it was rejected out of hand as a justification for censorship and suppression. When it was also raised as a major consideration by the Hutchins Freedom of the Press Commission in the United States in 1946, it was simply ignored.[26]

From the start, Unesco, with the U.S. delegation taking the initiative, made free flow of information one of its major concerns. In its account of the *first* session of the General Conference of Unesco, held in Paris in November–December 1946, the U.S. delegation reported that it had proposed to the subcommission on mass communications that "Unesco should cooperate with the Subcommission on Freedom of Information of the Commission on Human Rights in the preparation of the United Nations report on obstacles to the free flow of information and ideas. . . ."[27] In fact, a section on free flow of information was created in the Mass Communications Division of Unesco itself.

In the United Nations, similar initiatives for stressing and publicizing the free-flow doctrine were underway from the outset of that organization's existence. The United Nations Economic and Social Council established the Commission on Human Rights in February 1946 and, in June 1946, empowered this commission to set up a subcommission on freedom of information and the press.[28]

Earlier, the delegation of the Philippines Commonwealth had addressed to the Preparatory Commission of the United Nations, *for submission to the first part of the first session* of the U.N.'s General Assembly, a draft resolution that proposed an international conference on the press with a view "to ensuring the establishment, operation, and circulation of a free

26. See Llewellyn White and Robert D. Leigh, *Peoples Speaking to Peoples. A Report on International Mass Communications from the Commission on Freedom of the Press* (Chicago: University of Chicago Press, 1946).

27. First Session of the General Conference of Unesco, Paris, November 19–December 10, 1946. *Report of the United States Delegation, with Selected Documents* (Washington, D.C.: GPO, 1947), p. 17.

28. Resolution 2/9 of 21 June 1946, Economic and Social Council, *Official Records* (First Year, Second Session). Lake Success, N.Y.: United Nations, No. 8, p. 400.

press throughout the world."[29] With due respect to national sensibilities, it is impossible to imagine the Philippines' initiative, *preceding* the first General Assembly of the United Nations, without the support, if not encouragement and sponsorship, of the United States. The Philippines had been, since the end of the nineteenth century, and in a real sense still were in 1946, a dependency of the United States.

A new draft was introduced by the Philippines delegation to the General Assembly during the second part of its first session (in late 1946). This proposed that the international conference be extended to include other informational media such as radio and film. On December 14, 1946, the General Assembly adopted Resolution 59(1), which declared that "freedom of information is a fundamental human right, and is a touchstone of all the freedoms to which the United Nations is consecrated," and that freedom "implies the right to gather, transmit and publish news anywhere and everywhere without fetters."[30] The Assembly also resolved to authorize the holding of a conference of all members of the United Nations on freedom of information.

The United Nations Conference on Freedom of Information was held March 25–April 21, 1948, in Geneva. It provided the international ideological polarization the United States' policy managers had expected of it. William Benton, chairman of the United States delegation to the conference, explained: "Our Conference at Geneva, *as was to be expected* [italics added], is sharply divided. . . . The free are thus face-to-face with those whose ideology drives them toward the destruction of freedom." But, Benton continued, "we are not at Geneva to make propaganda. We are there to do all that we can to reduce barriers to the flow of information among men and nations." Yet among the main objectives of the American delegation, still according to Benton, and hardly compatible with his plea of nonpartisanship, was "to secure agreement upon the establishment of continuing machinery in the United Nations that

29. *Yearbook on Human Rights for 1947* (Lake Success, N.Y.: United Nations, 1949), p. 439.
30. *Ibid.*

will keep world attention focused on the vital subject of freedom of expression within and among nations."[31]

The conference's final act, embodying essentially U.S. views on free flow of information, was adopted by thirty votes to one (Poland's being the dissenting vote), with five abstentions (Belorussia, Czechoslovakia, the Ukraine, the USSR, and Yugoslavia). The Soviet proposal that the final act be signed only by the president and the executive secretary of the conference instead of representatives of all the attending governments did not please the U.S. delegation. Nevertheless, perhaps because of the uneasiness aroused by the conference's overtly provocative character, the Soviet recommendation was unanimously adopted.[32]

The conference voted also to refer the resolutions and its draft convention to the U.N. Economic and Social Council for consideration and eventual submission, for final adoption, to the General Assembly. In August 1948, after acrimonious and protracted debate, the Economic and Social Council submitted the entire parcel—three conventions and forty-three resolutions—without action or recommendation to the 1948 General Assembly, where it languished, without any actions being taken.[33] Despite the strong U.S. influence in the United Nations at the time, the organization's structure made it difficult to bulldoze all issues through the intricate web of committees, commissions, and the General Assembly.

The conference itself represented, in the eyes of U.S. observers, "in the main . . . a victory for American objectives. . . ."[34] Others saw it differently. The *Economist* (London), for example, though generally approving of the work

31. William Benton (chairman, United States delegation to the Freedom of Information Conference), address delivered before the Anglo-American Press Club, Paris, April 7, 1948. Published in *Department of State Bulletin* (April 18, 1948), pp. 518–20.

32. "Accomplishments of the United Nations Conference on Freedom of Information," *Documents and State Papers*. U.S. Department of State (June, 1948), 1(3).

33. United Nations documents E/Conf. 6/79 and E/1050, August 28, 1948.

34. John B. Whitton, "The United Nations Conference on Freedom of Information and the Movement Against International Propaganda," *American Journal of International Law* (January 1949), 43:73–87.

of the conference, noted:

it was the impression of most delegations that the Americans wanted to secure for their news agencies that general freedom of the market for the most efficient which has been the object of all their initiatives in commercial policy—that they regard freedom of information as an extension of the charter of the International Trade Organization rather than as a special and important subject of its own. And the stern opposition which they offered to Indian and Chinese efforts to protect infant national news agencies confirmed this impression.[35]

This assessment by the *Economist* reflected the continuing ambivalence of the United States' West European allies toward the issue of free flow of information. Though fully cognizant of the commercial threat the free-flow doctrine posed to their own communications industries, faced with the United States' media power, the Western market economies, especially Great Britain, nonetheless supported the principle as a means of embarrassing the Soviet sphere and placing it on an ideological defensive. On this question, a united Western position defending private ownership of the mass media took precedence over the internal conflicts in the Western world about who should dominate these instruments.

Though efforts to gain wide international support for the free-flow concept were at best inconclusive, the two decades following the Freedom of Information Conference in 1948 saw the realization of the doctrine in fact, if not in solemn covenant. New communications technology—computers, space satellites, television—combined with a powerful and expanding corporate business system, assisted the push of the United States into the center of the world economy.

Without public pronouncements, private, American-made media products and U.S. informational networks blanketed the world. Especially prominent were films, produced more and more frequently outside the country;[36] the exportation of

---

35. *Economist* (May 1, 1948), p. 701.
36. Thomas Guback. *The International Film Industry* (Bloomington, Ind.: Indiana University Press, 1969).

commercial television programs,[37] and international distribution of North American magazines and other periodicals. *Reader's Digest, Time, Newsweek, Playboy,* and Walt Disney Corporation productions reached millions of viewers and readers outside the United States. Moreover, foreign book-publishing firms disappeared into U.S. "leisure time" conglomerates. Along with these more or less conventional media penetrations, a variety of additional informational activities accompanied the global surge of private American capital. Foremost, perhaps, was the extension of the opinion poll and consumer survey, now undertaken all over the world, often under the auspices of American-owned research companies.[38]

Largely as a reaction to the flood of American cultural material and the usurpation of national media systems that were required to disseminate it, a new mood with respect to the doctrine of free flow of information became observable in the international community in the late 1960s and early 1970s. Besides the free-flow view, one began to see frequent references to cultural sovereignty, cultural privacy, cultural autonomy, and even admissions of the possibility of cultural imperialism.[39]

Another factor that perhaps is contributing to the shift of emphasis, outside the United States, away from the *quantity* to the *consequences* of free flow of information is the changed nature of the international community itself. Since 1945, more than ninety new national entities, most of them still in an early stage of economic development, have emerged to take their places in the community of nations. A paramount concern of these states is to safeguard their national and cultural sovereignty. Then, too, the results of two decades of *de facto* free flow of information have not gone unremarked. It is difficult, in fact, to escape the global spread of U.S. cultural styles featured in the mass media of films, television programs, pop records, and slick magazines. Their influence prompts senti-

---

37. Kaarle Nordenstreng and Tapio Varis, *Television Traffic—A One-Way Street?* Reports and Papers on Mass Communication, no. 70. (Paris: Unesco, 1974).

38. Herbert I. Schiller. *The Mind Managers* (Boston: Beacon Press, 1973).

39. *Ibid.*

ments such as that expressed by the Prime Minister of Guyana: "A nation whose mass media are dominated from the outside is not a nation."[40] . . . The 1948 comments of Robert D. Leigh, director of the staff of the Hutchins Commission on Freedom of the Press, have a prophetic ring:

> The main burden of my presentation is that in the present day, and especially across national boundaries, this faith in an omnicompetent world citizen served only by *full* flow of words and images is an oversimplification of the process and effect of mass communication. . . . *Barriers Down* standing by itself is not adequate policy in the international field. The focus changes from free individual expression as a right, to the primary need of the citizen everywhere, to have regular access to reliable information, and also, ready access to the existent diversity of ideas, opinions, insights, and arguments regarding public affairs. This does not deny freedom, but it joins freedom with a positive responsibility that freedom shall serve truth and understanding. *The concept of responsibility, carried to its logical conclusion, may even imply defining a clearly harmful class of public communication which falls outside the protection of freedom itself.*[41] (italics added in last sentence)

Finally, the possibility of direct satellite broadcasting from space into home sets without the mediation of nationally controlled ground stations, whether or not likely in the immediate future, has created a sense of urgency concerning the question of cultural sovereignty. This has been especially observable in the United Nations.

The Working Group on Direct Broadcast Satellites was established in 1969 "to consider mainly the technical feasibility of direct broadcasting from satellites."[42] It has met more or less regularly since that time, extending its range from the technical aspects to the social, legal, and political implications of direct satellite broadcasting.

40. *Intermedia* (1973), 3:1.

41. Robert D. Leigh, "Freedom of Communication Across National Boundaries," *Educational Record* (October 29, 1948), p. 382.

42. *Report of the Working Group on Direct Broadcast Satellites of the Work of Its Fourth Session*, A/AC. 105/117 (New York: United Nations, 22 June 1973), annex 1, p. 1.

Moreover, Unesco, the strongest advocate of the free-flow doctrine at one time, has veered noticeably away from its formerly unquestioning support. In its "Declaration of Guiding Principles on the Use of Satellite Broadcasting for the Free Flow of Information," adopted in October 1972, Unesco acknowledged that "it is necessary that States, taking into account the principle of freedom of information, reach or promote prior agreements concerning direct satellite broadcasting to the population of countries other than the country of origin of the transmission."[43] The U.N. General Assembly supported this view in November 1972, by a vote of 102 to 1—the United States casting the single dissenting vote.

Reactions in the private communications sector in the United States were predictably hostile and self-serving. Frank Stanton, one of the most influential American media controllers in the era of U.S. informational hegemony, wrote: "the rights of Americans to speak to whomever they please, when they please are [being] bartered away."[44] His chief objection to the Unesco document, he claimed, was that censorship was being imposed by provisions that permitted each nation to reach prior agreement with transmitting nations concerning the character of the broadcasts.

Stanton, along with a good part of the media's managers (including the prestigious *New York Times*), finds the right of nations to control the character of the messages transmitted into their territories both dangerous and a gross violation of the U.S. Constitution's provision concerning freedom of speech: "The rights which form the framework of our Constitution, the principles asserted in the Universal Declaration of Human Rights, the basic principle of the free movement of ideas, are thus ignored."[45]

Along with the hubris displayed in regarding the U.S.

43. Unesco Declaration of Guiding Principles on the Use of Satellite Broadcasting for the Free Flow of Information, Spread of Education and Greater Cultural Exchange, document A/AC. 105/109, 1972 (mimeographed).

44. Frank Stanton, "Will They Stop Our Satellites?" *New York Times*, October 22, 1972, pp. 23, 39.

45. *Ibid.*

Constitution applicable to, and binding law for, the entire international community is a second, even more questionable, consideration. Stanton and those in agreement with him matter-of-factly assume that the United States' constitutional guarantee of freedom of speech to the *individual* is applicable to the multinational corporations and media conglomerates whose interests they so strongly espouse. Yet more than a generation ago, Earl L. Vance[46] asked, "Is freedom of the press to be conceived as a *personal* right appertaining to all citizens, as undoubtedly the Founding Fathers conceived it; or as a *property* right appertaining to the ownership of newspapers and other publications, as we have come to think of it largely today?"

Stanton et al. extend the *property*-right concept of freedom of speech to all the advanced electronic forms of communication and expect universal acquiescence in their interpretation. But the national power behind this view is no longer as absolute or as fearsome as it was in 1945. The world is no longer totally dependent on, and therefore vulnerable to, the economic strength of the United States. A remarkable renewal of economic activity in Western Europe and Japan, significant growth and expansion of the noncapitalist world, and, not least, the experiences of the last quarter of a century have produced an altogether changed international environment.

This new atmosphere, as we have noted, is reflected in the voting patterns of international bodies—so much so, in fact, that U.S. spokesmen complain bitterly that the United Nations and Unesco, in particular, are practicing a "tyranny of the majority" that "brutally disregards the sensitivity of the minority."[47] Worse still, these organizations are being "politicized."[48]

It is worth quoting the response of the Algerian delegate to the United Nations to these charges. Abdellatif Rahal re-

46. Earl L. Vance, "Freedom of the Press for Whom?" *Virginia Quarterly Review*, (Summer, 1945), 21:340–54.

47. John Scali, U.S. delegate to the U.N., speech before the General Assembly, as reported in *New York Times*, December 7, 1974.

48. *New York Times*, Editorial, November 23, 1974.

minded the Assembly:

It may not be unimportant to begin by stressing that countries which today are rebelling against the rule of the majority are the very same which constituted the majority of yesterday, the same whose behavior at that time represented the best frame of reference for judging the behavior of today's majority. . . . Thus, if those who now criticize us protest the very rules which govern our work in this Assembly, they should remember that they themselves are the authors of these rules, let them not forget that the lessons they wish to give us today are worth little when compared with the examples they have already given us in the past.[49]

To be sure, the United States and its closest allies (and competitors) still emphasize the free-flow doctrine as the basis for peace and international security. The Helsinki Conference on Security and Cooperation in Europe, begun in mid-1973 and concluded in July 1975, made this very clear. In its preliminary consultations, the conference was instructed to "prepare proposals to facilitate the freer and wider dissemination of information of all kinds."[50] And it was this issue to which the Western delegates gave their greatest attention, seeking to make all other decisions contingent on a resolution of the free-flow question acceptable to themselves. British Foreign Secretary Sir Alec Douglas-Home, for instance, declared:

the item . . . on an agenda which deals with cooperation in the humanitarian field is in my judgment the most important item of our business. If our Conference is essentially about people and about trust then it is necessary that we do something to remove the barriers which inhibit the movement of people and the exchange of information and ideas.[51]

But despite the insistence of most of the political and economic leaders of Western, industrialized, market econo-

49. *New York Times*, December 12, 1974.
50. *Final Recommendations of the Helsinki Consultations* (Helsinki: Government of Finland, 1973), p. 15.
51. Sir Alec Douglas-Home, *Conference on Security and Cooperation in Europe, Verbatim Records, Part 1*, CSCE/I/PV.5, Helsinki, July 5, 1973.

mies on the continued importance of an unalloyed free-flow doctrine, alternate formulations are appearing. One was contained in the speech of Finland's President Urho Kekkonen, before a communications symposium in May 1973. Kekkonen, in a comprehensive review of the fundamental premises of international communications, singled out the free-flow doctrine for his scrutiny:

When the Declaration of Human Rights was drawn up after the Second World War, the Nineteenth Century liberal view of the world in the spirit of the ideas of Adam Smith and John Stuart Mill was the guideline. Freedom of action and enterprise—laissez-faire—was made the supreme value in the world of business and ideology, irrespective of at whose expense success in this world was achieved. The State gave everyone the possibility to function, but did not carry the responsibility for the consequences. So the freedom of the strong led to success and the weak went under in spite of this so-called liberty. This was the result regardless of which of them advocated a more just policy for society and mankind.

Kekkonen applied this general perspective to international communication and the free-flow doctrine. He noted:

At an international level are to be found the ideals of free communication and their actual distorted execution for the rich on the one hand and the poor on the other. Globally, the flow of information between States—not least the material pumped out by television—is to a very great extent a one-way, unbalanced traffic, and in no way possesses the depth and range which the principles of freedom of speech require.

These observations led Kekkonen to inquire: "Could it be that the prophets who preach unhindered communication are not concerned with equality between nations, but are on the side of the stronger and wealthier?" He remarked also that international organizations were in fact moving away from their original advocacy of the free-flow doctrine:

My observations would indicate that the United Nations and . . . Unesco have in the last few years reduced their declarations on behalf of an abstract freedom of speech. Instead, they have moved in the direction of planing down the lack of balance in international communications.

From all this, Kekkonen concluded: "a mere liberalistic freedom of communication is not in everyday reality a neutral idea, but a way in which an enterprise with many resources at its disposal has greater opportunities than weaker brethren to make its own hegemony accepted."[52]

Kekkonen's analysis is, in fact, the general conclusion, however long overdue, that is beginning to emerge with respect to *all* international and domestic relationships–not just those concerned with communications. When there is an uneven distribution of power among individuals or groups *within* nations or *among* nations, a free hand—freedom to continue doing what led to the existing condition—serves to strengthen the already powerful and weaken further the already frail. Evidence of this abounds in all aspects of modern life—in race, sex, and occupational and international relationships. Freedoms that are formally impressive may be substantively oppressive when they reinforce prevailing inequalities while claiming to provide generalized opportunity for all.

Not surprisingly, individuals, groups, and nations increasingly are seeking means to limit the freedom to maintain inequality. Measures aimed at regulating "the free flow of information" are best understood from this perspective.

52. Urho Kekkonen, "The Free Flow of Information: Towards a Reconsideration of National and International Communication Policies," address before Symposium on the International Flow of Television Programs, University of Tampere, Tampere, Finland, May 21, 1973.

10

The Many Worlds of the World's Press

GEORGE GERBNER and GEORGE MARVANYI

Gerbner and Marvanyi—collecting and analyzing data in their respective societies—provide a benchmark, cross-cultural study of the world's press. They studied one week's foreign news coverage from sixty daily newspapers representing nine capitalist, socialist, and nonaligned nations. Findings from this "snapshot" flow study are particularly useful in highlighting, by different systems, relative blind spots in the distribution of news attention. Part of their extensive bibliography related to world news flow is included in the reference list following this article.

DISTINCTIVE STANDARDS of reporting reflect conditions of industrial investment (including the manufacture of news), national security, and popular support. Studies of newsroom decision-making illustrate various aspects of newsroom climate resting on the real or assumed interests (or actual interventions) of publishers, stockholders, advertisers, parties, and

George Gerbner is professor of communications and dean of the Annenberg School of Communications, University of Pennsylvania, and editor of the *Journal of Communication.*

George Marvanyi is the program director for public affairs of Hungarian Television and a former staff member of the Mass Communication Research Center, Budapest.

This essay originally appeared in *Journal of Communication* (Winter 1977), 27(1):52–66.

other private or public organizations that set the terms of employment.

When the subject is foreign news, the process is even more variable; there is no effective reality check. Many different versions of the day's "world news" can be equally true and significant when judged by different standards of relevance.

This is the report of a multinational comparative study of foreign news coverage designed to explore the similarities and differences in the images of the "outside world" that each type of society projects for its members. The study included sixty daily papers published in nine countries of the capitalist, socialist, and "third" worlds. The countries were the United States, Great Britain, the German Federal Republic (West Germany), the Soviet Union, Hungary, Czechoslovakia, Ghana, India, and the Philippines. A total of 5,866 pages and 11,437 separate foreign news items were analyzed to probe dimensions of coverage affecting different societies' views of each other and of the rest of the world. . . .

We picked the week of May 24, 1970. There were elections in Ceylon, riots in Paris, and runoffs for the world soccer championships in Mexico. Israeli aircraft raided Lebanon, U.S. troops advanced into Cambodia, bombing and fighting raged in Vietnam. NATO ministers met in Rome, Arab leaders met in Khartum, and the Komsomol Congress met in Moscow. Sudan nationalized some industries and the Queen of England dissolved Parliament in preparation for new elections. These and hundreds of minor stories made up the news of the world of that week. If it was "unique" (and which week isn't?), it fits the typical categories into which each country dips for its own news.

Cross-Section of Readership

The newspaper samples were drawn to include various types of papers and to approximate a cross-section of news readerships. This required the selection of both elite and popular organs and of both mass-circulation and small newspapers. . . .

The characteristics of the samples reflect the relative circulations and sizes of the different newspapers. The United States press sample included two "elite" dailies of national circulation, the *New York Times* and the *Christian Science Monitor*. In the "popular" category of large circulation it also included the *New York Daily News*, and the medium circulation *San Francisco Chronicle*. Three newspapers of relatively low circulation (under 50,000) were included to represent the small local newspaper, and to provide additional geographic coverage. A total of nine U.S. newspapers of a combined circulation of almost 4 million copies and over 2,000 pages were analyzed.

The British sample included the London *Times* and *Daily Telegraph* as "elite" papers. The giant *Daily Mirror* was the "popular" daily, and other smaller papers represented other circulation and regional categories. The large circulation of national dailies brought the total British sample to over 8 million copies with only 900 pages.

The West German sample included the "elite" *Frankfurter Allgemeine* and *Die Welt*, the "popular" *Bild Zeitung*, and three other smaller circulation regional papers. The combined circulation of the sample was almost 5.5 million; its size was 924 pages.

The Soviet press sample included *Pravda* as the "elite" daily, three other papers published in Moscow, and four regional dailies. The combined circulation was nearly 14 million, but the size of the sample was 156 pages.

The Hungarian and Czechoslovakian samples each included ten papers in the respective categories, amounting to a combined circulation of less than 2 million with a total of over fifty pages each.

The nonaligned "third" world was represented by three papers each in Ghana, India, and the Philippines, each including one "elite" daily, and all printed in English. Their combined circulation was more than one million; the size of the sample was sixty pages.

We defined news as nonadvertising printed matter (text, picture, or tabular information) except editorials, cartoons, and comic strips, book reviews, indices, and tables of content, and Sunday magazine sections or other special supplements not part of the general weekday format of the newspaper.

The world, meaning the outside world, was defined as any territory outside of the geographical boundaries of the country in which the newspaper is published. Colonies or protectorates of the home country were to be considered foreign for purposes of our study.

Therefore, stories originating abroad (e.g., having a foreign dateline) were to be considered foreign news even if the subject matter involved domestic affairs. Second, when most of the information came from abroad or the story dealt mostly with foreign matter, or both, it was to be considered foreign news, even if it had a domestic dateline. Third, a story about foreign visitors was always to be considered foreign news. News originating in or written about international zones and their affairs (the U.N. in New York, Geneva, etc.; Berlin, East or West) was to be considered foreign in all papers.

The unit of analysis was the foreign news story or item, which we defined as a substantively and typographically distinct unit of relevant printed matter. Several items sharing the same headline were considered separate items if they were substantively and typographically distinct. Each item was to be marked, measured, and coded separately, except that a block of tabular information from abroad printed without other text, such as financial, weather, or sports statistics, was to be considered a single item.

Two coding forms were developed: one for a given issue of a newspaper in toto, and another for each item of foreign news within each issue. . . .

The analysis of the material was conducted simultaneously in Philadelphia and in Budapest following the procedure worked out jointly in advance. The U.S., Western European, and nonaligned press samples were analyzed in Philadelphia while the Soviet and Eastern European samples were analyzed in Budapest. Sample analyses were exchanged and recoded to improve coder reliability.

Findings

The American press ranked first on the average *length* of foreign news items. As table 10.1 shows, Western European papers carried nearly twice as many foreign news items *per day* as U.S. papers, with Eastern European papers second and the nonaligned press third. The press of Western Europe also led in the absolute amount of space per day, with nonaligned newspapers second and U.S. dailies third. In average length of foreign news items, U.S. newspapers were followed by nonaligned and Western European papers.

Large papers have more space, but much of that is devoted to advertising and other nonnews features (which is why they are large in the first place). Nearly 60 percent of U.S. newspaper space, and over 40 percent of Western Europe newspaper space was devoted to advertising matter. Ads occupied only 15 percent of Eastern European and 2 percent of Soviet

Table 10.1 Ranks and Measures of Foreign News Coverage

	United States		Western Europe		Soviet Union		Eastern Europe		Non-aligned	
	Rank[a]		Rank		Rank		Rank		Rank	
Number of foreign news items per newspaper per day	4	25.1	1	49.8	5	19.4	2	39.7	3	30.8
Square inches of foreign news space per newspaper per day	3	518	1	857	5	206	4	321	2	535
Square inches of foreign news space per item	1	20.7	3	17.2	4	10.6	5	8.1	2	17.4
Number of foreign news items per page	5	50.6	4	41.8	1.5	4.6	1.5	4.6	3	2.2
Square inches of foreign news per page	5	12.6	4	32.4	1	48.9	3	36.9	2	37.5
Foreign news space as percent of all nonadvertising space	5	11.1	2	23.6	4	16.5	1	37.5	3	22.8

[a] Items are ranked across rows.

newspaper space. The average amount of nonadvertising space per issue in U.S. newspapers was one-quarter larger than in Western Europe, twice as much as in the nonaligned countries, and almost four times as much as in Eastern Europe and in the Soviet Union.

The amount of foreign coverage can thus be measured in two ways. One is the absolute number of items and square inches of space devoted to foreign news. These measures are strongly influenced by physical characteristics. The other is the relative amount of available space or percent of the "news hole" devoted to foreign news. That is more a matter of editorial choice.

In absolute terms, the U.S. press used almost as much newsprint per issue as the other eight countries combined. While the U.S. dailies averaged forty-one (mostly large-sized) pages per issue, those of Western Europe averaged twenty-six, the nonaligned countries fourteen, Eastern European papers nine, and Soviet dailies four.

Relative allocations, however, present a different picture. As Table 10.1 shows, Soviet and Eastern European papers led in the number of foreign news *items per page*. The Soviet press was also first in the amount of *space per page* devoted to foreign news, with nonaligned papers second and Eastern European dailies a close third. Eastern European newspapers devoted the largest *percentage of nonadvertising space* to foreign news, with the press of Western Europe second, of nonaligned countries third, and of the USSR fourth. The U.S. newspaper sample ranked last on all relative measures.

The U.S. press, then, ranked low in comparison with the other areas on relative measures of attention to the outside world, reflecting low priority of editorial attention. The press of Western Europe led in absolute numbers of items and amounts of space, and the daily papers of the Socialist countries led in the proportion of available space devoted to foreign news. The nonaligned countries came in second and third on all measures.

Taking the percentage allocation of nonadvertising space as perhaps the most sensitive measure of editorial policy, we find that the leader is the German paper appropriately named *Die Welt*; it devoted 43.7 percent of its total nonadvertising space to foreign news. Five other papers gave more than 30 percent: the Soviet *Pravda* (38.0 percent); the Hungarian *Magyar Nemzat* (37.6 percent), *Nepszabadsag* (36.0 percent), and *Magyar Hirlap* (35.6 percent); and the Czechoslovakian *Lud* (30.1 percent). Another sixteen dailies, including the *Christian Science Monitor* (28.7 percent), gave more than 25 percent, but no other U.S., British, or Soviet paper did. The *New York Times* used 16.4 percent of its nonadvertising space for foreign news, the London *Times* 22.4 percent.

Less than 10 percent of available news space was devoted to foreign news by one Philippine, two Soviet, one British, and six U.S. daily papers. "Elite" papers gave generally more attention to foreign news than did the "popular" press.

An interesting comparison is made possible by the fact that six papers of our sample were also included in Jacques Kayser's study of the news in 1951. Table 10.2 shows that three of the six papers devoted about the same percentages to foreign news in 1951 as in 1970, and that the rank order of the six papers shifted only because the *Times of India* nearly doubled its foreign coverage, perhaps as a result of independence.

In general, there is an inverse relationship between commercial sponsorship (and the consequent demand for sales and localized news service) and foreign news coverage. On the whole, the publicly owned or institutionally managed

Table 10.2 Foreign News Content as a Percentage of Total News Space in 1951 and 1970

	1951	1970
New York Times	16	16
New York Daily News	2	7
London *Times*	25	22
Pravda	30	38
Rude Pravo	25	29
Times of India	14	25

press assigns higher priority to the outside world than does the strictly commercial press.

The "Worlds" of the Press Systems

To make the description of the global play of attention manageable, we divided the world into fifteen regions on the basis of a combination of geographical, political, and current affairs considerations. The regions are: (1) Western Europe, (2) Eastern Europe, (3) the Soviet Union, (4) the Mideast, (5) Israel, (6) North Africa, (7) Central Africa, (8) South Africa, (9) North Vietnam, (10) South Vietnam, (11) Eastern Socialist countries (China, Mongolia, North Korea), (12) South Asia and the Far East (including Burma, Cambodia, India, Indonesia, Japan, South Korea, Tawian), (13) Australia and Oceania, (14) Latin America, and (15) North America.

The first representation in figure 10.1 is a map of the world simplified into regions. The next five maps are the "worlds" of the five press systems scaled to the percentage of representation of each region in each press system.

Starting from the necessarily arbitrary assumption that each region has equal chance of newsworthiness, we first equalized the size of all regions, and then reduced each to the percentage of the equalized size that corresponds to its percentage representation in each press system (indicated on the map of each region).

Looking at the world of U.S. newspapers, we can see that foreign news events happening in Western Europe, South Asia and the Far East, North America, and the Middle East (including Israel), make up two-thirds of the U.S. foreign news map of the world. The war in Vietnam made that small region loom larger than all of Africa and China combined. The Mideast and Israel attracted more attention than the Soviet Union plus Eastern Europe.

In the world of British and West German newspapers

Figure 10.1

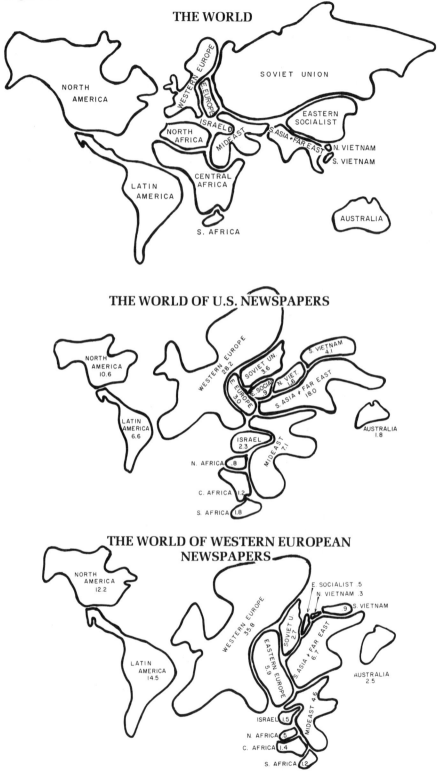

THE WORLD

NORTH AMERICA

WESTERN EUROPE

E. EUROPE

SOVIET UNION

EASTERN SOCIALIST

ISRAEL

NORTH AFRICA

MIDEAST

S. ASIA + FAR EAST

N. VIETNAM

S. VIETNAM

LATIN AMERICA

CENTRAL AFRICA

S. AFRICA

AUSTRALIA

THE WORLD OF U.S. NEWSPAPERS

NORTH AMERICA 10.6

WESTERN EUROPE 28.2

E. EUROPE 3.0

SOVIET UN. 3.6

E. SOCIAL .9

N. VIET. 1.6

S. VIETNAM 4.1

S. ASIA + FAR EAST 18.0

LATIN AMERICA 6.6

ISRAEL 2.3

MIDEAST 7.1

N. AFRICA .8

C. AFRICA 1.2

S. AFRICA 1.8

AUSTRALIA 1.8

THE WORLD OF WESTERN EUROPEAN NEWSPAPERS

NORTH AMERICA 12.2

WESTERN EUROPE 35.8

E. SOCIALIST .5

N VIETNAM .3

S. VIETNAM .9

SOVIET U 2.7

EASTERN EUROPE 5.9

S. ASIA + FAR EAST 6.7

LATIN AMERICA 14.5

ISRAEL 1.5

MIDEAST 4.6

N. AFRICA .5

C. AFRICA 1.4

S. AFRICA 1.2

AUSTRALIA 2.5

Figure 10.2

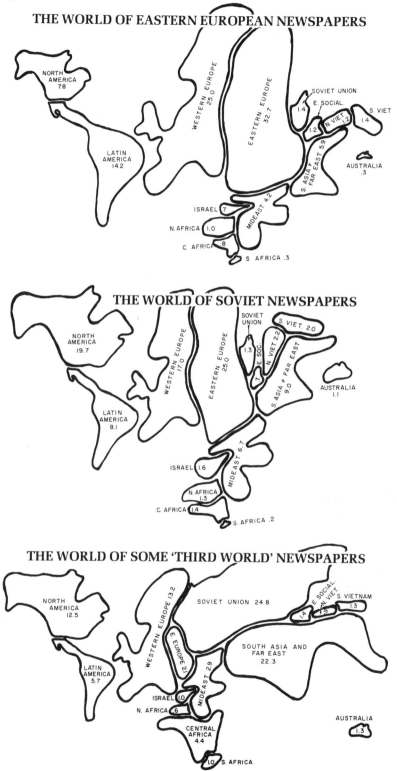

THE WORLD OF EASTERN EUROPEAN NEWSPAPERS

NORTH AMERICA 7.8

WESTERN EUROPE 25.0

EASTERN EUROPE 32.7

SOVIET UNION 1.4

E. SOCIAL. 1.2

N. VIET. 1.2

S. VIET 1.4

S. ASIA + FAR EAST 5.9

AUSTRALIA .3

LATIN AMERICA 14.2

ISRAEL 7

MIDEAST 4.2

N. AFRICA 1.0

C. AFRICA 8

S AFRICA .3

THE WORLD OF SOVIET NEWSPAPERS

NORTH AMERICA 19.7

WESTERN EUROPE 17.0

EASTERN EUROPE 25.0

SOVIET UNION 1.3

E. SOC. 7

N. VIET. 2.2

S. VIET. 2.0

S. ASIA + FAR EAST 9.0

AUSTRALIA 1.1

LATIN AMERICA 8.1

ISRAEL 1.6

MIDEAST 6.7

N. AFRICA 1.3

C. AFRICA 1.4

S. AFRICA .2

THE WORLD OF SOME 'THIRD WORLD' NEWSPAPERS

NORTH AMERICA 12.5

WESTERN EUROPE 13.2

E. EUROPE 2.1

SOVIET UNION 24.8

E. SOCIAL. 1.4

N. VIET .9

S. VIETNAM 1.3

SOUTH ASIA AND FAR EAST 22.3

LATIN AMERICA 5.7

ISRAEL 1.0

MIDEAST 2.9

N. AFRICA .6

AUSTRALIA 1.3

CENTRAL AFRICA 4.4

1.0 S. AFRICA

("Western Europe"), events in Western Europe, Latin America, and North America (in that order) occupied nearly two-thirds of all attention. These Western European papers paid less attention to Israel and to Vietnam than did the U.S., but more attention to Eastern Europe and Latin America,

Eastern European papers (figure 10.2) gave as much news to events about their own region as Western European ones did to theirs, but much more to Western Europe than vice versa. Otherwise, Eastern European press allocations followed fairly closely those of Western Europe. However, Eastern Europe devoted less attention to events in the Soviet Union than did any other press system, including that of the United States. Even Africa got more play in the press of Eastern Europe than did the Soviet Union.

The Soviet press, on the other hand, ranked Eastern Europe first and North America second (the highest rank of attention devoted to North America of all the press systems). Western Europe ranked third in the Soviet press. The three regions accounted for two-thirds of Soviet press attention to the outside world. (Yet neither the American nor the Western European press paid much attention to the Soviet Union.) The percentage of Soviet attention to Israel or South Vietnam or South Asia and the Far East was about half of that devoted to these regions by the American press.

The world of the Third World newspapers was the only one in which the Soviet Union loomed large, in fact the largest among all regions. Next were South Asia and the Far East, Western Europe, North America, and Latin America, in that order, together making up two-thirds of the world of the non-aligned press. In that world, the Mideast ranked lower and Central Africa ranked higher than in any of the others.

Western Europe Known Best

What can we conclude from these findings? Readers of all press systems know most about Western Europe. For American readers, non-Communist Asia and the Mideast are next. The relative blind spot of the American press is Latin America, at least in comparison with the other press systems.

The Western newspapers studied have little interest in the Socialist countries. News of the Soviet Union is also kept out of the press of Eastern Europe, but gets top play in newspapers of the Third World. Soviet readers get more news about the U.S. and Western and Eastern Europe than readers of those areas get about the Soviets. The regions of Africa, Australia and Oceania, and the Eastern Socialist countries of China, Mongolia, and North Korea were barely visible in the world's press of 1970.

This study suggests some dimensions underlying the present state of communication between different social systems. Our findings indicate where the process of reciprocal information may be out of joint. But our "snapshot" of the global flow of foreign news can only serve as a starting point for comparative analysis. Certainly the end of the war in Southeast Asia, and the relative rise in prominence of other areas, may have altered the distribution of news attention. More comprehensive and reliable insight into the "many worlds of the world's press" will come from indicators of trends over time and of the conceptions they cultivate in the minds of readers around the world.

Selected References

Budd, Richard W. "U.S. News in the Press Down Under," *Public Opinion Quarterly* (Spring 1964), 28:39–56.

Casey, Ralph D. and Thomas H. Copeland, Jr. "Use of Foreign News by 19 Minnesota Dailies." *Journalism Quarterly* (Fall 1958), 35:87–89.

Conrad, Richard. "Social Images in East and West Germany: A Comparative Study of Matched Newspapers in Two Social Systems," *Social Forces*, (March 1955), 36(3):281–85.

Cutlip, Scott M. "Content and Flow of AP News—From Trunk to TTS to Reader," *Journalism Quarterly* (Fall 1954), 31:434–46.

Dajani, Nabil and John Donohue. "Foreign News in the Arab Press: A Content Analysis of Six Arab Dailies," *Gazette* (1973), 14(3): 156–70.

Davison, W. Phillips. "Diplomatic Reporting: Rules of the Game," *Journal of Communication* (Autumn 1975) 25(3):138–46.

Galtung, Johan and Mari Holmes Ruge. "The Structure of Foreign News," *Journal of Peace Research* (1965), 2(1):64–91.

Gerbner, George. "Press Perspectives in World Communication: A Pilot Study," *Journalism Quarterly* (Summer 1961), 38:313–22.

Hart, Jim. "The Flow of News Between the U.S. and Canada," *Journalism Quarterly* (Winter 1963), 40:70–74.

Hester, Albert. "The News from Latin America Via a World News Agency," *Gazette* (1974), 20(2):82–91.

Kayser, Jacques. *One-Week's News: Comparative Study of 17 Major Dailies for a Seven-Day Period.* Paris: Unesco, 1953.

Ostegaard, Einar. "Factors Influencing the Flow of News," *Journal of Peace Research* (1965), p. 1.

Rosengren, Karl Erik and Gunnel Rikardsson. "Middle East News in Sweden." Paper prepared for the Seminar on East-West Communication, Beirut, May 1972.

Sande, Oystein. "The Perception of Foreign News," *Journal of Peace Research* (1971), 8:221–73.

Schramm, Wilbur, ed. *One Day in the World's Press: Fourteen Great Newspapers on a Day of Crisis.* Stanford: Stanford University Press, 1959.

Vilanilam, J. V. "Foreign News in Two U.S. Newspapers and Indian Newspapers During Selected Periods," *Gazette* (1972), 18(2):96–108.

White, David Manning. "The Gatekeeper: A Case Study in the Selection of News," *Journalism Quarterly*, (Fall 1950), 27:383–390.

11

International News Wires and Third World News in Asia
WILBUR SCHRAMM

Dr. Schramm, who has done as much as anyone to help both scholar and policy maker understand the structure, function, and impact of media flows internationally, focuses on Asia's news flow and needs in his essay. He examines what the new agencies "are reporting from and to the Third World, and how much and what kinds of news about the Third World were being taken from these and other sources and printed in fourteen newspapers from nine Third World countries, during one week in December 1977." His findings suggest, among other conclusions, that there is no shortage of wire news—"if there is anything wrong, it must be a shortage of coverage or a kind of coverage."

Wilbur Schramm is a distinguished researcher and former director of the Communication Institute of the East-West Center, Honolulu. Before joining the Center in 1973, he had been professor of communication and director of the Institute for Communication Research at Stanford University. He has done research on four continents and is the author of twenty books and more than a hundred articles. This article was prepared for the conference on the International News Media and the Developing World, April 2–5, 1978, Cairo, sponsored by the Edward R. Murrow Center of the Fletcher School of Law and Diplomacy, Tufts University. Additional materials were added in this revision.

THIS PAPER is not intended to "prove something" or recommend a policy, but rather to provide some solid evidence
that might be of help to those who must make the policy
decisions concerning the flow of news to and from the Third
World. We hope the paper will be read in that spirit: as a
record of what the news wires were reporting from and to the
Third World, and how much and what kinds of news about
the Third World were being taken from these and other sources
and printed in sixteen newspapers from nine Third World
countries, during one week in December 1977.[1]

Our concentration was on Asia. We obtained the complete
Asian news wires of the four big international news agencies[2]
twenty-four hours a day, for five days from December 5
through 9, 1977, and collected copies of the newspapers for
seven days, December 4 through 10. This took care of some
of the time overlap problems that beset studies like these.
Where possible at least two papers from each country were
included, so chosen as to make a significant comparison possible as, for example, between an Asian language paper and
an English language one, or a wide circulation paper and a
"prestige" paper.

Our procedure was to use the local news in the sixteen
newspapers, supplemented by the New York Times, Le Monde
and the London Times, for a picture of what was happening
in the Third World, particularly in those Asian studies rep-

1. A full report of this study can be found in Wilbur Schramm and L. Erwin
Atwood, Circulation of Third World News: A Study of Asia (Hong Kong: Press of
Chinese University of Hong Kong, 1981). The sixteen newspapers in the study were
as follows. Hong Kong: Sing Tao Jih Pao (Chinese language); South China Morning
Post (English). India: Ananda Bazar Patrika, Calcutta (English); Statesman, Calcutta
and New Delhi (English). Indonesia: Kompas, Jakarta (Indonesian). South Korea: Dong-
a Ilbo, Seoul (Korean language); Korea Times, Seoul (English). Malaysia: Nanyang
Siang Pau, Kuala Lumpur (Chinese language); New Straits Times, Kuala Lumpur
(English). Philippines: Philippine Daily Express, Manila (English); Pilipino Express,
Manila (Tagalog). Singapore: Sing Chew Jit Poh (Chinese language); Straits Times
(English). Sri Lanka: Ceylon Daily News (English). Thailand: Bangkok Post (English).
Later, three more dailies were added: Iran: Ettela'at (Farsi language); Kayhan Morning
News (English). Philippines: Bulletin Today, Manila (English).

2. The four agencies are the Associated Press, Reuters, United Press International,
and Agence France-Presse. TASS and Hsinhua were not available in time for inclusion
in the study.

resented in our study; then to examine the wires for a record of what they were reporting on *all* Third World countries; and finally, to study the newspapers to see what they were reporting on the Third World, and where the news came from. That provided an idea of the first three steps of the four steps along the news path. The fourth step, a readership survey in the Third World, was conducted later in the Philippines. Third World news content in both newspapers and wires were coded for five days, and the *entire* news contents for one day, in order to make comparisons between Third World and non-Third World coverage. Native speakers were used to do the coding, and the material was computer-analyzed and tabulated.

Before going into all the details of the study and findings, here are some general statements about the flow of news in the Third World countries of Asia:

• One of the first outcomes of this study was to put some hard figures on a phenomenon that is familiar to anyone who has examined the flow of international news: the amount of news decreases as it moves along the pipeline. That is, more potentially newsworthy events occur in any country than the newspapers of that country can publish. The local newspapers publish more than the international wires can pick up. The wires carry more than their clients can reprint. And these client-newspapers in second countries print more than their readers read. Thus, gatekeepers stand at every point of exchange, and the throughput constantly falls.

Figure 11.1

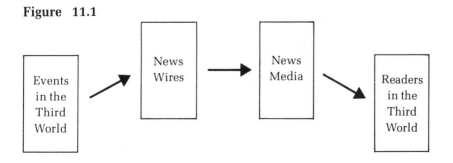

• The picture of Third World newspapers that emerges from this study is less different from non-Third World journalism than we might have expected. Third World newspapers, like others, are essentially local news media. They reflect the interests and information needs of the people around them. They are greatly interested in the Third World in general, and their region in particular. With the exception of a regional newspaper like the *Straits Times*, they devote about three-fourths of their stories to their own country—as do prestige papers in the United States.

• About half of the news content of the four international wires in the study, available in Asia, deals with the Third World, about 60 percent of that with Asia. This says nothing about the *quality* of the news—it is a purely quantitative measurement. But the quantity of Third World news circulating over these wires is rather impressive.

• One can hardly examine a week of news coverage in Asia without concluding that Asia is more than one news region. A major Pakistan story, for example, is covered basically in India, Pakistan, and Sri Lanka. An Indonesian story, on the other hand, gets almost exclusive attention from the press in Southeast Asia. The quality of news coverage depends, at least in part, on where news happens.

• The most disappointing feature of the limited coverage of development news was not the small amount of it, but rather the ignoring of stories that would seem important to developing countries and their readers. For instance, there was a Sri Lanka redevelopment plan that seemed to be an attempt to change the whole economic approach of the country. One wire and one paper carried it. One-third of the thirty major development stories that we traced in the study were not picked up anywhere. No one picked up India's literacy program, for example, or Philippine plans to build a nuclear power center, or Korea's plans for a new capital city.

• Third World countries are not yet ready to do without the international news agencies, from which they get two-thirds of their foreign news. But the enormous amount of unused copy on those wires—seven out of eight stories for the average Asian daily—suggests that there is plenty of room for negotiation and change if Asia is not satisfied with the wire news coming into it. The news agencies are conciliatory. The situation seems to call for a frank exchange of opinion and information on needs and capabilities.

The Week's Events

To a reader in Asia, the week of December 4 through 10 may well have seemed like a fairly typical news week, neither as quiet as some nor as stressful as others but full of interesting events. The week began with a shocking event—the crash of a hijacked airplane, killing all its passengers, in Malaysia on its way to the Singapore airport. This, of course, generated a great deal of copy out of Singapore and Kuala Lumpur. Throughout the world, however, Third World news was dominated by the Tripoli meeting and President Sadat's continuing peace initiative. All wires and almost all newspapers carried that story in detail. A war was underway in the Horn of Africa, and political violence occurred in many places: Rhodesia, the North African desert, Indonesia, Indochina, the southern Philippines, and Thailand among them. The full dimensions of an earlier disaster, the overwhelming storm in southern India, were just becoming apparent. More than 8,000 bodies had been recovered, and relief was being brought from many sources. Political developments were heated in most of the countries of Asia; these were covered intensively as local news, but reported surprisingly seldom in other countries. President Marcos was preparing for a referendum and considering the case of Aquino. President Suharto faced student demonstrations and was preparing to close newspapers. The new government in Pakistan was deciding what to do with Mr. Bhutto and some of his colleagues. A national commission in India was investigating Indira Gandhi's conduct as prime minster, and Mrs. Gandhi was attacking the commission and preparing for a political comeback in some of India's more troubled

states. The King of Thailand was celebrating his fiftieth an-
niversary. Textile-producing nations were negotiating for
higher quotas. China was quiet, but apparently restudying its
economic policy and the organization of its high command,
looking toward the Fifth Party Congress. A parade of diplomats
moved through the region, visiting their opposite numbers,
making friendly statements, and signing pacts of one kind or
another. And, appropriately for this report, a conference of
newspaper and news agency men, sponsored by Unesco, was
meeting in Sri Lanka to discuss the need for improved news
exchange in the Third World. The news output from this meeting was less than might have been expected.

Thus, in the perspective of history, it was a week like all
weeks. If there was one noteworthy feature about it, that was
the absence of any dominating story from the Big Powers. The
big news in the week of December 4 came from Cairo and
Tripoli, rather than New York or Moscow or London.

The Sources of the Week's News

Let us begin to analyze the flow of this news through Asia
with one noteworthy finding from our data: A little over three-
fourths of all nonlocal Third World news, during the five days
of the study, came to the Asian newspapers in our sample
from one or more of the four international news wire services
we have examined: Agence France-Presse, the Associated
Press, Reuters, and United Press International.

We were able to identify sources for more than 80 percent
of the total number of news items, other than local news, in
these dailies. The number of stories so identified totalled
1,365. We classified the sources under six headings: international wire or wires, national or regional wires, paper's own
correspondent, local coverage, special news service, and reprints. It may be well to say what we meant by each of these.

"International wire or wires" refers to the four international news services mentioned. The majority of stories listed only one agency as source. Some mentioned two; a few papers, usually in brief news roundups, credited "all agencies." A few references were to one of the international wires plus a national news service, for example, "Reuters, PTC" for some stories in the Ceylon Daily News. (PTC, the Press Trust of Ceylon, is a national service.) When we were able to ascertain that the story was transmitted from the original wire without rewriting, we credited it to the international wire. When we were unable to ascertain that this was the case, we credited it to the national wire. And of course, when a regional or national wire (such as Antara or Samarchar) is credited alone, or jointly with indication that the story has been rewritten, then the story is credited to "national or regional wire." The paper's own correspondent" is sometimes hard to identify, and there must be relatively few foreign correspondents on the staffs of Asian newspapers. We have coded it, however, when there seemed reason to do so. "Local coverage" of foreign Third World news occurs oftener than one might expect. Editorials on a foreign Third World topic fit into this class. So does local coverage of a foreign dignitary's visit to Asia. "Special news services" include, for example, such sources as the *New York Times* service, the *Washington Post-Los Angeles Times* service, or Depthnews. "Reprints" may be of an article from a magazine or another paper, a BBC broadcast, or similar source.

Given these definitions, the significance of the following figures is clear:

Of all the nonlocal Third World news stories in these fourteen Asian dailies, where we were able to identify the source, 76.4 percent came from one or more of the four international news wires.

3.9 percent came from national or regional wires
6.3 percent came from a paper's own correspondent
9.2 percent came from local coverage
3.3 percent came from special news services
1.0 percent came from reprints

It must not be assumed that these figures were uniform throughout the whole sample of papers. Actually the percentage of stories from the international wires ranged from 13 percent to 95 percent, but the low figures were in a native-language paper that carried only a few Third World stories from outside the country. The figures for "local coverage" and "own correspondent" may have been inflated somewhat by the crash of the hijacked airplane a few miles from the Singapore airport but across the border in Malaysia. Thus the very large Singapore papers could use some of their own staff to cover the story and could also depend to a special degree on representatives in Malaysia. But even with these possible additions, none of the other source categories is very large. The significant figure is that three out of four of all the stories of other Third World countries came from AFP, AP, Reuters, or UPI.

The Content of the Wires

We can simplify matters by imagining a sort of Composite Wire, averaging out the characteristics of the four Asian wires as they existed from December 5 through 9, 1977.

During those five days, this imaginary wire would have carried an average of a little over 26,000 words a day of Third World news. Actually there was a great deal of variation among wires. The amount of Third World news on different wires varied from a little over 10,000 to just under 35,000 words a day. Altogether, the four wires carried about 105,000 words a day, on the average, of Third World news.

To put it another way, our Composite Wire would have carried, on the average, about 100 Third World news stories a day. Together, the four wires carried 2,039 such stories in five days.

When we speak of Third World stories on the wires, we mean stories that deal either with Third World countries alone or in the same story with non-Third World countries (for example, a story of trade negotiations between Britain and India). "Third World stories," as we are using the term, distinguishes either of those types from stories about non-Third World countries alone: that is, a story about India alone or about India plus England, from a story about England alone. On the day in which we coded the entire content of the news wires (not merely the news dealing with the Third World), here was the distribution of these three kinds of stories:

	Stories	Percents
Third World only	227	24.7
Third World and other in the same story	223	24.2
Non-Third World	470	51.1

There is no very clear principle for dividing the second group of stories between Third World and others. Some stories emphasized the Third World, others the opposite, and in varying degrees. However, if we divide the second group evenly between Third and non-Third World, then we can estimate that about 339 stories (38.8 percent) on the four wires that day could be called Third World news. In other words, a good estimate is that a little over one-third of the Asian wires was used to cover the Third World. And about one-half of all the stories on these wires dealt to some extent with Third World countries.

What kind of news was it? The great bulk of it came from Asia, and this proportion might have been still larger were it not for the dramatic events in the Middle East. Asia accounted for 58 percent of the Third World stories during the five sample days; 24 percent came from the Middle East; only 11 percent was on Africa; 7 percent was on Latin America.

The distribution of coverage by countries followed the same general pattern. Despite the fact that only Third World news was coded during four of the five days of the study, still a few non-Third World countries emerged among the leaders in a number of stories. In one day, the United States was referred to in a little over 7 percent of all stories; the United Kingdom in just under 3 percent; Japan in 2.27 percent. No other non-Third World countries reached 2 percent. The Soviet Union appeared in 1.28 percent; Australia in 1.36 percent; France in 0.96 percent.

The heaviest concentration of coverage was on Middle Eastern countries. Egypt was in 7.26 percent of all the wire stories during the five days studied. A group of countries we called "Other Middle East" appeared in 4.98 percent of all stories. This group included South Yemen; the Emirates; countries like Morocco that were not among the main movers in the Tripoli meeting; and, most important, the Palestinians. We feel obliged to code the last as a unit despite their lack of national entity because they were treated constantly in the news as an entity, attending the Tripoli meeting, issuing statements, being treated in almost every respect as an organization, if not a government. Syria appeared in 2.99 percent of the stories. Algiers, Iraq, Jordan, Libya, and Saudi Arabia all received between 1 percent and 2 percent of the total coverage.

There was a concentration of coverage around Rhodesia, but very little other extensive coverage in Africa, even on the Somali-Ethiopian war. No country in Latin America received much attention—not even Cuba, which was already extending its activities in Africa. In Asia, however, as one would expect of Asia wires, a number of countries received substantial coverage. Malaysia was in 4.76 percent of the stories (the airplane crash), the Philippines in the same number (several interesting lines of political activity, and some large sports stories). China got 4.23 percent of the coverage. Here are the Asian Third World countries that got the most attention:

	Percent of All Wire Stories
Malaysia	4.76
Philippines	4.76
China	4.23
Indonesia	3.65
Thailand	3.48
India	3.40
Singapore	3.20
Pakistan	2.54
Vietnam	2.39
South Korea	2.37
Hong Kong	2.14

What kinds of news did the wires carry? A little over one story out of three (36 percent) dealt with relations between countries, friendly or unfriendly, direct or indirect, cooperative or otherwise. Some 15 percent of the stories were on economic matters; 11 percent on domestic politics and government matters; 7 percent on wars or other political violence or preparations for military activity. Contrary to some criticisms of news wires, a relatively small proportion of the news dealt with crime or disaster: 4 percent on crime or court trials, 5 percent on accidents and disasters, including the air crash and the Indian cyclone. But no less than 12 percent—one out of every eight stories—were about sports.

Let us be careful, however, not to assume that the Composite Wire we have been describing is any more than average. There are striking differences among the four wires, in addition to their variations in total length. Two wires carry a greater amount of non-Third World news than do the others. Two wires concentrate on international relations much more than do others. One wire specialized in very short items. Actually 40 percent of the Third World stories on that particular wire were two inches or less in length, about twice as many as on the other wires. There are considerable differences in the stories they cover. . . . The wires undoubtedly specialize in countries where they have the best news resources and the most clients. An example of this is the coverage of the cricket match between Australia and India, in Brisbane. Two wires did not report it at all. The other two carried about 9,000 words on the match. The story filled about 45 percent of the Indian news on one wire, 30 percent on the other. Obviously a great deal of this coverage was intended for India itself, and for a few other countries in which international cricket is of great interest.

Content of the Newspapers

If it is difficult to envisage a Composite Asian News Wire, it is incomparably more difficult to conceive of a Composite

Asian Third World newspaper. Newspapers in Asia, as in all other parts of the world, have personalities of their own and vary tremendously with support and clientele. For example, the amount of nonlocal Third World news in the thirteen newspapers . . . varies by a ratio of one to fifteen—from 3,000 to 46,000 words a day. If we had been able to include the remaining three papers in our sample, that ratio would have been still more striking: we have already noted that, to the best of our present information, the largest newspaper in India carried less than one non-Indian Third World news story a day.

It must be remembered that we are not coding local news, only the Third World news in these papers that deals, wholly or in part, with other countries. Considering that the greater part of most newspapers' content is local news, that means the Third World content of these papers is actually greater than our tables show.

To what extent do these Third World papers concentrate on Third World news? The best estimate we can make from data at hand is that on the average, the thirteen papers on which we have most data use 80 percent or a little more of their news space for Third World news, pictures, commentaries, and so on, counting both local and foreign news. When we estimate this from the number of stories, we get a figure near 80 percent; when we estimate it in terms of number of words, we get a figure in the high eighties.

These thirteen Asian daily newspapers carried altogether 1,646 nonlocal Third World stories during the five days we measured. These totaled nearly a million words. The mythical average daily in our sample, therefore, can be thought of as carrying 15,000 words a day, twenty-five stories, on the Third World outside its own country. It compares with the average wire like this:

	Stories Per Day	Words Per Day
Composite Wire	100	26,000
Composite Daily	25	15,000

One should not attribute too much magic to these figures. Even though the average daily carried about three-fifths as much foreign Third World news as the average wire, still the largest dailies may carry nearly twice as much as the average wire; and on the other hand, the largest dailies in many cases take all four services and thus have more than 100,000 words of wire news available to them each day.

In choosing Third World news from outside their own countries, the Asian dailies lean even more toward Asian news than do the Asian services. Here are the comparative percentages:

	Asia	Latin America	Middle East	Africa
4 Wires	58.2	7.0	23.5	11.3
14 Dailies	68.8	4.9	20.0	7.1

When we correlated the country focus in the composite Asian daily with each of the wire services, we discovered correlations of .57–.60. Thus we can say that the relationship with the wires apparently accounts for about one-half of the variation in the distribution within the papers of the news by countries. The rest of the difference is ascribable to the individuality of the papers, their editors, and their communities.

The newspapers' choice of news by content categories is very similar to that of the wires. Table 11.1 summarizes the comparison, using only percentages.

In both the newspapers and wires, foreign relations get far heavier coverage than any other kind of news. Economic news comes next, followed by domestic politics and sports, the latter two being almost even. The wires devote a little higher proportion of their news to foreign relations than do the newspapers, a little lower proportion to economic information and domestic politics, and about the same proportion to sports. Although the figures are small, it will be seen that the newspapers use a little higher proportion of human interest items, crime, and accidents than the wires offer.

Table 11.1 Subject Percentages of Newspapers, Wires

Category	14 Newspapers	4 Newswires
Military, political violence	5.1	6.7
Foreign relations	29.1	36.1
Domestic government, political	12.4	10.8
Economic	18.5	15.1
Science, health	0.9	1.1
Education	1.1	0.3
Accidents, disasters	6.6	5.3
Crime, judicial	4.9	4.0
Energy, environment	0.8	0.9
Human rights	1.4	2.7
Sports	12.0	11.5
Art, culture	1.4	0.7
Human interest	4.6	2.1
Religion	0.3	0.3
Miscellaneous	1.6	2.2

(tau correlation, wires and newspapers: .825)

But these differences are minor. News patterns, so far as they can be measured quantitatively, are strikingly similar between the wires and the newspapers. To demonstrate how similar they actually are, we applied correlational statistics to the Third World news content patterns of the newspapers and the wires for the entire five days of the study. We discovered correlations of .7–.86 across all content categories.

What is the significance of such a remarkable set of results? They are statistically significant far beyond the .001 level, far beyond the point where there is any reasonable likelihood the similarities could occur by chance. One seldom obtains correlations like that from research involving human elements and large numbers. The news pattern of the wires is apparently remarkably similar to that of the newspapers. The relationship is very little affected, as we thought it might be, when we separate out a group of Chinese language newspapers and compare them to the wires and to the English papers. The practical significance is that either the newspapers are following to an extraordinary degree the news agenda set by the wires, or the wires are meeting to an extraordinary degree the tastes of the newspapers, or the newspapers are following the lead of the wires, whether they like it or not, because they have no way of changing it and no suitable alternative.

Third World News in a Region

Let us now focus briefly on one region of the world. For this purpose, we have selected nine Asian Third World countries, most of which are represented by one or more newspapers in our sample; and, for comparison, three other countries. These others are Egypt, the country that made most news during the test week; Japan, the most affluent Asian country; and the non-Third World country cited most often on the news wires, the United States.

Table 11.2 gives the relative weight in percent of stories on each of these countries, as presented by the wires and by the regional newspapers. We simply list percentages: the percentage of the total number of Third World stories on the wires and in the fourteen newspapers, which were about each of the selected countries.

It is perhaps worth noting that whereas the correlation of the Composite Wire and the Composite Paper across the con-

Table 11.2 Percentage Distribution of Stories in Newspapers, Wires, by Country

Country	14 Daily Newspapers	4 News Wires
China	10.3	8.7
India	5.0	6.9
Indonesia	4.9	7.4
Malaysia	19.4	9.7
Pakistan	5.3	5.2
Philippines	5.5	9.7
Singapore	9.7	6.5
Thailand	5.8	7.1
Vietnam	3.8	4.9
Egypt	15.1	14.7
Japan	3.4	4.5
U.S.	11.8	14.6

tent categories was highly significant for Third World countries as a whole, the correlation of wires and papers over content categories, when only the nine Asian countries are included, does not quite meet accepted standards of statistical significance. This is apparently the effect of the regional situation at the time, notably the Malaysian airplane crash which threw the local attention to disaster news out of proportion to that of the wires. The crash was news everywhere, but in Asia it was almost local news.

What kinds of news picture were the newspapers of the region projecting for these nine countries during the sample week. Table 11.3 shows that of all the stories on economic matters in the region during that week, a certain percentage came from Singapore, a certain percentage from India, and so forth. Here we have included only the larger content categories—eight instead of the fifteen shown in Table 11.1.

During that week, then, it was chiefly to the Philippines, Indonesia, and Thailand that editors and readers looked for news of political violence and undeclared wars. It was obviously to Malaysia that they looked for news of accident and disaster: 70 percent of all stories in that category were about the crash of the hijacked plane! It was to Singapore that they looked chiefly for economic news. Pakistan had a domestic problem that was being discussed in terms of human rights. And so forth. India seemed to have a remarkably low profile in most categories during that week. The number of stories of China was quite large: the news from that country that proved most interesting was foreign relations and domestic government. One noteworthy feature of Table 11.3 is how nearly equal all the countries are in sports news. All of them (with the exception perhaps of Vietnam) were apparently interested in and interesting to others in sports.

Some aspects of such a regional profile must change from week to week, even day to day. Others may remain relatively unchanged. A disaster like the one in Malaysia would shift the region's attention overnight, for example, whereas Singapore will probably be a continuing source of economic information. To follow such news profiles through time might tell us a great deal about the flow of news through a region. . . .

Table 11.3 Coverage (in percent) of Nine Asian Countries by Fourteen Asian Daily Newspapers, December 4–10, 1977

	Military, political violence	Foreign relations	Domestic government, political	Economic	Accidents, disasters	Crime, judicial	Human rights	Sports
China	0	24.2	22.5	8.2	0	1.5	5.3	9.9
India	5.6	4.3	7.0	5.3	7.8	11.9	5.3	13.5
Indonesia	19.4	3.1	9.2	8.2	0	1.5	15.8	7.1
Malaysia	11.1	18.6	31.0	24.7	70.1	35.8	10.5	17.7
Pakistan	0	5.6	7.7	4.7	2.6	4.5	36.8	15.6
Philippines	38.9	8.7	17.6	1.2	3.9	3.0	0	9.9
Singapore	0	3.7	0.7	35.3	11.7	25.4	21.1	12.8
Thailand	19.4	11.8	3.5	7.1	3.9	14.9	0	12.8
Vietnam	5.6	19.9	0.7	5.3	0	1.5	5.3	0.7

A Note in Conclusion

This is a preliminary paper, a first look at a large mass of data—
more precisely, a look at the first output of data from a study
which will generate much more information and on which
additional analyses are underway and more are planned.

Therefore, this is no time for conclusions. Yet a few conclusions do seem to be emerging, and perhaps we may be
pardoned for setting down some notes about them.

For one thing, it is clear that the wire services are sending
large amounts of Third World news to Asia. The average daily
output, 100 stories per wire, is about four times as many items
of nonlocal Third World news as the average daily in our
sample carries, and 26,000 words of Third World news per
day on the average wire provides a great deal of leeway for
different needs and interests. Most of the dailies in our sample
receive more than one international wire; many of them receive three or four. Such a paper may have 100,000 words per
day of Third World copy available to it, and as many as 400
Third World stories. Thus, the measurements we have reported here suggest that there is no shortage of wire news; if
there is anything wrong, it must be a shortage of coverage or
a kind of coverage. The flow of news through the wires is
adequate for a varied service.

The evidence we have on news content is less clear. There
is, of course, the striking fact that three-quarters of all the
foreign Third World news copy in the sixteen Asian dailies
we have studied comes from the four services—AFP, AP, Reuters, and UPI. Considering that numerous other wires and services are available, and that local coverage generates a considerable amount of local coverage referring to other Third World
countries, the 76 percent figure for wire news seems quite
impressive.

So, too, is the very high degree of correspondence between
the wire services and the daily papers with respect to the kinds
of news they carry and publish. The differences we see here
are those one would expect between regional and local needs:

the wires have to supply more news of foreign relations and business to meet the diverse interests of their clients.

The distribution of coverage among zones of the world is also very similar among wires, papers and wires, and individual papers. And when the analysis is extended to coverage of countries, the correspondences throughout the sample are truly remarkable. The correlation between all wires and all papers, in coverage by countries, is .58; the composite paper correlates with each wire at about the same level; and the composite wire correlates with all the papers and with language subgroups of the papers except the two Indian papers, at a figure between .57 and .61. The correlation between the wires and the two Indian papers is somewhat lower, but is still at a level which could not occur 1 time in 100 by chance; and all the other relationships are over the .001 level.

These results say that, in general, the mix of news (kinds of news) in the papers and the wires is very much the same. They do not say that everyone is necessarily satisfied with that mix or with the particular items that go into it.

The expressions of desire for change, in recent years, need to be pinpointed more sharply. Are they dissatisfactions with the mix of news, the sources, the particular items selected, the treatment, or simply the control of the news exchange?

When we look more closely at the news flow, however, even at the present stage of the analysis, we begin to find large variations—quite different from the uniformity that was apparent in the aggregate data. The apparent similarity of wires and papers in categories of content does not extend to individual stories. The wires are quite different, not only in total size and length of stories, but also in the particular stories they choose to cover and the kind of coverage they give events within a country. All of them cover the Tripoli meetings and President Sadat's initiative, of course. All of them cover the Malaysian airplane crash. But, there is considerable variation in what else they cover, and the coverage they give events within a country.

More puzzling to us, however, is the wild variation in the Third World news carried by the newspapers. On the one hand, the largest newspaper in India apparently carried, during five days, only four items of Third World news from outside India. During the same time, the largest newspapers in Malaysia carried 147 and 215 items, respectively. A Korean newspaper carried a total of 900 words on India; a Philippine one, 1,100; but the *New Straits Times*, 5,000. Only five of the twelve non-Indian newspapers in Asia carried anything on the Shah Commission's investigation of Indira Gandhi during the five days of our study. Three Chinese-language newspapers, all well above the average in amount of Third World coverage, presented pictures of India which varied notably in tone and emphasis. Even the treatment of sports, which represented three stories out of eight in these Asian papers, likewise had its irregularities. Thus, although the papers were carrying about the same categories of news and the same percentage of wire news, they obviously were not carrying the same stories. As we continue to examine just what stories, rather than what classes of stories, are being carried by the different wires and the different papers, this will almost certainly continue to reveal wide disparities, but it may also contribute insights into the variations of taste and interest that a news exchange will have to satisfy.

An international news service will program its wire to make best use of its resources and to best meet the needs of its clients as it understands them. To a certain extent, the wires must specialize in their coverage and services. By the same token, a newspaper will select from wire service copy so as to tailor its product to the needs and interests of its readers, so far as it understands them. All of us know that the competition for space on any particular day, and the time of day when news becomes available, are going to affect what wire news gets into the paper. How much farther than that we can go, and whether we can really identify a set of principles that help to explain news flow and news selection—and consequently illuminate what is required of a news exchange—we do not know.

Our experience thus far suggests that it will be more difficult to say in general terms what kind of news a Third World country, or a Third World country at a certain level of development, wants in comparison to another Third World country or a non-Third World country, than to find some broad characteristics to help us understand the process of selection. For example, here are some kinds of questions that merit attention as we work on through the data.

- Other things being equal, will editors tend to prefer a short article with a current news peg to an analytical article? And if so, what are the characteristics of the analytical story (disregarding the availability of space) that will overbalance that choice?
- Will editors tend to prefer "futures"—that is, items which promise potential excitement—rather than items whose level of excitement is already known?
- All editors look for items about "names," but how do they define a name?
- Is it reasonable to suppose that a wire editor, other things being equal, will prefer a story involving two countries to a story about one country, because it should invite reading in both countries?
- How much does official standing raise the desirability of a story?
- What is the present attractiveness of feature material in the area we are studying? (We were a bit surprised by the relatively small amount of "soft" news we found, both on the wires and in the papers.)
- What evidence is there of distortion of Asian Third World news in the direction of Western interests or Western interpretation?
- How much attention is given to trivial stories with a feature angle, such as those the international wires have been accused of emphasizing?

We have no illusions that checking on a series of questions like these, or examining in detail the selections of sixteen newspapers, is going to explain all that it would help to know about news flow and news needs in Asia. We come to this point in the study, however, with some real hope that the final results will be helpful, especially if followed up with interviews with some newspaper and wire news editors, and some Third World readers.

Part III

Transnational News Agencies

THE MARKET FOR NEWS is virtually worldwide, and the large, highly competitive organizations most directly responsible for the success or failure of news to flow smoothly, reliably, accurately, and equitably are the transnational news agencies (TNNAs).

This section suggests how and why the Associated Press, Agence France-Presse, Reuters, UPI, and Visnews are expert news and information collectors, processors, and salesmen that reach more than 100 nations with literally millions of words and pictures every day. The essays address why these crucial news actors—because of their powerful, strategic position—should receive special attention if policies to redress intensely felt grievances among developing nations are to have far-reaching, long-term success. The TNNAs simply are not going to go away, despite all the complaints against them, and it is economically unrealistic to expect that additional, large-scale, general news services can easily be established to compete with or even supplement the dominant agencies.

In effect, the TNNAs (and, indeed, the whole transnationalization of communication phenomenon) are at one and the same time criticized and supported by virtually all nations—rich and poor, capitalist and socialist, industrial and nonindustrial. Without the global agencies, people and societies everywhere would be less informed than they are now. The existing world order of communication and international relations would quickly turn to disorder should the efficient TNNAs, with their high-capacity technology and near-global news collection channels, be disrupted. Understandably, the TNNAs and their information-rich home societies have a vested interest in maintaining the status quo. Reforms, of course, are acceptable, but a radical overhaul of the Western news organization and basic change in the assumptions about the nature of news are clearly unacceptable to the TNNAs as they now exist.

12

Reporting from
the Third World
MORT ROSENBLUM

Mort Rosenblum's essay addresses head-on the developing nations' problems and frustrations with international news coverage by the West. Focusing on what he calls the news-gathering system's severe difficulties and limitations, Rosenblum explains how the transnational news agencies operate and why "what is commonly referred to as the world flow of information is more a series of trickles and spurts." He documents how problems have been compounded by attempts of many Third World governments to inject their views into Western press coverage. These efforts include Unesco activities, national policies restricting foreign reporters' access to the news, and the advocacy of "developmental journalism." Rosenblum concludes that "there are no simple solutions to the basic conflicts underlying the Western and Third World approaches to the role of the press," but he points out that there are areas where progress has been and can be made.

Mort Rosenblum was editor of the *International Herald Tribune* in Paris from 1979 to 1981, and is author of *Coups and Earthquakes: Reporting the World for America.* From 1967 to 1979 he was an Associated Press correspondent in Africa, Asia, Latin America, and France.

This article was written while the author was with the Associated Press and originally appeared in *Foreign Affairs* (July 1977), 55(4):814–35.

A POPULAR MELODY has joined the reggae rhythms in Jamaican nightclubs; it is a song called, "The Foreign Press." In rich island dialect, the song accuses correspondents of besmirching Jamaica's good name with false reports throughout the world. It says that, between dispatches, reporters manage to frolic on the beach and in the nightspots, adding: "Why don't they write about that in the foreign press?"

It is no lighthearted calypso spoof. The wife of a prominent Jamaican cabinet minister told an American correspondent, with no trace of mirth: "You [reporters] don't know how you make us suffer with all your lies about communism and violence . . . and if you keep it up, the day will come that you will not be able to come here anymore or you'll have your throat cut." Already Jamaica, like scores of developing countries, is loath to grant entry to foreign correspondents.

Leaders in the Third World, with new and growing confidence, are translating into action their frustration with international news coverage.[1] Government criticism of the press is hardly new, but only recently have leaders acted so harshly on such a large scale. Reporters are banned, jailed, and, in some instances, tortured or shot. Dispatches are censored, and news sources are stringently muzzled. International news agency reports are controlled and foreign publications are seized. . . .

This trend is the tip of a political ice floe which shows every sign of resisting efforts to melt it. It reflects not merely a lack of mutual understanding but rather fundamental conflicts among differing concepts of a government's role in society and of a people's right to be informed. While Western newsmen generally act on the assumption that a free press is vital to a well-governed nation, many Third World leaders maintain that the greater goal of national development requires them to subordinate the ideal of free expression. Development of their countries requires unity, they say, and the press fo-

1. For a detailed analysis of the problems of the international news system and developing countries' complaints against the transnational news agencies, see Mort Rosenblum, *Coups and Earthquakes: Reporting the World for America.* New York: Harper & Row, 1979.

cuses on divisions. The Soviet philosophy of a controlled press supports their position and thus complicates efforts to seek common ground.

Third World Complaints

Third World concern appears to have focused on two principal complaints, articulated in conference after conference:

> −The Western press gives inadequate and superficial attention to the realities of developing countries, often infusing coverage with cultural bias. The traditional emphasis on the dramatic, the emotional, and the amusing—the "coups and earthquakes" syndrome—is seen not only as unbalanced but also as detrimental to the development process.
>
> −The Western monopoly on the distribution of news—whereby even stories written about one Third World country for distribution in another are reported and transmitted by international news agencies based in New York, London, and Paris—amounts to neocolonialism and cultural domination.

There is certainly some justification for these complaints. Yet it is also true, as Western newsmen argue, that the methods by which many Third World governments now seek redress cause serious distortions in the news. In addition, current efforts to form alternative Third World press agencies could further interfere with the free flow of accurate news. On both sides, storms of rhetoric have confused the picture. Some of the most vehement detractors of Western reporting are themselves responsible for the imbalances they decry. And some Western news executives who protest the loudest commit the most blatant misrepresentations of Third World attitudes.

Many on both sides, purposely or unwittingly, do not recognize how the problems of one are closely related to those of the other. Although it will not eliminate the real differences in interest, an increased and sincere attempt to achieve co-operation rather than conflict could help to lessen cultural misperceptions which serve neither the Western press nor the Third World.

"Trickles and Spurts"

In understanding the problems of Western coverage of the Third World, it is important to recognize that the international newsgathering system has severe limitations. What is commonly referred to as the world flow of information is more a series of trickles and spurts. News is moved across borders by surprisingly thin networks of correspondents for various types of news organizations with widely disparate purposes. Some correspondents, such as those working for television and most newspapers, report back to media in their own countries, and they approach the news from the viewpoint of specific readers and viewers. Others report to agencies which distribute their dispatches regionally or globally, or to internationally circulated magazines, and they attempt to achieve a more universal outlook, including details of interest to readers from many countries.

By far the largest distributors of information are the four Western-based global news agencies which provide separate reports for their home markets and for various regions in the rest of the world. The largest of these is the Associated Press, based in New York, with an annual budget of $100 million and a history dating back to 1848. The AP is a nonprofit cooperative owned by 1,350 member newspapers in the United States, with 3,500 subscribing radio and television stations. It sells its international news and photo services on a contract teleprinter basis to foreign newspapers and broadcasters with an estimated total audience of one billion people and deploys its staff and resources within the limits of its budget and according to the needs of its members. It has about 80 U.S.-based correspondents and bureau chiefs who are rotated among its overseas offices; it also has another 750 locally hired support personnel who assist the correspondents or who operate on their own in foreign bureaus unassisted by correspondents assigned from New York. Additionally, there are scores of "stringers," part-time reports with other jobs, who might contribute fewer than a half-dozen stories a year from the smaller capitals and cities. Dispatches from all these reporters are handled in two ways: one department in New York edits and sometimes rewrites stories that might be of interest to domestic members, and another department edits and relays stories destined for foreign subscribers. Separate overseas wires, in a variety of languages, carry the major international stories as well as minor stories of interest to the particular regions served by the individual wire.

The other three global agencies work similarly, but each has its own characteristics. United Press International, which also has headquarters in New York, is commercially organized and must bring in enough income to cover its costs. World news coverage is expensive, UPI executives say, and occasional profits are hardly excessive. Reuters, based in London, is owned by British and some Commonwealth news agencies. It operates somewhat like the AP, but its home market is much smaller, and it has specially tailored regional services. For example, about 30,000 words daily are sent to Africa, designed for African media. Reuters' worldwide news operations are partly financed by earnings from a separate economic news service and from income earned by sharing its communications facilities with other news organizations. The fourth major global agency, Agence France-Presse, has extensive regional coverage, with 790 Paris-based and national newsmen outside of France. Directly and through contracts with national news agencies, AFP dispatches reach 12,000 newspapers. AFP, although officially autonomous, receives large government subscription payments, which allow it to maintain uneconomical bureaus and to provide its services cheaply throughout the Third World. However, some editors say they prefer to rely on the other three main agencies in some cases, particularly when French interests are involved.

Goal of Objectivity

All four major news agencies have a stated goal of objectivity, which is harmonious with their practical considerations. Thousands of newspapers and broadcasters with positions ranging from the radical Left to the extreme Right receive each of the four services. Neighboring countries with centuries of enmity all rely on them for world news. For example, their subscribers include government-controlled Arab media and conservative Israeli dailies. Each subscriber demands immediate rectification if it feels a story has been distorted.

Apart from the main agencies, there are more than ninety regional and national news agencies which operate in a variety of ways. TASS of the Soviet Union and Hsinhua of China distribute highly politicized reports to a large number of developed and developing countries. Agencies like West Germany's Deutsche Presse-Agentur (DPA), Italy's Agenzia Nazionale Stampa Associata (ANSA) and Japan's Kyodo compete with the four main agencies in many areas. And many national agencies of Third World countries maintain correspondents in neighboring and in European capitals. The largest of these is Tanjug of Yugoslavia which has forty-seven correspondents abroad, mostly in industrialized countries. . . . Some agencies, such as ARNA of Libya and MENA of Egypt, cover contiguous geopolitical regions. And some of the smaller ones, such as the Gabonese News Agency, do little more than distribute officially sanctioned information within a country of 500,000 inhabitants.

Besides the news agencies, some large newspapers and newspaper chains syndicate their correspondents' work. The New York Times News Service carries stories from the *Times* of London and the London *Observer* as well as dispatches from *New York Times* reporters. It has more than 450 subscribers—about 5 percent of the AP's total but a select group of influential papers—more than 250 of them in the United States. Among others, the *Washington Post* and the *Los Angeles Times* also offer a combined service drawing on their foreign correspondents.

Costs and Correspondents

While a number of Western papers, magazines, and broadcast organizations also maintain correspondents abroad, the total is steadily dropping. Including salary, expenses, and communications, the costs of maintaining a single reporter overseas for a year can be well over $100,000. Provisions of the Tax Reform Act of 1976 lowering the income tax exemptions for U.S. citizens living abroad have increased the costs: the Chicago Daily News, which for years had kept a permanent staff of resident and roving correspondents overseas, disbanded its foreign service at the end of 1976, attributing its action at least in part to the new law.

Accurate statistics on reporters abroad are not available, but a good indication of the decrease is found in comparing the Overseas Press Club (of New York) directory of correspondents for 1975 with that of previous years. It listed 429 full-time American correspondents abroad compared to 563 in 1969. Foreign national employees of U.S. media were listed at 247 compared to 366 in 1969. (Of the 1975 total, 54 percent were based in nineteen European countries.) Even those totals are misleadingly high, since they include writers for specialized publications and some expatriates who retain accreditation from small newspapers for prestige purposes. Some areas are almost completely written off. The AP and UPI each has a single full-time correspondent, based in Nairobi, to cover all of black Africa north of Rhodesia; roving correspondents based elsewhere add to the news reports. Their stringers in other African capitals send little, and most are closely watched by their governments. Only a few news organizations keep correspondents in East or West Africa.

Some papers with few correspondents living abroad regularly send out reporters who travel. They vary widely in scope, and some of the best, like the *Christian Science Monitor*, have circulations which are small in relation to national readership. A number of major European and Japanese newspapers operate similarly, keeping a small group of correspondents based abroad with a regular staff of specialized reporters who make periodic visits to developing areas.

The larger newsmagazines also maintain their own foreign staffs overseas to send lengthy dispatches which are distilled by staff writers at home, combining correspondent reports with news agency material, information on file, and domestic sources. In early 1977, *Time* listed thirty-six staff members in seventeen foreign bureaus; *Newsweek*, twenty-two correspondents in eleven bureaus; and *U.S. News and World Report*, eight editors abroad. Additionally, each uses regular stringers who are paid according to their contribution.

The three U.S. television networks provide wide foreign coverage not only from crews based abroad but also from correspondents sent out from U.S. bureaus. Yet notwithstanding the enormous impact of television on the American public, Third World leaders seldom take into account television coverage because they do not normally see it. And few understand its import. Their quarrel is with the agencies, newspapers, and magazines.

Whatever the talents of the men and women involved, a press corps of that size can only sample the news. Even the *New York Times*, with thirty-three of its own full-time correspondents and a wide range of news agencies to draw on, runs only about 14,000 words a day from all over the world. That is much more than the half-dozen foreign stories carried in most newspapers, but it involves careful selection and editing.

Leeway to Interpret

As a general rule, newspaper reporters, particularly the European ones, have greater leeway to interpret news events

than do news agency correspondents. At the same time, newspaper correspondents normally have more space in which to
discuss opposing sides of a sensitive issue. Both, however, are
under great pressure to rush around covering major political
events and disaster stories, whereas stories on development
trends and social changes are regularly subject to delay. Because newspapers have only so much space and broadcasters
have only so much air time, editors feel they must select what
their audiences want, or they will lose the readers and viewers
who keep them in business. News judgment rests on the potential impact and interest of stories rather than on any sense
of international fair play. Even in the newspapers of most
Third World countries, news items are predominantly from
industrialized countries of the West and East, and stories from
other developing countries often conflict.

Sometimes the process itself causes imbalances. Correspondents knew the military was planning to overthrow Isabel
Perón in Argentina six months before the actual coup; the date
was revised repeatedly. Many were afraid to leave Argentina
to cover less dramatic stories for fear of missing the coup and
finding the border closed. . . . The smaller countries are
squeezed into rapid trips during lulls between major stories
in the larger countries. One Latin American scholar comments
wryly: "I'm always amazed to see how news breaks in South
America along the direct lines of the Braniff route.". . .

Because reporters tend to travel in packs, circumstances
can focus far more attention on a particular event than it might
ordinarily receive. Riots in Jamaica happened to coincide with
a major International Monetary Fund meeting there in early
1975, so scores of foreign reporters were on hand to report
them in chilling detail. Had there been no visiting correspondents, the local Jamaican stringers might not have seen fit to
write, and the disturbance might have been a tree falling unheard in a forest.

The situation is similar, or worse, in Africa and Asia. A
crisis in southern Africa (or a war in Vietnam) draws correspondents in droves, while the rest of the continent is neglected. Today, wide areas in both are rarely visited; for ex-

ample, the small island nations of the Pacific and Indian Oceans are all but completely forgotten.

A series of other difficulties and limitations affect foreign reporting. News organizations tend to send young inexperienced reporters to the Third World, transferring them to larger bureaus in industrialized countries as they gain seasoning. Correspondents frequently cannot speak the language of the country they are covering, and translators, if available, are rarely adequate. Unfamiliarity with baffling local customs and thought processes can be dangerously misleading. Under such circumstances, even the best have difficulty, and some reporters working abroad are simply not capable of untangling complicated situations and presenting them clearly to faraway readers. Correspondents are seldom specialists, and a reporter may write about politics, table tennis, budget deficits, and traffic accidents in the same afternoon. Inadvertent mistakes are also made in editing, rewriting, translating, and transmitting. . . .

Local stringers are generally poorly paid and have little motivation to provide more than a perfunctory relay of local newspaper reports. Because they may also be government employees, they are sometimes subject to extreme pressures, which often means one-sided or distorted dispatches. In addition, the scarcity of space in print or on the air provides a constant goad to reporters to portray the stories they are covering in the most dramatic light possible. This is particularly true with newsmagazines and television networks. Generally, foreign correspondents are responsible, with a keen sense of professional ethics, but there have been cases where some have exaggerated and even invented facts in order to lend strength to their dispatches.

Space limitations have another distorting effect. Correspondents often must use such shorthand terms as "right-wing dictatorship" and "pro-Peking" without further explanation, raising more questions than they answer. To the informed, and to many readers in the countries from which they are reporting, such meaningless labels and glib generalities may be seen as superficial and even insulting.

Finally, however hard a correspondent may try to exercise balance and objectivity, he is the prisoner of his own value system in judging a situation. . . .

Pressures on Correspondents

The efforts of many Third World governments to inject their perspectives into Western press coverage have in most cases compounded the problem. Many of them treat the Western press as a monolithic and hostile entity which, if properly controlled or cajoled, can be induced to act in a certain way. This philosophy normally leads to frustration and increased bitterness. The sectors of the press which were hostile to these regimes at the outset simply grow more hostile, and have more to criticize, when controls are imposed. And the sympathetic sectors are either prevented from saying anything—or are converted to hostility because of the measures taken.

Methods used to pressure correspondents vary widely. John Saar of the *Washington Post* made a trip to South Korea without difficulty, but no one would talk to him, at any level, because the *Post* had broken the story about questionable Korean lobbying in the United States. India cut the telephone and teleprinter lines of several foreign agencies in New Delhi but allowed them to use their neighbors' communications to send their material. Sometimes reporters are chided gently by low-level officials; sometimes they are obliquely threatened with death.

One common practice has been to expel a free-lance reporter with no major backing as an example to regular staff correspondents. However, after several countries recently expelled correspondents of major news organizations with only lukewarm response, there appeared to be a growing awareness that it is not so difficult to push around the foreign press. Organizations are often reluctant to ask the State Department to join in protesting expulsions because they want to keep themselves separate from government. In some cases, news executives want to keep peace with the government which expelled their correspondent, to make it easier to send a new one. Others, from inertia or lack of a guiding policy, just let the incident go.

The easiest way for a country to control coverage, of course, is simply to deny access. Ronald Koven, foreign editor of the *Washington Post*, negotiated for almost a year to get correspondent David Ottaway into Somalia. "We have the feeling that the Third World is closing down on us, little by little, almost on a monthly basis," Koven said in one of a series of personal interviews I conducted on this subject. "Visas for countries at peace with the United States are sometimes very difficult to get." The *Post*'s widely respected Africa staff is a good example of the problem. Ottaway, along with other reporters, was expelled from Ethiopia, where he had gone when barred from Kenya. Like others, he had serious difficulty obtaining visas to a number of countries. The *Post*'s Robin Wright avoids Angola because she was accused of links with the mercenaries, but few reporters get into Angola anyway. Koven says he does not send reporters to Uganda, even if permitted, for fear of their safety. (The problem is not limited to black Africa. It took years for Jim Hoagland of the *Post* to be allowed back into South Africa after doing his series from there, which won the 1971 Pulitzer Prize.)

When newsmen cannot get into a country, they must write about it from the outside, often relying on questionable dissident sources with little chance to balance their reports with remarks from authorized spokesmen, and the result is likely to cause even more bitterness from the leaders of that country. . . .

Strategies of Control

In addition to individual efforts on the part of Third World governments to manipulate the Western press, Third World leaders have been planning concerted strategies to increase their control over the flow of information.

An extreme move toward press restriction was put forward in a Soviet-sponsored draft resolution at the [1976] Unesco conference . . . in Nairobi. The key sentence in the proposed text—"States are responsible for the activities in the international sphere of all mass media under their jurisdiction"—would have endorsed measures taken against correspondents not only for their own actions inside a given country but also for the actions of their organizations elsewhere. Where authorities have been reluctant to expel reporters or to institute press controls for fear of damaging their international reputation, the sanction of an international body like Unesco could make a significant difference. . . .

At [another Unesco] meeting in Florence . . . discussions, exchanges were sometimes heated and bitter. Unesco's assistant director-general, Jacques Rigaud, identified a major point of contention: "Decolonization must be carried to its conclusion in the minds of men. It is uncomfortable to have to admit that supposedly universal values sometimes conceal a hard core of self-interest." He added later that values that had "for so long given a certain part of the world a clear conscience look different and are different if one is oppressed or well-endowed, developed or developing, or in danger of never developing."

The new feeling was evident in recent remarks by President Ferdinand Marcos of the Philippines, where until recent years the press was extraordinarily free. Marcos told the Philippine Broadcasters Association that there was freedom of speech and freedom of the press in the Philippines just as there was in the Western countries. "The only difference is . . . our policy requires that the media wholly participate in the government . . . as committed agents of the government . . . for development."

The Indonesian press director, Soekarno, was more specific in [a recent] interview with the *Washington Post* . . . : "These critical reports you've all been making lately hamper our speed of development. They draw the attention of the people away from development to other issues which creates frustration . . . if they [Western reporters] employ the Western tradition of hitting issues face-on, they will not achieve their mission [of creating better government]. They must follow the slower, more indirect Indonesian way, or else our government will ban foreign journalists and will ignore their reports." Indonesian Attorney General Ali Said earlier told local editors to stop printing Western news reports on the country. "Let them go to hell," he said.

Leonard Sussman of Freedom House in New York has labeled this concept "developmental journalism." Its thesis is that control of news is not only defensible but essential. Information itself and the means to transmit it are tools of development. Since governments must direct all resources toward the principal goal of development, any reporting that is critical or disruptive might hamper their progress. Governments, it is maintained, must focus attention on their achievements and protect their developing economies from the exposure of weaknesses; critical press coverage might dampen their people's spirits and lessen their chances for world sympathy.

Proponents of a more positive type of developmental journalism say that it is necessary for countries to share useful experiences and ideas which are not now adequately covered. Some liken this kind of journalism to the sort of reporting found in feature sections of Western papers, where readers in Dallas can learn how troublesome community problems were solved in Seattle or Miami. A low-cost housing program in Singapore could be a valuable model for dozens of other nations.

In order to share this sort of information, and to eliminate what many consider to be a Western bias in the information now available, a large number of Third World countries support expanding their own news facilities. The most significant steps in this direction were taken in mid-1976 with a ministerial meeting of fifty-eight nonaligned nations in New Delhi, followed by a summit in Colombo. The summit approved a resolution establishing a Third World news pool as a mechanism to centralize and distribute news items from developing countries around the world. . . .

The pool is already functioning, to a certain extent, with main relay points in Yugoslavia and India. . . . Under its constitution, any nonaligned nation can volunteer to collect and disseminate news from and to other countries provided it pays all reception and relay costs and does not interfere with the content of the incoming dispatches. Tanjug of Yugoslavia has been doing this on its own since January 1975, using four 38,000-watt transmitters outside of Belgrade which were reported to be part of a $13 million expansion program. Similarly, any nation can transmit its news for relay, and can receive relayed news, provided it pays all of its own costs. The framers of the pool arrangement encouraged countries to form national news agencies, if they had not already done so, to facilitate the exchange of news. . . .

At each international conference when news pools are discussed, numerous speakers repeatedly declare that their aim is not to supplant the major global agencies but rather to supplement them. According to this widely held moderate position, Western correspondents would not be affected by the changes developing countries advocate. However, an African ambassador to Unesco bluntly expressed a more radical view: "We don't want Western journalists in our countries. They should take their news from us." The difference is crucial.

Reactions by the West

Western responses to Third World complaints and controls range from defensive antagonism to efforts at expanding cooperation. While there is some sympathy for the benign type of comparative developmental journalism, the more radical variant is rejected out of hand by most Western journalists.

"In part the attacks [on the Western press] are justified

because attention to events is spasmodic and inadequate," observes Harvey Stockwin, a veteran correspondent for the *Far Eastern Economic Review*. "But they stem in large part from the fact that the Western press is the only one telling leaders what they don't want to hear." Western hostility to Third World positions revolves around that basic point: many leaders use such devices as news pools and developmental journalism as a convenient means to muzzle criticism and hide their own shortcomings.

Actual practice has shown this to be a justifiable concern. Where countries have refused access to correspondents but have provided a steady stream of government-vetted information by radio and by national news agencies, coverage has tended to be relatively uncritical and, by lack of balance, misleadingly favorable. This is particularly true in countries where there is not sufficient interest for reporters to seek out exiled opponents or neutral travelers to provide the needed balance.

Since there is some form of government control, subsidy, or guidance in almost every national news agency of the Third World, it would hardly be reasonable to expect completely balanced reporting on a voluntary basis. No government anywhere enjoys energetic probing by the press. . . .

At the [1976] Unesco conference, Western newsmen were vehement in their opposition to the Soviet proposal. George Beebe of the *Miami Herald*, chairman of the World Press Freedom Committee, told reporters in Nairobi that such curbs as the Soviet proposal would be "tragic." He said: "It is essential that we keep communication lines open in this rapidly changing world."

After the April [1977] conference in Florence, Beebe took a harder stance in a column for the *Herald*. He wrote: "The Unesco colloquium . . . convinced delegates from the West that we are fast losing the global war in the field of communications. What was billed as a conference on the 'Free and Balanced Flow of Information,' largely was a series of attacks on the U.S. news agencies and the Western media. This was led by the communists and leftists who exert a great influence on Unesco." Beebe then added: "There were few newspaper-men of stature from over the world. Instead there was a surplus of government officials, news agency representatives and several young radicals. . . . It was the consensus of the Western delegates that the most appropriate word for summarizing the future media outlook is 'frightening'."

Some contend that obstructing the flow of information violates the Universal Declaration of Human Rights.

Speaking for their Western readership, the newsmen make the point that if developed nations are to work cooperatively with developing nations in a new international economic order, they cannot do so in ignorance. As Philip M. Foisie of the *Washington Post* puts it: "We feel it is very important that the American reader and voter is informed by professionals about what is going on in other countries. As one example, if American voters are to spend tax dollars, they have a right to know what is going on."

While most admit inadequacies in their reportage, Western journalists also defend the job they are able to do under the circumstances. Executives emphatically deny any intentional bias or any form of conspiracy against anyone. Gerald Long, managing director of Reuters, noted in an interview that complaints often are made as a result of mistaken information about how news organizations work. He gave the example of an unnamed American ambassador in Africa who once charged that Reuters was guilty of worse distortion than TASS in reporting news from the United States because it transmitted only stories about racial strife. The ambassador was seeing only those few dispatches selected for publication by the local newspapers, a fraction of the complete Reuters report from the United States.

On the general subject, Long commented:

We are sometimes accused of not doing what we have not set out to do. How can you give a complete picture of India, in, say, 3,000 words a day? No, we're not and we can't. . . . We must operate on the principle of news as exception. Reuters tries to give a fair picture, a rounded picture, but we can only send a limited amount, and we must be selective.

With regard to cultural bias, Westerners also point out that most agencies employ nationals to write about their own countries, working in their own languages from the point of view of their own culture. Although most of what Uruguayans read about neighboring Argentina is from the global agencies, for example, the dispatches are almost all written originally in Spanish by Argentines with the idea in mind that they would be read largely by other Latin Americans.

The idea that a Third World news pool might solve some of these problems has been greeted by Western newsmen with a mixture of wariness, sympathy, and skepticism. Most global news agency executives say they have no objection to a Third World pool if the idea is only to supplement the existing reports and not to hamper correspondents' work or to close off markets. Stanley M. Swinton, vice president and director of World Services for the AP, phrased his personal view this way:

My basic theory is the more news the better so long as news from one source is not permitted to squeeze out news from international agencies in a twisted Gresham's Law way. . . . For the international news agencies, it is self-defeating to declare war on the Third World's efforts to intramurally distribute more information.

And according to a disinterested observer, Dr. Jacques Freymond, the Swiss director of the Geneva Institute for Graduate Studies and former vice president of the International Committee of the Red Cross:

This is a normal process of evolution of the Third World. We have been too ethnocentric in our reporting of things. Just as in early France all roads led to the capital in spoke and hub patterns with no connecting links, so it is with the patterns of reporting from these countries. If we resist their doing this [forming a pool], we will force them into an either/or situation; we will force the opposite of what we would want. At the same time, we should try to maintain our world agencies to offer the presence of a pluralistic solution.

Some agencies have offered advice and equipment to new nonaligned agencies, and some retired executives have said they might be available as consultants. In private, however, Western experts generally agree that internal ideological differences, political rivalries, and technical difficulties make it unlikely that any wide-based Third World pool would be functioning effectively soon. In fact, a number of eminent Third World journalists express similar skepticism.

For many, the limited response to Tanjug's efforts has shown that even sympathetic government-controlled papers do not want unwieldy streams of government press releases from other Third World countries unless there is some actual news value. Tanjug relays several hours of pool material daily, but little is used. And if the dispatches touch on the sort of sensitive political and economic issues that are of interest beyond national borders, they are often incomplete and unreliable. Also, many Third World leaders are reluctant to exchange domination by the international agencies for domination by a Third World agency. Already a rivalry has developed between [Yugoslavia and] India for leadership in the pool, and this is widely seen as evidence that some larger Third World countries want to use the pool as a means to exert their own political influence.

"In a river, there are big fish and small fish, and the small fish must beware," observes Elebe Ma Ekonzo, director general of the Zaire Press Agency and former ambassador to Belgium. Elebe prefers smaller regional groupings such as the Pan African agency, but even that, he said in an interview, could take years to organize because of the divisive factors at work.

No Simple Solutions

Obviously, there are no simple solutions to the basic conflicts underlying the Western and Third World approaches to the role of the press. Extremists on both sides must realize that some positions are virtually irreconcilable, and if they are concerned with an improvement they must seek some form of constructive compromise. This is complicated by the character of opposing forces. "Third World" is a convenient term, but it describes little. It covers scores of countries, each with its own national interests and policies. Similarly, there is no common position among news organizations of a single country, much less among all Western countries. Individual editors may become more sensitive, but they are not likely to subscribe to any overall code. With this in mind, there are specific areas where progress might be made.

- Both sides should drop politicized hyperbole and take a reasoned look at realities. At the working level, many of the goals passionately espoused at international meetings were realized long ago. Some are preposterously expensive and impractical. Disinterested experts could compile basic data showing how national and international agencies are already exchanging news, how correspondents operate and what they write, what the news media in developed and developing countries actually use, and what technical and organizational difficulties need to be overcome for further cooperation. A country-by-country survey could detail working conditions of correspondents and the flow of information, including visa restrictions and censorship rules. International discussion should include professional journalists as well as—or instead of—ideology-minded civil servants. Criticisms should be specific, citing particularly objectionable dispatches rather than merely putting forth general ideological condemnations.
- On the basis of realistic information, proponents of the various viewpoints should discuss means of accord and cooperation in private meetings. Such working level sessions as the Tunis conference in November 1976 between European and Arab agencies can provide the means for exchanging criticism and suggestions while preventing frustrations from turning into hostility. There are already scores of joint accords among large and small agencies to share their reporting, and these could be built into a more complete and workable international network.
- A significant Western contribution could be made in several areas. A number of leading American publishers and broadcasters have organized the World Press Freedom Committee—which plans to take in news executives from elsewhere in the

world—to encourage constructive cooperation. The initial proposal is to raise $1 million for several programs, including
training seminars to acquaint Third World journalists with
Western methods, visits by foreign journalists to American
professional meetings, and trips by Western experts to provide
technical assistance. The Committee can also help send Third
World journalists to Western universities. There are other possibilities. Although no agency or news organization has funds
for widescale training, governments could contribute jointly
to an organization which could administer transnational training programs. Cross-cultural training, it should be noted, has
limitations and dangers. Sometimes journalists may be frustrated in trying to apply the techniques of a free press in
countries where there is government control of information.
But a higher level of competence across borders can contribute
significantly to future understanding.

• Finally, Third World authorities must be persuaded to see for
themselves that their interests are enhanced more by cooperating with the Western press than by fighting it. Editors and
officials should use every opportunity to demonstrate that
Western reporting practices do not automatically mean hostility and conspiracy. And, in cases where pressure is applied,
they should protest vigorously at every possible level. News
organizations can use more imagination to find alternative
sources of information when borders are closed. If Third
World leaders can be shown that access to news will be defended—and that all countries will be covered whether or not
reporters are allowed to enter—they are likely to be more reluctant to attempt to manage news. Although much can be
gained by improving Western reporting and paying more attention to Third World viewpoints, Western editors must defend the right to report.

These measures are at least a beginning. Practical cooperation and Western defense of free-flowing information may
not resolve the basic conflict, but they will go a long way
toward ensuring that Americans, Argentines, and Angolans
alike will be more accurately informed about what is happening in their world.

13

Transnational News Agencies: Issues and Policies
JIM RICHSTAD

Richstad's essay deals with a framework of central issues concerning the transnational news agencies which have brought them from relative obscurity to the focal point of the crisis in international news. Dr. Richstad examines how the international agencies are closely related to national communication policies, and how these policies can often hinder the collection of international news. The relationship between internal news flows and policies and the quality of the international flow are examined. The development of strong national news agencies is seen as a key development toward a free and balanced flow, since the international agencies in many respects must rely on them for coverage of news events in their own countries. The movement of the agencies into "information services" is brought up, with questions of the legitimacy of the agencies in the news field.

THE FOCAL POINTS of the crisis in international news in the 1980s are the four major transnational news agencies—how they

An earlier version of this essay was presented to the Conference on Transnational Communication Enterprises and National Communication Policies, Honolulu, August 6–19, 1978.

are operated, owned, and controlled. The agencies are the Associated Press, Reuters, United Press International, and Agence France-Presse.[1] Little attention has been given to the even more predominant television news agencies, Visnews and UPITN. These six news agencies supply the world's mass media—print and broadcast—with most of their international news. Because of this, they exercise vast influence over the global news agenda.

Together, these agencies employ thousands of persons and have bureaus or offices in more than 100 countries. Their correspondents and stringers and reporter/camera teams number in the hundreds, and they control sophisticated, high-speed transmission facilities and make extensive use of communication satellites. The six agencies collect and disseminate millions of words and thousands of feet of newsfilm daily, to all parts of the world. They share a common stated goal to provide impartial, comprehensive, international news services. They operate in many languages, using English and French predominantly, and they have agreements with virtually all the national news agencies for the exchange of news.

Among news agencies, AP is undisputedly the largest. A *New York Times* report on the U.S. agency said:

The AP is a global giant whose reach wraps around the world and whose muscle is so vast that it cannot be measured. But it is a strangely anonymous giant and the millions of readers and viewers who unknowingly rely on it for most of their news about the nation and the world would be hard pressed to detail very much about it.[2]

1. The Soviet Union's Telegrafnoye Agentstvo Sovietskovo Soyuza (TASS) and China's Hsinhua are not included in the listing of global news agencies, although they share many of the characteristics of the "Big Four." Both agencies, however, are official government organizations. They rarely are judged by the same standards or get into the same kinds of controversies as the Western agencies, and they do not measure significantly in the global flow of news. They have the potential, however, of increasing their global importance, and present some balance to Western reports, at least in certain areas. Unesco is always careful to include TASS in its "Big Five" news agencies.

2. Deirdre Carmody, "The Associated Press is Developing Broader Perceptions of What Is News," *New York Times*, June 1, 1976.

After many years of relative anonymity, the agencies have suddenly become the center of worldwide political and academic attention. Stanley Swinton, head of World Services for AP, said the

attention is overdue. Only a few in the communications field and almost none of the general public understand the social role, the operative procedures, or even the history of the news agencies. It is a fascinating and important story. The Chinese invented the news agency, just as China invented gunpowder, and perhaps in the long history of man the news agency will turn out ultimately to have had more explosive effects over a longer historical period than even gunpowder now that we are going on to more disastrous explosives.[3]

From this attention in the 1970s, many factors began to emerge which increasingly led Third World critics to question the power and influence of the transnational news agencies. Under particular attack was the "free flow of information" policy and the qualitative and quantitative imbalances in the global flow of news.[4]

Concurrently, there came equally urgent demands from developing countries to mobilize or organize their domestic communication systems to support economic and social development, national unity and stability, and cultural preservation. As a framework to help achieve both the international and domestic objectives in communication, national communication policies were promoted by Unesco. Since most developing countries have few means and little power to influence the world news flow, national communication policies focused on national control. This caused great concern among Western media interests, who feared government control of the inflow and outflow of international news, through limiting access to official sources, visa restrictions, and other means. While the particular situation in a given country varies widely,

3. Stanley Swinton, in a public talk as part of the Jefferson Fellow Program at the East-West Communication Institute, Honolulu, June 14, 1979.

4. Herbert I. Schiller, "Freedom from the 'Free Flow,'" *Journal of Communication* (Winter 1974), 24:1.

the relationship of the flow of news through international agencies and national communication policies is important.

A new element affecting the role of international news agencies is the replacement in policy terms of the "free flow" principle with the "free flow and wider and better balanced dissemination of information." The policy statement is in the compromise Mass Media Declaration, adopted in November 1978 by the Unesco General Conference.[5] Exactly what the terms "wider and better balanced dissemination" will mean to transnational news agencies operations will become clearer over the years and through content study. The new phrase represents a clear departure from the post-1945 period when free flow was seen as virtually the only operating principle for the flow of international news.

This statement from Sean MacBride, who chaired the Unesco-initiated International Commission for the Study of Communication Problems, reflects the growing worldwide concern over responsibility for the kind of news people receive:

It is obvious that communication in the world today—in all its forms and at all levels—is vital to building a more humane, more just and more prosperous world tomorrow. Hence, I firmly believe the news agencies and media bear a heavy responsibility to inform the peoples of the world about the urgency and magnitude of the problems facing humanity.[6]

In general, the news agencies have responded to such comments by arguing that their services are simply the best available in a less than ideal world where pressures of speed,

5. The formal title of the Mass Media Declaration is "Declaration of Fundamental Principles Concerning the Contributions of the Mass Media to Strengthening Peace and International Understanding, the Promotion of Human Rights and to Countering Racialism, Apartheid and Incitement to War." See appendix F for full text of declaration.

6. Sean MacBride, "Opening Statement," International Seminar on the Infrastructures of News Collection and Dissemination in the World, a meeting in Stockholm conducted by the International Commission for the Study of Communication Problems, April 24–27, 1978.

accuracy, and balance are great. Associated Press's Swinton has argued:

man is imperfect, and news agencies by their nature are even more imperfect. Limitations of time, wordage, and editorial space make any news story a synthesis. Yet I think the critics of news agencies might well note one point: the Western news agencies have greater credibility globally than any other source.[7]

The three overriding concerns—the impact of and control over the international flow, and the use of communication resources—will continue to guide debate over transnational news agencies and the flow of news. Another major area of concern is the research needed for informed policy on international news. One of the frustrating aspects of the 1970s debate was that there was little hard data on the flow of news. In the past several years, however, many studies have been conducted, and the data on the quantitative flow from the industrialized countries to the developing countries has demonstrated the imbalance. Now, more sophisticated studies of news flow—especially ones dealing with the content on a qualitative basis—are needed and underway.

Out of these studies and numerous conferences, debates, and articles have come several widely accepted points concerning the flow of news and the transnational news agencies. While these are understood to be in terms of degree, they all have at least a substantial level of consensus or identify areas where there are clear differences in values.

1. The control of the international flow of news is essentially in the hands of six transnational communication enterprises with headquarters and policy control in three countries of the highly industrialized world—specifically the United States, Britain, and France, with Canada, Australia, and New Zealand sharing some of the British-based control.

2. There is a clear quantitative imbalance in the flow of news that is processed by the international news agencies, with a high proportion of the news about events or activities

7. Swinton, Jefferson Fellow Program.

in the essentially Western, industrialized world, and consequently less about other countries, particularly developing countries. Some recent studies, however, indicate the pattern may be changing.

3. The flow of news between the developed and developing world is largely one-way, with a high quantitative imbalance. Much more news flows from the industrialized world to the developing world than the other way, and much more international news of the industrialized world occupies space in Third World media than the other way. Again, this may be a changing pattern.

4. There is relatively little flow among the developing countries. Efforts toward news exchanges, the Nonaligned News Pool, and recent empirical evidence indicate this imbalance is lessening and is not entirely the result of the transnational news agencies' actions.[8]

5. Financially, the major consumers of the news provided by the agencies are in the Western countries, and hence the content of their news is designed for the Western market or audiences. The Associated Press, for example, receives only 1 percent of its revenues from subscribers in developing countries.[9]

6. After some initial Western suspicion and confrontation, there now seems wide agreement that the national news agencies and the News Agencies Pool of Nonaligned Countries offer means to improve the flow of news for the developing and developed countries. There is cooperation in development of national news agencies and at least token support for the

---

8. Wilbur Schramm, "International News Wires and Third World News in Asia." Paper for the conference on "The International News Media and the Developing World," April 2–5, 1978, Cairo. A version of this paper is included in this volume.

See also, Robert L. Stevenson, Richard R. Cole, and Donald Lewis Shaw, "Patterns of World News Coverage: A Look at the Unesco Debate on the 'New World Information Order'." Paper for the Association for Education in Journalism convention, Boston, August 1980; David H. Weaver, G. Cleveland Wilhoit, Robert L. Stevenson, Donald Lewis Shaw, and Richard R. Cole, "The News of the World in Four Major Wire Services." Paper for inclusion in the final report of the "Foreign Images" project of the International Association for Mass Communication Research for Unesco, 1980.

9. Swinton, Jefferson Fellow Program.

nonaligned pool by Western news agencies and governments. There remain many critical views of this development, and many professional journalists in and out of the Third World who see little achievement by the pool.[10]

There are many other important concerns on the issue of the flow of news, with varying degrees of support. They are evolving areas which require continued study, research, and dialogue. Several of them follow.

7. There is an awareness that to some degree the home country government and private business interests and politics influence the way international news is gathered, processed, and distributed. While this point is made repeatedly by news flow critics, the news agencies and others deny it, and evidence is hard to find.[11]

8. There are many critics, especially but not exclusively from a socialist viewpoint, who stress the commercial or market nature of the international news agencies, and they contend that this influences the news flow in ways that are detrimental not only to Third World countries but to all countries. Imbalance in the flow of news, for example, is viewed as a serious problem to the United States understanding of the world, particularly of the non-Western world.

9. Aside from the quantitative imbalances in the international flow of news, increasing concerns are expressed over the *qualitative* content of the news. This includes the concentration in coverage on certain subjects that are viewed as essentially of interest to the developed world but of little interest or even destructive to much of the rest of the world. It also includes the absence of news of interest to Third World countries—positive news on economic and social development matters.

10. Herbert I. Schiller, "Cultural Domination Adjusts to the Growing Demand for a New International Information Order." Paper for meeting on International Communication and Third World Participation: A Conceptual and Practical Framework, September 5–8, 1977, Amsterdam; Phil Harris, "A Third World News Deal? Part Two: Behind the Smokescreen," *Index on Censorship* (September/October 1977), 6(5):27–34.

11. For an example of how government policy can influence news coverage, see Ron Tiffen, "Australian Press Coverage of the Third World," *The Australian and New Zealand Journal of Sociology* (February 1976), 12(1):9–13.

10. One major factor often overlooked by news agencies critics is the limited resources given to the immense task of covering the world. The job is far beyond the resources of the transnational news agencies.[12] The discussion over flow of news should include an awareness of these limited resources involved and perhaps efforts to increase them. The largest of the four transnational news agencies, for example, ran on revenues of about $112 million in 1978.[13] For simple comparison purposes, the University of Hawaii, in a U.S. state with a population of less than one million persons, spends about 50 percent more each year than does the entire Associated Press global and domestic service. IBM, one of the largest communication transnationals, has annual sales of about $18 billion. So, while the Associated Press is the largest of the international news agencies, it is relatively small in the broader fields of education and communication enterprises. In numbers of employees, the comparisons are about the same. An AP field man can still express amazement at the small number of persons who run the AP foreign operations in its New York headquarters.[14] The transnational news agencies have influence far beyond that indicated by their relatively small business size.

11. Despite the relatively small-scale operations of the transnational news agencies, the gap between them and the smaller services, and particularly the national news agencies, is vast. Asok Mitra, an Indian scholar, says there is an imbal-

12. AP's Swinton said, "It is simply impossible to have a bureau, or even a staff correspondent, in Togo and Cameroons and all the small nations around the world, let alone the San Marinos, the Monacos, and the Andorras." Swinton, Jefferson Fellow Program.

13. Revenue figure is in "News Media Offered U.P.I. Partnerships," *New York Times*, September 23, 1979.

14. John Edlin, *AP Log*, July 24, 1978, and George Krimsky, "World Services: AP's Export Division," *AP Log*, January 19, 1981, p. 1. Krimsky says: "Visitors to APW (AP World Services) are often surprised at the relatively small size of a department that distributes news with the potential of reaching perhaps half the human race at a given moment. We have 29 staffers for around-the-clock service. But, like the General Desk, APW is an editing and control point and not primarily a news-originating department. Secondly, most overseas bureaus have the same capability as U.S. hubs to protect their own areas with regionals. New York is thus free to handle the main stories."

ance and growing gap between the international news agencies and the national news agencies.[15] The West predominates in news production and distribution resources, and its concentration of labor, capital, and technology far exceeds that of most national news agencies. A Thomson Foundation course to improve national news agencies concluded that the quality of the agencies news reports needs improvement: their material is too long, too late, badly written, and designed more for government officials than ordinary readers.[16]

Phil Harris, a critical British media researcher, sees the dominance by the Western agencies as stunting the potential of the national news agencies. "With their superior financial resources, with their computerized communications technology, with their massive corps of correspondents located worldwide, and with their services being beamed twenty-four hours a day to the farthest corners of the globe, these four news agencies have a monopoly of worldwide transmission of news and information."[17] Many of the proposed solutions to the problems of international news concern, of course, the development of strong, better national news agencies and the expansion of South-South information exchanges and telecommunication linkages among developing countries.

The concerns listed above are those of the U.N. system and the Third World generally. A closely related set of concerns has been generated by the international news agencies themselves, and involves the difficulties and dangers they experience in their operations. Basically, there has been strong concern for several years over the treatment of journalists and over the journalists' ability to gain access to information sources and to travel to the scene of news events. The Associated Press, for example, said the major obstacles it faces in the collection of news "are restricted access, explicit or im-

15. Asok Mitra, Keynote Address, Conference on Information Imbalance in Asia, Colombo, April 21–26, 1975.

16. Thomson Foundation, "Strengthening the National News Agency." Report on a specialist training course for senior staff of Third World news agencies, Cardiff, September 19–December 8, 1977.

17. Harris, "Third World News Deal."

plicit censorship and pressure against correspondents, extending in some cases as far as expulsion. . . . The most serious and widespread of these constraints is the inability to gain entry for professionally qualified AP representatives."[18]

The 1978 Mass Media Declaration, while it did not explicitly mention the transnational news agencies, dealt in several of its articles with the difficulties of journalists obtaining news. Concern over the safety of journalists was another major emphasis of the declaration, and the issue was vigorously discussed during the MacBride Commission deliberations but dropped from the final report because special status for journalists could lead to licensing. The final report also said "free access to news sources by journalists is an indispensable requirement for accurate, faithful and balanced reporting. This necessarily involves access to unofficial, as well as official sources of information, that is, access to the entire spectrum of opinion in any country."[19]

The problem goes beyond the correspondents to the news media in the various countries. When such media are themselves under close government control and other pressures, it is difficult for foreign correspondents to know accurately what is going on, and hence it is difficult for them to report to the rest of the world with adequate context and accuracy.

Extreme forms of pressure include beatings, jailings, humiliations, and even assassinations. A 1979 example was the on-film deliberate killing of a U.S. television correspondent who was covering the civil war in Nicaragua. Another example, one of many from the Iran situation of 1979–81, was the expulsion of many Western correspondents because of the nature of their reporting. Expulsion or nonadmittance of correspondents is a common tactic, and often serves to reduce the flow of news. Recent examples include events in Cambodia, Poland, and Afghanistan. Although correspondents are

18. Associated Press, "Monograph on the Associated Press (1977). Prepared at the Request of Unesco," January 1, 1978.

19. International Commission for the Study of Communication Problems. *Many Voices, One World: Communication and Society Today and Tomorrow* (London: Kogan Page, 1980), p. 263

not without means to learn about events under these circumstances, the danger is that their stories will be incomplete, biased, and inaccurate, since more distant and often less reliable sources are used.

Internal policies and practices of news gathering are expressions of national communication policies, and can have a direct impact on the quality and quantity of news that enters the international flow. Over recent years, for example, almost every country in Asia has declared martial law or emergency rule, or has followed political policies designed to ensure noncritical news coverage or no coverage at all. The transnational news agencies and other foreign correspondents were faced with a choice: Conform to the national policy, evade it, or depart. The reaction was not uniform. Some agencies decided it was more important to maintain complete editorial control over their work, and others, equally dedicated to journalism, decided it was more important to maintain continued representation in the countries involved. This particular issue caught world attention in late 1979 with the airing of an interview of an American hostage in Iran over the U.S. television network NBC, after the other two major networks, ABC and CBS, rejected offers from Iran to conduct interviews, citing the conditions the Iranians imposed.[20]

The international agencies are also concerned over the lack of knowledge among government officials and others of how the agencies operate, the professional and other constraints that affect them, and the expectations over what they can or should do. Gerald Long, the former chief of Reuters, stresses the magnitude of the problem in giving "a rounded picture of events," using India as an example. "The major difficulty in reporting India is India. It is a country of vast size, with an enormous population. Who knows in India, what is happening in India?" He says if the international news agencies are criticized because they don't report the whole truth, "they are being criticized for something which they have

20. *Facts on File*, 1979, p. 934 A3; *New York Times*, December 11, 1979, p. A1, A17; *New York Times*, editorial, December 12, 1979, p. A30.

never claimed to do and could never do." Long acknowledges the practice of "journalism of exception," although noting Reuters is trying to broaden its reporting.[21] Former UPI editor-in-chief Roger Tatarian, among others, has noted that relations between the West and the Third World are complicated by basic differences over what news is or should be:

In the developed countries of the West, the definition of news most often gives high importance to the immediacy of the event, to change, to the unexpected, to departures from the commonplace and from normalcy. Sudden change therefore usually commands greater attention and emphasis than slow, evolutionary change. The Western agencies assuredly do not ignore evolutionary change but an examination of their daily files will show where the emphasis of coverage is.[22]

The difficulties involved in reporting events around the globe that Long and Tatarian talk about focus attention on the apparently growing importance of the national news agencies, and their links with the international agencies. The importance of the national news agency in the international flow of news—both into and out of the agency's country—is well recognized. Rosenblum said the international agencies subscribe to scores of national agencies, "forming a layered global network almost too complex to plot accurately. . . . The national news services, where they exist, are principal sources for the international agencies."[23]

Swinton also stressed the key role of the national news agencies. He said the national agencies will continue to grow, and will be the main news suppliers for smaller media units. The larger media organizations, however, prefer to have news

21. "Reuters Chief Defends Western Coverage of Third World Countries," *IPI Report* (November 1976).

22. Roger Tatarian, "The Multinational News Agency." Commissioned by the Edward R. Murrow Center of Public Diplomacy, The Fletcher School of Law and Diplomacy, Tufts University, for Feasibility Conference in New York, September 12–14, 1979, p. 2.

23. Mort Rosenblum, "The Western Wire Services and the Third World," in Philip C. Horton, ed., *The Third World and Press Freedom* (New York: Praeger, 1978), p. 105.

service directly from the international agencies. The national news agencies, Swinton said, can cover their own countries in a way that the Associated Press or other transnationals simply cannot afford to do. The national agencies also play a critical role in overcoming language differences.[24]

Reliance on national news agencies has its problems. The national agencies, for various reasons, may not be able to report certain events or developments. Almost without exception, they are politically controlled. The agencies also tend to over-cover the capital areas and underreport the countryside.

The close link between the transnational and the national news agencies—with a tremendous variation in particular arrangements—clearly shows the important relationship between the internal communication systems and national policies, and the operations of the global news systems. This relationship shows that the flow of information within countries should be an integral part of the debate about the international flow—that one affects the other, and cannot be separated.

The imbalances resulting within countries have a bearing on the international flow issues. Indian journalist George Verghese, a member of the MacBride Commission, lists three internal imbalances in the flow of news: (1) between urban and rural areas; (2) between elite and masses; (3) between traditional and modern groups.[25] While there is a strong rationale for looking at the entire range of the flow of news—international and national and even to the community and individual levels—some argue that the international flow should be treated separately, as part of international relations. MacBride says "there is an obvious link between communication on the national and international levels. To isolate one from the other, to treat them separately, as often happens, would not only be a mistake, but is really impossible." He says that many of the complaints and criticisms on the inter-

24. Stanley Swinton, remarks made during Jefferson Fellow Program seminars at the East-West Communication Institute, Honolulu, June 14, 1979.

25. George Verghese, remarks in Working Group I, Seminar on the Infrastructures of News Collection and Dissemination in the World, International Commission for the Study of Communication Problems, Stockholm, April 25, 1978.

national level about monopolies, transnationals, imbalances, and cultural concerns are "certainly connected with what is often taking place inside various countries."[26]

Until recently, there was little attention in the United States—with an open communication system largely run by private interests—to comprehensive communication policy. With the growing controversies over the flow of international communication, however, and as the home country of two of the four major news agencies and involved with one of the television news agencies, the United States found itself without a clear policy to meet the many questions being raised in international forums. George Kroloff, as early observer of these events, feels it is still difficult for the United States to develop a domestic policy but that it can develop an international communication policy.[27]

A largely understudied area of policy research concerns the operations of the transnational news agencies themselves. While many of the news agency executives, such as Swinton and Long, feel the operations of their agencies are little understood by critics, or the public, others feel the agencies themselves put a professional cloak over many of their operations.

Another important development of the late seventies and early eighties is the gradual transformation of the transnational news agencies into transnational information services. Reuters, with about 80 percent of its operations devoted to business and information services, probably leads the way. UPI has recently become involved with the home computer business by supplying information for use by the Telecomputing Corporation of America. H. L. Stevenson, vice president and editor in chief of UPI, said: "We think of ourselves as an information service, not just a news agency. We are looking

26. Sean MacBride, Inaugural Presidential Address, International Commission for the Study of Communication Problems, Unesco, Paris, 1977.

27. George Kroloff, remarks at U.S. National Commission for Unesco Conference Toward an American Agenda for a New World Order for Communications, Athens, Georgia, December 12–15, 1979. His earlier observations are in: George Kroloff and Scott Cohen, "The New World Information Order." Report to the Committee on Foreign Relations, United States Senate, November 1977.

at other markets where we can take that basic information that we have gathered and utilize it."[28] The AP's Swinton also makes it clear: "The whole field is moving to information." The news agencies, by shifting into commercially based information services rather than focusing on news service, certainly move themselves closer to areas that are less strongly protected under free expression principles and traditions, and where their legitimacy as international news agencies can be challenged.

While recognizing that great changes are underway or have already occurred, the strength of the transnational news agencies remains strong, partly because there is no other single source that can provide the world news. Boyd-Barrett, while noting the growth of national and regional services, says "There is no strong evidence to suggest that over time the quantitative importance of the 'Big Four' agencies has diminished."[29]

The shape and character of the debate over the transnational news agencies and the flow of news has rapidly evolved over the past few years into one of the most important international policy questions. The major issues have been identified and documented, and a wide range of needs and views have been heard. Some changes have taken place, with the development of practical, professional cooperation between news agencies of the developing world and the transnational news agencies. This pragmatic cooperation does not, of course, greatly affect what are often fundamental, even irreconcilable differences in values and ideology over such questions as news values, the role of the press in reporting other societies, and the relationship of the press and governments. There still remains the great problem of securing sufficient resources for the collection, processing, and dissemination of news at the

28. "News Media Offered U.P.I. Partnerships," *New York Times*, September 23, 1979.

29. Oliver Boyd-Barrett, *The International News Agencies*. (London: Constable, 1980), p. 18. Boyd-Barrett's book provides a much-needed current look at the transnational news agencies, in the context of Third World concerns.

transnational and national levels. As the transnational news agencies seek to meet the changing needs of world news and at the same time create financially stable bases in the emerging information services, the questions of political and financial legitimacy will be matters of continuing policy concern.

14

Worldwide News Agencies—Private Wholesalers of Public Information
JEREMY TUNSTALL

*In his essay on the international news agencies as "private whole-
salers of public information," media critic Tunstall recognizes that
the Third World critique of the news agencies has considerable validity. But he emphasizes that these organizations are, in fact, relatively small and weak. The thrust of his analysis is that economics—
not political pressure—seems to be shaping the news agencies' somewhat bleak future as stable, global news endeavors. He argues that
their international operations do not produce great amounts of revenue and that of the big four agencies, only AP, a nonprofit cooperative, seems secure. Professor Tunstall predicts that one or two of
the four giants may even cease worldwide news distribution.*

If his assessment proves accurate, the news crisis might soon

Jeremy Tunstall is a British communication scholar and sociologist at the City University, London. He wrote *The Media Are American* and other books and articles on
journalism.

This essay is from an article for the Pacific Sociological Association meeting,
Anaheim, California, April 4–7, 1979.

*take on a new direction, as First and Third Worlds join forces to
ensure through subsidy and other means that the transnational news
agencies do not disappear, to the detriment of everyone.*

THE THIRD WORLD critique of the Western international
news agencies has considerable empirical validity. Two American agencies (Associated Press and United Press International), one British agency (Reuters) and one French agency
(Agence France-Presse) do indeed dominate the international
flow of news in all the non-Communist countries of the world.
Only about twenty newspapers and perhaps ten radio/televi-
sion networks in these same countries make a serious attempt
to gather much of their own foreign news; not one single news
organization in Africa, South America, or South Asia makes
a serious attempt to gather its own foreign news. Even a U.S.
television network like NBC relies heavily on AP and UPI for
initial information even on domestic stories. . . .[1]

A key reason for the continuing strength of the four Western agencies is that they have legitimacy—even in Third World
countries. The typical Third World country prefers to buy
foreign news from London or New York, with all its imperfections, rather than from a neighboring country.

Any government needs a digest of what other governments
around the world are saying and thinking; central banks require international financial news, and those newspapers and
radio/television stations which want foreign news must take
it from the least worst supply which is available. This is the
Western news agencies.

Part of the bitterness in the Third World critique may arise
from the recognition that there is no viable alternative. Seen
from the Third World, also, the four Western international
agencies—with their considerable similarities—look like an all
powerful cartel. But the inadequate coverage of the Third
World is a symptom of weakness, not of strength, and of "excessive" competition more than of cartel.

1. Edward Jay Epstein. *News From Nowhere* (New York: Vintage, 1974), p. 142.

"International" News Agencies?

The four Western news agencies are "international" only in their sphere of operations; each is securely based in, and controlled from, a single country. Each agency tends to be strongest in its home nation's traditional sphere of interest—the U.S. agencies in Latin America[2] and Reuters in former British imperial areas of Africa and Asia. Each agency aims for homogeneity of outlook and deliberately reflects the values of its home nation. All the agencies gear their operations toward marketing news to customers—they provide primarily what their most lucrative markets in the U.S. and Western Europe want. All four engage in fierce competition with each other. These news agencies have always been technological innovators and their present operations make heavy use of computers, satellites, and other modern methods of rapid data transmission processing and display.

Home market dependence is illustrated by its significance as a revenue source. Reuters is atypical in obtaining less than twenty percent of its revenue from Britain.[3] Both AP and UPI get at least seventy-five percent of their revenue from within the United States. The French agency gets a similarly high proportion of its revenue from France.

Public Information

These Western agencies have four main sources from which they collect information, and the same four also constitute the agencies' main customers for information.

2. An excellent description of international news agency activities which gives special attention to Latin America is: Al Hester, "International News Agencies," in Alan Wells, ed., *Mass Communications: A World View* (Palo Alto: National Press Books, 1974), pp. 207–26.

3. In 1976–77 Reuters obtained 17 percent of its revenue from Britain, 18 percent from the U.S.A. and Canada, 46 percent from Europe, and 19 percent from the rest of the world (Africa, Asia, Australia and Latin America). Anthony Robinson, "Metamorphosis in the Media," *Financial Times* (London) November 18, 1977.

1. *News media,* primarily newspapers but also radio/television stations are the most obvious customers of agencies; and newspapers, especially, are also the leading source from which information is collected in a foreign country.
2. *National news agencies* have a similar two-way relationship with international agencies. In many Third World countries, the Western agencies are not allowed to distribute to news media directly, but must distribute via a national agency. Often this national agency supplies its domestic service to the Western agency's local bureau in partial payment for the Western agency's world service.
3. *Governments*—typically the presidency and the foreign relations department—take international agency services. Governments, several studies indicate, are also the source of a high proportion of agency foreign news stories.
4. *Banks and other financial institutions* are also major customers, and for the British agency, Reuters, the predominant source of revenue. For both Reuters Economic Services and for AP-Dow Jones, financial institutions are obviously also the main source of information. This is the oldest sphere of agency operations—the two original international agencies, Havas and Reuters, both supplied stock market data before they had any newspaper customers.

The four Western agencies thus act as international go-betweens for newspapers in different countries, for news agencies, for banks, as well as go-betweens for governments. Foreign relations departments have their own diplomats and embassies upon which to rely. But for diplomats, the international agencies provide the basic service of fast news; and as the only supply of fast information . . . all the players in the world diplomatic game . . . hold in common, the international agencies inevitably play a large part in updating and setting the diplomatic agenda. Moreover, "these agencies do not merely play a major part in establishing the agenda, but they have done so now for a hundred years."[4]

Third World governments, which have fewer diplomats,

4. Jeremy Tunstall, *The Media Are American* (New York: Columbia University Press, 1977), p. 45.

foreign embassies, and reporting resources, paradoxically must rely more heavily on the Western agencies than do the U.S., British, and French governments. In the Third World also, where governments often directly own banks, news agencies, radio/television networks, and often newspapers as well, the Western agencies are dealing primarily with government both when collecting and when supplying information.

A Deviant Case of News Organization

One critique of the Western agencies is that, despite claims of neutrality and objectivity, they inevitably reflect the values and interests of their home countries. There is clearly some validity in this criticism. But normal Western news values, and the need to market news in many different foreign countries, ensure that these Western agencies must distribute around the world large quantities of negative news about their home countries. No two news organizations dispersed more news around the world about American failures in Vietnam than did AP and UPI. The fullest chronicler to the world audience of Britain's recent economic ills has been British agency Reuters. This, then, is a type of organization which relatively few governments in the world would want to have based on home soil. These agencies constitute a mix of commercial, governmental, political, and prestige elements which is unusual even for a news organization.

As news organizations, these agencies lack the most common sources of news organization revenue—no advertising, no mass market sales, no license fee (the major means by which television is financed in many countries).

Unlike most news organizations, these agencies, in their worldwide operations, have no single main deadline, nothing comparable to the first edition of the newspaper or the main evening news of the television network. These agencies operate a continuing moving belt, or a number of moving belts, of news around the world.

In some respects, computerization has made these organizations into extreme examples of centralization. But in other respects, computerization has led to flexibility and local control. Foreign bureaus can now code whole stories, and parts of stories, for particular destinations. A correspondent in Australia can code a particular story for, say, the Scandinavian capitals, and it may go automatically and unedited to these capitals via the computer in Reuters' head office in London. Clients also can increasingly choose stories to suit their own requirements.

The Revenue Against Legitimacy Dilemma

In their international operations, all four agencies face a central dilemma. These *international* operations do not produce much revenue—something in the $25 to $30 million a year range[5] in 1979—and costs are rising; yet the whole operation depends heavily upon legitimacy and it is difficult to develop new sources of revenue without very seriously risking legitimacy.

Havas and Reuters were both nineteenth century business buccaneers, primarily interested in making money. Not only did Havas start with stock exchange information, but Havas right up to 1940 always diversified its operations and exerted much of its power in France by being both a news agency and the leading advertising agency in France. This dual dominance during the 1930s came increasingly to be seen as both commercially and politically corrupt, and when after World War II, the French agency was reconstituted as Agence France-Presse, it was as a news agency alone. How was a French worldwide news agency to be financed? AFP has been sub-

5. It was estimated that AP's annual revenue in 1976 was $100 million (80 percent in the U.S.A.). UPI's revenue in 1976 was about $70 million (again about 80 percent in the U.S.A.). Agence France-Presse had 1976 revenue of $43 million and Reuters about $80 million (82 percent from economic news). "The News from Reuters," *The Economist* (London) October 29, 1977, pp. 72–3.

sidized by the French governments; all French government departments and embassies are compelled to take the AFP service, thus providing over half the agency's total revenue. AFP is widely regarded as a French governmental agency and this certainly reduces its legitimacy. AFP's reputation for providing an interestingly distinctive news service is closely identified with the French government's reputation for having an interestingly distinctive foreign policy; in the long run, this reputation could collapse. Moreover, some future French government may discontinue the subsidy and thus AFP's world service.

The United States agencies have handled the revenue-legitimacy dilemma in a different way. They have been fortunate in the large number of small yet affluent customers provided primarily by the daily newspaper press of the United States. These domestic newspapers still provide the bulk of both AP and UPI revenue. Both American agencies have diversified successfully into other forms of news—mainly wirephoto and special services for radio and television. The Associated Press has achieved the strongest diversification within the news field because AP-Dow Jones puts it internationally into partnership in the strongest traditional form of agency news (financial data) and with a financially strong American newspaper (The Wall Street Journal), and gives it a powerful position in providing general (not specialized) financial news in a form suitable for domestic U.S. news media. AP is the strongest world agency in another sense as well. The Associated Press—in its various manifestations over the last century—has always been a cooperative, relatively independent of the fortunes of any single enterprise.

UPI, on the other hand, is owned by a newspaper group (Scripps-Howard) and it could one day suffer the same fate as International News Service (INS) which was owned, and eventually closed, by Hearst. UPI is also generally agreed to charge less for its services and to have fewer of the more affluent morning newspapers among its clients (the large U.S. newspapers now all take both AP and UPI). UPI has tried to follow

AP's diversification into financial news, but on a much smaller scale.

While the American agencies have restricted their diversification largely to news and have thus preserved their legitimacy as *news* agencies, Reuters has recently diversified deeply into types of information which are unsuitable for media use; this deep involvement in financial data makes Reuters' strategy much the most risky both as business investment and in terms of risking its legitimacy as a news agency. When the American agencies made their challenge in the first decades of the twentieth century, Reuters lacked Havas' cushioning of advertising revenue and power. Reuters became dangerously dependent on the British government in both world wars. In the mid-1960s, Reuters made a decision to diversify heavily into financial news. This diversification has increasingly switched towards the provision of financial data to banks, stockbrokers, and commodity dealers—one of Reuters services has in recent years, in effect, created an electronic "market floor" for international currency dealings. Reuters' most lucrative market is Western Europe, but it has also entered more deeply into the U.S. domestic market in specialized financial data.

One of the legitimacy problems was illustrated in September 1977 when the chief editor of Reuters World Service resigned in protest at a set of developments which had led to Reuters news agency only getting 18 percent of its total revenue from media news. There are two other aspects of Reuters which together with this dominance of financial data must ultimately threaten its legitimacy as a world news agency. One is that the British national and provincial press, which owns 83 percent of Reuters, is now itself, as the result of a series of takeovers and mergers in the last decade, now largely owned by oil companies, conglomerates, and other companies whose main activities lie outside the media.

Reuters is the leading single news agency in Africa, the Middle East, and in South Asia. Afro-Asian criticisms of the Western agencies thus must inevitably focus upon Reuters more than upon any other single agency. Reuters must be vulnerable to the accusation that it is more interested in selling financial data to stockbrokers than in providing news for news media and that it is ultimately owned not by news organizations, but by oil companies and conglomerates.

Of the four Western international news agencies, the Associated Press is the only one which seems to have solved the revenue-legitimacy problem in a fairly permanent and consistent way. UPI, Agence France-Presse, and Reuters have all been relatively unsuccessful at solving this revenue-legitimacy dilemma. It must be highly possible that the four Western international agencies will be reduced to three and then, because the third agency would become relatively much weaker, to two.

Future News Agencies and World Media

In the future, the mass media will exist on three levels: (a) an international level dominated by United States media with mainly British assistance; (b) very local media appearing in provincial areas, in local languages—such as local newspapers and radio stations—and little influenced by the international media; (c) an intermediate level of mainly national media, partly peculiar to the country in question, partly influenced by the international media.

News agencies will probably fall into a similar pattern: (a) perhaps only two remaining international news agencies, of which one will be AP; (b) very local news agencies; (c) national news agencies which will continue as now to supply news to, and distribute the news of, the international agencies. However, within this category of national agencies, there is already one—Kyodo of Japan—that gathers nearly all of its own foreign news; and there are several others such as DPA (West Germany), Tanjug (Yugoslavia), ANSA (Italy), EFE (Spain), and MENA (Egypt) which have substantial teams of foreign correspondents and sell their services to some foreign media customers. We may well see an expansion of this category of more-than-national but less-than-international news agencies. These stronger national agencies will, of course, tend to appear in the countries with the strongest national media, where the international agencies previously had their best paying clients. This latter is another reason why the revenue of the present four international news agencies may be under increasing threat.

News Agencies and the Issues: Comments from the Transnational News Agencies

AGENCE FRANCE-PRESSE (AFP)
THE ASSOCIATED PRESS (AP)
REUTERS
UNITED PRESS INTERNATIONAL (UPI)
VISNEWS

One of the persistent complaints of the global news agencies is that their operations and problems are not well understood by Third World critics of news flow. This collection of comments by officials of the five major global news agencies, taken from a variety of sources, is designed to put forth the news agencies view on certain aspects of the international news system. Not all agree, as Gerald Long notes, that there is a news crisis at all.

In addition to the "Big Four" Western news agencies, the world's largest television news agency, Visnews, is included.

Correspondents Face Obstacles
AGENCE FRANCE-PRESSE (AFP)

BY AND LARGE, correspondents encounter—at the official level at least—few obstacles.

An exception must naturally be made in the case of censorship applied in time of war (Lebanon, 1977).

However, it is sometimes difficult to obtain visas for countries in which the Agency is not represented; in other cases, visas may be granted belatedly.

In countries in which it is represented, the Agency's correspondents all too frequently fail to obtain information, even official information, for lack of sources and contacts.

In too many countries, such information as can be obtained is of a purely political nature, and quite inadequate as far as economic and cultural affairs—precisely those which international agencies are taxed with neglecting—are concerned.

In some countries, travel by correspondents is subject to conditions (authorization, payment in certain currencies) that make it difficult if not ultimately pointless.

In two cases, the Agency's correspondent has been permanently or intermittently "tailed." Contact with potential opposition movements is disapproved of, and may be attended by certain consequences.

Certain agencies whose information constitutes the raw materials of correspondents' reports tend to neglect news items that, though of potential interest to the mass media throughout the world, are not transmitted because they are not in conformity with the government's position.

In one country, the correspondent cannot send news that

This essay is extracted from "Agence France-Presse (AFP)," in International Commission for the Study of Communication Problems, Monographs (I). Collection of news agency monographs assembled as background information for the International Commission for the Study of Communication Problems (Paris: Unesco, 1978), pp. 9–10.

has not first been disseminated by the national agency: in this case, the news is inadequate and may be biased.

On one occasion, one of the Agency's bureaus was "nationalized."

On several occasions, correspondents from the head office have been deported on the pretext of their "breaching the professional code," or "insulting" or "denigrating" the government in power, and replaced by local correspondents appointed with the government's approval.

One local correspondent has himself been tried, imprisoned, and deported without explanation.

In 1977, two journalists were detained by military forces and released after having been interrogated for five days on the source of certain reports.

Attempts are sometimes made simply to "browbeat" the correspondent by strongly advising him not to discuss a particular affair (e.g., abductions) or by denouncing him on the occasion of an international conference for having reported true—but disputed—facts.

It is sometimes difficult to make it understood that it is one of the functions of the Agency's correspondents to give an account of different—and sometimes conflicting—points of view in the countries covered by them; that to present an opponent's arguments is not to adopt them as one's own—but simply to inform.

Lastly, the guiding principles and ethic of news agencies are still frequently ill-perceived and little understood. It is here perhaps that lies the essential handicap with which correspondents must contend in the exercise of their professional functions.

AP: Covering the World
KEITH FULLER

ON A RECENT VISIT to China I was reminded that the word propaganda has an entirely different connotation in socialist countries. Propaganda, I was told, is information useful to the state. I submit that the subtle difference between news and propaganda is that news is what the head of every government needs and wants. Propaganda is what he or she passes on to the masses.

When we visited our hosts at Hsinhua in Peking, I was particularly impressed with the wire room . . . there dozens of teleprinters were clacking away bringing in information from agencies in a multitude of languages. As we walked down the line of printers, I kept looking for AP, of course. Having traversed the entire long room without seeing it, I was just to the point of asking our interpreter where it was when I saw off in a corner a single printer. I walked to it and it was indeed AP.

Not only that, but it was loaded with a three-carbon paper; I thought that silent tribute to our form of news reporting was the most singular compliment my agency ever received. I flatter myself to think that the most vociferous foe of Western news gathering would himself need, want, and indeed use the information we gather. Conversely, he would take little heed of the propagandized outpouring of state-sanctioned "news." I know that sounds smug but how can one say it? We are after hard information for the sake of fact alone—that has to be superior to any other motivation.

But good coverage of a good story is news everywhere. It wins as big headlines in Beirut as in Detroit. That's a big help in our efforts.

Keith Fuller is president of the Associated Press (AP). This essay was extracted from Keith Fuller, "Biased? Our Staff List Proves Not—AP Chief," *IPI Report* (June 1978), 27(5):10–11. Original source is a speech at the International Press Institute Assembly, Canberra, 1978.

So is the global pattern of news usage. Makeup and languages may vary but there's a striking similarity in news usage around the world. A 1972 AP study of sixty-four newspapers in eighteen countries showed that about one quarter of the news carried foreign datelines. The results varied only a percentage point or two between nations. For example, in the U.S., papers used 74 percent local and national news and 26 percent foreign. In the Soviet Union, the figure was 73.6 percent local and national and 26.4 percent foreign—just .4 percent difference.

Now abroad, AP distributes only international news. Considering the amount of space editors have for foreign news—about one-quarter, the survey showed—AP alone provides far more copy than any editor can use.

But do we give you what you want? A fair question.

I'm afraid neither AP nor any other news organization gives each editor precisely the foreign coverage he wants. But we try in many ways . . . to ensure that our report abroad is truly international and not simply a reflection of America media needs.

First, approximately six out of every seven full-time AP news people outside the United States are non-Americans. They are of dozens of nationalities and speak in many tongues. They were born to the language and cultures and societies on which they report.

The precise figures are 81 Americans and 478 full-time foreign nationals. The developing world is not slighted in that selection. In fact, AP staffers who carry the passports of developing nations also head a significant number of AP bureaus—Cairo, Bogata, Ankara, Kuala Lumpur, Istanbul, Jakarta, and Seoul, among others.

Second, foreign news distributed in the United States passes through AP's foreign desk. Without changing the facts or intent of the incoming dispatch, this desk inserts the background and explanatory material needed so that each story is meaningful to the average American reader.

Incoming stories from the field are relayed back overseas by a completely separate staff, that of the World Service desks.

The Latin American desk, which serves that continent, is completely manned by editors from Latin America or Spain. Another World Service desk controls the circuits going to the other continents. Its editors are a mix of Americans with specialized foreign area background and non-Americans who know the news needs of their home areas. A number are from the Third World.

From this I hope that . . . those from the developing world who read these remarks will realize that despite our big American base, AP is truly an international news agency.

At the same time, we are independent of all governments, including that of the United States. Our wide base of privately owned U.S. media gives us complete economic independence. AP has no financial ties, direct or indirect, with the U.S. government. We pull no punches in our coverage of Washington, as those in the U.S. government would be the first to tell you.

Our goal simply is to provide informed, untrammeled, and objective coverage of the United States and the world. Coverage of the developing world is increasingly important, for what is taking place in the Third World is significantly influencing both the present and the future. I expect AP's concern with the Third World to grow continuously.

In saying this, let me emphasize that AP's news interest in the developing world has nothing to do with business goals there. AP's total gross revenue from the lesser-developed countries is less than 1 percent of our income. Our coverage costs in those areas exceed our revenue many times over. Let me assure you AP would cover the developing world with equal objectivity and intensity if we had not 1 percent of revenue there.

Covering the Third World is not easy. I hope that with increasing understanding of each other's problems by journalists of the developed and developing world, there will come an easing of the problems AP and others face in providing fair and honest Third World coverage.

I refer to such constraints as inability to gain entry of professionally qualified AP news persons into nations whose importance merits, even demands, coverage. I refer to those countries, particularly in Latin America, which use implied threats to exert pressure on what correspondents report. I refer to implicit censorship, the self-defeating but common practice of inhibiting news coverage by denying correspondents access to those high-level official sources who can best explain the story of their countries to the world.

In return, we at AP want to cooperate in every way we can in assisting the growth of the communications industry and the media in the developing world. We are willing and eager to make available to the Third World what we have learned during 130 years in the news agency field—and this includes expertise in news, in photos, in communications, in administration, and in dozens of associated areas.

Reuters View on Unesco
GERALD LONG

THE ASPIRATIONS of those countries that feel they are badly reported, too little reported, or that they have too little possibility of being known to the rest of the world . . . are entirely legitimate. Many of the complaints that are made are well-founded, and it is the duty of all of us to help to fulfill their aspirations. That I would accept and affirm entirely. But it must be recognized that an international flow of information is only achieved by those countries which have a very well-developed internal flow.

In other words, you cannot have repression at home and enlightenment abroad. And insofar as that is an aspiration, it is one that is doomed to failure.

Gerald Long was managing director of Reuters, Ltd., when this essay was extracted from "Statement on Unesco," impromptu talk, International Press Institute meeting, Athens, Greece, June 19, 1979. He is now managing director, Times Newspapers of London.

It is said . . . that a certain style of information, this is a pejorative phrase obviously, current in the United States, is eroding the cultural identity of other countries. Those who say that leave out of account in my opinion two things: first, the fact that the United States, whether we like it or not, is undoubtedly the most powerful, the most influential and, therefore, the most interesting country in the world, and it is natural it should be very fully reported; and, secondly, the United States is that country in the world that has the largest internal flow of information, and this enormous amount of information which is flowing all the time within the United States provides the material for the external flow. I think that countries that aspire to have a good external flow of information should learn that lesson.

Unesco does not seem to me to learn it, nor to understand the nature of the situation at all, and, worse than that, Unesco is falsifying the whole context of this debate by seeing the situation entirely in terms of power. . . . I would like to say for myself as somebody concerned with international information, that I entirely reject the idea of information as power, that I believe that anyone working in the media, nationally or internationally, has to do that or they put themselves in the service of something which is not information and thereby corrupt the system that they should serve. . . .

We have the Unesco Director General in 1977 saying that communication often appears as the privilege of a tightly knit group of professionals or technocrats who hold populations, so to speak, at their mercy and can direct, if not manipulate, them at will.

That is nonsense. I would be very interested to see some support given by Unesco to the very wide-ranging and high-sounding affirmations that are made and for which no example whatsoever is adduced. I would like the Director-General to tell us how the manipulation is brought about, how it works, to give us some examples of it. I know none.

I know many examples where governments have attempted to manipulate the world and world events through the use, or rather the abuse, of information. That is something that happens all the time. There are outstanding examples of it that I will not quote here, but not by the media themselves.

Furthermore, as far as I am concerned, and I can speak only for my own organization, the mechanism by which one would direct or manipulate is totally absent. I can manipulate nothing. And I take good care that neither can anyone else in my organization. I think in that I act in common with my colleagues in the other similar organizations. This idea of direction, of manipulation of information by the major international news organizations is created by Unesco for Unesco's own purposes, purposes which appear to me extremely suspect. Let me say immediately what I think those purposes are. If you wish power to be organized, power to be transmitted, power to be handed over, that power must exist. It, therefore, has to be suggested that this power exists in the world in order that it may be regulated and directed, one has to suppose by Unesco. Unesco seems to me to have a rage to regulate. . . .

I direct one of the organizations that is often criticized in this so-called debate. I would suggest . . . that we are criticized for not doing those things that we have never set out to do, cannot do, cannot reasonably be asked to do. It is said, for example, that we devote too little time to the study of the problems of the Third World. The term Third World itself, of course, has no definition, can have no definition, and is not a useful term.

The judgment quoted shows a total misunderstanding of what news is. News is the search for truth in events and cannot be concerned with the study of problems. Other parts of the media do that. We do not.

I suggest that we are criticized for things we cannot do as part of the program to suggest that power exists which then must be reorganized or, as I would see it, usurped. I would claim, for my part, that there is in these organizations, or at least in mine—others must speak for themselves—no such power. Nor do we seek any such power. Far from it. We reject it. In my opinion, Unesco disqualifies itself on the basis of total misunderstanding from any claim to direct this debate.

UPI: Problems of International Coverage
FRANK TREMAINE

MANY DEVELOPING NATIONS complain that the international news services generate inaccurate pictures of their countries with incomplete or unfair reporting. They complain that not enough is reported from their areas and that what is reported concentrates on catastrophes, political upheaval, and other sensational material.

Such complaints are not without merit. There are several reasons for this, including problems of communications and the inhospitality of many of the complaining nations. There are at least three other reasons.

One is economics. Operating an international news service is an expensive proposition. Although UPI is a private enterprise organized for profit, it has not returned a dividend to its owners in more than twenty years.

UPI welcomes the opportunity to send its services to new areas. It is willing to tailor its services to the requirements of its subscribers, which means obtaining news from areas in which they are interested as long as factual, unbiased reporting is acceptable. But such subscribers must be willing to pay a fair price for the service and to keep their accounts current. Neither UPI nor other international agencies can afford anything else. However, the cost of their service would be far less to subscribers than the cost of supporting national news agencies in every country which wishes to improve its inward and outward flow of news by covering all or part of the rest of the world by themselves.

Frank Tremaine is senior vice-president of United Press International (UPI). This essay is from Frank Tremaine, "United Press International: Origin, Organization, and Operations," New York: UPI, January 1978, section 9.

Another problem relates to the technical strictures of producing newspapers and news broadcasts. The newspaper space or broadcast time which can be devoted to news from a particular foreign country is limited. Correspondents must write with that in mind. It is difficult to present a complete picture of a complicated subject in a 300-word story, yet many newspapers will use no more than that on any but the most important subjects of the day. A correspondent's work and the picture he presents, therefore, must be measured by the total of his work over a period of months or longer.

Of course, neither a correspondent nor his news service has any control over what the editors of hundreds of newspapers around the world select from the tens of thousands of words of news service copy they receive each day. News agencies file much more "positive" or "constructive" material than many critics realize because the critics do not see the full service of those agencies, only the stories published in the papers they read or broadcast by the stations they listen to. A serious report on economic development filed yesterday may be printed in only a few newspapers while the tragic story of today's catastrophe will be printed in hundreds.

Finally, there is the problem of quality. The newspapers and broadcasters which present an agency's news service range from excellent to poor in quality, and this is reflected in the way they handle news from abroad. Second, news agency reporters are like other humans, with all their good and bad points.

News agencies try to select their best people for foreign assignments. Mistakes can be made but the correspondents selected generally are above average and have the further advantage of working for organizations dedicated to the ideal of accurate, unbiased reporting. UPI has no political bias, no point of view. Its reporters and editors are schooled in the idea that their first responsibility is to be accurate. A former editor-in-chief of UPI, Roger Tatarian, wrote this to new employees:

For millions of people in this country and additional millions overseas, we are the only source of information on events outside their immediate localities. So our job is to be faithful stand-ins for people who cannot witness these distant events themselves. The test of our work is whether our reportage enables them to reach the same general impression, or gain the same understanding, that the event itself would have given them. To act as the extension of other individuals with different attitudes and different politics is to assume an enormous responsibility it may well be impossible to achieve with complete satisfaction, but that does not relieve us of the responsibility of trying to achieve it.

Visnews: TV News Flow and Satellites
PETER MARSHALL

THE INTERNATIONAL DEBATE about "free flow" and a "new information order" is being followed closely in the visual news agencies, with reactions ranging from detached astonishment to deep concern. Astonishment, because the debate does not often seem to recognize the real world in which we operate; concern, because of fears that the long-term, practical benefits which *could* emerge from such a debate might in the end be submerged by the rhetoric.

The real world is one in which Visnews has been able to build up, in the twenty-two years of our existence, the trust and acceptance of television organizations in ninety-eight countries, in every part of the world—developed and developing, East and West, North and South. We produce visual coverage of 45 or 50 worldwide news stories every day—that is, some 18,000 stories each year—and distribute this material,

Peter Marshall is general manager of Visnews. This essay is extracted from Peter Marshall, "Improving the Flow of Visual News," *Intermedia* (July 1978), 7(4):14–16.

daily, by the fastest possible methods available to us, to some 200 broadcasters.

For most of its first twenty years, the news service was primarily a film operation, with a steadily growing team of staff, contract, and stringer cameramen around the world. They now number more than 400. These cameramen provided most of the news coverage. The remainder is acquired from broadcasters under special arrangements in certain countries. . . .

A much greater change has been taking place, with increasing pace, during the past ten years, as more and more television stations began to take their news service by electronic means, with a parallel reduction in those requiring regular air-freighted film packages. Electronic distribution began with the growth of the daily Eurovision news exchanges, in which the agency contribution has increased year by year. . . .

But it was the arrival of satellite communications which brought about a major revolution in news distribution. After a period in which satellite transmissions were increasingly used on an ad hoc basis for top news stories, we were able to pioneer the first regular, daily satellite feed of news film in 1975. We sent a package of ten-minutes' duration, from London each night to Australia, so reducing by half the delivery time for most international news reaching the Antipodes.

There are now four such daily feeds; three transmitted from the Visnews headquarters in London and one from New York. They reach subscribers in Australia, New Zealand, Japan, Hong Kong, Singapore, the Middle East and Gulf States, North America, and South America. From some of these points, videocassettes are distributed to other nearby television stations who do not possess the resources to receive direct satellite transmissions. As a result, more than half of our subscribers now receive their daily news service by electronic means, rather than by film shipments, and the number continues to grow. . . .

The participation in daily satellite feeds has given a new dimension to world news. It brings "today's news today" within the reach of countries where international news film was usually two or three days old. New values have been created for broadcasters and agencies alike. One particularly satisfying outcome has been a big increase in the percentage of agency material used.

Major broadcasters who were once content to use no more than one or two stories a day from their package of air-freighted film now use between 50 percent and 75 percent of the satellited material. . . .

It is in London that Visnews has its headquarters. But this historical and geographical accident is not allowed to influence the journalistic objectivity and impartiality of the news service. Indeed, strenuous efforts are made to preclude such influence.

We recognize that the criteria governing what is news vary from country to country. We seek to reflect this in our news coverage policy and in the selection of material for distribution. The Visnews service contains not only headline-making events, but also background and feature stories, explanatory material, and reports of national success and achievement. Towards this end, and the better understanding of differing national criteria, our staff are based in most of the major capitals of the world.

This deployment enables them to experience and absorb each particular environment and to ensure that their reports and assessments are conveyed to the rest of the organization. Many of such staff are, in fact, nationals recruited locally; others are international journalists who gain valuable experience from successive periods in different parts of the world.

What can now be achieved by international pressure—perhaps by Unesco?—is in the direction of putting more resources into the provision of satellite ground stations and their associated equipment in the developing world. At the same time, greater unified influence might be brought to bear on the international telecommunications carriers to reduce and standardize the tariffs for satellite transmission. In this way it will be possible to bring daily news feeds (as well as other material) within the reach of all who wish to receive them.

We in the visual news agencies can play a part. Indeed, we have carried out much pioneering work in recent years to bring about reductions in the cost of satellite feeds for our subscribers by negotiating block-booking rates and shared cost arrangements. But at existing tariffs, even arrangements such as these are beyond the resources of most of the developing world. As the use of satellites increases, for a variety of purposes, so it should be possible for rates to be reduced; with, perhaps the arguments for a free and balanced flow of news justifying at least a measure of special treatment?

16

Visnews and UPITN: News Film Supermarkets in the Sky
JONATHAN KING

Most of the debate over the international news crisis has centered on the traditional print-oriented news agencies, but television is an increasingly important news medium in many parts of the world. The rapid growth of news dissemination through worldwide television news agencies, such as Visnews and UPITN, is analyzed in King's essay. It sheds light on the much-neglected subset of news agencies which specialize in film and it offers a case study of how a TNNA such as Visnews can affect the national policies and interests of Australia. Rapidly changing patterns—hard to keep up with—show the dynamic growth of global television news agencies in hardly a quarter of a century.

VISNEWS IS PERHAPS the closest thing to the concept of the "global village" first visualized by the Canadian media writer Marshall McLuhan. To the Visnews operators, the world is

Jonathan King is an Australian media critic and politics lecturer at the University of Melbourne. This essay was originally presented at the Conference on Transnational Communication Enterprises and National Communication Policies, East-West Communication Institute, Honolulu, August 6–19, 1978. It has been extensively revised and updated.

"one village" in which Visnews is now able to keep all the citizens in touch with each other. It is by far the largest television news service in the world, although there is healthy competition from its main rival UPITN.

This paper examines the operations of Visnews and UPITN and uses Australia to illustrate some issues raised by the news film agencies.

Visnews—which is a snappy name for Vision News—was created in 1957 by the British Broadcasting Corporation in an attempt to block American film syndicates from gaining a monopoly control over Britain and Europe. By creating this highly successful "profit-retaining trust" in which revenue is ploughed back into the organization to finance further development, the BBC gave birth to a global monopoly far greater than anything seen before in television news. By the mid-1950s, the rapid growth of television in the world had led—among other things—to the demise of the cinema newsreel and a fundamental change in the way most of the world saw the events and personalities in the news. New opportunities were presented, and these changes opened the way for the formation of Visnews—then known as BCINA, or the British Commonwealth International Newsfilm Agency.

Lord Radcliffe, the eminent British jurist who became the first Chairman of Visnews Trustees, expressed the company's guiding principles:

to create a service of pictorial television news clear of political control by anybody, impartial in its presentation, seeking to collect and distribute news on a world-wide basis, and organized so that it should not fall under the control of any one group, or influence, or person.

In March 1957, a small team, led by Kenneth Dick as managing editor and Norman Bull as the company secretary/chief accountant, started work in the North Acton premises left vacant by the closure of the Paramount Newsreel, absorbing twenty-five members of the Paramount staff. A cameraman network was created and the first news story was sold on April 12—from Nairobi. Gradually the momentum built up. By the end of May, fifty news stories had been filmed; by the end of 1957, trial services had been supplied to fifteen broadcast-bers and one—Cyprus Broadcasting Corporation—had signed a contract.

By 1966, there were 100 subscribers in sixty-five countries, and stories were being filmed at the rate of 1,000 a month. Aircraft throughout the world were carrying Visnews' packages every minute of every day. The new global news service had really taken off.

In addition to the BBC, the original owners were Reuters, the Canadian Broadcasting Corporation, the Australian Broadcasting Commission, and the Rank Organization. Pressures forced the Rank Organization out in 1968, and its place was taken by the New Zealand Broadcasting Commission. Today Visnews is owned by these five "Commonwealth partners" who have as their American affiliate the National Broadcasting Corporation (NBC).

Visnews Owners Today	*Percent of Shares*
1. BBC	33
2. Reuters	33
3. Canadian Broadcasting Corporation	
4. Australian Broadcasting Commission	33
5. Broadcasting Corporation New Zealand	

Affiliate
National Broadcasting Corporation (NBC)

GLOBAL OPERATIONS

Today Visnews Limited is an international company, providing, in addition to news film, a wide range of audiovisual services. The company employs journalists, cameramen, script writers, film directors, film technicians, and electronics engineers in offices in many major capitals around the globe.

The principal product of Visnews is its Television News Service. Each day, with more than 400 cameramen (mostly part-time) in the field, Visnews gathers forty to fifty news stories on film and videotape from around the world and sends them by satellite, terrestrial electronic circuits, or airfreight to

200 broadcasters in almost every country where television exists. The main objective of Visnews is to provide television stations everywhere with a comprehensive daily service of international news film. Visnews has been distributing daily "feeds" around the world since the early 1970s. The company aims to provide "an impartial unbiased news service" in which "news value" is the only criterion, and so it sifts the world for the "top stories" of the day for its service.

Visnews is certainly the world's leading supplier of international newsfilm. Each year it sends out at least 20 million feet of film (12 million in color and 8 million in black and white). Each week it sends 4,000 feet (more than 100 minutes) to the average subscriber. Each day Visnews sends out selections from its top news stories to different clients around the world. Each story is about 65 feet or 90 seconds long.

Although the operation is certainly world wide the headquarters has been in London since the start, and is now masterminded from Cumberland Avenue, NW 10. London was chosen as the headquarters over San Francisco—the main alternative—because U.S. $80,000 could be saved each year by operating out of London, the GMT time reference is a central one, airline flights and late European stories fit in well with the transmission times of many of the subscribers, and Britain shares the same PAL 625-line definition of picture that many of the Commonwealth subscribers use. Had the service been based in the United States, the NTSC 525-line definition would have been used and this would have meant expensive conversions for many of the clients.

There are sixteen bureaus around the world:

Bangkok	New Delhi
Beirut	New York
Buenos Aires	Paris
Cairo	Rio de Janeiro
Frankfurt	Rome
Hong Kong	Sydney
Lisbon	Tel Aviv
Nairobi	Tokyo

Visnews has a staff of 400, including at least 25 full-time cameramen and hundreds of stringers or part-time cameramen scattered around the world.

In addition to its own bureaus and staff, however, it has reciprocal arrangements with other television operations all around the world which gives it full access to news resources of many major international broadcasters. Contributions to the Visnews international feeds now include:

Visnews
British Broadcasting Corporation
Canadian Broadcasting Corporation
Australian Broadcasting Commission
New Zealand Broadcasting Commission
National Broadcasting Corporation (America)
Eurovision
NHK (Japan)
NIRT (Iran)
United Nations Television (United Nations, New York)

Visnews divides the world into four zones on the basis of shared time and common interest and sends a daily news package out to each of these zones to be shared among a group of countries in the same region. There is a producer in charge of each zone and this journalist gets to know what his zone likes or dislikes over the years. The four main zones are:

1. Australasia: Australia
                 China
                 New Zealand
                 Hong Kong
                 Japan
                 Singapore
                 South Korea
                 Brunei
2. Middle East: Iran
                 Dubai
                 Abu Dhabi

3. America: North America
                South America
4. South Africa: On request

These zones change from time to time as new groupings replace old ones. The number of feeds or daily packages also changes. In 1979 a new ten-minute feed was developed out of New York for Japan—which then had two feeds a day, one from London, one from New York. Australia, which at first occasionally took the second feed via New York, in April 1980 started taking two feeds daily. The New York feed means U.S. news can go directly to Asia/Pacific, providing fuller and more current service. With technology improving and satellite capacity increasing, the number and frequency of daily feeds can be expected to change. The zone groupings worked out on the basis of satellite placing and technological capabilities as well as time and common interest could change in the future. In addition Visnews "injects" single stories or "packages" of news into the Eurovision circuit, which serves Western Europe, where Visnews is the biggest single contributor, supplying 27 percent of all news stories transmitted on that network—1,700 stories a year. Visnews also now feeds the Intervision circuit which serves Eastern Europe and such single system nations as China Central Television (CCTV), which started daily satellite service in March 1980. It also has the facilities to supply "unilateral feeds" to specific countries on request or to specific stations—thus a commercial station in Australia could request a special exclusive coverage of an Australian football match played in London, or film of the funeral procession for Lord Mountbatten, or whatever. Thus there is very little that this transnational communication enterprise cannot do and there are few corners of the globe which it cannot reach.

Sending the News

Despite its ubiquitous coverage—Visnews says it covers 99 percent of the world's television receivers—the operation is surprisingly small and simple. Each day news stories are fed into the Cumberland Avenue headquarters from the contributors listed above. The stories have come in from all around the world by various means including satellite and airline freight— the American material comes in from NBC by air courier, having been selected by the Visnews bureau chief in New York City from the range of news stories available in America on the day.

Once all the stories are collected each day, the Visnews journalists sit down at 3 P.M. over steaming cups of coffee in the theater on the first floor of their three-story building, and review the stories on a movie screen. They then confer and put the stories into the different zones around the world. Then the stories are assembled, complete with a script and commentary, and sent off to the subscribers.

The selection is, of course, subjective and sometimes a single journalist has the job of choosing the stories that one entire zone of the world will have on any particular day. One journalist I interviewed who had run the operation many times single-handed said:

We are told to go for the top world stories of the day. Good ones include the Spanish disaster in which scores of holiday makers from different countries were killed by the gas explosion from an overturned lorry, and New York blackouts combined with violent looting.

The journalists argue that there is not much to choose from most days and the main limitation is the poor range of stories that are screened each morning. Different zones develop a different feeling, of course, and at one time it was commonly believed at Visnews that Australians prefer "bombs, earthquakes, car and train crashes, British strikes, and sporting stories," and so that is what Visnews journalists fed Australia.

Apart from "hard news," the Visnews journalists also try to throw in one "color" or human interest story in a lighter vein to cheer the viewers up. They also have the problem of serving more than one master, and, thus, if they put some Australian-style stories into the Australian feed one day they try to balance the feed the following day by putting in one story especially for Japan—another important client in that same zone.

The feeds or packages are normally ten minutes long and there are about five or six short stories in each package of about ninety seconds length. The stories are put together—given a "top and tail" (an introduction and a back-announcement for the broadcaster) and given a script based on the "dope sheet" that comes in with the film. The feeds are then sent out to the different zones in the afternoon (London time). Visnews, which has regular satellite time, has the use of five satellites in the Intelsat Global Satellite System for sending it news film—there are two satellites over the Atlantic Ocean, two over the Indian Ocean, and one over the Pacific Ocean.

There are now four major satellite transmissions a day to various zones of the world. Visnews serves twenty-one nations by satellite.

Australia, one of the twenty-one nations, offers an informative insight into a country receiving Visnews as its major source of international news film.

VISNEWS AND AUSTRALIA

The ten-minute package from London for Australasia is beamed off the Indian Ocean satellite and, in Australia, comes in through the "gateway" at Ceduna to the South Australian operations. It is then distributed to the three commercial and one public television networks. The package arrives at 7:30 A.M. and is recorded on tape and then screened for each television station, which selects what it wants for its news show that night. The new feed from New York, started on a regular basis in 1980, is timed for important morning news shows. Australia was until 1980 connected to the outside world through this one commercial lifeline, provided by this transnational communication enterprise with a virtual monopoly over news film. The other major sources for Australian viewers are the Australian Broadcasting Commission (ABC), which has ten major bureaus around the world in major centers such as London, Washington, and New York, and a newly established link with UPITN and the American CBS services.[1] News agency coverage from Reuters, Associated Press, United Press International, and Agence France-Presse is also available.

Visnews service is not free; the media have to pay for the daily satellite transmission to Australia—the commercial networks and ABC share costs. ABC—being a partner in Visnews itself—pays most of the $500,000 annual cost. Individual costs to networks and stations are considered confidential commercial matters by Visnews and the subscribers, and accurate figures are difficult to get.

Without the economies of scale enjoyed by Visnews, the operation would be prohibitive—a single camera crew costs about $50,000 a year. The increasingly high costs of wages, air fares, air freight, accommodation, film stock, and associated expenses force the transnational communication business into a virtual monopoly situation. Individual Australian stations could not afford to get the international news film on their own. News does not make money generally and in Australia the interest in international events is so low that foreign news makes even less money. The only way commercial television stations can make money is to attract advertisers. If the stories do not hold the interest of the viewers, then the stations have difficulty getting advertisers at good rates.

At the same time, news-gathering and transmission is a multimillion dollar operation. There are large financial outlays

---

1. The commercial television news film monopoly enjoyed by Visnews in the 1970s gave way to a more competitive context in 1980, when UPITN sold its daily satellite feed to the Channel 9 Network in Australia. The Nine Network also bought a satellite service from the American CBS network and paid A$1 million for the UPITN and CBS service together. Nine Network has a four-year contract with UPITN and a two-year contract with CBS. The network is so confident of the switch that it has dropped Visnews altogether. Nine's news director, John Sorrell, says, "We now have the upper hand in reporting overseas events."

The other stations do not agree. They say that the new services are untried, too costly, and that Visnews has improved lately. The other stations and Visnews have responded by adding a second daily feed to the news inputs from London to Australia. The general opinion in the news room, as I perceive it, is that this will balance the situation and bring the two news services into line with each other. Television critics are watching with interest as the rivalry unfolds but so far it has not altered the Anglo-American bias in the diet fed to Australians.

and low returns, especially for a country the size of Australia without a strong market for international television news. Australians are traditionally parochial, thus the news slot is poor for advertisers. Consequently, the television companies are not prepared to spend much on getting overseas news. As it is, they complain about spending as much as they do on Visnews.

The situation that Visnews enjoys as Australia's supermarket in the sky puts it in a position where it has an immense potential power. It may not exert this power but it certainly has the potential. For even by listing what products will be available on the shelves of its aerial supermarket it preselects what Australians, along with other countries, are going to be told about the rest of the world on any particular day.

In Australia, which has many of the characteristics of a Third World country, the impact of transnationals like Visnews is already so great that unless reforms are introduced soon the local culture will be irreversibly locked into that of the transmitting countries' principally Anglo-American value systems.[2]

DIVERSIFICATION

To survive as a transnational enterprise, Visnews has to diversify. To strengthen its operation, it has now developed services that include supplying transparencies of newsmakers (personalities) and places, leasing camera crews for special location work, providing archival footage to clients from its library of 35 million feet of film, providing laboratory processing services, and producing films. This latter enterprise, sponsored documentaries, is the most controversial because media critics argue that by making "public relations films" for

2. For a detailed analysis of data on international news shown over television in Australia, May–October 1979, see Derek Overton: "Television International News, a Tasmanian Perspective," 1980, available from the Communication Institute, East-West Center, Honolulu. The paper, which primarily deals with Visnews reports, closely complements Jonathan King's essay.

oil and automobile companies the Visnews organization may be forced to compromise its principles of objectivity.

The company has now produced, for a variety of sponsors, about 100 documentary films, ranging from short sales films to an hour-long documentary on the great annual Moslem pilgrimages to Mecca and Medina. The clients for these productions have included government departments, international and other organizations, charities, and industrial and commercial companies, spreading geographically over the United Kingdom, Europe, North America, the Middle East, Africa, and the Far East.

With the production service goes a distribution service, based on its technical and shipping facilities in London. Visnews also offers a worldwide location service to other filmmakers using its own technicians, production management, and technical services in London. The company also extends its influence to helping governments in developing countries establish their own film units, based on Visnews consultants and experts and using the backup of its own technical services in London. They now do very well in the field of technical equipment, as Visnews' full consultancy service is followed by supply, installation, maintenance, and training. This global giant also runs training courses in London in film-making techniques, drawing its student body mainly from developing countries.

In the United Kingdom, the Visnews Film Laboratory commercial service includes processing and printing, and as electronic and other means of audio-visual communications are developing, so the range of services offered by Visnews is growing and changing.

Despite these different avenues for making money, the economics of international news gathering are increasingly difficult. Visnews says that it only makes a 5 percent profit. It has been forced to cut back its staff and now uses skeleton staff in many of its operations. With less of an infrastructure, it thus has to rely more on the contributors that feed film into its system and this in turn makes it susceptible to pressures from these other interests.

UPITN, the Rival

Although it has a clear lead, Visnews is not alone in the international newsfilm market. Its major global competitor is UPITN, a transnational communications enterprise which combines the resources of United Press International and the British company Independent Television News (ITN). This organization is growing rapidly and soon will pose a serious threat to Visnews. UPITN now claims to have a $10 million turnover. According to this company, the network puts out "The world's greatest television news service."

According to company information, UPITN's daily television news service is screened by more than 200 television stations in over seventy countries—the news transmission can be seen by 90 percent of the world. In the United States, the American Broadcasting Corporation (ABC) and the National Broadcasting Company (NBC) feed UPITN's top international stories to vast networks of affiliated stations. In the United Kingdom, the Independent Television (ITV) companies subscribe to UPITN through ITN.

UPITN maintains its own network of editorial offices in New York, Washington, London, Paris, Frankfurt, Rome, Salisbury, and Hong Kong. Also, through the bureaus of UPI, the company is represented in practically every country in the world. Forty staff camera crews of many nationalities cover the day's news. They are backed up by almost 500 free-lancers worldwide. "All ready at a moment's notice to move in on a breaking story," the company notes.

UPITN's main servicing center is London, where at ITN House the headline stories of the day are fed in round-the-clock by satellite, microwave, and landline links. Their film laboratory (where copies are made for subscribers) processes 20 million feet (5 million meters) of film a year.

UPITN is increasingly involved in electronic deliveries. Every day from London, UPITN beams a forty-five-minute news package via the Atlantic satellite to major television stations and networks in the United States and South America.

From New York, another UPITN satellite transmission feeds news via Westar and the Pacific bird to Japan and the Far East. And in Europe, UPITN is also a major participant in the daily Eurovision news exchanges, contributing or matching about 25 percent of all news coverage handled by Eurovision each year.

This rival world television film agency has, like Visnews, also broadened its base and now provides film crews around the world, library footage, a weekly half-hour supermarket-style documentary for the "global shopper" called "Roving Report," and finally the usual commercial and industrial film productions needed to supplement the income from hard news.

Although UPITN has been gaining ground—notwithstanding the crippling U.K. strike during 1979—Visnews continues to lead the field and retain its grip in many of the countries which UPITN is threatening to invade. There are, of course, many nations which choose to take both services and so get the best of both worlds—in more senses than one. Which global news giant comes out on top could well depend on which one jumps the technological gun and develops cheaper, more efficient, and faster transmission techniques than the other. As the 1980s unfold, however, it appears that the veteran Visnews will have to change to meet rapidly changing technological realities faster than it has done in the past, or it might find itself neck and neck with this cheeky challenger. UPITN in some ways has a better management structure to cope with change since it is more free of the limitations of governmental or semigovernmental control. These matters slow Visnews down to some extent, since it has to coordinate a number of different owners of different nationalities.

Although UPITN offered its services free for one month to potential subscribers some time ago, the coverage was not considered as good as Visnews by some because, according to one journalist, UPITN was not "everywhere at the same time" the way Visnews was. Visnews is like an octopus, journalists say, with its tentacles around the world. If something happens anywhere one of the tentacles twitches and the message goes back to the center. It will take UPITN many years to match this comprehensive coverage of the world.

Thus having been first in the early seventies with the daily satellite transmissions around the world, Visnews has established a grip on many national markets.

IMPACT OF TRANSNATIONALS

In theory, it may seem harmless enough for a government that is interested in preserving democracy to leave the operations of communication businesses to market forces in the belief that this will produce a "diversity of opinion." In reality, however, as Australia illustrates, the absence of strong national policies can—in the absence of truly free enterprise market forces—give rise to a monopoly situation where there is only one voice. It has been shown through the Visnews example up to 1980 in Australia that the "market forces" in the international communications business tend to create monopoly structures.

The power enjoyed by transnationals like Visnews and UPITN is not a power over specific events or issues but rather a more general power—such as the ability to exert a general *conditioning* effect on viewers in particular countries, teaching them a particular type of "language," and passing on a particular set of values that protects the interests of organizations like Visnews—interested in making money by preserving the status quo.

Some disadvantages or problems with the transnational news film agencies include:

- The short feeds that limit countries' access to the outside world. The quantity is too limited. Unilateral feeds are too expensive as an additional supply, leaving a narrow range of choice.
- Much of the material is irrelevant due to the generalized selection on the part of journalists in London, limited financial outlays in the gathering of news by staff, and the desire to be "all things to all men" in the respective zones. In addition, most of the film usually has to be sent to London before it can

be passed on through the services, and this takes time and costs money.

- There is a cultural and political effect as the British bases also impose a particular view of the world. Everything is seen from the London headquarters as if London was the center of the globe, and the "angle" is not that of the subscribers. What may seem important in Sydney or Tokyo may not matter as much to someone in London.
- British and American values that are imported with the news film and that stress the desirability of the type of society and economy in the northern hemisphere are seen by some critics to be detrimental to other countries. These critics see the values contained in the newsfilm as helping to prepare audiences for the goods and services offered by the American/British suppliers. Thus the news film agencies help homogenize the world and extend the markets of the industrial countries into the southern hemisphere.

The basic problem for many of the small countries has been best expressed by Michael Symons: "Global monopoly has serious dangers—with too much power placed in too few hands—no matter how well-meaning."

Third World countries are increasingly complaining about the impact of the transnational media on their cultures. With the coming of electronic news-gathering and the technology that may enable countries like the United States to transmit television programs directly to receivers around the world, these complaints are likely to grow rather than disappear.

Selected References

Australia, Commonwealth of. *Broadcasting and Television Act, 1942–1977.* HMSO, Australia.

Curran, Charles and Kenneth Coyte, "The Visual Agencies." Paper for the International Institute of Communications conference, London, September 9–13, 1979.

Hamelink, Cees. *The Corporate Village: The Role of the Transnational Corporation in International Communications.* Rome: International Documentation and Communication Center, 1977.

McQueen, Humphrey. *Australia's Media Monopolies.* Melbourne: Widescope, 1977.

New Journalist, May 1972.

Rosenbloom, Henry. *Politics and the Media.* Melbourne: Scribe, 1978.

Schiller, Herbert I. *Mass Communications and American Empire.* Boston: Beacon, 1971.

Tunstall, Jeremy. *The Media Are American.* New York: Columbia University Press, 1977.

Visnews. "Visnews Extends Its Satellite News Operations to Peking," news release, March 21, 1980.

Visnews Limited, General Information Booklets.

17

What the Chinese Are Telling Their People about the World: A Week of the New China News Agency

WILBUR SCHRAMM

In the late 1970s, Wilbur Schramm, the distinguished American communication researcher, spent more than a year in Hong Kong teaching, doing research, and observing communication in the nearby People's Republic of China, which has recently been increasingly outward-looking.

   In this essay, Dr. Schramm presents a perceptive look at Hsinhua, the important New China News Agency, and what it is telling the Chinese people about the world. Although Hsinhua is not a transnational news agency, in the sense it is used in this collection, it obviously is an influential national and international news service. Dr. Schramm suggests that this unique, highly disciplined news operation is as important a collector of news and related information for China as it is a distributor of news outside of China. Comparing Hsinhua to other agencies, he says the Chinese agency "gives per-

This paper was prepared by the author in Hong Kong and circulated at the Flow of Communication Workshop, East-West Communication Institute, Honolulu, May 1978.

haps the greatest, proportional representation to Third World news, and, of course, to the news of China itself."

Hsinhua, the New China News Agency, is not quite like any other news agency in the world. It is the chief supplier of news to all the media of China, from the *People's Daily* to the smallest commune news sheet. It publishes *Ts'en-Kao Hsiao-Hsi* (Reference News) which circulates somewhere around 8 million copies to party leaders and cadre members and others who are permitted to subscribe, and consequently has some right to be called the largest newspaper in China. But it resists being thought of as a national or "internal" news service. Its function, as described by Wang Chi-hua as early as 1957, is to "distribute news to the length and breadth of the world. . . . The agency's early development into a world news agency is an urgent mission."[1]

Presently it maintains perhaps as many as 100 bureaus in cooperative countries, staffed almost entirely by indigenous Chinese. More than 100 employees work in the Hong Kong Bureau; more remote offices may have only one or two persons. These offices receive the news service from Peking, make it available to subscribing newspapers and broadcasters, issue news releases when appropriate, and, most important, keep a flow of news from their regions traveling back to Peking.

This last function of Hsinhua as collector of news and related information for China is apparently as important as its obligation to distribute the news outside China. Thus it is a complete nervous system, with the news currents flowing both ways, and both flows centering upon Peking. News to go out on the wire is selected in Peking, rather than by the bureaus. Therefore news gathered in the field must first go back to the capital, and this is one reason why, in comparison to wires like Reuters, AFP, AP, and UPI, Hsinhua often seems late with important news. Whether it disturbs the bureaus to have to make their stories available often a day or two later than the other wires, so that they get relatively little use in the foreign

---

1. Wang Chi-hua. "New China News Agency on the March." *Hsin-wen-yu Chupen* (News and Publishing). August 25, 1957.

press, we do not know, but a likely answer is that the time competition so important to Western news agencies is not a part of Hsinhua's concern.

Nor is the Western "all the news that's fit to print" of concern to Hsinhua. For example, during the week that we analyzed the New China News Agency wire as it came through the Hong Kong bureau, both the other news agency wires and the newspapers were full of President Sadat's initiative and the Tripoli meeting that came in reaction to it. This subject was never mentioned directly by Hsinhua; even when they reported that King Hussein of Jordan visited both Egypt and Syria they said that he talked with those leaders about "the situation"—never about *what* situation. In that same week the Asian papers, in particular, were preoccupied with the crash of a hijacked airplane in Malaysia on its way to Singapore. Hsinhua carried not a word about this either, although it reported carefully the Asia men's basketball championship tournament from Malaysia.

What the Chinese tell their people through Hsinhua can therefore only be understood in terms of *why* they tell them what they do. Like all the other Chinese media, Hsinhua is not intended to be essentially informative, but rather instrumental. It is expected to be at least in part an instrument of political policy and guidance. That is why it can take such a detached and timeless view of news breaks and getting there first with the news, why it feels it can omit many of the chief stories that excite other news agencies, and why it feels the need to concentrate on the Third World, as it does perhaps more than any other wire service. Hsinhua's view of the world is essentially that of Mao in his theory of the "Three Worlds."[2] Mao revised the older concept of a capitalist world, a communist world, and a developing world, and asked his readers to think of the three divisions as:

1. A First World consisting of two "hegemonist" powers, the USSR and the United States.

2. Mao introduced this concept of the "Three Worlds" in a talk with a visiting national leader in February 1974. Details were carried in *Peking Review* (November 4, 1957), 45:10 ff.

2. A Second World of powers like those in Europe and Japan, many of them affluent but none so hegemonistically inclined as the first two, and consequently potential allies of the developing countries in their resistance to the war-mongering First World.
3. A Third World of developing countries whose hope lies in creating a united front against the First World, and developing their own military and economic power for self-defense and preservation.

Given this world view, we can assume, then, that Hsinhua's news selection must be based upon instrumental goals like these:

1. The world must be made to see the hegemonist powers as enemies of peace and independence. At the moment, the USSR is the most dangerous country in the world, but a capitalistic country like the United States is capable of being just as dangerous if the decay of its system drives it to desperate measures.
2. It is necessary for other countries to stand up to this First World.
3. It is necessary for other countries to develop economic and military strength to resist the First World.
4. It is necessary for the other countries to cooperate—to face the First World with a United Front.
5. In this situation China will be a friend and aide to all who seek peace and who wish to defend their independence and dignity against the First World aggressors.

These themes, as will become apparent in the analysis that follows, run through Hsinhua's news report. Given such a world view and such long-term goals, it is not hard to see why the crash of an airliner does not fit into the Hsinhua news budget, or why the agency might prefer to say nothing about events in the Middle East that seem contrary to the idea of a united front. Or why Hsinhua is centered as much as it is upon the Third World. Or why news breaks, competition, even spectacular disasters or political maneuvers like those in the Middle East might seem unimportant at the moment. Better to wait and see how they fit into the Big Picture, Hsinhua might decide.

We have analyzed the Hsinhua news service, as available in Hong Kong, for the seven days, December 5 through 11, 1977. First, let us see what the agency was telling its readers, keeping in mind the themes cited above. Then let us add some quantitative measures and comparisons.

What Hsinhua is telling its users about——
- THE UNITED STATES
  1. Things aren't so good with capitalism.
     U.S. coal miners are on strike again, for the tenth time in thirty-five years.
     U.S. News and World Report says unemployment among black teenagers has reached 45 percent.
  2. The First World is looking ever more dangerous.
     U.S. and USSR step up firing of new missiles. American officials point out growth in Soviet military strength.
  3. But some small countries are standing up to the Big Powers.
     Panama's struggle with U.S. concerning sovereignty over Canal "represents victory for whole continent."
     Mexican petroleum company cancels order to U.S. for steel pipe, because U.S. insists on lower price for Mexican oil.
     Two U.S. congressmen visit Cuba to look for themselves and talk about aid (unofficially).
- THE SOVIET UNION
  1. Soviet hegemonism is widely denounced.
     Yomiuri, Japanese daily, denounces USSR for obstructing signing of Sino-Japanese Peace and Friendship treaty.
     Japanese fortnightly, Contemporary Asia, accuses USSR of hegemonism, and resorting to intimidation to prevent Japan from signing peace and friendship treaty with China.
     Spanish journal, El Lucha, organ of Central Committee of Spanish Workers Revolutionary Organization, denounces Soviet aggression in Africa.
     Somali foreign minister denounces Soviet intervention.
     Sadat denounces Soviet Union for attempts to sow discord among Arabs.
     "Signed article" in Somali daily, October Star, denounces Soviet hegemonism in Africa.

Somali weekly, *Vanguard*, denounces USSR for hegemonistic acts in Third World countries.

2. The USSR is becoming even more dangerous.
   U.S. officials point out rapid growth of Soviet military power.
   Step up firing of new missiles.

3. Some small countries are standing up to the USSR.
   Somali official explains decision to abrogate Somali-Soviet treaty.
   Japanese journal, *Northern Central News*, organ of Kansai Center for Promotion of Return of Northern Territories, carries article supporting Somalia's abrogation of treaty with USSR.
   Somalia protests Russian intrusion on fishing grounds.
   Japan rejects Soviet request for fishing port facilities.
   Interview with composer of Somali song of resistance against Soviet Union.

- WESTERN EUROPE
  1. Things aren't going so well with capitalism.
     Spanish building workers on strike.
  2. Dangers, tensions appearing.
     Spanish journal denounces "Soviet imperialist aggression and expansion in Africa."
     NATO urges strengthening of defenses against Soviet military buildup.
     EEC summit meets in Brussels.
     NATO foreign ministers meet.
  3. Many signs of friendship for China appear.
     British scholar lectures (in London) on China's contributions to world science and technology.
     Banquet is held in Peking for visiting Swedish Red Youth.
     President of Institute of Foreign Affairs in Peking meets with visiting deputy director of (English) International Institute of Strategic Studies.
     Finnish ambassador gives independence day reception in Peking, and Finland celebrates 60th anniversary of independence (including resistance to Russia).
     Vice minister in Peking receives West German minister.
     Vice premier meets outgoing Austrian ambassador.
     China wins table tennis tournament in France.
     Chinese musicians conclude visit to West Germany.
     Italian prime minister receives visiting Chinese journalist delegation.
     Chinese journalists' delegation leaves Italy for Switzerland.
  4. There are signs that Western Europe is ready to cooperate.
     Mauritania signs cooperative agreement with West Germany and France.
     Hungary-West Germany commission meets in Budapest.

Journal of Communist Party in Switzerland publishes Mao's article on "Three Worlds."

France cooperates with Arab emirates to raise military capabilities.

Somali delegation ends visit to Western Europe—U.K., France, West Germany.

And incidentally, new Swiss federal president elected.

- EAST EUROPE
  1. There are signs of development and growing strength.
     Hungary develops animal husbandry.
     Yugoslav women play big role in social, political, economic life.
     National conference of Romanian Communist Party closes. Yugoslavia participates in meeting of international bauxite association, adopting minimum-pricing standard.
     Hungary completes dam over River Koros.
  2. There are signs of cooperation.
     Hungary-West Germany commission meets in Budapest.
     Tito visits Romania.
     Tito concludes visit to Romania and returns home.
     Yugoslav official visits Spain.
     Minister of foreign affairs of Burundi visits Yugoslavia.
  3. Friendship for China is seen.
     Chinese vice-premier meets Romanian delegation.
     Guests from East Germany banqueted in Peking.
     Banquet is held for visiting scientific-technical delegation from Czechoslovakia.
     Chinese journalists' group leaves for Yugoslavia.

- THE MIDDLE EAST
  1. There is rather indirect treatment of existing tensions.
     Turkey and Egypt call for total withdrawal of Israeli forces.
     Sadat denounces Soviet Union for bringing discord to Arabs (no details and no mention of Tripoli meeting or negotiations with Israel).
     King Hussein of Jordan visits Egypt: no mention is made of Tripoli meeting.
  2. The Middle Eastern countries stand up to threats from outside countries.
     France cooperates with Arab emirates to raise military capabilities.
     Iraq and Iran issue joint communique on "struggle against imperialism."
     Malta prime minister says he will try to make Mediterranean a "lake of peace."
  3. These countries are cooperating.
     Meeting is held of governors of Arab bank for development.
     Saudi Arabia offers loan to Brazil.

Tunisian secretary of state visits Algeria.

Shah of Iran visits Oman.

Chilean foreign minister ends visit to Egypt.

  Prime minister of Malta ends visit to Algiers.

4. Friendship for China is seen.

Yemen Arab Republic receives Chinese ambassador.

Turkish prime minister receives Chinese sports minister.

Chinese observer attends sports council assembly in Damascus.

Chinese ambassador is received by premier of Yemen.

Visiting Chinese journalists are received by Tunisian prime minister.

Chinese team plays two basketball games in Turkey.

- AFRICA
  1. South Africa is denounced.

Southwest Africa Peoples Organization condemns South Africa.

Independence of Bophutswana is called "fraud and crime."

Bophutswana becomes independent; writer attacks South Africa.

Several African countries condemn South Africa's racist policies.

U.N. adopts resolution on decolonization aimed in large part at South Africa.

Blacks resist in South Africa.

U.N. Security Council adopts resolution for arms embargo against South Africa.

  2. Somalia, especially, stands up to the Russians.

Items previously mentioned, chiefly: protest intrusion into fishing grounds, denounced Soviet intervention, interview with composer of resistance song.

Somali weekly denounces intervention.

  3. Africa is developing and cooperating.

Conference on developing Lake Chad held in Nigeria.

Seminars on tuberculosis and leprosy held in Tanzania.

Ghana-Ivory Coast cooperation commission meets.

Nigerian head of state visists Mauritania.

Zambian president praises accomplishments of president of Somalia.

Nigeria and Mauritania sign economic cooperation agreement.

Re-elected President Mobuto of Zaire sworn in.

Election is held in Mozambique.

  4. Friendship for China is seen.

Hua sends greetings to Mobuto.

Chinese medical team leaves Cameroon after giving medical assistance.

Chinese friendship delegation leaves Benin.

- LATIN AMERICA
  1. Latin American countries are developing.
     Venezuela is trying to help Caribbean islands.
     Venezuela President says Latin America must integrate.
     Venezuela President says Latin America must develop its agriculture.
     New variety of maize is discovered in Mexico.
     Guyana has record rice output.
     Andean agriculture ministers meet.
     Latin American foreign ministers meeting on matters of Plata Basin.
     Meeting of Chile-Peru cooperation commission closes.
     420,000 have been trained in professions in Venezuela this year.
  2. Latin American countries stand in freedom and dignity.
     Panamanian struggle for sovereignty over Canal represents victory for entire continent.
     Peru celebrates anniversary of Battle of Ayacucho, which was important in achieving independence for Latin America.
  3. Latin America recognizes value of its culture and art.
     Silverwares fair is held in Mexico.
     Guyana holds national arts exhibition.
     Central American games will be held in El Salvador.
  4. Friendship for China is seen.
     Chinese women's basketball team leaves Peru for Ecuador.
     Chinese basketball team plays Ecuador team.

- THE SOUTH PACIFIC
  1. Friendship for China is seen.
     Chinese foreign minister meets former minister of New Zealand in Peking.
     Chinese and Australian gymnasts have friendly contest in Peking.

- JAPAN
  1. Things are not so good with capitalism.
     Nineteen Japanese shipyards have closed down this year—no reference is made to thriving Japanese economy.
  2. Japan stands up to the Soviet Union.
     Yomiuri says USSR is obstructing signing of Sino-Japanese treaty.
     Contemporary Asia, Japanese biweekly, accuses USSR of hegemonism in trying to obstruct Sino-Japanese treaty.
     Northern Central News supports Somali's abrogation of Soviet treaty.
     Japan rejects Soviet request for fishing port facilities.
  3. Friendship for China is seen.
     Chinese representatives to meeting on fishery leave Japan.

Japan and China take part in Western Pacific seminar on fertility.

Vice-premier meets Japanese friendship delegation in Peking.

Vice-premier meets delegation from Japanese military academy, apparently including some of his old classmates.

Banquet is held for visiting Japanese delegation.

Another Japanese delegation visits Peking.

Talks are held in Peking with visiting Japanese friendship delegation.

Luncheon is given in Peking for visiting Japanese Working Group Friendship delegation.

- ASIA
  1. Signs of development and cooperation are evident.

     Western Pacific seminar on fertility (in which China participated) ends in Manila.

     India and China sign trade pact in New Delhi.

     Pakistan gives Bangladesh cement.

     Bangladesh has built 2,368 miles of embankment along seacoast.

     Pakistan and Bangladesh agree to develop trade.

     North Korea signs trade agreement with Egypt.

     Indian prime minister visits Nepal.

  2. They stand up against Big Powers.

     Kim Il Sung, "Great leader of the Korean people," expounds tasks of workers party of North Korea.

     Iran signs joint communique with Iraq, promising struggle against imperialism.

     Thailand celebrates National Day.

  3. Friendship for China is seen.

     Reception in Peking celebrates birthday of Thai King.

     Reception is given in Peking for Iranian volleyball team.

     Iranian Ambassador gives banquet for Teng.

     Pakistan folk craft exhibition opens in China.

     Dinner is given in Peking for North Korea laser study group.

     Delegation from Korean tourist agency arrives in Peking.

     Chinese film delegation visits Vietnam.

     Vice-chairman of Chinese People's Congress is in Iran.

     Member of Chinese Central Committee tours province of Cambodia.

     Pakistan chief receives visiting Chinese football team.

     Vice premier tours part of Cambodia.

     Chinese tennis team visits Afghanistan.

     Chinese song and dance troupe arrives in Burma.

     Chinese vice chairman meets with vice chairman of Vietnamese National Assembly, in Peking.

     New Chinese ambassador to Malaysia leaves for post.

     Meteorological agreement is signed between China and Mongolia.

Basketball championship of Asian countries is held in Malaysia;
China won (numerous stories throughout week).
Iranian volleyball team loses to China in Peking.

News About China

Up to this point we have been cataloguing, with almost no
exceptions, *all* the stories in Hsinhua bearing on areas of the
world other than China. It will already have become apparent
that China is an actor in many of these stories. However, there
are also a number of stories dealing only with China. Together,
the number of stories dealing only with China or with China
and another country (or countries) represent 70 to 75 percent
of the total wire. On the first day of the week analyzed, for
example, twenty-five of thirty-five stories had to do directly
with China. To give some idea of the picture of China being
given the Chinese people by Hsinhua, let us catalogue the
stories on China that appeared on the wire during one day of
the week (December 5) only:

- CHINA
    1. China is developing, growing in strength.
       Ministry of Education drafts plan for developing fourteen sci-
          entific disciplines.
       Many Chinese factories, mines, and other enterprises are ahead
          of schedule in fulfilling plans.
       More than 300,000 Tibetan peasants are working on farm and
          pasture improvement.
       National conference on electronic industry closed yesterday.
       Rubber production is ahead of schedule.
       Editorial (carried entire) from *People's Daily* boosts electronics
          development.
    2. The Soviet Union is an enemy of China.
       Yomiuri of Japan accuses USSR of obstructing signing of peace
          and friendship treaty with Japan.
    3. China is cooperating with other countries.
       China participates in Western Pacific seminar on fertility, in
          Manila.

Chinese film delegation visits Vietnam.

Chinese minister of foreign trade has been in U.K. and now arrives in Paris.

Teng Ying Chao, vice chairman of Standing Committee of Chinese National People's Congress, is quoted at length on speech there.

China signs trade protocol in New Delhi with India.

China defeats Philippines in basketball, and advances in Asian Men's Basketball Championship, in Malaysia.

China B team loses to Turkey in basketball.

4. China is offering friendship to all countries that want to be friends.

Chinese vice-premier meets visiting Romanian delegates.

Birthday of Thai king is celebrated by reception in Peking.

Banquet is given for visiting Swedish Red Youth.

Luncheon is held for visiting Japanese Working Group Friendship delegation.

Foreign minister meets former New Zealand Minister, in Peking.

Talks are held with visiting Japanese Friendship delegation.

Reception is held in Peking for visiting Iranian volleyball team.

President of Chinese Institute of Foreign Affairs has meeting with deputy director of International Institute of Strategic Studies, from England.

Guests from East Germany are banqueted in Peking.

Another Japanese delegation is entertained in Peking.

A Few Quantitative Notes on Hsinhua

The New China News Agency does not provide a very large news service. The wire available in Hong Kong carried a little more than 53,000 words during the week of December 5–11—just over 7,500 words a day. By contrast, the four principal international news services—the Associated Press, Agence France-Presse, Reuters, and United Press International—carried an average of 26,000 words each per day on Third World news alone. Hsinhua carried 230 separate items during the week mentioned. The mean length was just over 225 words per item; the median, just under 200.

Hsinhua is distinguished, however, by the high proportion of attention it gives to Third World news, and especially to news of China. About 6,600 of Hsinhua's daily average 7,500 words are devoted to the Third World. Here are the percentages:

Non-Third World	12.2
Third World and Others	31.3
Third World only	56.5

So, 46.5 percent of all the stories during that week (108 out of 230) had China as their main actor. No other country was the main topic of more than 3 percent of the stories (Japan 2.6; Australia, Venezuela, Nigeria, and the U.S., 1.7 percent each). China was *an* actor, although not necessarily the principal one, in about 62 percent of the stories. For other countries, the corresponding percentages were much smaller (for example: USSR, 5.0; Japan, 4.5; South Africa, the U.S., and Australia, 2.0 percent each, and so on).

The focus of attention by regions of the world is also revealing. Here are Hsinhua's 230 items classified by the country or area of major interest:

	Percents
Non-Third World	12.2 (28 out of 230)
All Asia (except Japan)	47.0 (108)
Latin America	9.6 (22)
Middle East	11.3 (26)
Africa (except South Africa)	20.0 (46)

In this tabulation, of course, somewhere over 30 of the Asian 47 percentage would be attributable to China. In the other areas, a high proportion of the stories also would be about Chinese friendship or diplomatic representation or sports or cultural participation. Therefore the wire is very closely focused on China.

Almost exactly half of Hsinhua's stories deal with foreign relations, about 18 percent with economic news, and 10 percent with sports. Here is the division by categories of news, for the wire as a total, and as proportions of the non-Third World, the Third World News, and the items dealing with both.

Another way to look at the division by categories of news is to compare the emphasis on different types of news, within the news of non-Third World events, events involving both Third and non-Third World countries, and the Third World countries only. In the category with the highest frequency, foreign relations—with 115 articles—the percentages were 47.8, Third World only; 44.3, both Third World and non-Third World; and 7.8, non-Third World only. Economics was the next highest in frequency, with 41 items, and had percentages of 73.2, Third World only; 7.3, both Third World and non-Third World; and 19.5, non-Third World only. Sports was third highest, with 23 items, and percentages were 56.5, Third World only, 39.1, Third World and non-Third World; and 4.3, non-Third World only. Science was fourth highest with 17 articles during the week, with percentages of 82.4, Third World only; 17.6, Third World and non-Third World; and 0.0, non-Third World only. Similar imbalances in coverage were

Table 17.1 Categories and Proportions (in Percents) of News

Category	Total wire	Non-Third World	Third & Non-Third World	Third World only
Military and other political violence	3.5	2.6	0.9	0.0
Foreign relations	50.0	3.9	22.2	23.9
Domestic politics	5.2	1.3	0.4	3.5
Economic	17.8	3.5	1.3	13.0
Science	7.4	0.0	1.3	6.1
Education	2.2	0.0	0.4	1.7
Human Rights	0.9	0.4	0.4	0.0
Sports	10.0	0.4	3.9	5.7
Arts	2.6	0.0	0.4	2.2
Human Interest	0.4	0.0	0.0	0.4
N = 230 Total	100.0	12.2	31.3	56.5

present in most of the other categories, but with smaller frequencies.

To sum up, the New China News Agency sends a rather short news wire, highly focused on China but intended for other countries as well, highly centralized in Peking, highly disciplined, with a world view built on Mao's concept of "Three Worlds," and all of its news is interpreted against this consistent world view and political purpose. Of all the world's news services intended for international use, it gives perhaps the greatest proportional representation to Third World news, and, of course, to news of China itself.

Part IV

Evolving Directions in International Communication

FUNDAMENTAL CHANGES have recently taken place in international communication policies and practices, and more will inevitably follow. This concluding section describes some of the far-reaching developments, both completed and in progress. It indicates that new paths in news and information are being opened up in today's crisis-ridden, interdependent world, where communication is part of both the problem and the potential solution.

By the early 1980s, it was clear that one result of a decade of heated North-South debate and East-West confrontation over communication was an increasingly multi-polar international news environment. Various dynamic processes were evident in the way the existing news system was working and—more significantly—was being transformed. Particularly important were the unmistakable trends toward more explicit national and international communication policies and planning and the gradual evolution of a new conceptual and institutional foundation as the "New International Communication Order."

Not everyone, of course, is optimistic about any new order or the "decolonization" or "democratization" changes affecting how news is defined, collected, and disseminated. Media-strong countries like the United States stand to lose economically, politically, and militarily if "radical" new order proposals to increase South-South communication, or even if Unesco and other international organization resolutions, are implemented.

This section suggests why many in the West continue to be deeply troubled by what they perceive to be continuing bitter ideological conflicts and dangerous antidemocratic trends toward government control of domestic and international media and loss of human rights. They strongly reject the trend toward the remodeling of society and news and believe the world's communication problems can gradually be solved without a radical disruption of the present system and with less of what they see as "empty" or "inflammatory" rhetoric.

Both radicals and reformers recognize that much can and should be done to correct the historic news distortions and other problems with the existing system. The risks, of course, are great, and the times will place a premium on not only innovative ideas and policies but also on goodwill and patience among enlightened people everywhere.

18

Emerging Patterns of Global News Cooperation

MICHAEL H. ANDERSON

Dr. Anderson argues that despite all the conflict over highly contentious issues in the 1970s, more efficient and diversified communication is occurring over a wide front, in many different places, and part of the control over world and national news services is gradually shifting to a wider range of non-Western nations and organizations. He analyzes various emerging accommodation trends toward genuine global news cooperation and details how mutually reinforcing political, economic, and technological changes are underway within international organizations and the transnational news agencies, and, most importantly, within and between the developing nations.

DESPITE ALL the present-day conflict over some highly contentious issues, more efficient and diversified communication is occurring between nations, and alternatives to the status quo are being fostered.

Through practical bilateral and subregional, regional, and international interaction, a foundation for a more just and effective news system at world and national levels is being built, surprisingly calmly and constructively in light of the bitter ideological debates over a "new order" which almost tore Unesco apart in the mid-1970s.

All this is going on over a wide front, in many different places, and much of the control over world and national news service is shifting to a wider range of non-Western nations and organizations. A degree of genuine partnership and accommodation, albeit selective and fragile, was evident, and a modest but basic restructuring of news relationships was well underway. By the end of 1980, for example, Unesco member states at their Belgrade meeting had approved an International Program for the Development of Communication. This intergovernmental mechanism, under Unesco auspices, should help developing countries plan and fund practical ways to improve their communication infrastructures.

The purpose of this essay is to highlight some of the far-reaching improvements and changes in how the transnational news agencies (TNNAs) are operating unilaterally and relating to Third World nations, and how Third World nations themselves are relating to other developing nations.

"New Order" Trends

By the early 1980s, three important "new order" trends affecting *both* affluent, media-strong, politically powerful nations and relatively poor, media-deficient, and politically weak nations were evident:

1. News and information were increasingly being perceived in Third World nations as critical social commodities or resources (not only marketable goods) and as key sources of political power and self-determination.
2. The Western-based TNNAs were paying more attention—quantitatively *and* qualitatively—to Third World issues and concerns.
3. Third World governments and media were giving increased attention to developments among their neighbors and in other nations with similar problems and perspectives. This has led to a higher level of general cooperation among less developed societies.

Powerful nations like the Soviet Union and the United States have long recognized that propaganda and information are power, and they have put considerable effort into such international communication activities as foreign broadcasts, press and publications services, films, exhibits, and visitor and exchange programs. But only relatively recently have less developed nations seriously considered the urgency of gaining more control over sources and channels of mass communication.

Without such power, Third World nations realize that they cannot control their "window on the world," and they cannot effectively project a positive international image as independent nations working toward economic and social development.

At the national level, many Third World nations are trying to improve their communication facilities and are promoting such ideas as "development journalism" and "development support communication" programs. Internationally, they are assigning unprecedented importance to Unesco and other international organizations involved in aspects of communication, and they are emphasizing three needs:

—*Change* in the deeper, structural sense
—Greater *self-reliance*
—Explicit national and international development *policies* and comprehensive *plans* to coherently deal with the media and the use of communication in support of development.

These objectives and the debates over how to achieve them have put the Western media, as well as governments, clearly on the defensive and made them intensely troubled by the political thicket they recently have been forced into. At the same time, however, once hard-line TNNA and government officials have become more sensitized to Third World pleas, they no longer refuse to acknowledge that many of the criticisms do warrant action, and they have tried to respond pragmatically (and cautiously) to an increasingly impatient, even militant, Third World which almost schizophrenically both wants and rejects TNNA and other kinds of service and assistance. Tunisia, for instance, despite the fact that it has been an outspoken leader in the movement for a new world information order, feels that it cannot be isolated and that it must deal with the TNNAs. This is why in 1978 its Tunis Afrique Presses (TAP) not only opened a New York bureau at the U.N. but also completed an agreement with the Associated Press. The agreement means the Tunisian national news agency would distribute AP's international news within Tunisia and have access to AP training for its journalists. AP, in turn, would have access to TAP's domestic report for international distribution.[1]

Western news organizations, then, are not alone in having to change their ways and search for common ground. Some self-critical developing nations now admit that closer news exchange links with the TNNAs *and* unilateral changes within their own domestic borders can solve some of the pressing problems.

Many Third World nations also are recognizing the value of fostering direct ties with other developing societies, rather than relying on a few highly developed nations, for most of their economic, development, and other information.

Under the catchall phrase "new order," many Third World societies have moved toward policies and programs that emphasize the "balanced flow" concept of information. Some of these measures designed to eliminate various obstacles have fostered both confrontation and cooperation, and they have been closely followed by both transnational media and governments in the Western liberal democracies.

In general, the nations less than enthusiastic about the creation of any new order have vigorously asserted that an increasingly interdependent world needs to take steps that will widen—not narrow—the free circulation of information throughout a pluralistic world.

The United States would certainly lose if a new order

---

1. "AP, Tunisian Agency to Exchange News," *AP Log* (November 13, 1978), p. 2.

were implemented with various national and international communication policies on any wide scale. The concept does far more than challenge America's generally privileged position and its ability to influence trade, culture, and defense by freely selling communication software (not only news, but also advertising, movies, television programs, books, data, and music) and hardware (satellites, telephones, computers, telex). At its worst, a new order could seriously disrupt TNNA operations and threaten America's strong commitment to the philosophy that the media should be privately owned and "free and independent."

New order critics fear that Third World militants want a radically different communication (and economic) order that would sanction government control of information and prevent a free flow of goods, services, and ideas. These critics emphasize the free flow principle and strongly oppose international action in such areas as responsibilities and duties of the media, official codes of ethics for journalists, licensing of journalists, international right of reply, and special protective measures applying to journalists.

At the national level, critics of the new order are particularly suspicious of efforts to approach communication policies, both implicit and explicit, systematically as a means to meet international and domestic pressures. The notion of absolute national communication sovereignty, for example, is the kind of policy issue feared by the West and the TNNAs, who need to operate in a variety of foreign countries.

Despite about half a decade of relatively widespread usage and lengthy statements by new order advocates, the new world information order continues to be a disorderly, imprecise concept. Individuals and governments, even within the nonaligned movement itself, have different interpretations of how the concept should evolve, and how news organizations at home and abroad do and should function.

The TNNAs and Western governments tend to agree that the best route to solving the problems and misunderstandings is through an evolutionary process of cooperation rather than through confrontation. They want developing nations to expand their communication capacities by taking advantage of emerging technologies (admittedly developed in the West), strengthening private institutions and professionalism, and concentrating on change at local and national—rather than international—levels. They want what they call the "strident rhetoric" reduced and greater emphasis placed on gradual change through indigenous national development efforts, but also through the pragmatic cooperation of *both* First and Second Worlds.

Clearly, however, the new order consists of more than mere inflammatory talk or even evolutionary change at local and national levels. It is a very real and basic political concept having to do with the principle of national sovereignty and complex changes at both intra- and international levels. Despite its continued ambiguity, the new order in the early 1980s had come to symbolize a recognition that the status quo in news and international communication was no longer viable to much of the world. Even in the United States—with an extensive open communication system largely run by private interests and with many critics of the new order—there was an increasing recognition of the need to develop a comprehensive national communication policy.

The remainder of this essay will highlight some of the important changes and trends now underway within the Western-based TNNAs and among the Third World nations themselves. Most of the examples will be taken from AP and UPI because information is more readily available on them and because, together, they seem to attract more Third World attention than AFP, Visnews, or Reuters. This is not intended to lessen the importance of the non-American TNNAs—Visnews, for example, reaches about 99 percent of the world's TV audience with its news film service from London.[2]

2. For background on Visnews, see R. Cheek, "Visnews Ltd.: A Report." (Sydney: Visnews, 1979), and Visnews, "Visnews—The First Twenty Years 1957–1977" (London: Visnews Ltd., 1977). See also Jonathan King's "Visnews and UPITN: News Film Supermarkets in the Sky," in this volume.

Changes Within the TNNAs

The TNNAs are not really changing their organizational objectives or their ownership and management arrangements, but they *are* changing how and what they report and how they distribute the news.

AP, for example, continues in the legal form it has had since 1900 when it was incorporated in New York as the first nonprofit cooperative news organization. It continues to be controlled by "member" American newspapers, and it continues to be particularly influential in the United States and Latin American news markets. Worldwide, AP continues to deal in what it considers to be legitimate news and its policy is to be truthful and impartial.

What has changed within AP, however, are some of its approaches to news gathering and some of the tools it uses to transmit its reports. Also, the TNNA is no longer an unknown entity operating in isolation in midtown Manhattan. Global developments have forced AP to become a more open, flexible, and receptive organization that recognizes the world is not monolithic and that any news organization's policies and practices—even in as basic an area as defining what is news—are open to sincere, critical questioning.

As anyone who has walked into the headquarters of a TNNA recently knows, the most visible changes have to do with technical areas. In 1980, I visited the New York City world headquarters of both AP and UPI and saw first-hand how these TNNAs had invested millions of dollars in technology and product innovation specifically designed to transmit news faster, cheaper, further, and in larger quantities. Computers, satellites, video display terminals (VDTs), the Electronic Darkroom, and lasers are proof of the important role that the TNNAs have assigned to automation, high speeds, and research development.

The days when the TNNAs' reports were transmitted by tickers at the speed of 60 or so words per minute are rapidly disappearing. Today, hundreds of thousands of words are sent by cable and satellite at 1,200 words per minute. AP has a North American circuit that routinely operates at about 9,600 words per minute, and the TNNA is even able to make computer-to-computer transmissions at 56,000 words per minute.

In the late 1960s, UPI began implementing an electronic news gathering, editing, and distributing system called "Information Storage and Retrieval (IS&R)," and its New York bureau became the first completely electronic newsroom in the world. All UPI reporters and editors in the United States, Canada, Mexico, and Europe were using VDTs to write, edit, and transmit news stories by the end of the 1970s. Their stories were filed in a central New York computer, which editors anywhere in the system could tap for reediting and filing to meet requirements of subscribers in particular regions. The system cost about $12 million to design and implement, and it can handle up to 15 million words a day and hold two days' news files.[3]

In 1979, UPI broke away from its tradition of centralizing all facilities in New York when it established a $10 million technical service center in Dallas, Texas. This first-of-its-kind computer facility center was designed to link together journalists working at more than 400 VDTs in the United States and Europe into a single high-speed network. The facility has at least tripled UPI's data handling capacity.[4]

To a TNNA like UPI, the computer has literally become more essential than a typewriter or a telex machine. The agency has developed a highly sophisticated worldwide communication network around computers in Brussels (for Europe, Africa, and the Middle East) and Hong Kong (for Asia and Australia). UPI's vice-president Frank Tremaine has explained that technology makes it possible "for UPI to operate almost as though it were one huge, worldwide newsroom."[5]

---

3. Frank Tremaine, "United Press International: Origin, Organization and Operations" (New York: UPI, January 1978), sec. 4, pp. 3–4.

4. See Roderick W. Beaton, "UPI 1979 Progress Report" (New York: UPI 1979), p. 1, and UPI/The News Company," a UPI advertisement in *Editor & Publisher* (August 18, 1979), p. 1.

5. Tremaine, sec. 3, p. 5.

The satellite, too, has become indispensable to TNNA worldwide news dissemination. Transnational transmission by satellite has proven far cheaper, better in quality, and technically more flexible than traditional land-based means. UPI, for example, was an early user of satellite transmission of photos to and from Asia, and it now regularly serves Asia, Australia, and Europe by satellite. UPI has opened a full-speed satellite circuit between New Delhi and Hong Kong and between London and Bahrain and London and Abu Dhabi, and directly link Latin American nations like Bolivia and Paraguay to New York headquarters.[6]

AP is moving rapidly to a satellite delivery system. In 1981, for example, APRadio was already in service, and data transmission tests were underway in the United States on a growing satellite delivery system, bringing the agency's basic news report closer to satellite delivery. AP's financial services will be the first data services put on the Westar III satellite, but others will follow. Keith Fuller, AP president, has said that the satellite project "marks our full maturity in communications, which began with ownership of teleprinters and now is striding forward with an AP-owned, designed, installed, and managed satellite communications system for the 80's and beyond."

AP also has been a leader in photo transmission. In 1974, it broke new ground by introducing the use of lasers in an innovative facsimile newsphoto receiver called Laserphoto or Laserfax. By 1977, AP had introduced the remarkable Electronic Darkroom, a system built around a computer modified with special equipment to bring under electronic control functions traditionally performed in a photographic darkroom. And by 1980, AP was participating in five "information retrieval" projects. In one, for example, the TNNA and eleven member newspapers were joined in an experiment to test information retrieval service to home personal computers. For $5 an hour, a person with a home computer could dial special

6. Ibid., p. 6, and Beaton, p. 5.

telephone numbers to gain access to news, business data, and other information provided by AP and the newspapers.[7]

Other TNNA innovations are in the works. UPI, for example, is expanding its UPI NEWSTIME, the world's first satellite-delivered, all news cable TV channel in the United States.[8] The TNNA also is developing a service it calls Newshare, a computer timeshare enterprise that it believes could signal the beginning of electronic home delivery of information from local newspapers and its own databank.[9]

Despite undeniable technological progress, major doubts remain as to what long-term effects these TNNA innovations will have on news imbalances. Obviously, some of the new communications hardware has trickled down to the developing countries, and some national agencies and Third World-oriented organizations like Inter Press Service (IPS) are using some of it. But, given the economics of news gathering, the nagging question that remains is whether sophisticated innovations in the long run actually preserve—not change—the status quo. Some Third World nations suspect that the pace and direction of technological changes work to maintain—and even increase—various gaps between the haves and the have nots.

In nontechnical areas, the most significant change has to do with the nature of the actual coverage. Largely because of long-standing complaints from both home market and overseas subscribers that stories about unique, complex problems (such as Vietnam and the energy crisis) were not as balanced, complete, or meaningful as the average reader (or at least the media gatekeeping editor) felt desirable, the TNNAs have made changes in their news coverage. To some extent, the TNNAs have inched away from traditional "event journalism" and

---

7. "Satellite System Goal: Save $3.5 Million," *AP Log* (April 28, 1980), p. 1; AP, "The Associated Press. How it Came to Be and What It Has Become." (New York: AP, 1978), pp. 10–12; "AP, Members Join in Information Retrieval," *AP Log* (June 9, 1980), p. 1; and Larry Blasko, "Satellite Date Transmission Test to Start," *AP Log* (December 8, 1980), p. 1.

8. Beaton, "UPI 1979 Progress Report," p. 4.

9. For details on how a TNNA can use new technology, see Lean Rozen, "UPI Plugs News, Ads into Home Computer," *Advertising Age* (June 11, 1979), p. 4.

toward "process journalism" and are seriously asking themselves, "What is news?" And they are paying more attention at home to pressing problems like "pocketbook issues" and abroad to Third World perspectives generally. They are trying to address the complex, often emotional national development concerns raised by many Third World leaders and journalists.

Because of strong Third World feeling that the West ignores developing nations' achievements, the TNNAs have had to at least appear to be shifting their news focus somewhat. Mort Rosenblum, the former editor of the *International Herald Tribune* and AP foreign correspondent, explained:

Many editors, sensitized by the confrontation, have decided to take a more positive approach toward developing countries. Reporters are cautioned to avoid gratuitous sidelights which might be taken as slurs and to seek balancing "good points" when reporting on development setbacks. And they are asked to try to see things from the viewpoint of the society they are covering.[10]

In a sense, too, the TNNAs have consciously tried to improve the quality of their services and emphasize why foreign news is vital to everyone. They say they are trying to give greater attention to grass roots life and developments throughout a country rather than only in the capital city; about regions and areas rather than only nation-states; about subjects other than politics and economics; and about processes and trends rather than one-shot, spot news event, such as disasters, violence, and political crises.

One important factor behind some change in TNNA coverage is the increased competition at home and abroad. In the United States especially, specialized and supplement news services have grown in influence. Particularly important are the services run by the *New York Times* and, jointly, by the *Washington Post* and *Los Angeles Times*. They provide serious news and special features and analyses to media in the United States and abroad, and have special appeal to papers that want

10. Mort Rosenblum, *Coups and Earthquakes: Reporting the World for America* (New York: Harper & Row, 1979), p. 13.

prestige or reduced costs. To cope with rising production costs and shrinking news holes, many media feel they no longer need to take both AP and UPI. Therefore, they might drop one of the TNNAs—most likely UPI—and replace it with a comparatively inexpensive, compact supplementary service's package of "exclusives." In the United States, for example, about 18 percent of the 1,750-plus daily newspapers subscribe to both AP and UPI. This is a drop from 25 percent over about a decade.[11]

Technology is an area where increased formal sharing among the TNNAs may evolve. Recently, there has been evidence of American TNNA cooperation on satellites. UPI and AP and cooperating organizations like the American Newspaper Publishers Association have developed a domestic satellite delivery system which would permit the full array of news services to be received by subscribers on one small-dish ground satellite receiver only six feet in diameter.[12]

Official sharing of news is a more delicate area, and antitrust laws tend to encourage strong competition among the agencies.

Equally, if not more, sensitive to American media are suggestions that they work closer with the government. Despite the historic tradition of arm's-length relations, recent political developments have forced the TNNAs to have greater contact—informal and formal—with top-level American officials charged with formulating international communication policy and representing U.S. interests in various international meetings. For example, until 1979 AP was so wary of the Voice of America as a government propaganda organization that it refused to sell its news to the International Communication Agency's foreign broadcast operation.

Intense pressures and challenges, particularly at Unesco

11. For data on what TNNAs American dailies buy, see Edwin Emery and Michael Emery, *The Press and America*, 4 ed. (Englewood Cliffs, N.J.: Prentice-Hall, 1978), p. 307, and Daniel Machalaba, "UPI Struggles as It Loses Ground to AP, Other News Services," *The Wall Street Journal*, July 11, 1979, p. 1.

12. See Tremaine, sec. 4, p. 5; Beaton, p. 5; and "Satellites Play Major Role in UPI's News Distribution," *Editor & Publisher* (April 30, 1977), p. 52.

meetings in the mid-1970s, virtually forced American media and the State Department and the International Communication Agency, formerly the U.S. Information Agency (USIA), to start coordinating their efforts to respond to what they perceived as a genuine threat from the Soviet Union and the Third World. For example, senior American media representatives worked hand-in-hand with top American officials at the Unesco General Conference in Nairobi in 1976. These American government and media representatives, along with other Western governments and media, successfully lobbied against a Soviet-sponsored draft declaration on the use of the mass media.

Westerners generally felt that such a proposal was totally unacceptable because it would give an international seal of approval to state control of all media inside, entering, and/or leaving a country. Head-on confrontation at Nairobi was averted when the proposal was sent to committee for redrafting, the Unesco director-general appointed a prestigious group of sixteen "wise men" under Sean MacBride to study "the totality of communication problems in the modern world," and the United States acknowledged the existence of various problems and proposed multilateral help for Third World nations to develop their communication systems.

In the "spirit of Nairobi," a group of primarily Western journalistic organizations joined forces to establish the World Press Freedom Committee to work for a better relationship between developed and developing countries. The committee pledged to try to raise $1 million from the private sector to sponsor various assistance projects, to make used equipment available to Third World media, and to provide a manpower pool of journalism experts who could serve overseas as consultants and technicians.

By Unesco's 1978 General Conference, tensions had lessened, and a compromise declaration acceptable to all 146 Unesco member states was approved. Also at the conference, the United States emphasized the need for concrete and practical approaches to communication problems. John Reinhardt, ICA director, said the United States was committed to pro-

viding assistance to Third World regional centers of professional education and training in broadcasting and journalism
and to applying communication technology, specifically satellites, to economic and social needs in the rural areas of developing nations.[13]

One significant outcome from the various pressures on
American media and government has been a realization that
the United States was relatively unprepared for the international communication debate and that the American government—with advice from the media—had to move faster and develop more explicit communication policies. It is clear that
during the 1980s communication will remain an important
issue before various American government agencies, and that
practical actions will require joint actions from public and
private sectors. Unilaterally, the government cannot do much
to change how news flows at home or abroad. The economically weak TNNAs are limited in the amount of technical
assistance they can provide, and they certainly cannot force
their subscribers to use Third World dispatches.

Following the Nairobi debate, the TNNAs generally became more openly receptive to cooperative arrangements, particularly the provision of training, in the Third World. It must
be emphasized, however, that the TNNAs and many local
media, including national news agencies, have long had close,
mutually beneficial relations.

Cooperation, for example in the case of AP, has taken
various forms, including:

- "Agreements under which a national agency distributes AP
  news and/or newsphotos. Reciprocal access to the national
  agency's news and/or photos is a part of such arrangements."
- "Subscription to the news and/or photo service of a national
  or local agency with whom AP has no redistribution agreement. AP pays for the right of access to the agency's news and
  photos and AP use outside the country of origin."

13. For the American government's position at the 1978 Unesco General Conference, see John E. Reinhardt, "General Policy Statement." Paper delivered at Unesco
twentieth General Conference, Paris, November 3, 1978.

- Consultancies on "all aspects of news agency operation and planning" and "assistance in the communications area."[14]

The TNNAs, of course, are intensely interested in national news agencies for two important reason. First, some national news agencies relay TNNA materials to local subscribers. Second, national news agencies are principal sources of TNNAs' news. Since none of the TNNAs can afford to station a full-time correspondent or even a stringer in every place where news might develop, they all rely very heavily upon local media, particularly national news agencies, and want them strengthened.

These examples will suggest the variety of ways through which the TNNAs are cooperating with the Third World:

- In 1979, distribution of AP news was resumed after a news exchange agreement between AP and Cuba's national news agency, Prensa Latina, was signed (in 1969 the TNNA's Havana office was closed by the Cuban government). Under the agreement, AP's Spanish report from New York is sent to Havana for distribution by Prensa Latina, and the Cuban agency's news is sent to AP in Mexico City.[15]
- In 1978, UPI provided training to interns from Nigeria, Iran, Kuwait, the United Arab Emirates, South Korea, and Japan. UPI also provided technical assistance to Saudi Press Agency in Riyadh[16] for design and construction of a new, computerized editorial and news picture center.
- Over a twelve-month period in the late 1970s, AP participated in training or advisory programs with the news agencies of Argentina, Kuwait, Nigeria, Liberia, Indonesia, Ghana, and Iran.[17]
- In Latin America, Reuters in 1971 administratively and financially helped establish a regional agency, LATIN, as a cooperative among thirteen member newspapers from Mexico to Chile. Veteran Reuters executive Patrick Cross put LATIN

14. AP, "The Associated Press. How It Came to Be and What It Has Become," p. 13.

15. "AP, Cuban Agency to Exchange Reports," AP Log (August 20, 1979), p. 4.

16. Beaton, "UPI 1979 Progress Report," p. 4.

17. AP's Stanley M. Swinton in a public talk at the East-West Communication Institute, Honolulu, June 14, 1979.

into operation, and the two agencies shared an office in Buenos Aires.[18]

- In 1975, Reuters worked closely with thirteen Commonwealth Caribbean nations to establish CANA, the Caribbean News Agency. Based in Barbados, CANA was basically patterned on Reuters' former Caribbean Service. It distributes Reuters World File in the region and feeds its Caribbean file daily to New York and London.[19]

- Visnews has provided a variety of facilities, technical services, equipment, and training to such diverse nations as Libya, Saudi Arabia, Malawi, Zambia, and the Gulf States. Since 1977, Visnews has provided three fellowships a year for Third World journalists to study television in Europe and North America.[20]

- Deutsche Presse Agentur (DPA), the important, private West German news agency whose principal foreign partner is UPI, has loaned considerable equipment to Third World news agencies, and has had particularly close relations with the Arab World. It operates an Arab Service, beamed to Cairo and then relayed in Arabic by the Middle East News Agency (MENA) throughout North Africa and the Middle East. DPA also maintains an active news agency editorial and technical training program and consultancy service for Arab countries.[21]

Changes Within the Third World

While the developed nations in recent years have been scrambling for appropriate ways to respond to the new order chal-

18. Mort Rosenblum, "The Western Wire Services and the Third World," in Philip C. Horton, ed., *The Third World and Press Freedom* (New York: Praeger, 1978), pp. 109–10.

19. For the background on CANA, see Hugh N. J. Cholmondeley, "CANA: An Independent News Agency Launched by the English-speaking Caribbean Countries," *The Unesco Courier* (April 1977), pp. 10–11, and International Commission for the Study of Communication Problems, "Caribbean News Agency," *Monographs (II)* (Paris: Unesco, 1978), pp. 53–59. See also Marlene Cuthbert, "The Caribbean's Successful Model for a Third World News Agency," paper for Association for Education in Journalism Convention, Boston, August 1980.

20. See note 2.

21. International Commission for the Study of Communication Problems, "Deutsche Presse Agentur (DPA)," *Monographs (II)* (Paris: Unesco, 1978), pp. 59–69.

lenges, the Third World nations themselves have been taking unilateral steps to change the status quo and more explicitly to use news as essential support for their indigenous development efforts.

Certainly the most important development in news within the Third World has been the trend toward developing national news agencies and then strengthening them through various bilateral and multilateral arrangements. By the end of the 1970s, some 120 nations—many of them poor in information and everything else—had their own national agencies in one form or another.[22] This was an increase of about eighty agencies in a decade. News agencies in places as diverse as the Soviet Union, Japan, the People's Republic of China, Italy, the two Germanies, Iran, Cuba, Yugoslavia, India, Egypt, Tunisia, and Morocco were well established and influential far beyond their national boundaries.

Nearly all agencies take at least one of the Western TNNAs, and they generally oppose efforts to weaken the TNNAs. Pero Ivacic, head of Yugoslavia's Tanjug, is typical of national news agency executives who are critical of the TNNAs and want alternative sources but who also do not favor restricting their news gathering:

Without the presence of AFP, AP, Reuters, TASS, and UPI, the Yugoslav press and every other news media could never provide the scope and detail of international news coverage that it does, regardless of the development of its own foreign correspondents and its bilateral news exchanges with other national news agencies.[23]

In the industrialized nations of the West, the news agencies tend to be privately owned and often are operated as nonprofit media cooperatives. In the developing nations, agencies tend to be directly or indirectly controlled by the government.

Many of the same problems which severely restrict the

22. International Commission for the Study of Communication Problems, "The World of News Agencies." Document prepared for the commission (Paris: Unesco, 1978), p. 1.

23. Pero Ivacic, "The Flow of News: Tanjug, the Pool and the National Agencies," *Journal of Communication* (Autumn 1978), 28(4):160.

growth of local newspapers and broadcasting organizations also adversely affect the rise of national news agencies. Obstacles and problems vary from country to country, but generally include such well-documented difficulties as censorship, bureaucratic red tape, illiteracy, scarcity of trained personnel, low pay and status, high cost of news transmission, and lack of appropriate communications hardware. The combination of some of these problems makes many of the Third World news agencies ill-equipped to provide a viable domestic service, much less run an external service and maintain correspondents in bureaus abroad.

About forty nations, including twenty-four with populations of more than 1 million, have no national news agencies.[24] Papua New Guinea, Uruguay, and Ireland are without a news agency. This, of course, means they must depend heavily upon foreign news sources, usually the TNNAs, for news about each other.

But the trend toward national agencies and information self-reliance is irreversible. The feeling is strong among many Third World nations that they should hear news of their neighbors directly from them. In late 1980, for example, the government of Papua New Guinea proposed a Pacific Regional News Agency to improve "communication of ideas, information and events" in the Islands.

Since the early 1960s, Unesco has actively assisted a number of nations to develop local media and agencies. For example, Unesco has advised the Caribbean Area News Agency (CANA) and has helped Malaysia, Somalia, Libya, Cameroon, Nepal, and Upper Volta plan their news agencies.[25] Unesco has also been active in the establishment of various training and/or research institutes. An important example is the Asia-Pacific Institute for Broadcasting Development (AIBD), a re-

24. International Commission for the Study of Communication Problems, "News Agencies Multilateral Cooperation." Document prepared for the commission (Paris: Unesco, 1978), p. 3.

25. For details of Unesco's various activities, see special issue of *The Unesco Courier* entitled "A World Debate on Information: Flood-Tide or Balanced Flow?" (April 1977).

gional intergovernmental training institution in Kuala Lumpur, established in cooperation with the government of Malaysia.

In addition to the growth of national news agencies, there also is a trend toward greater cooperation among the national agencies. These examples will suggest emerging patterns of increased Third World news exchange at subregional, regional, and even transnational levels:

- Since 1972, the news agencies of three nations—Pars News Agency, Iran; Anadolu Agency, Turkey; and Associated Press of Pakistan—have cooperated in exchanging news and personnel.[26]
- Regional cooperation within the English-speaking Caribbean region has been greatly stimulated by the growth of CANA. Since 1976, it has been independent of Reuters and has gained a reputation as a professional, successful regional news agency. It is owned by a unique mixture of public and private organizations from Belize in the north to Guyana in the south.[27]
- Discussions through the Organization of African Unity have been underway in Africa to establish the Pan-African News Agency (PAFNA), which would strive to disseminate news about the region, regional cooperation, and African political unity both within and outside of Africa.[28]
- Discussions also have been conducted among Islamic nations on the feasibility of a full-fledged International Islamic News Agency (IINA).
- Interregional cooperation between Arab and European news agencies has been promoted by meetings in the mid- and late-1970s between the heads of East and West European news agencies and of Arab agencies. Initiative for this Euro-Arab cooperation has come from Tunis Afrique Presse (TAP).[29]

26. International Commission for the Study of Communication Problems, "News Agencies Multilateral Cooperation." Document prepared for the commission (Paris: Unesco, 1978), p. 3.

27. See note 19.

28. International Commission for the Study of Communication Problems, "News Agencies Multilateral Cooperation," p. 5.

29. Ibid., pp. 7–8.

- The Middle East News Agency (MENA), Cairo, is typical of many national news agencies which are increasing their arrangements for exchange of news among themselves. For example, MENA has offices in eleven other Arab countries, as well as Belgrade, East Berlin, London, and Paris, and exchange agreements with eleven Asian and European agencies. In addition, it subscribes to two of the TNNAs and exchanges news with another.[30]
- In 1969 the Press Foundation of Asia (PFA), an independent organization founded by Asian editors and publishers and with headquarters in Manila, began DepthNews. Airmailed to subscribers, the service appears weekly and is the only Asia-based feature service with a distinct development orientation. In 1980, PFA was helping coordinate the newly organized Committee of Asian Editors on Communication Issues. The body of senior media practitioners was formed to consider the complex issues raised by the UNESCO-appointed MacBride Commission and to develop an action program to "democratize" the region's media.[31]
- In the vast Pacific basin region, the South Pacific Commission in 1974 began experimenting with a satellite regional news exchange project, and the exchanges are continuing weekly with the Cook Islands, Kiribati, Tuvalu, New Caledonia, Niue, Papua New Guinea, the Solomon Islands, Tonga, Northern Marianas Commonwealth, New Zealand, and Hawaii. The project, under PEACESAT (Pan Pacific Educational and Communication Experiment by Satellite), is explicitly to link the relatively small, isolated Pacific islands for exchange of news about one another.[32]

Three other cooperative efforts warrant attention. One

30. International Commission for the Study of Communication Problems, "The World of News Agencies," p. 5.

31. S. M. Ali, "DepthNews: A Model for a Third World Feature Agency," in Horton, The Third World and Press Freedom, p. 191, and "Asian Editors Submit New Measures for Just Information Order," DepthNews (August 30, 1980).

32. For an overview of PEACESAT, see Jackie Bowen, "PEACESAT Regional News Exchange Project, 1974–1976." Paper for Flow of Communication Workshop, East-West Communication Institute, Honolulu, May 1–5, 1978; and John Bystrom, "A Satellite Communication System: Global Development and Cultural Imperialism," in Jim Richstad, ed. New Perspectives in International Communication (Honolulu: East-West Communication Institute, 1977), pp. 149–79.

scheme is the noncommercial system of intra- and interregional television news exchange, which is best illustrated by the successful Eurovision News Exchange (EVN) and Intervision (IVN). The other two transnational schemes are print- and Third World-oriented agencies. One, the News Agencies Pool of Nonaligned Countries, distributes news within the nonaligned group of developing nations. The other is the relatively unknown and nontraditional and more manifestly political news agency called Inter Press Service (IPS). Under Dr. Roberto Savio, IPS has developed close ties to many Third World news agencies and several U.N. agencies. It has stressed the need for increased international partnership and collective self-reliance among developing nations through the use of satellite channels.

The spread of formal television exchanges beyond ad hoc or bilateral transmissions has improved the quantity and quality of television program flow among nations whose demand for news, particularly about their region, has greatly increased. The Geneva-based EVN began a daily, multilateral exchange of hard news within Western Europe in 1960, and has primarily served members of the European Broadcasting Union, including developing nation members such as Turkey, Algeria, and Morocco. IVN, headquartered in Prague, has had a daily news exchange since 1970. It was created by the International Radio and Television Organization (OIRT) to serve the Soviet Union and other Eastern European socialist states.[33]

Despite political differences, EVN and IVN share a close working relationship when it comes to exchanging news and special event coverage—especially sports—with one another. Each has increased its use of satellites to expand service into other regions. In the Third World, too, professional organizations, like the Asia-Pacific Broadcasting Union, and governments are encouraging satellite exchange. In Indonesia, the

33. For background on EVN and IVN, see Regis de Kalbermatten, "The European Broadcasting Union—Past, Present and Future," *Intermedia* (December 1977), 5(6):25–30; Charles E. Sherman and John Ruby, "The Eurovision News Exchange," *Journalism Quarterly* (Autumn 1974), 51(3):478–85; and Wacaw Wygledowski, "Intervision: The Growth of an Exchange," *Intermedia* (June 1978), 6(3):24–27.

government is trying to organize its Association of Southeast Asian Nations (ASEAN) partners to support greater intra-regional cooperation by joining a regional satellite communication system. In 1976, Indonesia became the first Asian nation to have its own domestic satellite, and countries like India, Japan, Australia, and China plan their own systems in the 1980s.

The idea for a Third World pool developed out of political and economic recommendations made in Algiers in 1973 at the Fourth Summit Conference of Nonaligned Countries. By early 1975, Tanjug in Yugoslavia was collecting and redistributing news reports from the nonaligned world. In July 1976, information ministers and news agency directors from sixty-two countries met in New Delhi to give their approval to the pool's statute and to a coordination committee.[34]

The News Agencies Pool of Nonaligned Countries operates very simply: several of the stronger national news agencies (India, Yugoslavia, Iraq, Tunisia, Mexico, etc.) serve as regional collector-distributor centers of lightly edited reports. These reports are chosen and sent to the pool by more than forty participating national news agencies, each of which bears all the expenses of its own participation.

To date, the pool has operated very modestly on limited resources. The volume of daily news exchange via the pool is about 40,000 words per day, and it has in no way threatened the TNNAs, as Westerners initially feared. Tanjug's Ivacic, the pool's chairman since 1979, has emphasized:

The pool is a tangible example of cooperation among equals, on a voluntary and democratic basis. From the outset, it was never conceived as a supranational news agency of the nonaligned countries. We believe it will help to enhance mutual knowledge among the nonaligned countries and to reinforce their unity. We are also fully aware that the nonaligned movement is in no way a monolithic block, nor in any way subject to the will of a single center. It is a

34. For an overview of the important 1976 news pool meeting in Delhi, see *Communicator*, a publication of the Indian Institute of Communication (April–July 1976), pp. 13–46.

movement marked by great diversity, but also by strong, identical interests.[35]

Although all pool members are theoretically equal, the older, better-staffed members—particularly the Yugoslavian and Indian agencies—are clearly the most influential. Intra-Third World rivalry over wider issues of ideology and political leadership has led to considerable coordination problems within the pool.

By TNNA standards, the major problem with the pool is its lack of credibility. Most of its participating news agencies are directly controlled by governments, and this fact has restricted the pool's ability to go much beyond official information or handouts to carry frank political reporting.

By the early 1980s, the pool concept was still emerging, and it was far too early to assess what kind of an impact it has had or will have on correcting various imbalances. Michael Dobbs of the *Washington Post* summarized the situation most accurately:

It is easy for Western journalists to criticize the lack of professionalism in the pool. Yet given the political and economic pressures it is subjected to, perhaps the most remarkable thing about the pool is that it functions as well as it does.[36]

The IPS is a nontraditional news organization that has operated from Rome since 1964.[37] Since the early 1970s it has geared its coverage to Third World subscribers interested in

35. Pero Ivacic, "The Non-Aligned Countries Pool Their News," *The Unesco Courier* (April 1977), p. 20.

36. Michael Dobbs of the Washington Post Service, "Third World News Agency Discovers It's Not So Easy," *Honolulu Advertiser*, November 18, 1978, p. D-16.

37. For an overview of IPS, see Al Hester, "Inter Press Service: News for and about the Third World," *Studies in Third World Societies, Publication #9*, Third World Mass Media: Issues, Theory and Research. William and Mary College, Department of Anthropology. 1980, pp. 83–101; Phil Harris, "Putting the New International Information Order into Practice: The Role of Inter Press Service" (Rome: Research and Information Unit, IPS, February 1979); and International Commission for the Study of Communication Problems, "News Agencies Multilateral Cooperation," pp. 11–12.

reports clearly sympathetic to the nonaligned movement. IPS calls itself "an international nonprofit-making journalists' cooperative" and explicitly states its services "are in line with the ideals of 'decolonization of information'."[38] Its coverage deliberately avoids the conventional spot news orientation of the TNNAs. Instead, IPS claims to be an alternative news agency that concentrates on Third World and developmental news and analysis. By 1979, it was working closely with the United Nations Development Program (UNDP) and a number of developing countries on plans to create a computer-driven "development information network" that would facilitate the exchange of mutually supportive development information within the Third World. (For a fuller look at IPS, see Phil Harris' "News Dependency and Structural Change," in this volume.)

There has been considerable talk—but no real action—on a host of sketchy proposals for a Third World-run transnational agency—not a pool—that would operate as an independent, commercial news agency competing head-on with the TNNAs.

Two proposals are built around variations of a joint venture among existing news agencies. One general proposal originates in the Third World and another, more specific proposal in the First.

Indian Journalist Narinder K. Aggarwala, now with the UNDP in New York, has argued for a truly independent, Third World News Agency (TWNA), capable of projecting multiple Third World perspectives. His proposal is for an organization built around a loose conglomerate of autonomous regional or subregional news agencies, which in turn would draw upon, as much as possible, existing national news agencies for local news. The TWNA, however, would have its own independent offices in the world's major news centers.[39]

Former UPI executive Roger Tatarian has introduced the concept of the "Multinational News Agency," or "North-South News Agency," that would be "directed jointly by professional

38. Inter Press Service, "IPS Third World News Agency" (Rome: IPS, n.d.)
39. Narinder K. Aggarwala, "News with Third World Perspectives: A Practical Suggestion," in Horton, *The Third World and Press Freedom.* p. 204.

journalists from both areas" and "serve as a central production and distribution mechanism for news of social, economic, cultural, and other development activities in the Third World."[40]

Under Tatarian's proposal, an agency would be organized around a directorate with participation from North and South on an equal basis. The agency's correspondents would consist of twelve experienced journalists—six each seconded from news agencies or media in developed and less developed nations. All twelve would work for the proposed agency for a year and would continue to be paid by their regular employers. The correspondents would be sent to a country other than their own and would write news emphasizing national development programs and projects. They would not cover day-to-day "hard" news, particularly about politics. Their reports would be transmitted simultaneously to all participating media.

Aggarwala's proposal was still in the idea stage in the early 1980s, and Tatarian's scheme was getting increased attention. Funding for the Tatarian agency would come from both private and official sources in both worlds. For the idea to work, an annual budget of about $780,000 would be needed and—more importantly—Western media would have to accept the idea of working closely with governments and mixing private and governmental funding.[41]

One innovative project along private lines that was struggling to take shape in the 1980s was a plan from the International Institute of Communications, headquartered in London, and the Twentieth Century Fund, a private New York research foundation interested in communications, international affairs, and other public policy areas. They want to form an independent international committee, made up of leaders in communications from the industrialized countries and the Third World, to monitor, evaluate, and report on ways and means of resolving problems raised by imbalances in the flow

40. Roger Tatarian, "The Multinational News Pool." Paper for the Conference on the International News Media and the Developing World," Cairo, April 2–5, 1978, p. 1.

41. Roger Tatarian, "The Multinational News Agency." Paper for Feasibility Conference in New York, September 12–14, 1979, p. 13.

of information around the world.[42] The Twentieth Century Fund was a leader in a consortium which created the National News Council in the United States in the early 1970s, and it is not inconceivable that the proposed joint IIC/Fund venture could gradually evolve into some form of an "international news council" that might serve as a forum for public complaints against the media and as a defender against government interference with press freedom.

Conclusions

By the start of the 1980s and despite considerable continued resistance in certain Western media and government quarters, some of the structural outlines of an emerging new order were taking shape. Third World nations were increasingly getting their news and views presented in the developed nations and having greater direct contact—so-called horizontal communication—with fellow developing nations.

It was equally clear, however, that progress toward quantitative and qualitative improvement in news flow would be slow because of entrenched interests. Building any kind of new order would be a long and difficult process, as the MacBride Commission discovered by the time it had finished its study of the world's complex communication problems in 1980.[43] The obstacles and difficulties, including semantics, were truly vast and some individuals, institutions, and nations firmly believed that the problems could only be solved by radical change.

42. The creation of an independent international committee was first recommended by an independent Twentieth Century Fund Task Force. See Colin Legum, *A Free and Balanced Flow: Report of the Twentieth Century Fund Task Force on the International Flow of News* (Lexington, Massachusetts: Lexington Books, 1978).

43. International Commission for the Study of Communication Problems. *Many Voices, One World: Communication and Society, Today and Tomorrow*. (London: Kogan Page, 1980). The 312-page MacBride Commission's final report details the progress and problems involved in a new communication order.

This essay has presented evidence of considerable multidimensional news cooperation, and more will inevitably follow. But achieving consensus on communication solutions on any worldwide scale will be exceedingly difficult and inevitably linked to wider economic and other aspirations *and* to internal national developments.

19

The Western Media and the Third World's Challenge
LEONARD R. SUSSMAN

In an essay advising Western media how to respond to Third World challenges, Leonard Sussman explains that developing nations' complaints are "real, pervasive, and will not disappear if ignored." He advocates further sensitizing of Americans to the problems and the establishment of better links between the West and the Third World. As a strong supporter of "a free but badly performing press" over "an efficient, government-controlled press," Sussman views freedom and balance as mutually exclusive rather than complementary.

While there may be movement toward press freedom in a Third World country, Sussman concludes, there are "no halfway houses" between a government-run media system and a system independent of government.

THE WESTERN NEWS MEDIA should recognize that an information revolution of historic proportions lies just ahead.

Leonard R. Sussman is executive director of Freedom House, a New York City organization that has long been identified with liberal democracy and support of press freedom and individual liberties. He has been a journalist in New York and in the Caribbean. This essay originally appeared in "Mass News Media and the Third World Challenge," *The Washington Papers* (Beverly Hills: Sage, 1977), 5(46):59–68.

The impending changes will probably have far greater impact on both developed and developing worlds than the discovery of the telegraph and its application to news communication 100 years ago. Technological development again empowers the new revolution, but the primary catalyst this time is the *content* of the message. The Third World means to have its news heard and understood wherever it chooses. It believes the newer, former colonial nations cannot develop their economies and maintain their full sovereignty, particularly in the cultural field, without drastic revisions in international informational exchanges. . . .

Obstacles appear, however, at two important levels:

1. Given the best intentions on both sides, enlarging the coverage of Third World developments could be prohibitively expensive, and transmitting "constructive" news from [Third World countries] could require a degree of access to official information that [they] resist, and an assurance of favorable coverage that Western journalists cannot provide without subverting standards of independent journalism.
2. The valid Third World complaints against the Western news media are highly ideologized by both the Soviet Union/Marxist mechanisms, and the diverse nationalisms of the Third World itself.

Any ameliorative effort by the Western media must therefore be preceded by the clear understanding that a list of valid demands is being exploited for widely divergent ideological purposes.

How, then, can the U.S. media managers proceed?

First, by recognizing the heterogeneity in the Third World on many aspects of information policies. Twenty-one Latin American nations stood together at San Jose in 1976 to demand "balanced" North-South reporting—unobjectionable in theory—through implicitly restrictive procedures. Of these, five may be regarded as "free" countries, ten as "partly free" and six as "not free."[1] Some of the most authoritarian regimes in

1. R. D. Gastil, "The Comparative Survey of Freedom," *Freedom at Issue* (January–February, 1977), p. 9.

the Third World (e.g., Cuba and Haiti) and several of the most democratic (e.g., Costa Rica and Venezuela) joined in framing and approving press-control recommendations. To be sure, their motivations differ, but the consequences of their actions may be the same.

To strive for more constructive consequences, U.S. media managers should understand the diversity of ideologies that confuse the media issues in the Third World. . . . This suggests which Third World countries may be receptive to constructive U.S. approaches for improving North-South news coverage. The analysis generally eliminates, at present, the hard-core Marxist and Marxist-oriented states but suggests some possibilities in the mixed socialist-capitalist economies, even though they presently limit the freedom of their own journalists. We suggest the far greater likelihood of, and necessity for, constructive approaches to the bare 14 percent of free states in the Third World.

In all such efforts, however, it will be essential to recognize that there are journalists in many [developing countries] who strain impatiently at the chains their regimes have placed on all forms of mass communication. A young editor of a West African national news agency . . . raised the question of his country's participation in the nonaligned press pool. He clearly had misgivings. He already suffers too many restrictions in editing his government-run news file. Once a part of the nonaligned pool, he fears, he may be expected to transmit domestically only what he receives from the pool (largely government communiques), and one day he may be cut off entirely from the incoming AP and Reuters wires. Even while questioning his government's communication policy, however, it was this editor who asked, "Why do your wire services continue to refer to South African freedom fighters as 'terrorists' and Ian Smith as 'Prime Minister'?"

An American seeking constructive negotiations with such an African journalist should understand the moderating distance he tries to maintain from his own government and his difficulty in observing even rudimentary standards of editorial press freedom. Failure to acknowledge such realities can only deepen the philosophical gap between North and South.

There are courageous Third World journalists, even now, who try to moderate their country's press-control policies. A dramatic example was provided by the *Weekly Review* of November 8, 1976. It was published in Kenya while Unesco's biennial conference met in that country to consider the USSR's press-control declaration. The *Review* carried the text of Kenya's information minister, Darius Mbela. He noted that efforts to secure a "free and balanced flow of information" and other improvements in national communication policies were under a "barrage of attacks mainly from the United States and un-African black allies." Mbela said that America is a "rebel society," has been since its breaking away from Britain, and still needs a "rebel mass media." But, he added, "we in Africa do not need a rebel mass media. Neither do we need one that operates under the fear of persecution for telling the truth. What we need are totally committed African mass media based on African socioeconomic-cum-political policies and not a replica of either the East or the West."

When Mbela had finished, Hilary Ng'weno published in the *Review* his eloquent response, "All Freedom is at Stake." Every American news editor and manager who processes a news file beamed either to or from the Third World should examine Ng'weno's words.

Ensuring Ghana's right to report news from China is not nearly as important—given Ghana's limited resources—as the flow of information into and within Ghana, says Ng'weno. While they have not adopted Communist ideology, many Third World countries share the concerns of the Communist states: foreign newsmen gather information and beam it back for the inhabitants of those countries. "Many young countries," says Ng'weno, "have fragile political structures that cannot withstand endless scrutiny by the news media of the shortcomings of those in power or the failures of economic and social development programs." He chided Western newsmen for looking at the Third World in cold-war terms. . . .

Third World countries may properly seek a "middle ground" between Western and Communist political ideologies. But on the issue of the press, "there simply happens to be no middle ground" between the Soviet Union's press-control proposal and the West's viewpoints, Ng'weno continued:

The reason is simple: The conflict is not between Western and Communist ideology, but rather between the proponents of government control of the mass media and those of an independent press that is not controlled by the government. . . . Control of the press by those in authority is inherent in a totalitarian system of government, whether the government is of the right-wing type such as during the Nazi period in Germany or the greater part of Franco's rule in Spain, or a left-wing type such as is to be found in the Soviet Union, Cuba, or China. There is no point in fooling oneself that it is possible to get the good aspects of government control of the press and marry them with the good aspects of an independent press. . . . Good aspects there are in both systems of the press, but they are not attributes of the press which exist independently of the systems in question. They are not like fruit which can be picked from different trees to make up a basket that would be appetizing to a customer; they are part and parcel of the system of communications in which they are manifest.[2]

For this reason, he maintained, "Third World nations will have to stop trying to sit on the fence hoping for an opportunity to present itself that would help them establish a halfway house between government control of the media and independent media."

Ng'weno concluded by admitting that it may be theoretically possible for a government-controlled press to operate freely—that is, by placing the interests of the citizenry above the narrower interests of the regimes. "In practice," he added, "this has not been the case anywhere." It is unwise, he added, for Third World nations to support blindly the Unesco press-control proposals. Not only is the freedom of journalists at stake, he concluded, but the "freedom of millions of inhabitants of Third World nations."

2. Hilary Ng'weno, in *The Weekly Review* (Nairobi), November 8, 1976.

Steps in Response

American media managers should not read the second part of Ng'weno's essay (the defense of freedom) without absorbing fully his earlier recounting of the developing nations' complaints. They are real, pervasive, and will not disappear if ignored. . . .

It is not sufficient to respond by pleading that press cable tolls have just risen 400 percent (as they have); that high-speed technology, common in Western communications systems, is very expensive to install (as it is); or that Africa's land lines run north and south but insufficiently link the continent's interior, a holdover from European (not American) colonial patterns. New technology may be needed. The West can help finance and install it. More likely, however, existing techniques, intelligently applied and requiring modest expenditures, could help.

Radio, long and shortwave; the telegraph; even the mimeograph where no printing press exists, may provide additional facilities for communication in the short term. It is not likely that satellites or even domestic television will provide the necessary improvement in the volume of information exchanges in the immediate future. No part of the economic development story will be covered with more verve by Third World journalists than the demonstration that American publishers and broadcasters are ready to help. The U.S. Government, however, should not participate in this phase of the response. To do so would suggest to some that the U.S. is seeking ideological influence or is following the pattern of government involvement it professes to oppose. . . .

Part of an American media manager's argument to Third World leaders may include a frank discourse on the value of an untrammeled news flow to the [developing countries] themselves. It should readily be agreed that the West needs more information from developing countries. Many of the international crises originate there. In the years before deep U.S. involvement in Southeast Asia, there were only a handful of American correspondents permanently stationed on the entire continent of Asia. There are few there today. The expense is great ($100,000 per correspondent per year abroad, one newspaper estimates), but roving correspondents and local stringers fill in adequately—if Third World governments permit access to their countries and to news sources. The present press-control trend is not promising. [Developing countries] should be told that their press gaps place development programs in jeopardy. Western citizens who pay foreign aid bills through their taxes are not likely to support indefinitely countries that have shrouded their activities in secrecy. Indeed, U.S. capital investment—private or governmental—is not likely to flow to a nation that bars access to data and news.

A new international economic order can hardly develop without dependable, verifiable information about many aspects of a country's social, political, and economic development. And in this era of great concern over human rights, Americans in particular will scarcely want to assist regimes that mask cruel and inhuman treatment of their own citizens behind controls over domestic and international journalists. Scholars of the Western world, also barred from examining reliable information, cannot contribute to the proper understanding of the Third World, particularly by Western governments, if facts and figures are denied them. And, it must be admitted, we all need to know much more about the realities of the Third World.

Finally, more information, not less, is required to help stabilize the Third World. Despite routine charges that the Western press exaggerates troubles, the news media also serve as conveyors of information that may clarify the unknown and remove some suspicion. To be sure, the press can be guilty of error and exaggeration, but it can also clarify mistakes, sometimes even its own. The stabilizing factor of the international news media should not be underestimated. Imagine the Third World with *only* the nonaligned press pool to provide its daily news budget; in a short time, countries would be responding to the unreal statements of "reality" projected by as many national agencies as there are participants in the pool.

Crux of the Matter

To challenge, says Webster, is to invite into competition (not only to demand as a right or call to a duel). The Third World's challenge to the Western mass media shows signs of growing competitiveness within the Third World as well as between it and the industrially developed countries. This should be encouraging to those nurtured on the value of the free marketplace of ideas. There are . . . alternative information channels within the Third World. They seem to be developing distinct differences in approach to news coverage, although all aim to please their respective governments. The fact is, those governments represent widely diverse socioeconomic and political philosophies. That is the other side of the coin of sheer anti-Westernism.

Similarly, dissent from Western journalistic procedures may not necessarily lead to Third World intransigence. . . . The major news services . . . seem to signal they are ready to help if the Third World chooses to improve its domestic and transnational information coverage. . . . The Third World news-media conflict, Ng'weno reminds us, "is not between Western and Communist ideology, but rather between the proponents of government control of the mass media and those of an independent press that is not controlled by government."[3]

That has been the crux of the matter from the beginning, and few see it as clearly as Ng'weno. A moderate Indian journalist, Chakravarti Raghavan, attacks the Western news media for promoting those skills and values which differentiate rather than unite individuals in a society. He wants the news media to fulfill a social function, yet he fears "manipulation by an elite, whether governmental or nongovernmental." Needed, he says, "is a definition of the broad social and cultural milieu and its norms, and the creation of legal, administrative, political and economic instruments toward these

3. Ibid.

ends." Yet, he insists "the widest freedom must be given to the practitioners," the journalists.[4]

Elites *do* manipulate information, even as Raghavan fears. And the current Third World challenge to the Western press can readily follow that pattern in country after country. For that reason, the status of press freedom in the world may well determine the outcome of many geopolitical struggles. . . . The free press takes seriously the social assumption that governments are created to serve the citizen, and not the individual to serve the state. In many places, that is a revolutionary concept. In furthering it, the free press ranges itself in philosophical opposition to the regime. No rationalization can long cloud that fundamental relationship, not even the claim that economic development is essential and information a sine qua non of development.

There are indeed serious inadequacies in the coverage of Third World events and social movements. The Third World's reporting of its own events to itself—both within and between the developing nations—is perhaps even less satisfactory than Western reportage of the same countries. That is not an excuse for a lessened Western response. On the contrary, it calls for greater collaboration between the Western news media and the developing countries. But on which philosophical basis?

Is truth to spring full-blown from the presses and broadcasts of governments? Or is it to emerge, laboriously incomplete, sometimes belatedly, from the tension between government, on the one hand, and a nongovernmental and relatively free press on the other?

It comes down, then, to the realistic expectations of the masses of people in the world, and the extent to which their rulers will permit the satisfying of those expectations. The inalienable rights Americans refer to are not American rights. They are universal. The essence of humanity is personal free-

---

4. C. Raghavan, "A New World Communication and Information Structure." Paper for Seminar on the Role of Information in the New International Order, Mexico City, 1976.

dom. That is exercised in many forms, not the least in employing the right to know and understand. That is quite distinct from the government's "right" to inform.

It is claimed there is an unfairness in the market system. The wealthy nations control vast communications systems, and over them portray aspects of their national power. There is indeed an asymmetry of power in the world, and the Western and Eastern bloc information media naturally reflect that reality. The economic and political balance is not likely to be affected in favor of the Third World as a consequence of stringent controls over the Western press or even competitive Third World news agencies. Indeed, there is a likely counterproductive effect: American taxpayers may ultimately refuse to provide economic or other aid to countries whose restrictive information policies defy accurate reporting. The Congress has already warned it may mandate automatic rejections of transnational loans to countries that violate the human rights of their own citizens; and U.S. investors are less likely to provide corporate capital to countries that deny access to a regular flow of dependable domestic information.

These are no small concerns within the Third World. Yet the clamor for a press responsive to the regime motivates even a democrat like President Carlos Andres Perez of Venezuela. He told Unesco that "international regulation of communications is required to ensure the sacred right to information by guaranteeing that only the truth will be reported and to safeguard the unrestricted right to express opinions."

The free journalist does not have to display a social responsibility in order to earn his freedom. He must be responsible to the craft of journalism. The craft, at its best, is understood to demand high standards of truth, personal integrity, a sense of inquiry, and commitment to the commonweal. That standard need not be spelled out in a code such as Unesco will now try to create. Sooner or later some government is likely to insist on enforcing that code. Then, even the best code becomes another noose of government, appropriate only for authoritarian societies.

It will be argued that truly free journalism is restricted by economic and national interests; that Third World peoples are unprepared for freedom and their economic and political structures too flimsy to withstand brisk words of controversy; and that newer political philosophies and social models favor mass over individual rights to information as to all else.

There is indeed some degree of truth in each of these contentions. But in the final analysis, as Ng'weno stated eloquently, the choice is only between a government-run system and a system independent of government. There are no other real alternatives, no halfway houses.

At its base, therefore, the primary question is not press performance; it is press freedom. A free but badly performing press serves its peoples far better than an efficient, government-controlled press. There is thus a greater danger in Unesco's effort to create an international guide to news media performance. It will inevitably, diplomatically, provide a spectrum of "acceptable" views: the control of news media by governments will be cited as a form equally as appropriate as press services kept independent of governments. That shopping-list approach to a basic human-freedom issue is in itself an erosion of freedom.

The objection to aiming governmental power at journalism extends even to a government professing to compensate for past injustices and present imbalances. The concept of affirmative action, devised as a compassionate American response to old domestic injustices, has raised complex constitutional issues in the United States. There, such concepts can be ultimately and equitably resolved within a democratic system. No such system exists in the international arena in which the news media controversy appears. On the contrary, too many of the actors are committed demagogues or authoritarians for whom there are no checks and balances.

Developmental journalism is an increasing threat to the existing free press, and in the Third World itself, a bar to the development of free political as well as journalistic systems. For developmental journalism, like deferred political liberty, presupposes that citizens of developing nations cannot be trusted to examine competing viewpoints, but must hear only a single voice.

Where they are given the choice . . . the citizens of the Third World prove their humanity. They strive to hear new and competing voices, and to raise their own freely.

20

News Dependence and Structural Change
PHIL HARRIS

Phil Harris presents an argument for structural change from vertical to horizontal communication systems in international news as a long-term way to end what he considers to be the cause of imbalances between North and South—the dependence of the South on the North. Harris develops these arguments based on his extensive empirical research for Unesco on news agencies and flow, and comes to many of the same conclusions as Mustapha Masmoudi and others. He then, in the part of his larger article published here, proceeds to examine alternative news structures—using Inter Press Service for illustrative purposes—and a shift from vertical news systems to horizontal structures.

IN RECENT YEARS, there has been growing concern about, and often vociferous condemnation of, the inequalities in the

Phil Harris is coordinator, Research and Information Unit, Inter Press Service (IPS) Third World News Agency. IPS, which has its headquarters in Panama and its telecommunications center in Rome, is closely identified with "new order" efforts to promote collective self-reliance and expand South-South communication links between developing countries. He is a former research associate with the Center for Mass Communication Research, University of Leicester, England. This article is taken from a longer paper "The International Information Order: Problems and Responses," written in 1978.

international information order. These inequalities have taken various forms but among the more serious have been the poverty of the Third World and the dominance of the developed world in terms of media resources, the dominant unidimensionality of news and information flow from the developed world to the Third World, and the qualitative imbalance in the content of news and information flowing through the international news system. . . .

In looking at the international information order, many analysts have argued that this order can be characterized by "media imperialism" or "media colonialism" by the North (the developed world) of the South (the Third World underdeveloped countries). While I can agree with the basic argument that the information order is characterized by imbalance between the North and the South . . . this imbalance is more accurately characterized as one of "media dependence"—the South is dependent on the North. . . .

The main thrust of the Third World critique has been that the present international information order is imperialist, is Northern-dominated, and provides a biased version of news. . . .

On the basis of my research[1] . . . I suggest that the following conclusions can be drawn:

- The present international news agency network owes its origins to the development of an international news media network geared directly to the expansion of interests (both economic and political) of the major colonial powers.
- The major influence on the development of indigenous news media in the underdeveloped areas has been foreign ownership of the media which has led to the growth of a demand for the types of services provided by the Northern news agencies. In addition, the establishment of indigenous news agencies was carried out largely with the assistance of these same Northern news agencies with the obvious implications for the ways in which the new agencies now operate.

1. The research referred to was carried out by the author for Unesco between 1974 and 1978. The Final Report, "News Dependence: The Case for a New World Information Order," is awaiting publication by Unesco.

- The present international news media network is still dominated by the major Northern international news agencies.
- The service provided by the Northern news agencies to the underdeveloped news media consists of a Northern-oriented image of reality.
- The services provided by the Northern news agencies to their markets in developed Northern societies portray an imbalanced image of the role of the Third World in the international arena.

On the basis of my research, it is possible to comment on the claims and criticisms raised by the Third World from a position supported by empirical evidence. The evidence available indicates that the Third World nations have a strong case. The present international information order *is* Northern dominated, *does* owe its origins to the interests of the imperial colonial powers, and *does* provide a Northern-oriented image of reality.

Responses to Third World Critique

As I suggested . . . the responses can take various forms, not all of which will necessarily be beneficial. The range of responses can extend from, at one extreme, what I call "benevolent cosmetic surgery" to, at the other extreme, fundamental structural changes not only in the information order but also in the economic order.

Benevolent cosmetic surgery appears an attractive response for many. It incorporates such various modes as an increase of financial aid from the North to the South, donation of equipment and technology, training programs for newsmen from the South, and undertakings to increase the quantity and quality of coverage from the Third World.

On the other hand, structurally oriented responses are directed toward fundamental alterations in the relationships between sectors of the world, in particular in the relationships of dominance and dependence between North and South.

In my view, the cosmetic response, while it clearly has a role to play, should not be regarded as a definitive solution. In fact . . . it is clear that deeply-rooted structural factors condition the particular form which the present international information order takes. If we wish to make changes in the information order, ultimately we must recognize that change is necessary in the infrastructural relationships which condition the form of the information order.

There is a danger in the cosmetic response, which may not necessarily be consciously motivated on the part of its proponents, that such a response will do little to improve the problem and may, indeed, lead to a further strengthening of Northern domination. For example, a proposal widely voiced in many quarters is that the sole remedy lies in the developed world helping the Third World countries to improve communication capacities, whether in the fields of technology or professionalism. In this latter case, we arrive at the critical question of training, which all too often takes the form of a benevolent paternalism which assumes first, that Third World newsmen are incapable of developing their own journalistic practices, and second, that the Northern style of journalism is the "right" style of journalism. . . .

This ethnocentrism spills over into another critical area—the question of press freedom. I say "critical" because many in the North have mounted a strong campaign against the Third World and its demands for a New International Information Order (NIIO), arguing that this new order would be inherently destructive of press freedom. This campaign is another example of ethnocentric arrogance which assumes that custody of "press freedom" rightly belongs to the North.

As Martin Woollacott[2] of *The Guardian*, writing on this tendency, has correctly observed, it "reflects the West's deep disillusion with nearly all post-colonial societies as well as our assumption that we are still the ultimate arbiter of the rest of the world." The Third World, taken *en bloc*, is assumed to

2. Martin Woollacott, "Western News-Gathering—Why the Third World Has Reacted," *Journalism Studies Review* (June 1976), 1(1):12–14.

be incapable of self-regulatory freedom not only in the field of communications, but also in the broader functioning of society. This type of argument conveniently labels all Third World countries with the same tag and extrapolates from the obvious documented cases of suppression of press freedom (which are not in any case a preserve solely of the Third World) to the general indictment of the Third World as antidemocratic and antifreedom.

There is the potential danger that this view could become linked with the cosmetic response to the problems of the international information order. One form which this linkage might take may be the extension of Northern finance and assistance under certain conditions. It may be that some aid donors would attempt to tie information aid and assistance for Third World countries to certain conditions pertaining to the political conduct of Third World state systems. The motivation behind such attempts would be the desire to ensure that Third World information systems "fitted" with the Northern concepts of information rather than that Third World autonomy was recognized.

Structurally Oriented Response

This latter point—Third World autonomy—brings me to the second type of response to recognition of problems in the international information order: a structurally oriented response. If we look at the present international structure of information, it is clear that it is dominated by a *vertical* structure, both at national and international levels. Within societies, elites dominate the masses; at the international level, the North dominates the South. However, the real nature of the process of communication is that it is intrinsically a *horizontal* process— the exchange of information between individuals, between social groups, and between nations. To this extent, the structures which presently exist are incapable of accommodating a *real* communication process.

The structurally oriented response recognizes this and directs its effort toward a restructuring of the information order in such a way as to make horizontal communication possible. The aim is to maximize, to as great an extent as is possible, the access of individuals and the various social sectors to the information system, thus eliminating verticalism. Encompassing this response is the growth of the concept of the "right to communication" under which access to the media is given to the protagonists in the social process—to the mass of the people.

For example, as communications costs fall dramatically . . . a wide-reaching potential is opened up for achieving access to communications.

Behind structurally oriented responses to the problems of the international information order lie the principles of achieving national autonomy in information, regional cooperation between Third World countries, and an international information order based on international equality, mutual respect, and the right of national autonomy.

Contrary to the fears expressed by many . . . this response is not an attempt to violate or restrict freedom. What the proponents of a structurally oriented response recognize very clearly is that it is unacceptable that the vast majority of people are structurally denied access to communications. The present demands for a restructuring of information are based on the search to increase the potential for horizontal communication. . . .

Of course, structural solutions to the problems of the international information order are not likely to be attainable overnight. What is important, I feel, is that it should be recognized that cosmetic approaches, while they may go some of the way toward rectifying some of the more obvious manifestations of imbalance, cannot in the long term provide meaningful solutions to a problem which is deeply and historically rooted. Nor can piecemeal approaches which divide international affairs into clearly identifiable categories (such as communications, economics, politics, education, etc.) provide adequate solutions.

Solutions must be based on the recognition of the inter-relationships between the various sectors of the international system. Isolating communications from the economic sector, for example, cannot lead to more than surface solutions. At root level, moves have to be made toward rectifying the imbalances in the relationships of power and domination between the various sectors of the international community.

This is not to argue, however, that we are faced with the decision either to accept immediate, short-term, surface solutions or to wait for long-term structural change. Modes of action which can be utilized now provide immediate improvement but also recognize the desirability and inevitability of long-term, fundamental action. In this context, I suggest that the role and activities of Inter Press Service (IPS) Third World News Agency provide an illustrative example.

IPS: A Structural Response

In line with its policy of support for all moves toward greater international social justice, IPS has consistently backed progressive attempts to establish a new international information order. As an international news agency dedicated to the principles of alternative information and increased Third World integration, IPS has largely been a lone voice among the international news media.

Established as an international, nonprofit-making, cooperative of journalists, IPS now has an international network comprising Latin America, Africa, Asia, Western Europe, and Eastern Europe. Approximately 200 full-time journalists (the majority of them from the Third World) work for IPS worldwide, and the agency transmits daily bulletins in three languages (Spanish, English, and Arabic) totaling some 90,000 words per day.

The agency's operational principles have been formulated in response to the Third World critique of the existing international information order, and its objectives accommodate the recognition that structural changes in the information order is not only desirable but necessary.

However, the agency also recognizes that steps can be taken at various levels to provide solutions to the problems identified in the information order. To this extent, IPS is engaged in a two-level strategy to facilitate the establishment of NIIO. On the first level, IPS is concerned to supply an *alternative* news service with a view to rectifying immediate problems in the nature and quality of news circulating throughout the international news media system. On the second level, IPS is concerned to bring about structural change in the information order, and to this extent incorporates *horizontal* communication as its primary operational objective. By adopting this two-level strategy, IPS combines modes of action which provide immediate improvement in the information order and which also lead toward structural change in this order.

Alternative News

One of the major distinguishing characteristics of IPS is that it is concerned to provide an information service which is an alternative to the services provided by the transnational news and information system. In order to achieve this objective, IPS recognizes that it is necessary not only to focus on Third World events and affairs but also to adopt a new approach to the question of information.

One of the key elements in the demands for NIIO is the need for a type of information which has a content and a function appropriate for the Third World. It is not enough merely to increase the quantity of news flows. . . . The formats of news and information currently employed by the transnational media system (and against which the Third World has reacted) are focused on "spot news," on the immediate and visible. Social process is excluded from the information system.

For the Third World, the problem is further exacerbated

by the fact that the "cultural distance" of the Third World from the North means a generally lower level of news coverage and a generally negative focus when coverage is given. In its attempt to rectify these aspects of the problem, IPS has adopted a style of journalism which focuses directly on the processes of development. This alternative style is an attempt to provide systematic and processual coverage of the successes and problems of development in the various Third World countries.

From the negative point of view, this means minimizing coverage of "protocolarian news" (the doings and sayings of political and other elites, airport meetings, etc.). From the positive point of view, this means increasing analysis and background and increasing the importance of nonelite news. Further, it means coverage of the realities of the Third World— not the reality of the Third World as seen from the North but as seen from within the Third World itself.

IPS aims to provide a systematic and synchronized view of national development processes, of Third World problems, and of processes which are of vital importance for development, independence, anticolonialism, antiracism and the non-aligned movement. The agency recognizes the multidimensionality of the Third World and the different approaches which are adopted by Third World nations in their search for national autonomy, but rather than following the traditional line of the transnational system in accentuating the uniqueness of each situation, IPS assists the solidarity of the Third World by examining the commonality of interests, problems, and perspectives. . . .

To achieve this, IPS has identified three major themes for its alternative news service:

- Facts related to the needs of the people of the Third World and the efforts being made to satisfy them
- Facts related to potential factors for an autonomous and self-reliant development
- Facts related to the efforts to transform socioeconomic structures

Within each of these categories, specific subject areas are

covered. Thus, under the first heading, the agency provides continuous information about the efforts being made to satisfy the needs of Third World populations in the fields of hunger and malnutrition, health and disease, housing and overcrowding, population policies, unemployment, illiteracy, and cultural marginality. Under the second heading, IPS covers potential factors for autonomous and self-reliant development in such fields as economic processes, production, and exploitation of resources, regional cooperation, technology, industrialization, and technical cooperation among Third World countries. Under the third heading, IPS carries information about land reform, rural development, reform of ownership structures, interventions in the commercial sectors for a more socially responsible goal, and educational reform.

It is the view of the agency that this type of focus, in combination with a more analytical and systematic treatment, leads to an alternative news service which begins to meet the requirements of a new international information order. On a second and more fundamentally based level, however, IPS has adopted a strategy aimed at facilitating the establishment of this new order of information—the strategy of providing horizontal communication.

Horizontal Communication

As I argued earlier, the nature of the information order as it is constituted at the moment is of verticality rather than horizontality. However, the real nature of the communications process is that it is the horizontal exchange of information.

With a view to contributing toward a *real* process of communication, IPS has directed its energies toward the horizontal linkage of Third World countries in the field of information. The aim of IPS is to escape the traditional vertical processes of communication by operating a horizontal system in which the basic units in the information system—the journalists— interact together to bring to the system a dialectic process within which policy is formulated. While IPS does not deny its manifestly political orientation, the agency's view is that, since this orientation is the product of journalistic interaction, it escapes the problems of traditional vertical structures in which one power or authority invests the news organization with a particular orientation.

This has become particularly important in the Third World, where the success of a Third World news exchange system depends on equal and mutual interaction of the participating agencies. In this sense, IPS offers a horizontal communication system in which all Third World news agencies are offered the opportunity of becoming partners through the journalists employed by them under exchange agreements.

In offering a horizontal system of information exchange to the Third World, IPS is concerned not to assume, or to be forced to assume, a leadership role within a Third World information system. Rather, IPS attempts to guarantee the success of such a system by maintaining its own status as just one instrument of information among others, to be shared by as wide a public as possible, and by maintaining its willingness to collaborate with any other information medium or other organization which shares the IPS philosophy.

This philosophy can be outlined in the following terms. The term *Third World* is very much a mechanistic concept which gained currency in the 1940s and 1950s and refers to those countries which have gained formal independence and formal sovereignty but which have not yet gained *real* independence and *real* sovereignty. The Third World exists in a state of dependence which is the result largely of external factors. While the Third World consists of countries with different regimes and different stages of political, economic, social, and cultural development, all share a common denominator—the inability to escape dependence.

Within this broad categorization, IPS identifies three trends which represent Third World interests and which define not only those countries which IPS terms "Third World" but also those countries which can be seen as compatible with IPS's aims. The first of these trends is a move toward real democracy—the integration of the people with the destiny of the country. This may take several forms—parliamentary democracy, one-party rule, two-party rule, etc.—but it must be directed toward the societal integration of the people within the country. The second trend is a move toward social and internal justice through reforms which make all citizens equally capable of utilizing opportunities for development. The third trend is the move toward real national sovereignty over national resources, including such cultural resources as information and communication.

Within this philosophy, and underpinning the collaboration of IPS with national news agencies in the Third World, is a conceptual model of the information process in which IPS sees its role. This conceptual model consists of a four-step cycle embracing orientation, production, distribution, and control. For IPS, the orientation and control of information (which exist in all societies) are factors which must be respected by the agency, but in the case of production and distribution IPS has a role to play.

Due to the historical development of the information order, these two processes have remained underdeveloped, with production directed largely toward an industrial, urban elite market and with distribution facilities severely limited. In both processes, the Third World news agencies are severely limited in terms of international structures.

Thus, IPS with its extensive international network collaborates with Third World news agencies in production, either by accepting material as it stands or, through mutual agreement, by revising material to improve its quality. Through its distribution network, IPS can then transmit this material to numerous destinations. As far as orientation and control are concerned, it is the view of IPS that these are conditioned by the three trends mentioned above, which define Third World interests. If a Third World news agency is compatible with these trends, IPS is open to collaboration with such an agency and is in a position to negotiate a bilateral agreement for news exchange.

In connection with the news pool of the nonaligned countries (which is a Third World-based attempt to counter some of the negative implications of the existing information order), IPS recognizes the variety and disparity of the news agencies comprising the news pool and collaborates with the news pool by distributing its news in line with its policy of support for multilateral moves in the interest of the Third World. What IPS offers is the use of its communication network while preserving the individual autonomy of the national news agencies utilizing these facilities.

The agreements which IPS has negotiated with Third World news agencies reflect the nature of its role within a Third World information network. The most common form of agreement reached is a dual arrangement which involves:

> –Direct exchange of news between two news agencies, either or both of which can then use the other news agency's material in its own services
> –A technical arrangement whereby IPS guarantees to transmit untouched the other news agency's material directly to IPS's subscribers

In the former case, IPS will always, if it decides to incorporate the other news agency's material in its own services, append a double byline to indicate the original source of the material. In the latter case, IPS will not append its own byline and will not alter the content or "line" of the material (even if it is reedited).

By operating within the guidelines outlined above, IPS hopes that the verticalism of traditional international communication can be replaced by a horizontalism which permits greater national autonomy and improved regional cooperation.

21

The Nonaligned News Pool

D. R. MANKEKAR

Displeasure with the transnational news agencies has led many Third World nations to support the creation of their own news agency to exchange news of common interest and develop a new style of journalism that gives priority to positive, nonsensational events and processes. In the mid-1970s, the News Agencies Pool of Nonaligned Countries became a reality, largely through the efforts of the Yugoslav news agency Tanjug and a few key Third World governments.

In 1976, India became the first head of the pool's coordination committee, which D.R. Mankekar chaired until late 1979. In his essay, he suggests how the self-financing pool has been operating to supplement existing transnational news sources, what its short-comings are, and what challenges lie ahead.

THE NEWS AGENCIES POOL of Nonaligned Countries is simply an arrangement for exchange of news between nonaligned countries, the kind of news they don't get from the Western

D. R. Mankekar, veteran Indian journalist, is the former chairman of the Coordination Committee of the News Agencies Pool of Nonaligned Countries. Author of *Media and the Third World* and *One-Way Free Flow—Neo-Colonialism and the News Media*, Mankekar has been the editor of the *Times of India* and a correspondent for Reuters and Associated Press of India. For a longer version of this essay, see Mankekar's *Media and the Third World* (New Delhi: Indian Institute of Mass Communication, 1979), esp. chs. 6 and 7.

transnational news agencies to which our media subscribe for foreign news. Its constituents are the news agencies of the nonaligned countries, and it seeks to supplement—not supplant—the major Western transnational agencies.

The pool is not a news agency in the sense of Reuters or the Associated Press. It does not have a central headquarters, a general manager, a board of directors, or even a budget and a staff. Its nearest equivalent to a board of management is the Coordination Committee of the News Agencies of Pool of Nonaligned Countries. The committee has a chairman but the post rotates every three years.

The constituent nonaligned countries have devised for the pool a self-financing structure—the sender of the news pays for its transmission. The news they exchange, which now totals about 40,000 words daily, is primarily of special interest to the nonaligned and developing countries and of the type which is generally ignored or neglected by the Western agencies. Reporting spot news is not the prime concern of the pool.

The architects of the pool are not content with the prevailing definition of news—that is, an event that is out of the ordinary, exciting, sensational, of the "man-biting-dog" variety. They would stretch the definition to include and emphasize "constructive" news, embracing stories on social change; economic development; socioeconomic, agricultural, technological and industrial progress; news that highlights the cultural side of life and promotes trade and commerce and cordial and cooperative relations between nonaligned countries.

These take the form of news features, special articles, situationers, and backgrounders. Most of such material is bound to be somewhat lengthy and would not be affected by the time element, and therefore could, with advantage, rely upon the air mail for their transmission, reserving the expensive telecommunication transmission channels to important spot political stories of special interest to the developing countries.

There are international political developments which could have a special developing countries' angle to them and may therefore also serve as occasions for special political coverage on the part of the Nonaligned Pool. The black/white confrontation in southern Africa would, for example, be a fit subject for such exclusive political stories.

Considering that we get hardly any news from South America, Africa, and Asia other than of military coups, terrorism, and natural calamities, there will be plenty of worthwhile stories to transmit among pool partners, if the service is competently organized and imaginatively directed.

Common charges against the pool are that the majority of the nonaligned countries contributing have authoritarian regimes, that many of them do not even have independent news agencies and, therefore, the news contributed by them to the pool comprises governmental propaganda and handouts issued by authoritarian regimes. The news issued by the pool, therefore, would not be objective or credible.

Reply to Critics

Those who have made these charges have not taken the trouble to look for evidence to support their charges in the news service actually supplied to newspapers by the pool. I have studied the incoming file of the Indian News Pool Desk for two years and I was gratified that I could not find a single news item put out by the News Pool Desk in New Delhi which could be described as either propagandist or a boost for the regimes of the countries from which the news emanated.

The constitution of the Pool provides that the recipient desk is free not to use any news item received from other partners. Indeed, the Indian Pool Desk has displayed mature news judgment and efficiency in editing and, where necessary, killing items which in their opinion did not deserve to be published for legitimate reasons, such as news of propagandist nature, news which violates good taste and decorum or amounts to libel, or news calculated to promote tensions and ill-feeling between countries.

The analysis showed that the content of most of the news issued by the Indian Pool Desk related to topics of economic, developmental, commercial, and trade interest, and also news of special interest to nonaligned and developing countries.

The news on commercial, financial, economic, and agricultural topics has generally been used in full by India's financial and economic newspapers like the *Economic Times* and the *Financial Express*. News of developmental and political interest concerning nonaligned countries has found a place in the columns of the general newspapers.

In the first two years, the News Pool Desk in New Delhi was putting out on an average 1,000 words a day of news received from more than a dozen nonaligned news agencies. The output will improve appreciably, and so will its content and quality when the recent steps taken to vamp up the service get into stride.

Accompanying the charge that the pool news is propagandist is the accusation that the pool news lacks credibility. Credibility stems from (a) accuracy and quality of news; and (b) the antecedents of the disseminator of the news, which in this case is the Nonaligned News Pool, representing news organizations scattered over four continents and composed of agencies with varying standards of professional skills and levels of journalistic evolution.

It is premature to pronounce a verdict on performance of the pool. To be able to do so, the critics must wait until the measures taken to resolve the twin obstacles in the way of its more efficient operation—the communication bottleneck and paucity of trained personnel—are in full gear.

The orientation of the deskman—the gatekeeper—is an important factor. You may produce the best news service, but if you give it to a desk team whose minds are trained and oriented to the West, you are wasting your news service. So you have to train your men to look at news more discriminatingly and from developing countries' viewpoint. So, this is another aspect which should be remedied by the Nonaligned News Pool.

All the big four global news agencies—AP, UPI, Reuters, and AFP—belong to countries which are ideologically on the same side of the fence and reflect broadly the same line of thinking on international politics. Therefore, they do not serve as alternatives to one another or offer the "other viewpoint" on a given international controversy.

Between them, they are in a position to determine what world news the newspaper readers shall and shall not read in developing countries. Indeed, in the years since World War II ended, we have known quite a few international issues on which the Western news agencies have ganged up to project a particular viewpoint.

The Third World news grievances largely stem from the fact that the agencies primarily gather, compose, and edit news for their home market—in other words, to meet the news needs of home newspaper readers, as dictated by their norms and values. Their clients in developing countries are served out of this basket of news, and it is inevitable that readers in developing countries should find such news out of tune, irrelevant, or unsympathetic, woefully inadequate, and even prejudicial and destructive.

The pool is an attempt to remedy such vital gaps in the Western agencies' services, by the nonaligned countries' own efforts, through a system of pooling their news resources and exchanging regional news and news of interest to nonaligned and developing countries.

That is what the Nonaligned News Pool is all about. Indeed the pool partners are fully aware of the shortcomings of their venture, but are not prepared, on that account, to be discouraged from going ahead with a project considered so vital and mutually beneficial by the entire community of nonaligned nations. They are determined, in the process of its operation, to rectify those shortcomings.

There is, however, not much that the nonaligned countries can do to rectify the distortions of their image committed by the transnationals in their outward service—unless the pool is able to get a regular and systematic outlet for their news services in the media of the rest of the world, and particularly of the West. Nor is it easy to persuade any of the Western media to agree to disseminate, through its channels, a stipulated wordage daily from the pool. Nevertheless, persistent efforts are being made in this direction either through access to indigenous news agencies or to the columns of individual newspapers.

It is in the sphere of regional exchange of news that the pool will play a vital part because it is practically an untapped area. Western transnationals do not consider it worthwhile or viable to gather and distribute the regional type of news because their home markets are not interested in it. But the countries of the region or those belonging to the nonaligned group are very much interested in the happenings in their neighborhood, apart from their community of interest. This prompts greater exchange of information about each other in the region. Developmental news, sociocultural activities, agricultural progress, social reform, and news of human interest are all grist to the mill of regional news.

The deficiency in quantitative and qualitative news flow in the Western agencies is also in a large measure within the capacity of the news pool to rectify. Here the remedy lies in those nonaligned news agencies who can afford to expand their corps of foreign correspondents, particularly in key centers like the United Nations, Unesco, Food and Agricultural Organization and other important U.N. agencies, and also in key cities in America, Western Europe, and the Socialist group. In this respect the Yugoslav news agency and center for the pool, Tanjug, has already a network of arrangements with other news systems in Eastern Europe, North Africa, Latin America, and China, in addition to its already smoothly functioning news pool.

Can the pool deliver the goods? Can it effectively fill the deficiencies found in the news services supplied by Western news agencies that the nonaligned countries complain about?

The answer depends entirely upon the professional competence and organizational and technological skills injected into the operations of the News Pool. Do we possess the requisite professional competence and organizational skills? In view of the fact that the community of nonaligned nations comprises a widely scattered group of nations, distributed over four continents, in varying stages of development, all of them do not command competence and skills in equal degree; but collectively they certainly do have the capabilities. Since the pool represents a collective and cooperative venture, they could, with advantage, draw upon the professional and organizational skills available among the more advanced partners within the pool.

The question is often asked, even by journalists, "News is news. What does it matter who writes and reports it?" If this were true, we could get the United Nations to run a single world news agency for the entire press of the world, and save a lot of money by abolishing all the powerful national news agencies of U.S.A., U.K., France, and the Soviet Union, whose very multiplicity tends to confuse and create tensions.

First Step in New Order

The pool constitutes the first concrete and significant step toward the establishment of a New International Information Order which, to quote from the Declaration adopted at the Colombo Summit of Nonaligned Countries, "is as vital as a New International Economic Order." It is heartening that the importance of rectifying serious imbalances in the flow of global information has not only been highlighted in recent years by the nonaligned movement but has come to be recognized by the world community as reflected in the resolutions of Unesco and the mandate given to the International Commission for the Study of Communication Problems.

Some sixty years ago when Britannia ruled the waves as well as the airwaves and Reuters held a monopoly of world news, Reuters shut off the Associated Press of America from the international arena of news. Kent Cooper, then general manager of AP, vigorously protested against Reuters' monopoly with the argument: "Americans want to look at the world through their own eyes, and not through the British eyes."[1] That, indeed, is the very essence of international news coverage.

1. Kent Cooper, Barriers Down (New York: Farrer and Rinehart), 1942.

Cooper went on to complain that Reuters gave a distorted image of America to the world, an image of a wild uncivilized country of Negro lynchings and racial violence. It is a strange irony that today other countries should be making the same charge against the American news media! We in India, of course, know too well what kind of image of India is presented to the world when prejudiced eyes look at our country.

I have cited this interesting episode to underline the remarkable parallel between the charges levelled by developing countries against the Western media in the 1970s and the American wail against the British world news monopoly in the 1920s. Indeed you have only to substitute the term "U.S.A." for the words "developing countries" and Kent Cooper would appear to be speaking most effectively for developing countries in the present era.

All that nonaligned countries are asking for is that they too want to look at the world through their own eyes instead of through the eyes of the Western news media.

It is to be noted here that in the electronic, satellite, and computer era, the potentialities of a monopoly placed in the hands of single group of Western media could be a hundred times more dangerous than such a monopoly was sixty years ago, when the sole means of communication was the submarine cable.

There are indications that the Western transnational news agencies themselves have given up their initial confrontational attitude and are getting reconciled to the idea of the developing countries organizing themselves to meet one another's regional news requirements. Indeed, I have received a letter from Stanley M. Swinton, vice-president of the Associated Press, expressing support for the Nonaligned News Pool concept and "offering to make available AP's more than 125 years of news agency experience to young national agencies on a consultancy basis." The AP Delhi correspondent also conveyed to me a proposition which offered the news desk at the Delhi point the use of an AP satellite channel. I understand the Asian News Agencies Group has also received a similar offer from UPI.

Nevertheless, there are still some diehards in the West who seem, for some inexplicable reason, to continue to be hostile to the very idea of the developing countries' developing their own communication system. Then there are others who jeer at our project and aver that it would never get off the ground.

The best riposte that we could give to the Western skeptics is to produce a strictly objective professional news service that will at once earn credibility for itself and belie the fears and doubts felt about it by our friends as well as critics. This could be best achieved by firmly adhering to the triple news virtues of truth, objectivity, and accuracy.

Tasks Ahead

With this end in view we must concentrate on pivotal issues like the setting up of distribution centers, resolving communication bottlenecks, organizing crash programs for professional and technical personnel, and redefining news so as to conform to the news needs of developing countries and the new world economic order we are aspiring to usher in.

We need to divide the widely scattered nonaligned world into conveniently sized zones with each zone in charge of a distribution center. To overcome the prevailing slow and ineffective transmission communication channels, a satellite channel is being established between Delhi and other important nonaligned news agency countries. There is a further need for rationalization of press cable rates between developing countries.

I recall the British penny-a-word press cable rate introduced within the British Commonwealth countries before World War II. This news strategy paid fabulous dividends to Britain and its empire in terms of more British news published in the Commonwealth press as well as the press of the rest of the world, thereby helping British culture and news dominate the world's news map.

We of the nonaligned world should emulate the British example and agree to introduce a low press cable rate among the nations of the nonaligned world, a rate which would be within the means of the poorest among us. The introduction of the Press Bulletin Service on satellite channels by many countries may go a long way toward solving our problem in this respect.

The next, and perhaps even more important, problem before us is that of organizing facilities for training in news agency journalism. A crash program of an eight-month training course in news agency journalism is being established in five institutes of journalism in different nonaligned countries. The Indian Institute of Mass Communication in New Delhi, for example, conducted its first course beginning in December 1978. Some of us are also in a position to loan the services of news agency experts to other developing countries to help them set up a nucleus for their own national news agency.

One of our major tasks and duties—Unesco has rightly emphasized this aspect of the question—is to encourage developing countries to start their own national news agencies if they do not have one. These national news agencies would contribute to the regional news pool and provide the new infrastructure for a worldwide News Agencies Pool of Nonaligned Countries.

If then a national news agency is a must for a state, it behooves the state to help realization of that objective, if necessary even by subsidizing it.

Indeed in the international sphere no news agency, however powerful and affluent, can afford to be independent in its news policies vis-a-vis the government of its country. Independence is therefore a relative term when we discuss its functioning in the international arena.

We must also devise plans for cooperation between the regional efforts towards news exchange systems and the intraregional News Agencies' Pool of Nonaligned Countries that we are building so as to avoid wasteful overlap and evolve more economical and mutually beneficial methods of coordination between them and the pool.

The pool symbolizes an effort to forge collective self-reliance among nonaligned countries for the emancipation and development of their national information media through exchange of greater information, in the first place among ourselves. We can turn the pool into an important instrument for furthering our plans and programs for political and economic growth and cultural regeneration.

22

Communication Tomorrow

INTERNATIONAL COMMISSION FOR THE STUDY OF COMMUNICATION PROBLEMS (THE MACBRIDE COMMISSION)

The International Commission for the Study of Communication Problems (the MacBride Commission) presented its basic recommendations at a press conference in February 1980, more than two years after it had started its work. The recommendations were "founded on the firm conviction that communication is a basic individual right as well as a collective one required by all communities and nations." The commission completed its task in December 1979, the date of the Final Report recommendations. The almost 500-page document was not publicly available until mid-1980, when Unesco published the report as a book, Many Voices, One World: Communication and Society Today and Tomorrow. The commission struggled with many conflicting ideological and cultural values and perspectives amid the concerns of East-West and North-South relations. Many points raised in its 1978 Interim Report

This essay is an excerpt from Part V of the *Final Report* of the International Commission for the Study of Communication Problems. Copyright © 1979 Unesco. Reprinted by permission. A list of Commission members is given in "Communication Problems Today" in this volume, with the addition of Sergei Losev, director-general of TASS, as the Soviet member for the *Final Report*.

had to be put aside for later discussion—matters concerning pro-
tection of journalists, codes of ethics, right of reply, and so forth.

The 1980 General Conference of Unesco accepted the MacBride
Final Report and by the end of that year the UN General Assembly
had passed a resolution that nations should "take into account" the
commission's recommendations.

The eighty-two recommendations in the Final Report are pre-
sented here, with introductory materials and some details of rec-
ommendations deleted. The recommendations are intended to show
the direction "the world must move to attain a new information and
communication order." Many of the recommendations are getting
wide global acceptance, while several of them continue to provoke
sharp Western reactions. In all, they provide a provocative inter-
national new agenda for the 1980s and beyond.

THE SURVEY CONTAINED in this Report has recorded a dramatic expansion of communication resources and possibilities. It is an expansion that promises great opportunities, but
also raises anxieties and uncertainties. Everything will depend
on the use made of the new resources—that is, on crucial decisions, and on the question of who will make the decisions.
Communication can be an instrument of power, a revolutionary weapon, a commercial product, or a means of education;
it can serve the ends either of liberation or of oppression,
either of the growth of the individual personality or of drilling
human beings into uniformity. Each society will have to make
its own choice in its own way. But the task before us all is to
find ways of overcoming the material, social and political constraints that impede progress.

We have already considered many suggestions for further
development. Without repeating them it might be useful to
begin our recommendations by summarizing previous main
conclusions:

1. Our review of communication the world over reveals
a variety of solutions adopted in different countries—in accordance with diverse patterns of social, economic and cultural
life—their traditions, needs and possibilities. This diversity is
valuable and should be respected; there is no place for the
universal application of preconceived models. Yet it should

be possible to establish, in broad outline, common aims and common values in the sphere of communication, based on common interests in a world of interdependence. . . .

2. The review has also shown that the utmost importance should be given to eliminating imbalances and disparities in communication and its structures, and particularly in information flows. Developing countries need to reduce their dependence, and claim a new, more just and more equitable order in the field of communication. . . .

3. Our conclusions are founded on the firm conviction that communication is a basic individual right, as well as a collective one required by all communities and nations. Freedom of information—and, more specifically the right to seek, impart and receive information—is a fundamental human right; indeed, a prerequisite for many others. . . .

4. For these purposes, it is essential to develop comprehensive national communication policies linked to overall social, cultural and economic development objectives. . . .

5. The basic principles which are developed at length in the body of our Report are intended to provide a framework for the development of a new information and communication order. We see its implementation as an on-going process of successive changes in the nature of relations between and within nations in the field of communications. . . . Crucial decisions concerning communication development need to be taken urgently, at both national and international levels. These decisions are not merely the concern of professionals, researchers or scholars, nor can they be the sole prerogative of those holding political or economic power. The decision-making process has to involve social participation at all levels. This calls for new attitudes for overcoming stereotyped thinking and to promote more understanding of diversity and plurality, with full respect for the dignity and equality of peoples living in different conditions and acting in different ways.

Thus our call for reflection and action is addressed broadly to governments and international organizations, to policy-makers and planners, to the media and professional organizations, to researchers, communication practitioners, to organized social groups and the public at large.

I. Strengthening Independence and Self-Reliance

COMMUNICATION POLICIES

. . . .

We recommend:

1. Communication be no longer regarded merely as an incidental service and its development left to chance. Recognition of its potential warrants the formulation by all nations, and particularly developing countries, of comprehensive communication policies linked to overall social, cultural, economic and political goals. . . .

2. As language embodies the cultural experience of people, all languages should be adequately developed to serve the complex and diverse requirements of modern communication. Developing nations and multilingual societies need to evolve language policies that promote all national languages even while selecting some, where necessary, for more widespread use in communication, higher education and administration. . . .

3. A primary policy objective should be to make elementary education available to all and to wipe out illiteracy, supplementing formal schooling systems with non-formal education and enrichment within appropriate structures of continuing and distance learning (through radio, television and correspondence).

4. Within the framework of national development policies, each country will have to work out its own set of priorities, bearing in mind that it will not be possible to move in all directions at the same time . . . .

STRENGTHENING CAPACITIES

. . . .

5. Developing countries take specific measures to establish or develop essential elements of their communications systems: print media, broadcasting and telecommunications along with the related training and production facilities.

6. Strong national news agencies are vital for improving each country's national and international reporting. Where

viable, regional networks should be set up to increase news flows and serve all the major language groups in the area. Nationally, the agencies should buttress the growth of both urban and rural newspapers to serve as the core of a country's news collection and distribution system.

7. National book production should be encouraged and accompanied by the establishment of a distribution network for books, newspapers and periodicals. The stimulation of works by national authors in various languages should be promoted.

8. The development of comprehensive national radio networks, capable of reaching remote areas should take priority over the development of television, which, however, should be encouraged where appropriate. Special attention should be given to areas where illiteracy is prevalent.

9. National capacity for producing broadcast materials is necessary to obviate dependence on external sources over and beyond desirable program exchange. This capacity should include national or regional broadcasting, film and documentary production centers with a basic distribution network.

10. Adequate educational and training facilities are required to supply personnel for the media and production organizations, as well as managers, technicians and maintenance personnel. In this regard, cooperation between neighboring countries and within regions should be encouraged.

BASIC NEEDS

. . . .

11. The communication component in all development projects should receive adequate financing. So-called "development support communications" are essential for mobilizing initiatives and providing information required for action in all fields of development—agriculture, health and family planning, education, religion, industry and so on.

12. Essential communication needs to be met include the extension of basic postal services and telecommunication networks through small rural electronic exchanges.

13. The development of a community press in rural areas and small towns would not only provide print support for economic and social extension activities. This would also facilitate the production of functional literature for neo-literates as well.

14. Utilization of local radio, low-cost small format television and video systems and other appropriate technologies would facilitate production of programs relevant to community development efforts, stimulate participation and provide opportunity for diversified cultural expression.

15. The educational and informational use of communication should be given equal priority with entertainment. At the same time, education systems should prepare young people for communication activities. . . .

16. Organization of community listening and viewing groups could in certain circumstances widen both entertainment and educational opportunities. Education and information activities should be supported by different facilities ranging from mobile book, tape and film libraries to programmed instruction through "schools of the air."

17. Such activities should be aggregated wherever possible in order to create vibrant local communication resource centers for entertainment, education, information dissemination and cultural exchange. . . .

18. It is not sufficient to urge that communication be given a high priority in national development; possible sources of investment finance must be identified. Among these could be differential communication pricing policies that would place larger burdens on more prosperous urban and elite groups: the taxing of commercial advertising may also be envisioned for this purpose.

PARTICULAR CHALLENGES

. . . .

19. A major international research and development effort to increase the supply of paper. . . .

20. Tariffs for news transmission, telecommunications

rates and air mail charges for the dissemination of news, transport of newspapers, periodicals, books and audiovisual materials are one of the main obstacles to a free and balanced flow of information. This situation must be corrected, especially in the case of developing countries, through a variety of national and international initiatives. . . .

21. The electromagnetic spectrum and geostationary orbit, both finite natural resources, should be more equitably shared as the common property of mankind. . . .

II. Social Consequences and New Tasks

INTEGRATING COMMUNICATION INTO DEVELOPMENT

. . . .

22. Promotion of dialogue for development as a central component of both communication and development policies. . . .

23. In promoting communication policies, special attention should be given to the use of non-technical language and comprehensible symbols, images and forms to ensure popular understanding. . . . Similarly, development information supplied to the media should be adapted to prevailing news values and practices. . . .

FACING THE TECHNOLOGICAL CHALLENGE

. . . .

24. Devising policy instruments at the national level in order to evaluate the positive and negative social implications of the introduction of powerful new communication technologies. . . .

25. Setting up national mechanisms to promote participation and discussion of social priorities in the acquisition or extension of new communication technologies. . . .

26. In developing countries the promotion of autonomous research and development should be linked to specific projects

and programs. . . . More funds are necessary to stimulate and support adaptive technological research. . . .

27. The concentration of communications technology in a relatively few developed countries and transnational corporations has led to virtual monopoly situations in this field. To counteract these tendencies national and international measures are required, among them reform of existing patent laws and conventions, appropriate legislation and international agreements.

STRENGTHENING CULTURAL IDENTITY

. . . .

28. Establishment of national cultural policies, which should foster cultural identity and creativity, and involve the media in these tasks. Such policies should also contain guidelines for safeguarding national cultural development while promoting knowledge of other cultures. . . .[1]

29. Communication and cultural policies should ensure that creative artists and various grassroots groups can make their voices heard through the media. . . .

30. Introduction of guidelines with respect to advertising content and the values and attitudes it fosters, in accordance with national standards and practices. Such guidelines should be consistent with national development policies and efforts to preserve cultural identity. Particular attention should be given to the impact on children and adolescents. In this connection, various mechanisms such as complaint boards or consumer review committees might be established. . . .

REDUCING THE COMMERCIALIZATION OF COMMUNICATION

. . . .

31. In expanding communication systems, preference should be given to non-commercial forms of mass commu-

---

1. Comment by S. MacBride [Ireland]: "I wish to add that owing to the cultural importance of spiritual and religious values and also in order to restore moral values, policy guidelines should take into account religious beliefs and traditions."

nication. Promotion of such types of communication should be integrated with the traditions, culture, development objectives and sociopolitical system of each country. As in the field of education, public funds might be made available for this purpose.

32. While acknowledging the need of the media for revenues, ways and means should be considered to reduce the negative effects that the influence of market and commercial considerations have in the organization and content of national and international communication flows.[2]

33. That consideration be given to changing existing funding patterns of commercial mass media. In this connection, reviews could be made of the way in which the relative role of advertising volume and costs pricing policies, voluntary contributions, subsidies, taxes, financial incentives and supports could be modified to enhance the social function of mass media and improve their service to the community.

ACCESS TO TECHNICAL INFORMATION

. . . .

34. Developing countries should pay particular attention to: (a) the correlation between educational, scientific and communication policies because their practical application frequently overlaps; (b) the creation in each country of one or several centers for the collection and utilization of technical information and data, both from within the country and from abroad; (c) to secure the basic equipment necessary for essential data processing activities; (d) the development of skills and facilities for computer processing and analysis of data obtained from remote sensing.

35. Developed countries should foster exchanges of tech-

---

2. Comment by E. Abel [U.S.A.]: "At no time has the commission seen evidence adduced in support of the notion that market and commercial considerations necessarily exert a negative effect upon communication flows. On the contrary, the commission has praised elsewhere in this report courageous investigative journalism of the sort that can be sustained only by independent media whose survival depends upon their acceptance in the marketplace, rather than the favors of political leaders. The commission also is aware that market mechanisms play an increasingly important role today even in so-called planned economies."

nical information on the principle that all countries have equal rights to full access to available information. . . .

36. Developing countries should adopt national informatics policies as a matter of priority. . . .

37. At the international level, consideration should be given to action with respect to: (a) a systematic identification of existing organized data processing infrastructures in various specialized fields; (b) agreement on measures for effective multi-country participation in the programs, planning and administration of existing or developing data infrastructures; (c) analysis of commercial and technical measures likely to improve the use of informatics by developing countries; (d) agreement on international priorities for research and development that is of interest to all countries in the field of informatics.

38. Transnational corporations should supply to the authorities of the countries in which they operate, upon request and on a regular basis as specified by local laws and regulations, all information required for legislative and administrative purposes relevant to their activities and specifically needed to assess the performance of such entitities. They should also provide the public, trade unions and other interested sectors of the countries in which they operate with information needed to understand the global structure, activities and policies of the transnational corporation and their significance for the country concerned.

III. Professional Integrity and Standards

RESPONSIBILITY OF JOURNALISTS

. . . .

39. The importance of the journalist's mission in the contemporary world demands steps to enhance his standing in society. . . .

40. To be treated as professionals, journalists require broad educational preparation and specific professional training. . . .

41. Such values as truthfulness, accuracy, respect for human rights are not universally applied at present. Higher professional standards and responsibility cannot be imposed by decree, nor do they depend solely on the goodwill of individual journalists, who are employed by institutions which can improve or handicap their professional performance. The self-respect of journalists, their integrity and inner drive to turn out work of high quality are of paramount importance. It is this level of professional dedication, making for responsibility, that should be fostered by news media and journalists' organizations. In this framework, a distinction should be drawn between media institutions, owners and managers on the one hand and journalists on the other.

42. As in other professions, journalists and media organizations serve the public directly and the public, in turn, is entitled to hold them accountable for their actions. Among the mechanisms devised up to now in various countries for assuring accountability, the Commission sees merit in press or media councils, the institution of the press ombudsman and peer group criticism of the sort practiced by journalism reviews in several countries. In addition, communities served by particular media can accomplish significant reforms through citizen action. . . . Voluntary measures . . . can do much to influence media performance. Nevertheless, it appears necessary to develop further effective ways by which the right to assess mass media performance can be exercised by the public.

43. Codes of professional ethics exist in all parts of the world, adopted voluntarily in many countries by professional groups. The adoption of codes of ethics at national and, in some cases, at the regional level is desirable, provided that such codes are prepared and adopted by the profession itself— without governmental influence.

TOWARD IMPROVED INTERNATIONAL REPORTING

. . . .

44. All countries should take steps to assure admittance of foreign correspondents and facilitate their collection and

transmission of news. Special obligations in this regard, undertaken by the signatories to the Final Act of the Helsinki conference, should be honored and, indeed, liberally applied. Free access to news sources by journalists is an indispensable requirement for accurate, faithful and balanced reporting. This necessarily involves access to unofficial, as well as official sources of information, that is, access to the entire spectrum of opinion within any country.[3]

45. Conventional standards of news selection and reporting, and many accepted news values, need to be reassessed if readers and listeners around the world are to receive a more faithful and comprehensive account of events, movements and trends in both developing and developed countries. The inescapable need to interpret unfamiliar situations in terms that will be understood by a distant audience should not blind reporters or editors to the hazards of narrow ethnocentric thinking. . . .

46. To this end, reporters being assigned to foreign posts should have the benefit of language training and acquaintance with the history, institutions, politics, economics and cultural environment of the country or region in which they will be serving.

47. The press and broadcasters in the industrialized world should allot more space and time to reporting events in and background material about foreign countries in general and news from the developing world in particular. Also, the media in developed countries—especially the "gatekeepers," editors and producers of print and broadcasting media who select the news items to be published or broadcast—should become more familiar with the cultures and conditions in developing countries. Although the present imbalances in news

3. Comment by S. Losev [USSR]: "This paragraph doesn't correspond to the Helskinki Final Act (see section 2 - information, point (c)), contradicts the interests of developing nations and therefore is completely unacceptable and I object against it being included. I suggest to replace this recommendation by the following text: 'All countries should take appropriate measures to improve the conditions for foreign correspondents to carry out their professional activities in the host countries in accordance with the provisions of the Helsinki Final Act and with due respect to the national sovereignty and the national identity of the host country'."

flow call for strengthening of capacities in developing countries, the media of the industrialized countries have their contribution to make toward the correction of these inequalities.

48. To offset the negative effects of inaccurate or malicious reporting of international news, the right of reply and correction should be further considered. While these concepts are recognized in many countries, their nature and scope vary so widely that it would be neither expedient nor realistic to propose the adoption of any international regulations for their purpose. . . .

49. Intelligence services of many nations have at one time or other recruited journalists to commit espionage under cover of their professional duties. This practice must be condemned. . . .

PROTECTION OF JOURNALISTS

. . . .

50. The professional independence and integrity of all those involved in the collection and dissemination of news, information and views to the public should be safeguarded. However, the Commission does not propose special privileges to protect journalists in the performance of their duties, although journalism is often a dangerous profession. Far from constituting a special category, journalists are citizens of their respective countries, entitled to the same range of human rights as other citizens. One exception is provided in the Additional Protocol to the Geneva Conventions of 12 August 1949, which applies only to journalists on perilous missions, such as in areas of armed conflict. To propose additional measures would invite the dangers entailed in a licensing system since it would require some body to stipulate who should be entitled to claim such protection. Journalists will be fully protected only when everyone's human rights are protected and guaranteed.[4]

4. Comment by S. MacBride: "I consider this paragraph quite inadequate to deal with what is a serious position. Because of the importance of the role of journalists and others who provide or control the flow of news to the media, I urge that they should be granted a special status and protection. I also urge that provisions should

51. That Unesco should convene a series of round tables at which journalists, media executives, researchers and jurists can periodically review problems related to the protection of journalists and propose additional appropriate measures to this end.[5]

IV. Democratization of Communication

HUMAN RIGHTS

. . . .

52. All those working in the mass media should contribute to the fulfillment of human rights, both individual and collective, in the spirit of the Unesco Declaration on the Mass Media and the Helsinki Final Act. The contribution of the media in this regard is not only to foster these principles, but also to expose all infringements, wherever they occur, and to support those whose rights have been neglected or violated. Professional associations and public opinion should support journalists subject to pressure or who suffer adverse consequences from their dedication to the defense of human rights.

53. The media should contribute to promoting the just cause of peoples struggling for freedom and independence and their right to live in peace and equality without foreign interference. This is especially important for all oppressed peoples who, while struggling against colonialism, religious and racial discrimination, are deprived of opportunity to make their voices heard within their own countries.

54. Communication needs in a democratic society should be met by the extension of specific rights such as the right to

be made to enable a journalist to appeal against a refusal of reasonable facilities. My views on these issues are embodied in a paper entitled *The Protection of Journalists* (CIC Document No. 90) which I submitted to the Commission; I refer in particular to paragraphs 1–17 and 35–53 of this paper."

5. Comment by S. MacBride: "I urge that such a Round Table be convened annually for a period of five years; I refer to paragraphs 50-57 of my paper on *The Protection of Journalists* (CIC Document No. 90)."

be informed, the right to inform, the right to privacy, the right to participate in public communication—all elements of a new concept, the right to communicate. In developing what might be called a new era of social rights, we suggest all the implications of the right to communicate be further explored.

REMOVAL OF OBSTACLES

. . . .

55. All countries adopt measures to enlarge sources of information by citizens in their everyday life. A careful review of existing laws and regulations should be undertaken with the aim of reducing limitations, secrecy provisions and other constraints in information practices.

56. Censorship or arbitrary control of information should be abolished.[6] In areas where reasonable restrictions may be considered necessary, these should be provided for by law, subject to judicial review and in line with the principles enshrined in the United Nations Charter, the Universal Declaration of Human Rights and the International Covenants relating to human rights, and in other instruments adopted by the community of nations.[7]

57. Special attention should be devoted to obstacles and restrictions which derive from the concentration of media ownership, public or private, from commercial influences on the press and broadcasting, or from private or governmental advertising. The problem of financial conditions under which the media operate should be critically reviewed, and measures elaborated to strengthen editorial independence.

6. Comment by S. Losev: "This whole problem of censorship or arbitrary control of information is within the national legislation of each country and is to be solved within the national, legal framework taking in due consideration the national interests of each country."

7. Comment by S. MacBride: "I also wish to draw attention to the provisions of Article 10 of the European Convention for the Protection of Human Rights which I consider as wholly inadequate. I urge that Articles 13 and 14 of the Inter-American Convention on Human Rights (1979) are much more comprehensive and effective than the equivalent provisions of the European Convention. The matter is discussed in paragraphs 26–29 of my paper on *The Protection of Journalists* (CIC Document No. 90)."

58. Effective legal measures should be designed to: (a) limit the process of concentration and monopolization; (b) circumscribe the action of transnationals by requiring them to comply with specific criteria and conditions defined by national legislation and development policies; (c) reverse trends to reduce the number of decision-makers at a time when the media's public is growing larger and the impact of communication is increasing; (d) reduce the influence of advertising upon editorial policy and broadcast programming; (e) seek and improve models which would ensure greater independence and autonomy of the media concerning their management and editorial policy, whether these media are under private, public or government ownership.[8]

DIVERSITY AND CHOICE

. . . .

59. The building of infrastructures and the adoption of particular technologies should be carefully matched to the need for more abundant information to a broader public from a plurality of sources.

60. Attention should be paid to the communication needs of women. They should be assured adequate access to communication means and that images of them and of their activities are not distorted by the media or in advertising.

61. The concerns of children and youth, national, ethnic, religious, linguistic minorities, people living in remote areas and the aged and handicapped deserve also particular consideration. They constitute large and sensitive segments of society and have special communication needs.

8. Comment by E. Abel: "Regarding (a) and (c), anti-monopoly legislation, whether more or less effective, is relevant only in countries where a degree of competition can be said to exist. It is a travesty to speak of measures against concentration and monopolization in countries where the media are themselves established as state monopolies, or operate as an arm of the only authorized political party. (b) Transnational corporations are expected to comply with the laws of the countries in which they do business. (d) Where it can be shown to exist, the influence of advertisers upon editorial content or broadcast programming would warrant careful study. But a sweeping demand that such influence be reduced, without pausing to examine or attempting to measure that influence in particular circumstances, is a symptom of ideological prejudice."

INTEGRATION AND PARTICIPATION

. . . .

62. Much more attention be devoted to use of the media in living and working environments. Instead of isolating men and women, the media should help integrate them into the community.

63. Readers, listeners and viewers have generally been treated as passive receivers of information. Those in charge of the media should encourage their audiences to play a more active role in communication by allocating more newspaper space, or broadcasting time, for the views of individual members of the public or organized social groups.

64. The creation of appropriate communication facilities at all levels, leading toward new forms of public involvement in the management of the media and new modalities for their funding.

65. Communication policymakers should give far greater importance to devising ways whereby the management of the media could be democratized—while respecting national customs and characteristics—by associating the following categories: (a) journalists and professional communicators; (b) creative artists; (c) technicians; (d) media owners and managers; (e) representatives of the public. Such democratization of the media needs the full support and understanding of all those working in them, and this process should lead to their having a more active role in editorial policy and management.

V. Fostering International Cooperation

PARTNERS FOR DEVELOPMENT

. . . .

66. The progressive implementation of national and international measures that will foster the establishment of a new world information and communication order. The pro-

posals contained in this report can serve as a contribution to develop the varied actions necessary to move in that direction.

67. International cooperation for the development of communications be given equal priority with and within other sectors (e.g., health, agriculture, industry, science, education, etc.) as information is a basic resource for individual and collective advancement and for all-round development. . . .

68. The close relationship between the establishment of a new international economic order and the new world information and communication order should be carefully considered by the technical bodies dealing with these issues. Concrete plans of action linking both processes should be implemented within the United Nations system. The United Nations, in approving the international development strategy, should consider the communications sector as an integral element of it and not merely as an instrument of public information.

STRENGTHENING COLLECTIVE SELF-RELIANCE

. . . .

69. The communication dimension should be incorporated into existing programs and agreements for economic cooperation between developing countries.

70. Joint activities in the field of communication, which are under way between developing countries, should be developed further in the light of the overall analysis and recommendations of this Report. In particular, attention should be given to cooperation among national news agencies, to the further development of the News Agencies Pool and broadcasting organizations at the nonaligned countries, as well as to the general exchange on a regular basis of radio, television programs and films.

71. With respect to cooperation in the field of technical information, establishment of regional and sub-regional data banks and information processing centers and specialized documentation centers should be given a high priority. . . .

72. Mechanisms for sharing information of a non-strategic nature could be established particularly in economic matters.

Arrangements of this nature could be of value in areas such as multilateral trade negotiations, dealings with transnational corporations and banks, economic forecasting, and medium- and long-term planning and other similar fields.

73. Particular efforts should be undertaken to ensure that news about other developing countries within or outside their region receive more attention and space in the media. Special projects could be developed to ensure a steady flow of attractive and interesting material inspired by news values which meet developing countries' information needs.

74. Measures to promote links and agreements between professional organizations and communication researchers of different countries should be fostered. . . .

INTERNATIONAL MECHANISMS

. . . .

75. The Member States of Unesco should increase their support to the Organization's program in this area. Consideration should be given to organizing a distinct communication sector, not simply in order to underline its importance, but to emphasize that its activities are interrelated with the other major components of Unesco's work—education, science and culture.[9] In its communications activities, Unesco should concentrate on priority areas. Among these are assistance to national policy formulation and planning, technical development, organizing professional meetings and exchanges, promotion and coordination of research, and elaboration of international norms.

76. Better coordination of the various communication activities [is needed] within Unesco and those throughout the United Nations system. . . .

77. It would be desirable for the United Nations family to be equipped with a more effective information system, in-

9. Comment by M. Lubis [Indonesia]: "I strongly believe that the present set-up in Unesco (Sector of Culture and Communication) is adequate to deal with the problems of communication."

cluding a broadcast capability of its own and possibly a communication satellite. . . .[10,11]

78. Consideration might be given to establishing within the framework of Unesco an International Center for the Study and Planning of Information and Communication. Its main tasks would be to: (a) promote the development of national communication systems in developing countries and the balance and reciprocity in international information flows; (b) mobilize resources required for that purpose and manage the funds put at its disposal; and (c) assure coordination among parties interested in communication development and involved in various cooperation programs and evaluate results of bilateral and multilateral activities in this field; (d) organize round tables, seminars, and conferences for the training of communication planners, researchers and journalists, particularly those specializing in international problems; and (e) keep under review communications technology transfers between developed and developing countries so that they are carried out in the most suitable conditions. The Center may be guided by a tripartite coordinating council composed of representatives of developing and developed countries and of interested international organizations. . . .[12]

10. Comment by M. Lubis: "I am of the opinion that the present communication potential of the U.N. system has not been effectively and efficiently used and managed. And I cannot foresee for a long time to come that the U.N. system will be able to speak with one voice on the really relevant issues of the world, disarmament, peace, freedom, human rights. . . ."

11. Comment by S. MacBride: "I would point out that the phenomenal growth of international broadcasting highlights the absence of a U.N. International Broadcasting System. Some thirty countries broadcast a total of 12,000 hours per week in one hundred different languages. I urge that the U.N. should establish a broadcasting system of its own that would broadcast 24 hours around the clock in not less than 30 different languages. See my paper on *The Protection of Journalists* (CIC Document No. 90, paragraph 46) and the paper on *International Broadcasting* (CIC Document No. 60)."

12. Comment by B. Zimmerman [Canada]: "Although I agree that a coordinating body in the field of communication development could serve a useful purpose, I cannot support this precise recommendation. All members of the Commission did not have the opportunity to discuss thoroughly the advantages and disadvantages of various objectives and structures for such a coordinating body. As a Unesco Intergovernmental Conference is to be held in 1980 to cover that topic, I feel the Com-

Footnote 12 continued bottom next page

TOWARDS INTERNATIONAL UNDERSTANDING

. . . .

79. National communication policies should be consistent with adopted international communication principles and should seek to create a climate of mutual understanding and peaceful coexistence among nations. Countries should also encourage their broadcast and other means of international communication to make the fullest contribution toward peace and international cooperation and to refrain from advocating national, racial or religious hatred, and incitement to discrimination, hostility, violence or war.

80. Due attention should be paid to the problems of peace and disarmament, human rights, development and the creation of a new communication order. Mass media, both printed and audiovisual, should be encouraged to publicize significant documents of the United Nations, of Unesco, of the world peace movements, and of various other international and national organizations devoted to peace and disarmament. The curricula of schools of journalism should include study of these international problems and the views expressed on them within the United Nations.

81. All forms of cooperation among the media, the professionals and their associations, which contribute to the better

---

mission should welcome the careful study that the Unesco Conference is in a position to give the matter, rather than offering any recommendation at this time."

Comment by E. Abel: "This proposal is premature, unnecessary and unwise. The design of an appropriate mechanism for promoting and coordinating communications development demands more time and resources than this Commission possesses. Essentially the same proposal here advanced was one of two submitted to a Unesco experts meeting in November [1979]; neither one was endorsed. The question is on the agenda for an intergovernmental meeting at Unesco in April [1980]. The U.N. General Assembly has now taken a strong interest in the matter and has requested the Secretary-General to intervene. As it stands, this proposal can only deter the necessary cooperation of both the competent U.N. bodies and the developed nations whose cooperation is indispensable to further progress."

Comment by S. MacBride: "I suggest that if any steps are taken in this direction prior consultation and accord should be reached with journalists' organizations and other NGOs [nongovernmental organizations] involved in the mass media."

knowledge of other nations and cultures, should be encouraged and promoted.

82. Reporting on international events or developments in individual countries in situations of crisis and tension requires extreme care and responsibility. In such situations, media often constitute one of the few, if not the sole, link between combatants or hostile groups. This clearly casts on them a special role which they must be expected to discharge with objectivity and sensitivity.

. . . .

Our study indicates clearly the direction in which the world must move to attain a new information and communication order—essentially a series of new relationships arising from the advances promised by new communication technologies which should enable all peoples to benefit. The awareness already created on certain issues, such as global imbalances in information flows, suggests that a process of change has resulted and is under way. The power and promise of ever-new communication technologies and systems are, however, such as to demand deliberate measures to ensure that existing communication disparities do not widen. The objective should be to ensure that men and women are enabled to lead richer and more satisfying lives. . . .

It is important to realize that the new order we seek is not only a goal but a stage in a journey. It is a continuing quest for ever more free, more equal, more just relations within all societies and among all nations and peoples. This Report represents what we believe we have learned. And this, above all, is what we wish to communicate.

23

International News: Looking Ahead

**JIM RICHSTAD and
MICHAEL H. ANDERSON**

*In this final essay, Jim Richstad and Michael H. Anderson, editors
of this collection, examine where the contemporary international
communication crisis is headed in terms of a freer and more balanced flow of information and a new order that would increase
mutual understanding, at both national and international levels.*

*The thrust of their article is that the world is moving forward
in some promising policy directions and that the spirit of the 1980s
and beyond could be one of pluralism, harmony, and positive cooperation. The risks, however, are great, and the times will place
a premium on not only innovative ideas but also patience and public
diplomacy. The fiery responses to the MacBride Commission's recommendations and the work of Unesco in news and broader communication areas from American and British news executives continues and portends a renewal of the hostility similar to the mid-
1970s over international news. Several critical study and research
areas are outlined for the 1980s and beyond.*

THE POLICIES and prospects for communication in the 1980s

are challenging to assess and difficult to predict. There seem to be some certainties, however, that will influence policy in this unruly decade, and point out new, cooperative directions for international communication and news.

Since this book of readings has focused primarily on the relationship between the interconnected First World and the Third World in the news field, these conclusions are weighted in that area. Before going to the particular dynamics of that relationship, however, some broad elements in the communication and news environment, as they emerged in the 1970s, are still strong influences in the 1980s and should be examined.

The nature of communication changed tremendously in the 1970s—there emerged an almost entirely new and highly politicized communication environment in which the whole concept of news and communication and information was reevaluated and great shifts occurred in priorities and possibilities. The sharp clashes of views, basically over decolonization and protectionism policies and processes, created a world crisis in news and information. The changes, amplified by tremendous technological advances and the "communication explosion," were of the magnitude that a new, more "open" information or communication order was emerging from the crisis. People and governments everywhere were recognizing the strategic and economic nature of information and generally were becoming more dependent upon it as a vital resource.

American media products, in particular, continued to be important though imperfect for much of the world. William Read has explained:

U.S. private mass media are far from perfect channels of international communications. They neglect some regions, are forbidden to operate in others, and efficiently distribute inappropriate information to still other audiences. Nonetheless they are regular, repetitive, normally dependable sources of information. Just as major government leaders need "hot lines," lesser mortals also require communications networks to share information useful in shaping their portion of an interconnected, if not yet fully interdependent world. U.S. mass media are major contributors to such networks.[1]

The American media are almost universally perceived as having significant impact abroad. Read has enumerated some often cited conclusions: "American media influence foreign media; an international (or transnational) information elite has developed; mass media contribute to the spread of an Americanized world culture; and the media are helping shape an interdependent world."[2]

One of the first steps in policy formation is developing a clear, more sophisticated statement of the problem, which obviously extends far beyond the simplistic notion that sprawling U.S. or European media and news agencies are "the" problem, or that there are only minor problems that can be tinkered away. Through the 1970s there were urgent demands to restate the news and information problems in inter- and intranational terms that widen the concepts and perspectives of global news and information policy to include several new sets of interests—mainly those of the politically emergent and developing nations of the Third World. The work of the MacBride Commission has been seminal in clarifying major world communication problems and issues and documenting various growing Third World nations' concerns over their dependence in matters of communication, especially news. In addition, the development of communication technology, particularly in sophisticated computers, lasers, and satellites, provided new and economical means of increasing the flow of news and information and establishing new patterns for the flow. That is, no longer is it necessary because of the communication structures for developing countries to communicate through a developed or center country—it is now easily possible (although often financially impossible) for any two

1. William H. Read, "U.S. Private Media Abroad," *The Role and Control of International Communications and Information*. Report to the Subcommittee on International Operations of the Committee of Foreign Relations, United States Senate (Washington, D.C.: GPO, June 1977), p. 35.

2. *ibid.*, p. 26.

spots on earth to be in instant communication with each other, to exchange news and information about each other. This opens the potential for increased all-round dialogue and for wide horizontal news and information networks.

Several of these South-South arrangements are already functioning along with the more established North-North exchange systems.[3] There seems to be no real technological limit for developing countries—all countries—to get the kind of news information and data they want, from whom they want it. This is a central guiding factor for the 1980s—the breaking up of "feudal network," in Norwegian peace researcher Johan Galtung's term[4]—in the development of a global news and information policy. Many of the bitter complaints by the Third World that emerged in the 1970s, while often fully justified, are simply no longer relevant in the technological context of the 1980s. The lesson for policy formation is that the problems of the 1970s may no longer be relevant or are less relevant, that the problems are shifting in nature, and that as one problem is solved or ameliorated, others grow from it or emerge separately. Policymakers should not, as Arthur Clarke warns, be looking in a rear-view mirror at the problems that are left behind by technological, political, and other developments.

Some of the key problems in the 1980s seem clear; others require more policy-relevant study, dialogue, research, and testing. None of them will be solved through one global design. None of them will be solved overnight—or even over the decade. None of them will be solved without confrontation or at least very strenuous, time-consuming negotiation. All of them will

3. The News Agencies Pool of Nonaligned Countries and the Inter Press Service are two operating South-South agencies, among several. For information on exchange of development information, see "Development Information Network for Cooperation Among Developing Countries," United Nations Development Program, New York, 1980, and Erskine Childers, "TCDC: Facing the Challenge of Contact Deprivation," *Intermedia* (December 1977), 5(6). For an exposition on what the new South-South information region developments portend, see Jim Richstad and Tony Nnaemeka, "Information Regions: Context for International News Flow Research," paper for Association for Education in Journalism Convention, Boston, August 1980.

4. Johan Galtung, "A Structural Theory of Imperialism," *Journal of Peace Research* (1971), 8(2):81–117.

relate somehow to a series of Third World concerns over communication sovereignty, content, resources, accountability,
and—above all—equity.

The central problem in the 1980s for news and information policy and processes is the correction in the imbalance
of news, as evident in the developed world, and more particularly in the United States. The United States is especially
important in this discussion because of its still predominant
position in world communication, and in economic, social,
political, and cultural areas. What has emerged with devastating and chilling clarity in the 1970s is that the people of
the United States are relatively insular and, in MacBride Commissioner Elie Abel's words, in "substantial ignorance" of conditions in the rest of the world.[5] Veteran foreign correspondent
Mort Rosenblum has made this observation about Americans:

When crisis impends, they are not warned. When it strikes, they are
not prepared. They know little about decisions taken on their behalf
which lessen their earnings, restrict their freedoms and threaten
their security. In their blissful unawareness, they give up their
chance to have a hand in events and leave themselves vulnerable
in an increasingly competitive world.[6]

Despite heavy foreign news on crises like Vietnam, Afghanistan, or Iran, Americans generally tune out world events.
They do not know how people in other parts of the world live
or think or act, and they do not know how this lack of knowledge can vitally affect their own and the world's peace and
well-being. The news media of the United States present a
sketchy, distorted, and clouded picture of the world, a simplistic picture, and, perhaps, a very dangerous picture. This
is part of the reason for the ignorance in the United States of
the rest of the world—an ignorance that is viewed by some in
the Third World as an arrogance in not caring to learn about

5. Elie Abel, in remarks from the podium at 43d Annual Meeting, U.S. National
Commission for Unesco, Athens, Georgia, December 12–15, 1979.
6. Mort Rosenblum, *Coups and Earthquakes: Reporting the World for America*
(New York: Harper & Row, 1979), pp. 1–2.

other peoples and cultures, particularly those of the developing countries.[7]

The media need to do more to expand their international coverage and disseminate more foreign-produced materials. Television programming studies in the 1970s, for example, found that the United States was the second most closed system in the world—behind the People's Republic of China.[8] Here is a country with one of the most advanced communication systems—a superpower in communication—that sees less of the world's television production than other countries.

Ironically, in the mid- and late-1970s, China—after several decades of isolation—opened itself to outside and Western influences (transnational media and others), a lead the United States could follow. One encouraging sign on the television horizon for the early 1980s was the Time-Life Films plan to begin BBC in America, a cable television network using satellites to bring British programs into American homes. If public broadcasting ratings are any indicator, however, few Americans will choose to watch comparatively sophisticated documentaries and dramas from Britain or anywhere else.

Another compelling problem on the agenda for the 1980s—one that will require immense collaborative research and dialogue among many countries—is a clarification of the responsibility of the news media and the role of news in the affairs of the world. The great "irreconcilable" differences of the post-1945 period require concerted and continuous effort on the part of many to find a multicultural, multi-ideological framework suitable for global news and information policies and processes. This is not a new problem—it has been with us from the beginning of the news media. What is new is that the world is sharply divided on this intensely political issue and insisting on some concrete resolution. It is at the heart of what

7. Ratu Sir Kamisese K. T. Mara, prime minister of Fiji, made a reference to "arrogance among Europeans" (which includes Americans) toward the developing countries of the Pacific Islands, during the conference, Development the Pacific Way, Honolulu, March 26–29, 1980.

8. Tapio Varis, "Global Traffic in Television," *Journal of Communication* (Winter 1974), 24(1):104, 107.

we call the crisis in international news. Although the conflict in values—looking back—has always been there, never have so many people and organizations and countries been unwilling to accept the status quo, or the old order. Never have so many voices been demanding harmonizing communication policies in support of a new world news and information order. Never has the potential for serious international conflict been so great, should old existing communication systems become jammed or somehow be put out of order.

From the Western perspective, controversial new resolutions and further national-level official restrictions on foreign correspondents are a real possibility in the 1980s. Despite significant lessening of international tensions surrounding news (but certainly not surrounding economics and politics), many observers fear that Western governments and media may be running out of time to make good on pledges made in the 1970s. Warren Agee, a University of Georgia journalism professor, has concluded that far more must be done at various levels if the magnitude of the problems are to be lessened and reprisals averted:

An overall appraisal of the situation indicates that efforts must be *considerably increased* to alert Western media editors and owners, and the general public as well, to the perils to democratic, industrialized nations implicit in the prospect that additional vast areas of the world may be blocked off from Western news-gatherers or reported almost solely through state-controlled news agencies. Such indeed is the very lively possibility should the Western media fail in their attempts to help correct the current imbalance in news communication between the First and Third Worlds and within the LDCs [less developed countries] themselves.[9]

Finally, and most importantly to the Western media, never have foreign correspondents been more openly manipulated for propaganda and other purposes by those in political power.

9. Warren Agee, "Drying Streams of International News: Journalism Organizations Respond to Threats to World Press Freedom." Paper presented to the International Communication Division, Association for Education in Journalism Annual Convention, Houston, Texas, August 7, 1979, p. 35.

The 1979–81 Iranian crisis was a classic example of how media coverage to a large extent influenced world opinion and created news. For example, Iranian radio reports heard in Pakistan directly contributed to the attack on the American Embassy in Islamabad in November 1979, and throughout the Iranian crisis the Khomeini government and the revolutionaries skillfully used media diplomacy, particularly through television, not only to influence their own people but also to communicate instantaneously through satellite with the American government and try to influence world opinion. The use (and abuse) of foreign and local media, of course, is nothing new, but by the start of 1980s the severity of abuse substantially increased. Foreign journalists covering controversial stories found themselves more vulnerable than ever to censorship, information-control tactics, and even murder and terrorism. The "rules of the game" of international reporting seemed to be under attack, as correspondents increasingly found themselves not merely covering a fast-breaking crisis but actively and unwillingly participating in it.

These new twists to foreign news gathering have intensely troubled Western journalists, who traditionally have not perceived themselves as political actors but rather as passive, objective observers. To some extent, events have forced journalists to take a closer look at how news has traditionally been defined. Western norms, which maintain that "bad" news is better than "good" news and support "accuracy" and "fairness," are under serious attack in the Third World, and Western journalists have had to become more conscious than ever that news values are closely correlated to individual, institutional, and cultural perceptions.

Journalism has become a more dangerous, difficult, powerful, and political profession. An acute observer, Pulitzer Prize-winning David Broder, writing in the *Washington Post* in late 1979, points to the growing anguish and dilemma journalists face:

We, in the press, are . . . troubled by the definition of our responsibility. Journalists, for the most part, crave the comfortable position of neutrality so long as the story comes out, as long as we get to cover it every step of the way. By the same token, we hate to become part of the story we are covering.

But Iran has robbed us of that luxury. We are not neutrals in this struggle and we find our values being turned inside out on us. All of us defend our professional obligation to seek access to all of the decision-makers on this drama—including the captors. But many of us cringe when we see how the competitive scramble for that access is being exploited by the captors to make us serve their propaganda purposes.[10]

Throughout the 1970s and in the early 1980s, foreign correspondents frequently found themselves having to operate under extremely difficult and hazardous working conditions, or banned entirely from a developing story.

The MacBride Commission stimulated considerable worldwide discussion of issues related to free access to all news sources, including opposition groups, and protection of professional journalists. Sean MacBride himself was particularly concerned about the need to protect journalists and generally formulate international norms governing freedom of information:

In recent years, the freedom of journalists has been increasingly restricted in many parts of the world; in other cases journalists have been subjected to harassment, imprisonment and even assassination. These attacks not only infringe the rights of journalism but they constitute attacks on the right of the people to be informed.

Surely, it is time to draw up national and international standards on journalistic practices, not only to protect journalists on perilous assignments, but to guarantee their freedom in carrying out professional tasks. The definition of such standards may be difficult, but the problem must be seriously faced by all those concerned with improving the veracity of news content and increasing the free and balanced flow of information.[11]

10. David Broder of the Washington Post Writers Group, "Journalists Turn Introspective," *Sunday Honolulu Star-Bulletin/Advertiser*, December 23, 1979.

11. Sean MacBride, "Opening Statement." Prepared for International Seminar on the Infrastructures of News Collection and Dissemination in the World," Stockholm, April 24, 1978, p. 10.

While the MacBride Commission in its final report came out strongly for "free access to news sources by journalists," and abolishment of censorship, it dropped the idea of giving journalists a special status and protection. An international code of ethics was deferred by the commission, as well as a "right to reply" to what are considered inaccurate news stories.[12]

The problem of how journalists can perform their duties with the needed access to news sources and physical security is a continuing challenge for the 1980s. The issue presents another dilemma for Western journalism and particularly for the international media and news agencies. While journalists support the idea, of course, of protection and access, they do not like the mirror part of the proposition as it was presented during the MacBride Commission deliberations and elsewhere. To be eligible for protection as a journalist, journalists must be identified, and the fear was that eventually a system of licensing would be imposed. Another Western concern that will take much working out is responsibility. To the private, Western media, responsibility is something they practice, and something that no one outside of journalism should police. They fear that if governments take it upon themselves to determine when a journalist or news agency is acting responsibly, as a condition for protection and access to sources, then a whole series of political questions arises. Western journalists are adamantly unwilling to let others judge their responsibility in any enforceable way (aside from the traditional legal sanctions on libel, obscenity, and similar matters). This Western media view on responsibility is not entirely accepted even within the Western countries.

A third major problem for the 1980s, well-recognized in the 1970s, is the need for more equitable distribution of communication resources throughout the world, and less news dependence by the Third World.

The Western and industrialized nations continue predom-

12. International Commission for the Study of Communication Problems, *Final Report*. (Paris: Unesco, 1979), pp. 456–462.

inance in communication resources, particularly in telecommunications, and this in and of itself is widely seen as a destabilizing and inequitable situation. The demands made in the name of the new communication and information order are that the use of these resources be more widely shared, and that there be a transfer of some of these resources from the developed to the developing world. What concerns the policymakers and professionals of the 1980s is the magnitude of this shift of resources, and how it can be carried out. The Western nations made clear commitments in the late 1970s to share these resources, to help the developing world build their communication infrastructures. Difficult operational questions remain—how much is the West willing and able to share with the developing countries, and how effective will such transfers be in easing resource inequities? The question of the mechanisms and procedures for transfers of resources are just beginning to be addressed, and will need patience, compromise, and good will.

While some observers see the need for a major restructuring of the world news and communication systems under a new order, the immediate outlook seems to be for the growth of alternative structures for news and communication that meet, particularly, the nonmarket-oriented needs of the developing nations. Along with these new structures—such as the News Agencies Pool of the Nonaligned Countries and the Inter Press Service—important changes will be made in the present structure, particularly by the central actors, the transnational news agencies. The world news agencies, like the broader group of multinational corporations, are not all likely to disappear or change radically over the next several years. What is likely, and well underway, is an increased sensitivity to broader international concerns, particularly those of the developing countries, in the way the global agencies are organized and operate. Another important development, encouraging for better news flow, is the cooperation between the established news agencies and the developing new structures, to their mutual benefit. Some form of Roger Tatarian's "North-

South Agency"[13] scheme could develop, for example. The economics of global news agencies, however, could bring about important changes in the global systems. Economic factors could combine to force one or more of the four Western news agencies out of business. UPI, for example, is having major financial problems and serious questions are being raised about its future as America's second largest news agency. Its longtime parent company, E.W. Scripps, has been trying to divest itself of UPI because of the agency's continuing financial losses. By 1980, efforts to broaden UPI's ownership by persuading a limited number of U.S. newspapers and broadcasters to buy into the agency failed. Although the limited partnership offer has been cancelled, Scripps continues to be serious about finding partners from American media or else selling the agency outright to a non-media—perhaps even a non-American—owner.

Even if serious political differences could be set aside, and major changes were politically possible quickly, funding remains an overriding problem. A price tag is impossible to specify but clearly no one organization—certainly not Unesco—or one government—not even the United States—is in a position to finance the kinds of massive infrastructure, training, and other improvements necessary to substantially alter the existing world news system. Somehow, ways of multilateral cooperation and collaborative consultation need to be devised to establish priorities and internationally raise and administer the funds necessary for large-scale changes. Early efforts on such a funding and organizational scheme were underway with intergovernmental planning meetings sponsored by Unesco in Washington in 1979 and Paris in 1980. The United States sought to have a "communication consultative group" outside of Unesco to channel aid to strengthen Third World news and communication structures, and Mustapha Masmoudi, a lead-

13. Roger Tatarian, "The Multinational News Agency." Paper commissioned by the Edward R. Murrow Center of the Fletcher School of Law and Diplomacy, Tufts University, for Feasibility Conference in New York, September 12–14, 1979.

ing Third World spokesman on news, proposed a new institute within Unesco itself. At the 1980 meeting, the Unesco approach was adopted by consensus after eight days of politically charged discussion, although the United States and some of the other Western countries expressed reservations and did not make any immediate financial pledges. The matter went before the 1980 Unesco general conference in Belgrade, and can be seen as supporting new international information order advocates.[14]

At the Unesco conference itself, a major step forward in international cooperation did take place—although not very amicably—when an International Program for the Development of Communication (IPDC) was approved. Established as a mechanism within Unesco and under a 35-member intergovernmental council, the program will serve—at least during its initial three years—as a modest clearinghouse with a small secretariat. Its purpose is to help developing countries define their information needs and then find bilateral, private, or international funding sources through which practical training and other projects can be implemented.

The United States half-heartedly supported the IPDC concept, and it continues to voice major reservations about Unesco's expanding role as the preeminent international forum not only for "new communication order" debate but, more significantly, action. Politically as well as economically, the U.S. government under both the Carter and the Reagan administrations was in no mood to support a special international fund for communication development or to contribute large sums to operate IPDC outside of Unesco's regular program, which gets about one-fourth of its funds from the United States. Also, the United States was not happy about the possibility that IPDC might be used by the Third World or the Soviets to try to implement some of the more "radical" ideas suggested in the MacBride report.

14. "Unesco Agrees on Mechanism for Information." *International Herald Tribune*, April 22, 1980; "Unesco: Call for New Institutions," *Intermedia* (January 1980), 8(1):4; John Reinhardt, "General Policy Statement." Delivered at 20th General Conference of Unesco, Paris, November 3, 1978, pp. 19–20.

At the end of the 1970s, the United States had pledged both government and private media assistance. The record, however, even with the most favored look, is far from encouraging. The World Press Freedom Committee, organized by the Western media to combat threats to press freedom and help developing countries establish strong press systems, so far has failed in its goal of raising 1 million dollars, collecting about half of that amount by the end of the 1970s. And 1 million dollars was acknowledged, even by the WPFC, as a start, and wholly inadequate to the problems. The efforts of the U.S. government, which pledged practical Third World assistance as part of its Unesco strategy in fighting the Mass Media Declaration in 1976 and 1978, had produced little new in tangible assistance or ideas at the start of the 1980s. Initiatives put forth seem less than innovative and are little different than traditional U.S. technical assistance proposals. The directions of U.S. aid, as outlined by John Reinhardt of the International Communicaton Agency (ICA), have been toward promotion of "suitably identified regional centers of professional education and training in broadcasting and journalism in the developing world" and the application of "the benefits of advanced communications technology—specifically communications satellites—to economic and social needs in the rural areas of developing countries."[15] The ICA, incidentally, is the government agency charged with handling "public diplomacy" and implementing a two-way flow of communication between the United States and the rest of the world. While this is an extremely difficult task for a government agency in the free and private media context of the United States, the commitment has been made, and means to achieve a balanced flow of news must be found to maintain U.S. credibility in the continuing debate on international news.

It is too early to say whether ICA as a bureaucracy will be able to implement new ideas and officially take the lead in defining communication issues for the whole American government. But by the start of the 1980s a consensus among

15. Reinhardt, "General Policy Statement," pp. 15–17.

international communication professionals was emerging on what the new government information entity should not be. The post-Cold War, post-1970s thinking was that ICA should not be a "salesman" or "America's agent" in a popularity or propaganda context. Glen Fisher, a former State Department advisor now with Georgetown University School of Foreign Service, has offered a more creative, realistic, and long-range view of ICA:

Its future ability to persuade will be more a product of its credibility, its capacity for adding missing information in the interest of accuracy and a fuller comprehension of American methods and objectives, and its contribution to the health of the larger information and image flows of which ICA is only a part.[16]

When ICA was established in 1978 to include the former U.S. Information Agency, the Voice of America, and the State Department's Bureau of Educational and Cultural Affairs, President Jimmy Carter asked the new agency to help develop and execute a comprehensive national policy on international communications, designed to encourage the maximum flow of information and ideas among the peoples of the world. "Such a policy," Carter said, "must take into consideration the needs and sensitivities of others, as well as our own needs."[17]

Even a kind assessment of achievement in this area of give-and-take dialogue and mutual understanding has to rate it as a partial failure. In general, the United States government at the beginning of the 1980s continued to have a less-than-clear, less-than-comprehensive policy toward Third World media and other communication needs. The lack of long-range planning and strong coordination among the various government agencies involved with admittedly highly complex, overlapping communication issues continues to be a problem within both ICA and the State Department. Neither of these

16. Glen Fisher, *American Communication in a Global Society* (Norwood, N.J.: Ablex, 1979), p. 135.
17. Reinhardt, "General Policy Statement," p. 14.

American official agencies appears to be doing much beyond addressing short-term problems and "fire-fighting." Crisis-oriented planning for the next round of international meetings, and their inevitable sharp debates, seems the rule. To much of the world, the American government and media toward the end of the 1970s appeared defensive, insensitive, and uninterested in proposing positive, creative ways that change could be fostered through American (and others') participation.

Except at the time of Unesco general conferences when the United States is under intense world pressure to show that "something is being done," news flow has not been a clear priority on the American government agenda. Officials generally have been unreceptive to the following kind of advice, offered in a 1977 staff report to the U.S. Senate Foreign Relations Committee:

Most nations of the world, it appears, would welcome U.S. participation in their efforts to reshape the information order. But they will go ahead without us, if need be. Thus, if the United States does not soon address the problems of worldwide information arrangements, it is conceivable that in 1999 Uganda and the Central Africa Empire, the U.S.S.R. and Czechoslovakia, Sweden and France will have done more to reorder major aspects of world society—and our society—than the citizens and the government of the United States.[18]

By 1980, however, a more positive, forward-looking and aggressive U.S. stance began emerging, and it could not only enhance American credibility but also promote world understanding. George Dalley, a State Department official responsible for Unesco relations, implicitly seemed to recognize problems with America's international communication position throughout the 1970s when he declared:

We feel it is high time we devoted less time to defending ourselves from complaints and reacting to the initiatives and prescriptions of others and sat down to think out what we believe should be done

18. George Kroloff and Scott Cohen, "The New World Information Order." A Report to the Committee on Foreign Relations, United States Senate, Washington, D.C., November 1977, p. 4.

to improve the global system of communications. In other words, we believe it is time to stop *reacting* and begin *acting* to foster our ideas and conventions.[19]

This shift in approach was apparent also at the decade-closing conference sponsored by the U.S. National Commission for Unesco, Toward an American Agenda for a New World Order of Communications.[20] The conference, chaired by Elie Abel, recognized the validity of many Third World concerns, and recommended positive measures to assist development of Third World media, promote press freedom and free flow of news, protect journalists, and assist in training of journalists.

Three major international developments in international communication policy occurred in the late 1970s, and should have a profound, positive effect for policy formation throughout at least the 1980s. The 1978 Unesco General Conference in Paris reached a compromise agreement on the Mass Media Declaration after several years of often acrimonious debate, and the 1979 World Administrative Radio Conference (WARC) spent several productive weeks planning the use of the radio spectrum and related questions for the next two decades. A third major achievement of the late 1970s, although officially discussed in 1980 at the Unesco General Conference in Belgrade, is the work of the International Commission for the Study of Communication Problems, or the MacBride Commission. Again, much of its final report put aside ideological conflicts and presented a comprehensive view of international news and its problems, and offered several pragmatic areas for cooperation between the West and the Third World.

These three developments, while far from perfect or conflict-free, offer an excellent opportunity to move ahead on a fair and equitable world communication policy. The term "fair

19. George A. Dalley, "Third World Communication Needs and the U.S. Government." Speech prepared for Association for Education in Journalism Annual Convention, Houston, Texas, August 7, 1979, p. 18.

20. The conference was part of the 43d Annual Meeting, U.S. National Commission for Unesco, hosted by the University of Georgia, Athens, Georgia, December 12–15, 1979.

world communication policy" is used here to denote a set of international communication principles and policies that provide for equitable, mutlicultural, nondominating use of global communication resources. Such a policy, as it develops, will recognize differences in communication capabilities and needs among countries, and attempt to establish conditions under which all nations can exchange news and opinion and other communication on a fair basis.

The Mass Media Declaration came only after long and hard negotiations between the Western governments and media interests, and, primarily, with Third World interests. The intervention of the director-general of Unesco proved a key element in the compromise, and the result is a strong document that recognizes the need for "a free flow and a wider and better balanced dissemination of information." The declaration also states that "the exercise of freedom of opinion, expression and information" is recognized as a human right and fundamental freedom, and that access to a diversity of sources and means of information should be provided. An important section for improving the content of news flow about developing countries urged that "information on the aims, aspirations, cultures and needs of all people" be reported. Several other important points are made in the declaration and, on the whole, provide a strong policy base for international news. The key thrust of the declaration is that all peoples should be fairly represented and reported, that there be better exchange of information and opinion, and that a free and more balanced flow of information should be encouraged. Gone entirely from the declaration were earlier references that had been perceived in the West as sanctioning government control of the media.[21]

WARC-79 demonstrated the kinds of conflict and dilemmas facing the use of global communication resources. Here the question was the allocations and fairness of the uses of a natural resource—the radio or broadcast spectrum. As in other communication resources, the Western and developed world, particularly the United States and Soviet Union, had acquired

---

21. See appendix F for text of Mass Media Declaration.

extensive use of this resource, far beyond a fair share. The first come, first served principle that had guided allocation of this resource to almost the end of the 1970s ran into the same type of Third World opposition faced by the free flow principle earlier, for many of the same reasons. Both principles favor those nations that had attained extensive communication infrastructures, strong financing and capitalizing ability, and highly skilled and trained personnel. And they had a need for extensive communication systems to support their business, military, and cultural activities around the world.

The initial report of WARC-79 presented by the U.S. Department of State called the session "successful" and noted that some of the expected political difficulties were resolved at the beginning of the session. A pragmatic negotiating pattern developed—with the U.S. finding itself "in alliance with different groups based on common interests rather than any fixed ideological mind set."[22] Several issues were put over to special WARC conferences in the years ahead. While this U.S. assessment of WARC-79 does not change the fundamental differences of opinion, nor the demands of Third World countries for a larger share of the broadcast resource, there seem to be greater opportunities for an equitable restructuring of the global telecommunication resource allocation without what could be divisive political struggles. The political issues remain, however, and will surface if the carry-over issues of WARC-79 are not solved in the coming special conferences. Although the outcome of WARC and the Mass Media Declaration seem to promise a stable environment for developing a fair world communication policy, deep and serious disagreements can easily arise over the years of negotiations and dialogue. Vital national interests are at stake.

The MacBride Commission report is another case of international accord on the major communication problems and the solutions that seem required or are possible. The remark-

22. U.S. Department of State, "World Administrative Radio Conference: Summary Report No. 9," n.d. For a U.S. newspaper industry publication's review of the impact of WARC on news, see Joseph P. Rawley, "Calls to Regulate News Fail at WARC," *Presstime* (January 1980), p. 10.

able thing about the MacBride Commission is not just the report and the many excellent resource articles the commission generated and published, but also the mandate of the commission: to look at *world communication problems*. That challenge could become a global necessity for survival and growth in the years ahead.[23]

The research and study challenges of the coming years are related generally to the major problem areas of news imbalance, lack of communication among developing countries, needs in personnel development and communication infrastructure, technology transfer, redefinition of news, and so forth. There are many other broader questions, however, that link communication problems to the political problems. One major task, for example, is research on the question of whether the present communication system is the result of a conspiracy for dominance of the developing world by the West, as posited by neo-Marxist thinkers and others, or whether it is the result of early and rapid communication development in the West, giving a few countries a great and decisive head start in establishing communication systems and predominant global influence and control. Much heat has been radiated over these questions, and some clarity and new evidence is needed to put the problem of dominance in better perspective, and perhaps point to the more productive solution areas.

Another overriding research and theoretical challenge deals with the role of communication in society and communication as a human right. The right to communicate concept, barely a decade old, has proved for some to be a useful framework within which to address many of the problems of international communication and communication's role in society. The flow of news, imbalances, access to media and information, and the right to cultural privacy are just some of the obvious issues the right to communicate can address. Glen Fisher views the right to communicate as a concept the United

23. George E. Brown, Jr., "Freedom and Order in Future International Communications." Paper for conference on "Toward an American Agenda for a New World Order of Communications," 43d Annual Meeting, U.S. National Commission for Unesco, Athens, Georgia, December 12–15, 1979, p. 6.

States will have to deal with, since it is being used in the efforts to get a more equitable world communication system.[24]

An emerging research question, noted by the MacBride *Interim Report* and vigorously pursued at the late 1979 conference, Toward an American Agenda for a New World Order of Communication, is the relationship between intranational and international communication. It is a convincing Western tactic in international communication debates, for example, to answer Third World critics of "cultural imperialism" by pointing to what are usually very controlled, manipulative, elite-oriented communication systems in Third World countries. As Mort Rosenblum and others note, much of the flow of international news is dependent on the national flow. And where that flow is biased, distorted, or inadequate, the international flow will reflect this, and perhaps even compound it. While these points are made at many meetings, little research has been done to show the relationship between the internal and external flows. One of the problems of Pacific island communication, for example, is the lack of flow among the islands. But part of the reason for that is the relatively skimpy news gathering structures within the islands, producing little for the external flow.[25]

Another great imbalance problem is the poor representation of women and minority groups when it comes to media ownership and control. Part of the reason for such groups' less-than-equal ability to influence media is that relatively monolithic local and national media are insufficiently committed to serving the needs of diverse social and cultural groups. Transnational media organizations are unlikely to end any unfair practices in hiring or reporting until, for example, the status of women or linguistic minorities is improved within nations. A hint of an increased international focus on these "intranational justice" issues surfaced in ICA Reinhardt's Unesco General Conference policy statement in 1978.

24. Fisher, *American Communication*, p. 70. See also Jim Richstad and L. S. Harms, "News and the Right to Communicate," in Anne Van Der Meiden, ed., *Ethics and Mass Communication* (Utrecht: State University of Utrecht, 1980), pp. 56–77.

25. Jim Richstad, "News Flow in the Pacific Islands: Selected Cases," *Communications and Development Review* (Summer 1978), 2(2), p. 10.

He told the intergovernmental meeting that the United States has been "making major efforts in recent years to encourage ownership and operation of media outlets by blacks, women, Hispanics, and others—to the end that the distinctive voice of each of these developing groups within our own society can make itself heard in its own way."[26] Research theory and practice will certainly need to give greater explicit attention to the relationship between communication and these kinds of pressing social policy issues.

An important policy research question concerns the priorities given to communication in various countries,[27] and the relationship of these priorities to the quality of news structures internally and externally. The costs of international news agencies are rather small in comparison to other activities. The policy research envisioned here would broaden some of the traditional economic analysis models for investment, to see what other relevant political inputs and values could be in the analysis when considering investment in communication structures.

There are many directions international news development can take in the years ahead. The future will be invented, as Dennis Gabor says, and there can be many communication futures to choose among.

Two contrasting futures for world communication and news systems were outlined by political scientist Harold D. Lasswell in a 1972 paper, and they apply both nationally and internationally.[28] Lasswell presented two models of human organization, an oligarchic model and a participatory model.

26. Reinhardt, "General Policy Statement," p. 6.

27. An example of national priorities bearing on communication policy was given as: "The way societies tend to think about communication policy reflects their very natures. In the United States, the emphasis is on speed and efficiency, and on open and fair access to information and the basic principles of pluralism and diversity. There is a concern for privacy and confidentiality and most people and institutions try to restrain malicious behavior and misuse of information. There is a desire for freedom of speech and freedom of choice." Joseph E. Slater, "Foreword," in Glen O. Robinson, ed., Communications for Tomorrow: Policy Perspectives for the 1980s, (New York: Praeger, 1978), p. v.

28. Harold D. Lasswell, "The Future of World Communication: Quality and Style of Life." Papers of the East-West Communication Institute, no. 4. Honolulu: East-West Center, September, 1972.

The oligarchic model is power-oriented and designed to control and manipulate people. Communication, under this model, Lasswell said, was "used to indoctrinate and distract." The participatory model uses "intermediate, resource-parsimonious technology," and is designed to "strengthen a universal and differentiated sense of identity and common interest." The oligarchic model is well suited to mass media and vertical communication systems with central control and one-way communication. In other words, it is the type of system that would generate the kinds of Third World complaints that arose in the 1970s. The participatory model develops strong horizontal, multiway, interactive, user-driven communication systems, where control is dispersed. While the Lasswell models are provocative for analysis, the choice of paths in the years ahead will not be clear. There will be complex mixed systems, and changes from one emphasis to the other over time. The two communication models will coexist in varying strengths throughout the world.

There are at least two broad approaches to solving the problems of international news, and they relate directly to how the problem of news is defined. Both of these approaches are going on at the same time and even in the same places.

One, consistently followed by neo-Marxists but also by others, views news as part of the political and social struggles in societies, and therefore news problems can only be viewed in a broad historical, political, and social context. This approach focuses on basic structural changes in society and the news systems, and links the dependencies of Third World countries to news imbalances and other problems.

The second, certainly the favored view by Western media and government interests and with some support in the Third World, is to take a pragmatic approach to particular problems, such as inadequate training of news agency personnel, high newsprint costs, lack of access to satellites, not enough news about the Third World in the news agencies file, and so forth. The approach here is to try to improve the present world news system—to provide more professional training, work for lower newsprint costs, seek access to satellites and data banks—

through aid, counsel, and cooperation with Third World journalists and news organizations.

Part of the irony and difficulty of the international debate on news is that Western proposals to improve the present news system are sometimes seen as cosmetic or even detrimental to the task of basic reform in the broader international orders, especially the economic and information orders.

At the least, an awareness of these different levels of approach is essential to an understanding of the debate over the crisis in international news.

The fundamental, intriguing question that must be answered in the years ahead is a highly political and perilous one: Whose version of a more just and effective "new order" will be implemented and at what costs and benefits to "reformers" and "radicals"?

A jarring note to the international debate came from Western media executives in mid-1980. In an unusually outspoken speech in New York, Gerald Long, managing director of Reuters, called upon the industrialized nations to withhold funding for special Unesco communication programs because the organization was trying to secure "worldwide control of the development of the media," and he said he doubted whether the MacBride Report "has any merit whatsoever." The American Newspaper Publishers Association, in a letter to Unesco, said it was "troubled" by several of the MacBride recommendations. Allen S. Neuharth, a leading U.S. newspaper executive, said "Unesco is going to continue to consider controls over the world's media and a 'New Information Order'" whether the West likes it or not, and that journalists should "sound the alarm."[29] These deeply felt concerns by Western news executives over Unesco and freedom of the press will remain a major focus of the debate, along with the Third World concerns.

Exactly what official steps will be taken to address con-

29. "Reuters Chief Urges Nations Refuse Funds to Unesco," *Diplomatic World Bulletin*, May 19, 1980, p. 1ff.; Letter from Jerry W. Friedheim, American Newspaper Publishers Association, to Amadou-Mahtar M'Bow, Director-General, Unesco, May 29, 1980; News Release, American Newspaper Publishers Association, May 29, 1980.

crete international communication problems in the 1980's remain uncertain. Following President Reagan's election, for
example, major questions were being raised about what role
the United States should play in international communications issues. The new administration seemed to reflect the
view that the West in recent years has given in to Third World
and Soviet pressures, and American media continued to project an overwhelmingly negative image of Unesco.[30] In the early
days of the Reagan presidency, serious attention was even
being given to a high-level proposal that the United States
withdraw from Unesco. Such a move would not only save U.S.
taxpayers millions, but it would also signify that the U.S. government sees Unesco's communication activities as impinging
on Western journalistic freedoms and threatening commercial
interests.

Regardless of how the Reagan administration attends to
international communication affairs, the times clearly demand
greater attention to intercultural relations. Michael Weyl, a
former American foreign service information officer, made this
point in a 1980 study:

America is a country much more dependent than previously on
developments and decisions beyond its borders. Its survival as a
prosperous nation at peace requires genuine understanding of the
U.S. abroad and an increased American competency to deal with
global issues and foreign economic competition. And as a nation
that is no longer intellectually and technologically more advanced
than a growing number of other countries, the sharing of thought,

---

30. See, for example, A. H. Raskin, "Report on News Coverage of Belgrade Unesco
Conference." New York: The National News Council, March 6, 1981. This study said
that American press coverage of the important 1980 Unesco conference was neither
comprehensive nor objective and tended to focus on the negative aspects of the Unesco
intervention in media matters. It reported:

> Not one story emanating form the six-week conference dealt with any of the
> reports, speeches or resolutions on Unesco's basic activities in combatting illit-
> eracy, developing alternative energy sources, protecting historic monuments,
> broadening educational programs for scientists and engineers, sponsoring basic
> research in food production and ocean sciences and scores of other fields. By
> contrast, there were 173 news and feature stories dealing with the debate over
> communications policy. This was also the central topic for 181 editorials.

knowledge and skills becomes much more beneficial to the U.S. than in the earlier, postwar era.[31]

Meanwhile, the debate will continue between those favoring balanced flows and those favoring free flows, and many of the world's media will have little choice but to continue to depend heavily upon the Western news agencies for much of their foreign news.

We close with this hope, expressed in the Kuala Lumpur Declaration on communication policy:

People and individuals have the right to acquire an objective picture of reality by means of accurate and comprehensive information through a diversity of sources and means of information available to them, as well as to express themselves through various means of culture and communication.[32]

We add our view and hope that the news and information people will need will be increasingly available to them through the evolving international news system.

31. Michael Weyl, "U.S. Educational Exchange: An Agenda for the '80s," *Chronicle of International Communication* (January 1981), 2(1):6.

32. "Kuala Lumpur Declaration." In Unesco, *Final Report*, Intergovernmental Conference on Communication Policies in Asia and Oceania, Kuala Lumpur, February 5–14, 1979, p. 31.

Appendix A

Declaration on Mass Communication Media and Human Rights, Council of Europe, 1970

A. Status and Independence of the Press and the Other Mass Media

1. The press and the other mass media, though generally not public institutions, perform an essential function for the general public. In order to enable them to discharge that function in the public interest, the following principles should be observed:
2. The right to freedom of expression shall apply to mass communication media.
3. This right shall include freedom to seek, receive, impart, publish and distribute information and ideas. There shall be a corresponding duty for the public authorities to make available information on matters of public interest within reasonable limits and a duty for mass communication media to give complete and general information on public affairs.
4. The independence of the press and other mass media from control by the state should be established by law. Any infringement of this independence should be justifiable by courts and not by executive authorities.
5. There shall be no direct or indirect censorship of the press, or of

the contents of radio and television programs, or of news or information conveyed by other media such as newsreels shown in cinemas. Restrictions may be imposed within the limits authorized by Article 10 of the European Convention on Human Rights. There shall be no control by the state of the contents of radio and television programs, except on the grounds set out in paragraph 2 of that Article.

6. The internal organization of mass media should guarantee the freedom of expression of the responsible editors. Their editorial independence should be preserved.

7. The independence of mass media should be protected against the dangers of monopolies. The effects of concentration in the press, and possible measures of economic assistance require further consideration.

8. Neither individual enterprises, nor financial groups should have the right to institute a monopoly in the fields of press, radio, or television, nor should government-controlled monopoly be permitted. Individuals, social groups, regional or local authorities should have—as far as they comply with the established licensing provisions—the right to engage in these activities.

9. Special measures are necessary to ensure the freedom of foreign correspondents, including the staff of international press agencies, in order to permit the public to receive accurate information from abroad. These measures should cover the status, duties, and privileges of foreign correspondents and should include protection from arbitrary expulsion. They impose a corresponding duty of accurate reporting.

B. Measures to Secure Responsibility of the Press and Other Mass Media

It is the duty of the press and other mass media to discharge their functions with a sense of responsibility towards the community and towards the individual citizens. For this purpose, it is desirable to institute (where not already done):

(a) professional training for journalists under the responsibility of editors and journalists;

(b) a professional code of ethics for journalists, this should cover interalia such matters as accurate and well-balanced reporting, rectification of inaccurate information, clear distinction between reported information and comments, avoidance of calumny, respect for privacy, respect for the right to a fair trial as guaranteed by Article 6 of the European Convention of Human Rights;

(c) press councils empowered to investigate and even to censure instances of unprofessional conduct with a view to the exercising of self-control by the press itself.

C. Measures to Protect the Individual against Interference with His Right to Privacy

1. There is an area in which the exercise of the right of freedom of information and freedom of expression may conflict with the right to privacy protected by Article 8 of the Convention on Human Rights. The exercise of the former right must not be allowed to destroy the existence of the latter.

2. The right to privacy consists essentially in the right to live one's own life with a minimum of interference. It concerns private, family and home life, physical and moral integrity, honor and reputation, avoidance of being placed in a false light, nonrevelation of irrelevant and embarrassing facts, unauthorized publication of private photographs, protection against misuse of private communications, protection from disclosure of information given or received by the individual confidentially. Those who, by their own actions, have encouraged indiscreet revelations about which they complain later on, cannot avail themselves of the right to privacy.

3. A particular problem arises as regards the privacy of persons in public life. The phrase "where public life beings, private life ends" is inadequate to cover this situation. The private lives of public figures are entitled to protection, save where they may have an impact upon public events. The fact that an individual figures in the news does not deprive him of a right to a private life.

4. Another particular problem arises from attempts to obtain information by modern technical devices (wire-tapping, hidden microphones, the use of computers, etc.), which infringe the right to privacy. Further consideration of this problem is required.

5. Where regional, national, or international computer-data banks are instituted the individual must not become completely exposed and transparent by the accumulation of information referring even to his private life. Data banks should be restricted to the necessary minimum of information required for the purposes of taxation, pension schemes, social security schemes, and similar matters.

6. In order to counter these dangers, national law should provide a right of action enforceable at law against persons responsible for such infringements of the right to privacy.

7. The right to privacy afforded by Article 8 of the Convention on Human Rights should not only protect an individual against interference by public authorities, but also against interference by private persons or institutions, including the mass media. National legislations should comprise provisions guaranteeing this protection.

Appendix B

Nonaligned Summit Statement on Communication Issues, Algiers, 1973

XIII. Developing countries should take concerted action in the field of mass communications on the following lines in order to promote a greater interchange of ideas among themsèlves:

    (a) Reorganize existing communication channels which are the legacy of the colonial past, and which have hampered free, direct, and fast communications among them;

    (b) Initiate joint action for the revision of existing multilateral agreements with a view to reviewing press cable rates and facilitating faster and cheaper intercommunication;

    (c) Take urgent steps to expedite the process of collective ownership of communications satellites and evolve a code of conduct for directing their use;

    (d) Promote increased contact between the mass media, universities, libraries, planning and research bodies, and other

From Articles XIII and XIV of the "Action Program for Economic Cooperation," approved by the Fourth Conference of Heads of State or Government of Nonaligned Countries in Algiers, September 5–9, 1973. See Odette Tankowitsch and Karl P. Sauvant, The Third World Without Super Powers: The Collected Documents of the Non-Aligned Countries (Dobbs Ferry, N.Y.: Oceana, 1978), pp. 225–26.

institutions so as to enable developing countries to exchange experience and expertise and share ideas.

XIV. Nonaligned countries should exchange and disseminate information concerning their mutual achievements in all fields through newspapers and periodicals, radio, television, and the news media of their respective countries. They should formulate plans for sharing experience in this field, interalia through reciprocal visits of delegations from information media and through exchange of radio and television programs, films, books, photographs, and through cultural events and art festivals.

Appendix C

Statement by the Participants in the Dag Hammarskjold Third World Journalists' Seminar, New York, August 29– September 12, 1975

1. The satisfaction of human needs and the creation of a habitable environment on the basis of self-reliance and harmony with the values and aspirations of each society are the main purpose of *another development*, which implies a new world system through the establishment of the New International Economic Order.
2. The New International Economic Order requires a new framework of world information and communications. As the 1975 Dag Hammarskjold Report on Development and International Cooperation states,

   A near monopoly of international communications—including those

From *Development Dialogue* (1976), no. 1, pp. 106–9. The ten signatories were from Algeria, Peru, Senegal, Sri Lanka, Pakistan, Venezuela, India, Chile, Mexico, and Tanzania.

among Third World countries—by transnational corporations, linked to their dominance of many and influence in almost all Third-World-country media, is a basic element of the present hierarchical pattern of Center ideological and cultural domination.

3. This situation cannot continue. True political liberation is endangered and efforts for economic liberation will continue to be strongly handicapped unless steps are taken to break the hold that news agencies reflecting interests which are not those of the Third World have on the information sent to or originating in Third World countries. For the New International Economic Order to emerge, peoples of both industrialized and Third World countries must be given the opportunity of understanding that they share a common interest in creating international conditions that will permit *another development* of societies in all parts of the world. Changes in the present unjust international structures must be seen as a precondition for peace and security tomorrow.

4. This common interest cannot be adequately perceived unless communication patterns are also liberated from the market-oriented sensationalism approach to news. Such reporting will never permit public opinion in the industrialized world to have full information about the Third World, its true reality and its urgent needs.

5. The Third World nations must protect themselves from the distortion of their cultures and ways of life implicit in present communications dependence. Information is a nonmaterial commodity that is bought and sold in a highly oligopolistic market. This must be changed. An end to such a system and thus a widening of the capacity to inform is a fundamental component of the New International Economic Order, permitting a valid interplay of different cultures and national realities.

6. The structural and substantive deficiencies of the United Nations system in general are particularly noticeable in its information/communication sector.

7. To redress the situation, action has to be taken at different levels, including:

–National and collective self-reliant action by Third World countries
–Action directed towards the true reflection of the interdependence of nations
–Changes in the policies and structures of the information services of the United Nations system.

I. The Right to Inform and Be Informed

8. The participants at the seminar endorse Point 6 of the 1975 Dag Hammarskjold Report on Development and International Co-operation, which reads as follows:

   Citizens have a right to inform and be informed about the facts of development, its inherent conflicts and the changes it will bring about, locally and internationally.

   Under present conditions, information and education are only too often monopolized by the power structure, which manipulates public opinion to its own ends and tends to perpetuate preconceived ideas, ignorance and alienation.

   A global effort should be made to give the new international relations their human dimension and to promote the establishment of genuine cooperation between peoples on the basis of equality and recognition of their cultural, political, social and economic diversity. The image of the Other should reach each of us, stripped of the prevailing ethnocentric prejudices, which are the characteristic feature of most of the messages currently transmitted.

   Such an effort should be concerned both with information and with education in the broadest sense of the word; it should be directed towards "conscientization" of citizens to ensure their full participation in the decision-making process.

II. National and Collective Self-Reliant Action by Third World Countries

9. On the basis of collective self-reliance, Third World nations as a whole, at the regional and interregional levels, should take steps to ensure that information and communication networks are used to further and promote the establishment of the New International Economic Order and the objectives of *another development*.

10. To facilitate fundamental transformations to this end, governments should take action within their own countries to create, foster, and strengthen national structures, based on self-reliance, for information and communication that will enable them to change existing systems in this field.

11. National news agencies of Third World countries should co-operate directly with each other through bilateral arrangements and through multilateral exchanges already in existence or to be set up.
12. National governments should take urgent steps to implement the program of action agreed upon at the meeting of foreign ministers of the nonaligned countries, held at Lima, in August 1975, in the resolution on cooperation in the field of diffusion of information and mass communication media, particularly in part three of that resolution:

    To revise cable tariffs for the press and to facilitate more economical and faster intercommunication.

    To cooperate in the reorganization of communication channels still dependent or which constitute a colonial inheritance and obstruct direct and rapid communication among nonaligned countries.

    To exchange and disseminate information on mutual national achievements through newspapers, radio, television and news communication media.

    To share experiences in connection with information media.

13. Early steps should be taken to set up a Third World information center to serve Third World needs and to help in the dissemination of information on the Third World in both industrialized and Third World countries. It should also organize a research and development effort in order to achieve the objectives of the New International Economic Order in the field of information and communication.
14. All these actions indicate the urgent need for a high-level investigation which should be supported by interested organizations. . . .

III. Action Directed towards the True Reflection of the Interdependence of Nations

15. A massive effort must be made in industrialized countries to explain and make known the legitimate nature of the aspirations of the Third World countries for the establishment of the New International Economic Order. Third World communications

networks should be prepared to create direct relationships with any interested group and to supply all data, information, and analysis that might be required for their work.

16. Links with institutions established in the industrialized world that promote, in their own public opinion, the ideas and values of *another development* for all societies should be created and their activities supported. Specifically, the International Center for Development Alternatives . . . should contribute in creating conditions for the understanding of interdependence.

IV. Changes in the Policies and Structures of the Information Services of the United Nations System

17. The United Nations system's information/communication sectors, concerning both media and non-governmental organizations, should be transformed so as to:

Ensure that its activities are geared to the primary goal of promoting a better mutual understanding among societies and nations in their rich cultural and socio-economic diversity.

Promote a dialogue, beyond purely intergovernmental action, among the peoples of the United Nations.

Promote in particular a real awareness in the industrialized countries of the realities of the development process, including the role of the transnationals, which should be controlled in the interests of the peoples of both industrialized and Third World nations.

Contribute to the attainment of self-reliance in Third World countries, through *inter alia* the promotion and systematic utilization of horizontal links between Third World countries and regions.

Improve drastically the flow of concrete information on the research activities of the many institutions and bodies of the system.

Redirect its financial and staff resources and its productive capacity to serve the above-mentioned objectives.

18. The Ad Hoc Committee on the Reform of the Structure of the United Nations system should give serious attention to the information/communication sectors of the secretariats. . . .

Appendix D

Conference on Security and Cooperation in Europe, Final Act, "Information," Helsinki, 1975

Information

The participating States . . . make it their aim to facilitate the freer and wider dissemination of information of all kinds, to encourage cooperation in the field of information and the exchange of information with other countries, and to improve the conditions under which journalists from one participating State exercise their profes-

This excerpt on information is taken from the "third basket" of the Helsinki Agreements. The other "baskets," as the four main sections were called, deal with security in Europe, cooperation in economics, science, technology, and the environment, and continued cooperation on the Agreements. The "third basket"—Cooperation in Humanitarian and Other Fields—covered also human contacts and cultural and educational exchanges. Thirty-five heads of state from Europe and North America signed the agreement. Many in the West, particularly in the United States, stress the information freedoms of the "third basket" as the priority for peaceful relations and security, while the socialist countries put priority on the security provisions as a prerequisite to freer information flows.

sion in another participating State, and *express their intention* in particular:

(a) IMPROVEMENT OF THE CIRCULATION OF, ACCESS TO, AND EXCHANGE OF INFORMATION

(i) *Oral Information*
To facilitate the dissemination of oral information through the encouragement of lectures and lecture tours by personalities and specialists from the other participating States, as well as exchanges of opinions at round table meetings, seminars, symposia, summer schools, congresses and other bilateral and multilateral meetings.

(ii) *Printed Information*
To facilitate the improvement of the dissemination, on their territory, of newspapers and printed publications, periodical and non-periodical, from the other participating States. For this purpose:

- They will encourage their competent firms and organizations to conclude agreements and contracts designed gradually to increase the quantities and the number of titles of newspapers and publications imported from the other participating States. . . .

To contribute to the improvement of access by the public to periodical and non-periodical printed publications imported on the bases indicated above. In particular:

- They will encourage an increase in the number of places where these publications are on sale;
- They will facilitate the availability of these periodical publications during congresses, conferences, official visits and other international events and to tourists during the season;
- They will develop the possibilities for taking out subscriptions according to the modalities particular to each country;
- They will improve the opportunities for reading and borrowing these publications in large public libraries and their reading rooms as well as in university libraries.

They intend to improve the possibilities for acquaintance with bulletins of official information issued by diplomatic missions and distributed by those missions on the basis of arrangements acceptable to the interested parties.

(iii) *Filmed and Broadcast Information*
To promote the improvement of the dissemination of filmed and broadcast information. To this end:

- They will encourage the wider showing and broadcasting of a great variety of recorded and filmed information from the other participating States, illustrating the various aspects of life in their countries and received on the basis of such agreements or arrangements as may be necessary between the organizations and firms directly concerned.
- They will facilitate the import by competent organizations and firms of recorded audio-visual material from the other participating States. . . .
- [They will] grant to journalists of the participating States the right to import, subject only to its being taken out again, the technical equipment (photographic, cinematographic, tape recorder, radio and television) necessary for the exercise of their profession.

(b) COOPERATION IN THE FIELD OF INFORMATION

To encourage cooperation in the field of information on the basis of short- or long-term agreements or arrangements. In particular:

- They will favor increased cooperation among mass media organizations, including press agencies, as well as among publishing houses and organizations;
- They will favor cooperation among public or private, national or international radio and television organizations, in particular through the exchange of both live and recorded radio and television programs, and through the joint production and the broadcasting and distribution of such programs;
- They will encourage meetings and contacts both between journalist's organizations and between journalists from the participating States;
- They will view favorably the possibilities of arrangements between periodical publications as well as between newspapers from the participating States, for the purpose of exchanging and publishing articles;
- They will encourage the exchange of technical information as well as the organization of joint research and meetings devoted to the exchange of experience and views between experts in the field of the press, radio and television.

(c) IMPROVEMENT OF WORKING CONDITIONS FOR JOURNALISTS

The participating States, desiring to improve the conditions under which journalists from one participating State exercise their profession in another participating State, intend in particular to:

- Examine in a favorable spirit and within a suitable and reasonable time scale requests from journalists for visas;
- Grant to permanently accredited journalists of the participating States, on the basis of arrangements, multiple entry and exit visas for specified periods;
- Facilitate the issue to accredited journalists of the participating States of permits for stay in their country of temporary residence and, if and when these are necessary, of other official papers which it is appropriate for them to have;
- Ease, on the basis of reciprocity, procedures for arranging travel by journalists of the participating States in the country where they are exercising their profession, and to provide progressively greater opportunities for such travel, subject to the observance of regulations relating to the existence of areas closed for security reasons;
- Ensure that requests by such journalists for such travel receive, in so far as possible, an expeditious response, taking into account the time scale of the request;
- Increase the opportunities for journalists of the participating States to communicate personally with their sources, including organizations and official institutions;
- Enable journalists of the other participating States, whether permanently or temporarily accredited, to transmit completely, normally and rapidly by means recognized by the participating States to the information organs which they represent, the results of their professional activity, including tape recordings and undeveloped film, for the purpose of publication or of broadcasting on the radio or television.

The participating States reaffirm that the legitimate pursuit of their professional activity will neither render journalists liable to expulsion nor otherwise penalize them. If an accredited journalist is expelled, he will be informed of the reasons for this act and may submit an application for re-examination of his case. . . .

Appendix E

Declaration of San Jose, Unesco Intergovernmental Conference, Costa Rica, 1976

The representatives of the governments of the States of Latin America and the Caribbean, members of the United Nations Educational, Scientific and Cultural Organization (Unesco),

Meeting at the Intergovernmental conference on Communication Policies in Latin America and the Caribbean, convened in San Jose (Costa Rica) from 12 to 21 July 1976.

Hereby declare:

That man has a vital need to express himself and that therefore his free and spontaneous right to establish relations within his own community should be guaranteed.

That this human attitude is encountered at all times, everywhere and in every type of society.

That man, in his urge to communicate, has created a wide diversity of forms and media that constitute the whole range of cultural expression.

That access to the entire range of cultural resources and the free and

From Intergovernmental Conference on Communication Policies in Latin America and the Caribbean, *Final Report*, San Jose, Costa Rica, July 12–21, 1976 (Paris: Unesco, October 1976), pp. 23–24.

democratic participation of all men in the diverse manifestations of the spirit is a human right.

That the growth of the population and the consequent increase in its spiritual and material needs have led men to apply their scientific talent to the creation of more and more efficient media and instruments that facilitate closer relations and communication between human beings.

That those media form part of the resources of society and the scientific heritage of all mankind, and therefore constitute fundamental components of universal culture.

That there are sectors of the population which have yet to emerge from the isolation in which they live and be helped to communicate with one another and to be informed about national and world-wide affairs.

That all the members of a society are responsible for ensuring the peaceful and beneficial use of communication media.

The States have social, economic and ethical obligations and responsibilities in all matters relating to simulation, support, promotion and dissemination of the resources of the community in the interest of its overall individual and collective development.

That they should therefore encourage individuals and peoples to become aware of their present and future responsibilities and their capacity for autonomy, by multiplying opportunities for dialogue and community mobilization.

That it should be the joint responsibility of the State and the citizen to establish plans and programs for the extensive and positive use of communication media within the framework of development policies.

That national communication policies should be conceived in the context of national realities, free expression of thought and respect for individual and social rights.

That communication policies should contribute to knowledge, understanding, friendship, cooperation and integration of peoples through a process of identification of common goals and needs, respecting national sovereignties and the international legal principle of non-intervention in the affairs of States as well as the cultural and political plurality of societies and individuals, with a view to achieving world solidarity and peace.

That the United Nations and the agencies of its system, especially Unesco, should contribute, to the fullest extent that their possibilities allow, to this universal process.

Appendix F

Mass Media Declaration, Unesco, Paris, 1978

DECLARATION ON FUNDAMENTAL PRINCIPLES CONCERNING THE CONTRIBUTION OF THE MASS MEDIA TO STRENGTHENING PEACE AND INTERNATIONAL UNDERSTANDING, THE PROMOTION OF HUMAN RIGHTS AND TO COUNTERING RACIALISM, APARTHEID AND INCITEMENT TO WAR

Preamble

. . .

ARTICLE I

The strengthening of peace and international understanding, the promotion of human rights and the countering of racialism, apartheid and incitement to war demand a free flow and a wider and better balanced dissemination of information. To this end, the mass media have a leading contribution to make. This contribution will be the more effective to the extent that the information reflects the different aspects of the subject dealt with.

From General Conference Twentieth Session, Unesco, "Compromise Text Proposed to the Director-General with a View to Consensus." 20 C/20 Rev. (Paris: Unesco, November 21, 1978).

ARTICLE II

1. The exercise of freedom of opinion, expression and information, recognized as an integral part of human rights and fundamental freedoms, is a vital factor in the strengthening of peace and international understanding.
2. Access by the public to information should be guaranteed by the diversity of the sources and means of information available to it, thus enabling each individual to check the accuracy of facts and to appraise events objectively. To this end, journalists must have freedom to report and the fullest possible facilities of access to information. Similarly, it is important that the mass media be responsive to concerns of peoples and individuals, thus promoting the participation of the public in the elaboration of information.
3. With a view to the strengthening of peace and international understanding, to promoting human rights and to countering racialism, apartheid and incitement to war, the mass media throughout the world, by reason of their role, contribute effectively to promoting human rights, in particular by giving expression to oppressed peoples who struggle against colonialism, neo-colonialism, foreign occupation and all forms of racial discrimination and oppression and who are unable to make their voices heard within their own territories.
4. If the mass media are to be in a position to promote the principles of this Declaration in their activities, it is essential that journalists and other agents of the mass media, in their own country or abroad, be assured of protection guaranteeing them the best conditions for the exercise of their profession.

ARTICLE III

1. The mass media have an important contribution to make to the strengthening of peace and international understanding and in countering racialism, apartheid and incitement to war.
2. In countering aggressive war, racialism, apartheid and other violations of human rights which are *inter alia* spawned by prejudice and ignorance, the mass media, by disseminating information on the aims, aspirations, cultures and needs of all people, contribute to eliminate ignorance and misunderstanding between peoples, to make nationals of a country sensitive to the needs and desires of others, to ensure the respect of the rights and dignity

of all nations, all peoples and all individuals without distinction of race, sex, language, religion or nationality and to draw attention to the great evils which afflict humanity, such as poverty, malnutrition and diseases, thereby promoting the formulation by States of policies best able to promote the reduction of international tension and the peaceful and the equitable settlement of international disputes.

ARTICLE IV

The mass media have an essential part to play in the education of young people in a spirit of peace, justice, freedom, mutual respect and understanding, in order to promote human rights, equality of rights as between all human beings and all nations, and economic and social progress. Equally they have an important role to play in making known the views and aspirations of the younger generation.

ARTICLE V

In order to respect freedom of opinion, expression and information and in order that information may reflect all points of view, it is important that the points of view presented by those who consider that the information published or disseminated about them has seriously prejudiced their effort to strengthen peace and international understanding, to promote human rights or to counter racialism, apartheid and incitement to war be disseminated.

ARTICLE VI

For the establishment of a new equilibrium and greater reciprocity in the flow of information, which will be conducive to the institution of a just and lasting peace and to the economic and political independence of the developing countries, it is necessary to correct the inequalities in the flow of information to and from developing countries, and between those countries. To this end, it is essential that their mass media should have conditions and resources enabling them to gain strength and expand, and to cooperate both among themselves and with the mass media in developing countries.

ARTICLE VII

By disseminating more widely all of the information concerning the objectives and principles universally accepted which are the bases of the resolutions adopted by the different organs of the United Nations, the mass media contribute effectively to the strengthening of peace and international understanding, to the promotion of human rights, as well as to the establishment of a more just and equitable international economic order.

ARTICLE VIII

Professional organizations, and people who participate in the professional training of journalists and other agents of the mass media and who assist them in performing their functions in a responsible manner should attach special importance to the principles of this Declaration when drawing up and ensuring application of their codes of ethics.

ARTICLE IX

In the spirit of this Declaration, it is for the international community to contribute to the creation of the conditions for a free flow and wider and more balanced dissemination of information, and the conditions for the protection, in the exercise of their functions, of journalists and other agents of the mass media. Unesco is well placed to make a valuable contribution in this respect.

ARTICLE X

1. With due respect for constitutional provisions designed to guarantee freedom of information and for the applicable international instruments and agreements, it is indispensable to create and maintain throughout the world the conditions which make it possible for the organizations and persons professionally involved in the dissemination of information to achieve the objectives of this Declaration.
2. It is important that a free flow and wider and better balanced dissemination of information be encouraged.
3. To this end, it is necessary that States should facilitate the procurement, by the mass media in the developing countries, of ad-

equate conditions and resources enabling them to gain strength and expand, and that they should support cooperation by the latter both among themselves and with the mass media in developed countries.

4. Similarly, on a basis of equality of rights, mutual advantage, and respect for the diversity of cultures which go to make up the common heritage of mankind, it is essential that bilateral and multilateral exchanges of information among all States, and in particular between those which have different economic and social systems be encouraged and developed.

ARTICLE XI

For this Declaration to be fully effective it is necessary, with due respect for the legislative and administrative provisions and the other obligations of Member States, to guarantee the existence of favorable conditions for the operation of the mass media, in conformity with the provisions of the Universal Declaration of Human Rights and with the corresponding principles proclaimed in the International Covenant on Civil and Political Rights adopted by the General Assembly of the United Nations in 1966.

Selected
Bibliography

This selected bibliography reflects the increasing attention to the crisis in international news over the past decade. Although publications in this field have increased greatly in the past few years, most of the authors, whatever side of the issues they represent, are from the United States and Great Britain. However, a broadening of the input seems apparent, and should increase in the years ahead. This bibliography is limited to some fifty books directly on questions of news and the news crisis. There also is a sprinkling of books that touch on major aspects of the news debate, but not on news itself, such as the dependency question. These few citations are not comprehensive—they are designed to open a line of inquiry for those interested. In addition to books, there are hundreds of relevant reports and journal articles. Some of the key journals include *Journal of Communication, IPI Report, Freedom at Issue, Democratic Journalist, Journalists' Affairs, Media Asia, Communicator, Asian Messenger, Gazette, World Broadcast News, Journalism Quarterly, Communication Research, ABU Newsletter, EBU Review, Journal of Broadcasting, Telecommunication Journal, Intermedia, Telecommunications Policy, Development Dialogue,* and *Dialogue.*

The largest recent collection of materials on international communication was gathered by the International Commission for the Study of Communication Problems, the MacBride Commission. In addition to the 1978 *Interim Report* and the *Final Report,* dated 1979 but not widely released until 1980 (as *Many Voices, One World: Communication and Society, Today and Tomorrow*), the commission published almost 100 essays and collections of readings. The other major source on the news developments is

Unesco itself, through its publications on research, conference proceedings, and other materials.

Academy for Educational Development. *The United States and the Debate on the World "Information Order."* Washington D.C.: Academy for Educational Development, 1978.

Barnet, Richard and Ronald Muller. *Global Reach: The Power of the Multinational Corporation.* New York: Simon & Schuster, 1974.

Batscha, Robert. *Foreign Affairs News and the Broadcast Journalist.* New York: Praeger, 1975.

Bell, Daniel. *The Coming of Post-Industrial Society: A Venture in Social Forecasting.* New York: Basic Books, 1973.

Boyd-Barrett, Oliver. *The International News Agencies.* London: Constable, 1980.

Cardoso, Fernando Henrique and Enzo Faletto. *Dependency and Development in Latin America.* Translated by Marjory Mattingly Urquidi. Berkeley: University of California Press, 1979.

Casmir, Fred L., ed. *Intercultural and International Communication.* Washington, D.C.: University Press of America, 1978.

Cherry, Colin. *World Communication: Threat or Promise?* New York: Wiley, 1978.

Cohen, Bernard C. *The Press and Foreign Policy.* Princeton: Princeton University Press, 1963.

Cooper, Kent. *Barriers Down: The Story of the News Agency Epoch.* Port Washington, N.Y.: Kennikat Press, 1942.

Dake, Anthony C. A. *Impediments to the Free Flow of Information Between East and West.* Paris: North Atlantic Treaty Organization, 1973.

Davison, W. Phillips. *International Political Communication.* New York: Praeger, 1965.

Desmond, Robert. *The Information Process: World News Reporting to the Twentieth Century.* Iowa City: University of Iowa Press, 1978.

Epstein, Edward Jay. *News from Nowhere.* New York: Vintage, 1974.

Fascell, Dante B., ed. *International News: Freedom Under Attack.* Beverly Hills: Sage, 1979.

Fisher, Glen. *American Communication in a Global Society.* Norwood, New Jersey: Ablex, 1979.

Fisher, Heinz-Dietrich and John C. Merrill, eds. *International and Intercultural Communication.* New York: Hastings House, 1976.

Gans, Herbert. *Deciding What's News—A Study of CBS Evening News, NBC Nightly News, Newsweek and Time.* New York: Pantheon, 1979.

Gerbner, George, ed. *Mass Media Policies in Changing Cultures.* New York: Wiley, 1977.

Hachten, William A. *Muffled Drums: The News Media in Africa.* Ames: Iowa State University Press, 1971.

Halberstam, David. *The Powers That Be.* New York: Knopf, 1979.

Hamelink, Cees. *The Corporate Village: The Role of Transnational Corpo-

rations in International Communications. Rome: International Documentation and Communication Center, 1977.

Harms, L. S. and Jim Richstad, eds. *Evolving Perspectives on the Right to Communicate.* Honolulu: East-West Communication Institute, 1977. Distributed by University Press of Hawaii, 1970.

Heacock, Roger. *Unesco and the Media.* Geneva: Instituit Universitaire de Hautes Etudes Internationales, 1977.

Hoggart, Richard. *An Idea and Its Servants: Unesco from Within.* London: Chatto and Windus, 1978.

Horton, Philip C., ed. *The Third World and Press Freedom.* New York: Praeger, 1978.

Instant World. Ottawa: Information Canada, 1971.

International Commission for the Study of Communication Problems. *Final Report.* Paris: Unesco, 1979. The report was subsequently published as a book, *Many Voices, One World: Communication and Society Today and Tomorrow.* London: Kogan Page, 1980.

International Commission for the Study of Communication Problems. *Interim Report on Communication Problems in Modern Society.* Paris: Unesco, 1978.

International Press Institute. *As Others See Us: Studies in Press Relations.* Zurich: IPI, 1954.

International Press Institute. *The Flow of News.* Zurich, 1953.

Katz, Elihu and George Wedell. *Broadcasting in the Third World: Promise and Performance.* Cambridge: Harvard University Press, 1977.

Kayser, Jacques. *One-Week's News: Comparative Study of 17 Major Dailies for a Seven-Day Period.* Paris: Unesco, 1953.

Lasswell, Harold, Daniel Lerner, and Hans Speier, eds. *Propaganda and Communication in World History.* 3 vols. Honolulu: University Press of Hawaii, 1980.

Legum, Colin. *A Free and Balanced Flow: Report of the Twentieth Century Fund Task Force on the International Flow of News.* Lexington, Mass.: Lexington Books, 1978.

Lent, John A., ed. *Asian Newspapers: Reluctant Revolution.* Ames: Iowa State University Press, 1971.

——. *Broadcasting in Asia and the Pacific.* Philadelphia: Temple University Press, 1978.

Lerner, Daniel and Jim Richstad, eds. *Communication in the Pacific.* Honolulu: East-West Communication Institute, 1976.

Lerner, Daniel and Wilbur Schramm, eds. *Communication and Change in the Developing Countries.* Honolulu: East-West Center Press, 1967.

Lippmann, Walter. *Public Opinion.* New York: Macmillan, 1922.

Mankekar, D. R. *Media and the Third World.* New Delhi: Indian Institute of Mass Communication, 1979.

——. *One-Way Flow: Neo-Colonialism via News Media.* New Delhi: Clarion Books, 1978.

McHale, John. *The Changing Information Environment.* Boulder, Colo.: Westview, 1976.

Merrill, John C. and Harold A. Fisher. *The World's Great Dailies: Profiles of 50 Newspapers.* New York: Hastings House, 1980.

Morehouse, Ward. *Opening or Closing Our Window on the World? The Media and the Academy in International Affairs.* New York: Council on International and Public Affairs, 1979.

Nordenstreng, Kaarle and Herbert Schiller, eds. *National Sovereignty and International Communication.* Norwood, N.J.: Ablex, 1979.

Nordenstreng, Kaarle and Tapio Varis. *Television Traffic—A One-Way Street?* Reports and Papers on Mass Communication, no. 70. Paris: Unesco, 1974.

Porat, M. U. *The Information Economy.* 10 vols. Washington, D.C.: U.S. Department of Commerce, Office of Telecommunications, 1977.

Pye, Lucian W., ed. *Communications and Political Development.* Princeton: Princeton University Press, 1963.

Read, William. *America's Mass Media Merchants.* Baltimore: Johns Hopkins University Press, 1976.

———. *Rethinking International Communication.* Cambridge: Harvard University Press, 1980.

Richstad, Jim, ed. *New Perspectives in International Communication.* Honolulu: East-West Communication Institute, 1977.

Righter, Rosemary. *Whose News? Politics, the Press and the Third World.* London: Burnett Books, 1978.

Robinson, Glen O., ed. *Communication for Tomorrow: Policy Perspectives for the 1980s.* New York: Praeger, 1978.

Rosenblum, Mort. *Coups and Earthquakes: Reporting the World for America.* New York: Harper & Row, 1979.

Roshco, Bernard. *Newsmaking.* Chicago: University of Chicago Press, 1975.

Rubin, Barry. *International News and the American Media.* Washington Papers, no. 49. Beverly Hills: Sage, 1977.

Schiller, Herbert I. *Communication and Cultural Domination.* New York: International Arts & Sciences Press, 1976.

———. *Mass Communications and American Empire.* New York: Kelley, 1969.

Schramm, Wilbur and L. Erwin Atwood. *Circulation of Third World News: A Study of Asia.* Hong Kong: Press of Chinese University of Hong Kong, 1981.

Schramm, Wilbur, ed. *One Day in the World's Press: Fourteen Great Newspapers on a Day of Crisis.* Stanford, Calif: Stanford University Press, 1959.

Schramm, Wilbur and Daniel Lerner, eds. *Communication and Change: The Last Ten Years—and the Next.* Honolulu: University Press of Hawaii, 1976.

Siebert, Fred S., Theodore Peterson, and Wilbur Schramm. *Four Theories of the Press.* Urbana: University of Illinois Press, 1956.

Smith, Anthony. *Geopolitics of Information: How Western Culture Dominates the World.* London: Faber & Faber, 1980.

——. *Goodbye Gutenberg: The Newspaper Revolution of the 1980s.* Oxford: Oxford University Press, 1980.

——. *The Politics of Information: Problems of Policy in Modern Media.* London: MacMillan, 1978.

Sommerlad, E. Lloyd. *The Press in Developing Countries.* Sydney: Sydney University Press, 1966.

Sussman, Leonard R. *Mass News Media and the Third World Challenge.* The Washington Papers, No. 46. Beverly Hills: Sage, 1977.

Teheranian, Majid, et al., eds. *Communication Policy for National Development.* London: Routledge & Kegan Paul, 1977.

Tiffen, Rodney. *The News From Southeast Asia: The Sociology of Newsmaking.* Singapore: Institute of Southeast Asian Studies, 1978.

Tuchman, Gaye. *Making News.* New York: Free Press, 1978.

Tunstall, Jeremy. *The Media Are American.* New York: Columbia University Press, 1977.

Unesco. *World Communications: A 200-Country Survey of Press, Radio, Television and Film.* New York: Unesco, 1975.

U.S., Congress, House Committee on Government Operations, "International Information Flow. Forging a New Framework." Washington: GPO, 1980.

Wells, Alan. *Picture Tube Imperialism? The Impact of U.S. Television on Latin America.* Maryknoll, N.Y.: Orbis Books, 1972.

Wells, Alan, ed. *Mass Communications: A World View.* Palo Alto, Calif.: National Press Books, 1974.

The Contributors

Elie Abel

Harry and Norman Chandler Professor of Communication, Stanford University, and American member of the International Commission for the Study of Communication Problems. Dean, Graduate School of Journalism, Columbia University, 1970–79. Long career as foreign correspondent, *New York Times*, NBC News.

Jean d'Arcy

French communications consultant. President, International Institute of Communications. President of a French communication company, VIDEO-CITES, Paris.

Keith Fuller

President and General Manager of the Associated Press, New York City, since 1976.

George Gerbner

Professor of Communications and Dean of the Annenberg School of Communications, University of Pennsylvania, and editor, *Journal of Communication*.

Phil Harris

Chief, Research and Information Office, Inter Press Service (IPS) Third World News Agency, Rome. Former Research Associate, Centre for Mass Communication Research, University of Leicester, England. Author of *News Dependence: The Case for a New World Information Order*, report for Unesco.

Jonathan King — Australian media critic and Politics Lecturer, University of Melbourne.

Gerald Long — Managing Director, Reuters Limited, until 1981 when he became Managing Director, Times Newspapers of London.

D. R. Mankekar — Veteran Indian journalist and recent chairman of the Coordination Committee, News Agencies Pool of Non-Aligned Countries. Author of *One-Way Free Flow: Neo-Colonialism via News Media.*

Peter Marshall — General Manager, Visnews, London, since 1975. Former News Editor, BBC, and newspaper and radio reporter.

George Marvanyi — Program director for public affairs of the Hungarian Television. Former staff member, Mass Communication Research Center, Budapest.

Mustapha Masmoudi — Tunisia's permanent delegate to Unesco and member of the International Commission for the Study of Communication Problems. In 1977 elected President, Intergovernmental Coordinating Council for Information of Nonaligned Countries. Former General Manager, Tunis-Afrique Press.

John C. Merrill — Dean, School of Journalism, Louisiana State University. Former journalism professor, University of Maryland and, for fifteen years, University of Missouri. Author of nine books and many articles on international communication and philosophy of journalism, with the most recent *The World's Great Dailies.*

Y. V. Lakshmana Rao — Unesco project coordinator, Paris. Former Secretary-General of the Asian Mass Communication Research and Information Center (AMIC), Singapore.

Rosemary Righter

Development Correspondent of *The Sunday Times*, London. Author of *Whose News? Politics, Press, and the Third World*.

Mort Rosenblum

Editor, *International Herald Tribune*, Paris, 1979–1981. Former AP correspondent in Africa, Asia, Latin America, and France. Author of *Coups and Earthquakes: Reporting the World for America*.

Herbert I. Schiller

Professor of Communications, Third College, University of California, San Diego. Author of *Mass Communications and American Empire*, *The Mind Managers*, and *Communication and Cultural Domination*.

Wilbur Schramm

Communication researcher and author of *Mass Media and National Development* and *Process and Effects of Mass Communication*. Former director, East-West Communication Institute, Honolulu, and Institute for Communication Research, Stanford University.

Leonard R. Sussman

Executive Director, Freedom House, New York City. Former journalist in New York and the Caribbean.

Frank Tremaine

Senior Vice-President responsible for overall direction of planning and special projects, United Press International (UPI), New York City. Former UPI Vice-President in charge of international operations.

Jeremy Tunstall

British media critic and Professor of Sociology at the City University, London. Author of *The Media Are American*.

The Editors

Jim Richstad, a research associate with the East-West Communication Institute since 1970, holds a B.A. in journalism from the University of Washington and a doctorate in Mass Communication from the University of Minnesota. He has worked for newspapers in Illinois, Washington, and Hawaii. His teaching experience includes the University of Washington and the University of Hawaii, where he is an affiliate of the Graduate Faculty. At the Communication Institute, he specializes in international communication policy, flow of news, Pacific Islands journalism, and the right to communicate. His publications include *Communication in the Pacific, New Perspectives in International Communication,* and *Evolving Perspectives on the Right to Communicate.*

Michael H. Anderson, an information consultant with UNICEF in New York, did his work on this collection as a member of the East-West Communication Institute's Communication Policy and Planning Project. He holds a B.A. and M.A. from the School of Journalism and Mass Communication at the University of Minnesota, and a Ph.D. in Political Science, earned at the University of Hawaii while on an East-West Center scholarship. Anderson has newspaper reporting experience in Minnesota and journalism teaching experience at the University of Minnesota and the University Science Malaysia. In 1970–71, he was assistant to the director of a regional journalism training center in Kuala Lumpur, Malaysia. In 1977–78 he conducted field research on transnational advertising in Southeast Asia. Anderson's research interests focus on Third World development and international communication and policy issues.

Index